Conflict Management a

Conflict Management and Resolution provides students with an overview of the main theories of conflict management and conflict resolution, and will equip them to respond to the complex phenomena of international conflict.

The book covers these four key concepts in detail:

- negotiation
- mediation
- facilitation
- reconciliation.

It examines how to prevent, manage and eventually resolve various types of conflict that originate from inter-state and inter-group competition, and expands the existing scope of conflict management and resolution theories by examining emerging theories on the identity, power and structural dimensions of adversarial relationships. The volume is designed to enhance our understanding of effective response strategies to conflict in multiple social settings as well as violent struggles, and utilizes numerous cases studies, both past and current. These include the Iranian and North Korean nuclear weapons programs, the war in Lebanon, the Arab–Israeli conflict, civil wars in Africa, and ethnic conflicts in Europe and Asia.

This book will be essential reading for all students of conflict management and resolution, mediation, peacekeeping, peace and conflict studies, and international relations in general.

Ho-Won Jeong is Professor, the Institute for Conflict Analysis and Resolution, George Mason University, USA. He has published nine books in the field of international relations, peace and conflict studies. He is also a senior editor of the *International Journal of Peace Studies*.

Conflict Management and Resolution

An introduction

Ho-Won Jeong

Routledge
Taylor & Francis Group

LONDON AND NEW YORK

First published 2010
by Routledge
2 Park Square, Milton Park, Abingdon, Oxon OX14 4RN

Simultaneously published in the USA and Canada
by Routledge
270 Madison Ave, New York, NY 10016

Routledge is an imprint of the Taylor & Francis Group, an informa business

© 2010 Ho-Won Jeong

Typeset in Times by Wearset Ltd, Boldon, Tyne and Wear

British Library Cataloguing in Publication Data
A catalogue record for this book is available from the British Library

Library of Congress Cataloging in Publication Data
Jeong, Ho-Won
Conflict management and resolution: an introduction/Ho-Won Jeong
p. cm.
1. Conflict management. I. Title. HD42.J45 2010
658.4′053–dc22

2009021854

ISBN10: 0-415-45040-3 (hbk)
ISBN10: 0-415-45041-1 (pbk)
ISBN10: 0-203-86497-2 (ebk)

ISBN13: 978-0-415-45040-9 (hbk)
ISBN13: 978-0-415-45041-6 (pbk)
ISBN13: 978-0-203-86497-5 (ebk)

For My Mother

Contents

Tables

Preface

This book covers processes and methods adopted to end ethnic and other types of conflicts which have drawn international attention. The imposition of state hegemony has provoked protracted struggles between governments and ethnic minorities in many parts of Africa, former Yugoslavia, the former Soviet republics, Sri Lanka, and elsewhere. Power asymmetric relationships have permitted the continued imposition of harsh rule in Tibet, Burma, Spanish Western Sahara, and Chechnya with little prospect for relieving the suffering of the marginalized populations.

For the last two decades, we have observed a plethora of activities many of which have yielded peace accords. Protracted conflicts in South Africa and Northern Ireland eventually ended with the establishment of new governing structures designed to mend deep layers of social and political rifts. Even after the fighting is over, however, the massacres of innocent civilians and genocide in Sudan, Bosnia-Herzegovina, Guatemala, and Rwanda have left big scars to heal in the future. Reconciliation has become an important cornerstone of transforming adversarial relationships for coexistence.

The complexities of intractable conflicts defy any easy, simple generalization of social, political processes to regulate, mitigate, settle and eventually resolve seemingly irreconcilable differences. Yet many of these experiences, both failed and successful, can be comprehended in conceptual knowledge which can be applicable to other conflicts which continue to flare up. In doing so, the manuscript offers theoretical perspectives that illustrate different features of strategies aimed at changing social, psychological dynamics of destructive fights.

In covering a various range of conflict management and resolution activities, the main features of this book center on linking negotiation, mediation, and facilitation methods to different stages of conflict. In protracted conflict, mutual understanding of the necessity for talks can be forged through dialogue or other informal facilitation methods which promote deeper analysis of the causes and exploration of a way out. When deep mistrust and suspicion dominate negotiation, mediation can be introduced to improve communication and change perceptions of each other. These processes can be better illuminated by our knowledge about conflict relationships embedded in power, identity, and structures which are directly or indirectly related to inducing changes in antagonistic behavior.

In completing this manuscript, I am very grateful for the ten anonymous reviewers who offered valuable comments on shaping various aspects of the manuscript. I also appreciate the help given by Routledge editor, Andrew Humphreys, for initiating this project as well as providing editorial comments and suggestions for revisions. My research has been stimulated by the encouragement of such founding scholars of peace and conflict studies as Chadwick F. Alger, John W. Burton, Johan Galtung, Elise Boulding, Milton Esman, David Singer, Janice Stein, Jurgen Dedring, the late Paul Smoker, and many others.

In understanding the major international conflicts often referred to in this book, I have certainly benefited from direct and indirect consultation with the following area specialists. Regarding the Middle Eastern peace process, I depended heavily on William Quandt's insightful books on the Camp David and US engagement in the conflict between Israel and its neighbors. In understanding conflict between the US and North Korea, I have taken advantage of work done by Robert Gallucci and Jack Pritchard who shared their valuable insights of being direct participants in the negotiation process with many of their audiences. Sean Byrne and John Darby's work has been the most useful in illuminating peace processes in Northern Ireland. My comprehension of conflict transformation has been strengthened by Charles Reilly's analysis of a peace process in Guatemala and other Central American countries. Andrea Bartoli's work on informal intermediary intervention in Mozambique has deepened my understanding of a non-state actor's role in overcoming an adversarial relationship between deeply entrenched foes. Daniel Lieberfeld has presented an excellent illustration of negotiation for ending the apartheid system in South Africa.

I have also greatly benefited from the insights of many of my colleagues, including Charles Lerche, Charles Snare, Earl Conteh-Morgan, Johannes Botes, and Karen Andrews, who have reviewed various chapters. My graduate assistants Sudha Rajput and Kate Romanova have devoted a lot of their time and efforts to bibliographic research and organization of references. Sally Moreland, Rick Langille, Jason Reader, Tammy Rutledge, John Kelly, and my other students reviewed this manuscript from readers' perspectives and offered valuable input. Finally Mary and Nimmy have inspired me to complete this manuscript.

Ho-Won Jeong

Part I

The anatomy of conflict resolution and management

1 Perspectives on conflict resolution

Conflict is manifested through adversarial social action, involving two or more actors with the expression of differences often accompanied by intense hostilities. The conditions of scarcity (for instance, caused by soil degradation or depletion of water in river basins or lakes in Central Africa) and value incompatibilities can become a continuing source of contention. Most significantly, protracted conflict arises from the failure to manage antagonistic relationships. Despite economic difficulties and cultural diversity, South Africa and many other societies have been able to eventually overcome inter-communal rivalries and develop various types of institutions which can renegotiate opposing economic and political interests democratically.

In Switzerland, the Netherlands and other advanced democratic countries, regional and cultural divergence has not created social disruptions or armed violence. Indeed, opposing roles and positions have been harmonized and institutionally accommodated without the destruction of the social fabric. In contrast with the coexistence of multi-ethnic communities in Western Europe and North America, religious, language and racial differences have served as a means to rally various rival groups in a struggle for power and territorial gains in many other parts of the world, stretching from the Middle East, Central Asia, the Balkans, and the Caucasus to Latin America. The eruption of uncontrolled violence has cost the loss of many lives, destroyed homes and economic devastation in war-torn societies, most notably Sudan, the Democratic Republic of the Congo, Sri Lanka, and Bosnia-Herzegovina. In understanding conflict, we need to examine the quality of relationships that reveals the way we relate to each other socially, economically and culturally as well as how political decisions are made.

Even though conflict has been treated like an uncontrolled fight in chaotic, lawless societies (as exemplified in Somalia and Afghanistan), differences between opponents can be handled in a non-adversarial manner. In order to establish functional relationships, the solution should be found through negotiated agreements rather than resorting to violent tactics. The opposing positions can be examined for persuasion via verbal arguments.

Traditional models of settling diverse interests focus on the management of disagreement and tension within the constraints of the prevailing system. Various dispute resolution mechanisms in communities, corporations, and government agencies have been institutionalized to promote a more rule-governed society by handling complaints arising from employment relations, poor quality of services, claims over property ownership among neighbors, or opposition to development projects.

In a more destructive, large-scale conflict, deeper sources of resentment might be related to economic disparities and political oppression. The United Nations, Organization of Security and Cooperation in Europe, African Union, and other regional organizations have developed conflict mitigation and management mechanisms ranging from fact-finding missions in the cases of human rights abuses or minority rights violations to good offices (designed for assistance in communication between adversarial states in support of easing tensions).

Removing misperceptions of adversaries is regarded as a vital step toward settling differences and institutionalizing a new relationship. Indeed, reduced enemy perceptions play a crucial role in initiating a collaborative process. Minimizing value incompatibilities has to touch upon reconciling a different sense of identity by acknowledging each party's needs, intrinsic to their survival and maintenance of dignity. Most importantly, the process and outcome of negotiating different values and incompatible interests reflect not only perceptual, subjective differences but also power relations between dominant and subordinate groups.

It is essential to shed light on diverse phenomena, extending from group dynamics to structural adjustment in an adversarial social system in order to accommodate the vital interests and needs of those who have been alienated and suffered from injustice. Whereas a complex conflict has many underlying sources (both structural and psychological), it is necessary to define conflict in a specific pattern of interactions between opponents being influenced by identity differences and overarching social relations as well as power asymmetry.

One of the primary tasks of conflict resolution is to avert the recurrence of destructive conflict by qualitatively altering antagonistic relationships. Beyond responding to a few manifest, contentious issues, mutually acceptable outcomes stem from finding remedies for power imbalances and inequitable social and economic relations which are often the main source of grievances. The nature of adverse relationships needs to be transformed by supporting consensus on power sharing, enhancement of individual and group well-being as well as a guarantee of security.

A large map of conflict formation and transformation can reveal the nature of a struggle as well as the processes for changing psychological perceptions. There are wide differences among conflicts in terms of their scope and group dynamics, as is illustrated by a comparison between the guerrilla warfare in Chechnya and the nonviolent protest against brutal Chinese rule in Tibet. In transforming adversarial relationships, we need to investigate how group processes are linked to structural conditions. Inter-group relations are constrained by a superimposed political structure as well as by internal group dynamics such as rivalry between factions which take different attitudes toward conflict.

The book's objectives

This book is designed to examine how to manage and resolve conflict, in part, by shedding light on the styles and methods of communication in overcoming differences along with the efforts to minimize the harmful aspects of struggle. It is important to explore diverse modes of interpreting conflict in tandem with the illumination of different ways of tackling a range of problems arising from competitive relationships within and between societies. The manner of our societies' response to conflict has broad implications for human well-being and social change. The volume treats reconciliation, along with transformation of repressive relations, as an essential part of a conflict resolution process.

Keeping the above objective in mind, this book consists of three parts. In Part I, the author presents the conceptions of conflict management, settlement and resolution as well as the examination of processes and strategies to transform conflict. Some conflicts are

harder to mitigate due to a deep rooted history of animosities, institutionalization of dominant relations and difficulties in changing an entrenched system of exploitation and suppression. These themes are echoed and conceptualized in the chapters of Part II on identity,
power and structure. The chapters thus cover identity formation, the effects of power in
conflict outcomes, and the changes in social and political institutions needed to forge new
relationships.

Part III looks at different forms of conflict settlement and resolution, ranging from adjudication to arbitration to collaborative problem solving. Various features of negotiation are
illustrated by different stages of bargaining and outcomes. Negotiation between warring
parties often faces challenges, creating the need for the involvement of mediators who can
facilitate communication and assist in forging compromise. Facilitation is essential to initiating dialogue and promoting understanding of difficult issues which divide communities
with the aim of building consensus for problem solving. Overall, the main ethos of this
book is to illustrate both the past and current human endeavors to settle and resolve conflict
in such a way as to enhance reconciliation and justice.

Multiple facets of conflict

Despite its application to a variety of situations, the definition of conflict has traditionally
been relegated to competition for resources or other interests, value differences or dissatisfaction with basic needs. Incompatible economic and political interests develop an attempt
to suppress other groups often with threats and actual use of force. The discovery of oil,
uranium and other minerals in Morocco, Nigeria, and Sudan has resulted in government
attempts to tightly control ethnic minorities along with the refusal of fair sharing of
incomes from mineral exploitation. The growing resentment ignited armed resistance
which has been followed by government retaliatory attacks on many civilians, causing
destruction of properties, indiscriminate killing, rape, and other abuses which sometimes
reach genocidal levels (as has recently been illustrated in Darfur, Sudan).

The perception of scarcity often worsens competitive situations by generating an even
stronger desire to have access to the limited resources. The level of competition is thus
affected by the availability and value of the territories or other objects sought simultaneously by rival groups. In the absence of agreeable decision-making rules and accepted
norms on the conduct of behavior, the contest can turn into activities aimed at the destruction of each other.

For instance, the 1994 genocide in Rwanda can be attributed to simmering tensions
which originated from competition between Hutus and Tutsis over arable land for producing coffee beans that generate a major source of export income. The rivalry has naturally
grown into an attempt to control state institutions involved in decision making on the allocation of land and export income. The contest has been further fueled by exclusive ethnic
ideologies alongside the colonial legacy which granted disproportionate wealth and power
to minority Tutsis.

Power struggle is inevitably involved when each group attempts to impose its own language, religious or social values on other groups which have their own unique traditions
and histories. As communal conflict in Sri Lanka and Kashmir for the last several decades
vividly demonstrates, minority groups have a strong desire for autonomy and self-control
of their destiny. In establishing or maintaining a superior status, dominant groups may discriminate against minority ethnic culture or language. Then the newly created hierarchy is
used to further control subordinate religious, racial, or linguistic groups.

Regardless of wide differences in the types of relationships, "incompatibility of goals" features general characteristics of conflict (Jeong, 2008; Kriesberg, 1998; Mitchell, 2002; Rubin *et al.*, 1994). The pursuit of different objectives leads to interference in each other's activities to prevent an opponent from attaining what one group desires. These conditions of conflict can result in either a sustained conflict or compromise solutions unless a superior party overwhelms and subdues the other side rather quickly. A minority group may seek outright independence, but the state controlled by a majority ethnic group may oppose the aspiration and even suppress rights to ethnic language and religion. As happened to the independence of East Timor, the matter can be determined by a popular referendum after decades of struggle. In other tense conflict situations, ethnic groups made a compromise and gave up independence in return for self-rule and the guarantee of expanded political and cultural rights. In the late 1990s and early 2000s, negotiations following serious clashes and armed revolts by ethnic Albanians in Macedonia eventually gave them freedom to teach ethnic languages at various levels of academic institutions and increased political representation in the government.

In an unregulated competition, claims to scarce status, power, and resources may result in an attempt to injure or eliminate rivals (Coser, 1956). Incompatible preferences are a more acute source of tension and struggle especially when each party seeks distributive outcomes which satisfy one group's interests at the expense of others. A competitive struggle often arises from a situation where each party's aspirations cannot be fulfilled simultaneously. The difficulties in dealing with extremist terrorist groups such as al-Qaeda are that their actions are not motivated by obtaining specific, tangible, negotiable objectives but by broad, ideological doctrines which seek the total destruction of an enemy society (blamed for collective responsibility for the misery in Islamic societies).

In a contentious struggle, one group's perspectives are organized around the primacy of their own interests, as each party competes for maximizing gain. In a conflict seen as zero-sum (where one's gains become the other's loss), one party has to be induced or forced to yield or withdraw from their quest in the competition in order to avoid serious confrontation. A power-based contest becomes the primary means to determine a winner when contentious competition turns into an unregulated fight.

Each group attaches different degrees of importance to their struggles and outcomes, developing divergent perceptions of the incompatible interests. The more desirable one party feels winning in contention, the more intense efforts the party is likely to make. Value and identity differences along with economic and social inequality create an intractable source of conflict. Beneath a struggle for territory and wealth lie pride, identity and security. Whereas emotional threat generates the fear of losing what one values, a sense of insecurity creates loyalty to one's own group and hatred toward rival groups.

In the absence of a past history of cooperation, aggressive actions are more likely to be ignited in polarized communities where leaders develop antagonistic attitudes toward each other. A long period of conflict entrapment increases the likelihood of greater rigidity and polarization with the reinforcement of mistrust, enemy perceptions and feelings of victimization. The stereotypes of an enemy and misunderstanding of their motives justify the denial of the legitimacy of opposing claims.

The institutionalization of negative interactions is inherent in conflicts fueled by many years of accumulated hostilities. This is vividly represented by recurrent provocations and confrontations between the Sudanese government and southern provinces which seek independence. When an intense struggle permeates the social fabric with its effect on individuals and institutions, a vicious cycle of destructive struggles touches multi-faceted layers of adversarial relationships. As every aspect of social life is dominated by violence, the necessity to cope with conflict influences mundane daily decisions. For instance, Israelis (exposed to rocket and mortar fire from Gaza) have to curtail their outdoor activities while Palestinians (hit by frequent Israeli military strikes) need to look for safe shelters.

In addition, conflict preoccupies political and intellectual agendas filtered through the public domain. Even cultural and educational systems are adapted to the support of the justification of ideologies and values mobilized for the conflict. While Jewish school trips to holocaust sites in Poland are intended for the remembrance of past sufferings, they unintentionally re-traumatize the new generation and turn them into supporters of harsh government measures against Palestinians. As the quality of life further deteriorates owing to the Israeli closure of their borders, Palestinians in Gaza develop further resentment, passing it on to their children who grow up with the language of hatred and demonization of Jews.

In a deadlocked conflict rooted in historical, collective memories (of centuries of foreign occupation and war, for instance, in the Balkans), winning a conflict becomes a matter of survival. Individuals and groups are adapted to conflict realities filled with new and old animosities and prejudices against opponents. Old memories are evoked to strengthen the will to fight on regardless of continuing suffering and loss. Inter-group differentiation is made clearer by an emphasis on exclusive symbols attached to the group's current experience and history, reflecting on a sense of legitimacy about one's own claims and feelings of victimization. These symbols further intensify the dividing lines between us versus them.

The tensions between Unionists and Nationalists in Northern Ireland have been symbolized by the Orange Order marches which celebrate the Protestant victory over the Catholics at the Battle of the Boyne in July 1690. The migration of unemployed rural Catholics to parts of the traditional routes of the marches created controversy, as Catholics interpret the celebration as a provocation to show who is superior. Protestants regard any attempt to restrict their freedom to walk through what have been the traditional routes for centuries as a move to marginalize their Protestant identity.

The politicization of religion and other identity bases creates difficulties in reconciling different positions. In a deeply rooted power struggle, every issue becomes perceived as incompatible and non-negotiable by partisans. As differences are not regarded as reconcilable, it is difficult to moderate or change one's behavior that is deemed necessary for bringing the fight to an end. In a total conflict, every member of an adversary group becomes a potential object of indiscriminate attacks.

Behavioral and psychological aspects of pathological conflict

In antagonistic group mobilization, a high degree of tension is manifested in the threatened use of force as well as verbal confrontations. Indeed, anger, hatred, and dehumanization are amplified by demeaning verbal communication and degrading nonverbal behavior. The initial use of violence may be aimed at achieving limited objectives and demonstrating one's unyielding commitment and will often combine with the manifestation of frustration. The uncontrolled emotional, psychological aspects of conflict can be an obstacle to resolving differences in substantive issues. As observed in many internal wars in Africa, the destructive side of a complex conflict can be ascribed to perceptual, attitudinal, and behavioral distortion which even entails gross humanitarian crimes often characterized by killing and rape in front of family members and forcing them to pay for the bullets after the execution of loved ones.

When the conduct of struggles begins to involve the abandonment of established rules and norms accustomed to constrain each other's behavior, oppression and violence become an unrestrained means of control over enemy "others." During the Guatemalan civil wars (in the 1980s–1990s), indigenous women were often sexually assaulted by government security forces and their affiliated paramilitary group members. In the Bosnian war, Serb militias used rape as a weapon of ethnic cleansing. In civil wars in the Democratic Republic of Congo, women were forced to eat the dead bodies of their family members as well as being abducted as sexual slaves for armed gang members. Many undisciplined armed groups in Burundi, Sierra Leone, Uganda, and other places in Africa have used children as tools of unspeakable crimes such as killing adults with stones. The pathological aspects of conflict can certainly not be reversed without the restoration of some kind of order which imposes discipline on armed militias not subject to control by any responsible leadership.

Adaptation mechanisms

The effects of conflict on the psychology of individuals and society grow deeper along with the progression of the struggle. In a protracted conflict, opponents develop social mechanisms to continue the struggle and justify one's own action internally as well as externally. In order to overcome the adverse effects of suffering inflicted on them in a continuing contest of will, each party ought to have physical endurance from the destruction of violent assault, ranging from suicide bombings to guerrilla campaigns to bombings of residential areas in total warfare. In particular, each party has to psychologically cope with the loss of economic livelihood and the deaths of their community members. Even in nonviolent struggles, those who have to absorb physical injuries and psychological terror (in such cases as the Tibetan monks protesting against Chinese rule) need to maintain high morale and preserve their own spirits as well as hopes for a better future in the midst of an oppressive reality.

In general, the psychology of conflict drives the attitudes and behaviors of individuals and groups toward more polarized views of the world. Perceived injustice is often a source of anger which feeds continuing protests and a demand for justice. Ever-increasing degrees of hostile activities can be mobilized in confrontations against enemies under the name of group survival. Conflict over matters of values and identities is posed as a total concern with survival and furnishes new meaning in life.

Societies have to develop mechanisms for responding not only to death, injury, and material loss but also to anxiety and other psychological stresses which are even harder to measure. Physical and psychological hardships can be endured by an emphasis on readiness for personal sacrifice, unity, and a call for courage. In the solidification of a conflict, a collective emotional orientation supports mistrustful attitudes toward opponents, strengthening the internal group bond and social identity. Given the feelings of pain and grief as well as the sense of a lack of control and helplessness, intra-group solidarity is needed to maintain a determination to fight and ability to endure.

In fact, conflict changes beliefs about one's own images and others as well as aspirations, goals, norms, and values. In particular, emotions related to threat and other enemy images tend to be associated with extreme groups' beliefs such as exclusive nationalistic ideologies. The beliefs incorporated into stereotypical thinking, myths, and collective memories serve as a motivational basis to keep up morale. Threatening situations increase cognitive closure, as groups tend to get more strongly attached to their in-group beliefs. Psychological mechanisms in support of stress management are needed to sustain mental and physical capabilities to cope with enemy attacks.

Conflict settlement versus resolution

The removal of misperceptions may be sufficient enough to end hostile activities if there is a consensus on desirable conditions for resolving differences. Unfortunately, many conflicts are attributed to unsatisfactory social relations rather than miscommunication. Institutional arrangements (in support of the maintenance of the existing hierarchy) may merely protract the challenges from those who are alienated from the system.

Once understanding is reached regarding mutually agreeable goals, opposing groups can concentrate on the means to achieve them. For instance, in the early 1990s when the minority white government in South Africa finally realized that it would no longer be feasible to maintain their power by excluding the majority black population, the main task had become how to guarantee coexistence among different racial groups in the country. The agreement on the establishment of a new constitutional government elected by the majority popular vote led to efforts to control violence by the leadership of both the government and the African National Congress.

Mutually acceptable solutions arise from a collaborative search for strategies to put an end to a struggle. A voluntary process to resolve differences stems from a willingness to jointly analyze interests and needs underneath divisive issues. In spite of the settlement of a few specific issues, underlying relationships may remain contentious, short of complete satisfaction due to a lack of procedures to explore deeper causes. An eventual agreement can be developed by the analysis of sources related to the failure of an existing system and a commitment to the establishment of new social relationships based on the guarantee of political opposition, free elections, power sharing, land reform, etc. These reform measures constituted a basis for the negotiation to end decades of civil wars in El Salvador and Guatemala in the early and mid-1990s.

Resolution strategies can be distinguished from a settlement process in which compromises can be achieved without a satisfactory removal of deeply entrenched, contentious issues. In the absence of serious examination of the real sources of grievances, the same type of conflict can recur. For instance, in Kenya, repeated post-election violence is expected to continue as long as inter-tribal rivalry persists in the failure to reduce economic inequity and to guarantee more proportionate power sharing deemed to be fair by opposing groups. When its main focus is on achieving compromised solutions in diffusing an imminent crisis, settlement is likely to be oriented to temporary adjustment, while keeping the economic, social, and political status quo.

In fact, conflict settlement has been contrasted with conflict resolution in terms of end result. Despite the 2005 accord between the Sudanese government and the Southern People's Liberation Movement, the unresolved issue of control over the oil-rich region on the border between the north and south provoked government attacks on residents of the southern town of Abyei in May 2008. The prospect for peace has been darkened by fear and animosity. In clarifying issues representing points of confrontation, conflict resolution is supposed to explore opportunities for forging new relationships by facilitating peaceful change and reconciliation.

The imposition of settlement terms by coercive bargaining may lead to short-term acceptance of the outcome. One of the protagonists may be forced to change their behavior and strategies under unfavorable circumstances. Temporary behavioral change may not last long in the absence of the modification of an adversarial relationship. When fundamental goals (such as a quest for self-rule) remain unsatisfied, antagonistic relations may submerge but can eventually resurface. If one party is forced to give in to the demand of another party owing to fear or threats, it will surely not bring about attitudinal changes. In many situations where relative degrees of power determine the outcome of conflict, a dissatisfied party is likely to look for future opportunities to redress old issues with a shift in power balance.

Indeed, conflict can certainly be settled in the manner of abandoning coercive tactics aimed at hurting the other party, opening the door for a long process of relationship transformation. The termination of violence or other arrangements to decrease the intensity of a destructive struggle leave breathing room for exploring strategies to overcome key differences if the adversaries are willing to search for a harmonious relationship. As the 1998 Good Friday Agreement designed to end sectarian fighting in Northern Ireland indicates, the cessation of violence may eventually contribute to reaching substantive deals which provide a foundation for fundamental arrangements on power sharing, social integration, or economic interdependence. However, regarding the cessation of active hostilities in the Western Sahara occupied by Morocco, Cyprus, Armenia–Azerbaijan and other frozen conflict situations, mitigation efforts have merely been confined to cease-fire, withdrawal of active hostilities, and limited confidence-building measures.

In peace talks determining the future status of Northern Ireland during the late 1990s, a commitment to ending sectarian fighting propelled the recognition of the needs for democratic participation of all sectarian groups and rights to self-governance. A firm obligation to a cease-fire by the Irish Republican Army (IRA) was a precondition to the resumption of substantive political negotiations which centered on power-sharing arrangements. At the same time, behavioral changes such as the complete abandonment of violence and demobilization of the IRA have been sustainable due to a successful conclusion of the far-reaching agreement on the embracement of the Catholic community in a new governance structure.

As illustrated above, the term conflict resolution refers to a process of not only modifying and eventually ending a contentious struggle but also removing its sources such as alienation from a political process. The process to find a formula for resolving conflict is far more complex than the mere settlement of differences in peripheral issues. In fact, pragmatic solutions which evade central concerns can bring about short-term settlement, but an improved environment is necessary to resolve more complicated, difficult issues. The 1994 US–North Korea Agreed Framework diffused a crisis by halting North Korean nuclear programs, but growing antagonism and mistrust (developed since the establishment of the Bush administration) provoked a complete collapse of the denuclearization deal in the early 2000s.

As opposed to a status quo approach of settlement, conflict resolution indicates a movement from one condition to another which can be more acceptable on a long-term basis. In South Africa, system transformation accompanied by the agreement between the white minority government and the African National Congress has granted the black majority a control over the government while guaranteeing civic, social, and economic rights for the white minority population. In Northern Ireland, a power-sharing government has emerged after many years of struggle between Protestants and Catholics over how to dissolve such deadlocked issues as a shift in territorial boundaries and political power as well as strategies to disarm paramilitary groups. Although it may take time to develop a more amicable relationship, conflict resolution generally brings about a new framework for coexistence which eliminates the necessities of continued engagement in an uncontrolled fight for domination.

In a search for the deeply rooted foundation of conflicts, a general understanding has been forged that violent behavior cannot be simply eradicated by the mere injection of fear.

Most importantly, a shift in prejudiced group values and attitudes toward others has to go along with structural changes in conflict dynamics. The process of resolving conflict entails synchronization in the alteration of underlying behavioral patterns designed to end violence in tandem with improved communication. Perceptual and attitudinal changes are aimed at reducing tensions, which can, in turn, improve an atmosphere of searching for ultimate solutions. In the end, the creation of interdependent, symbiotic relationships serves as a prerequisite for the development of lasting peace (which has been observed in Franco-German relations since World War II).

When conflict has been handled constructively, all the parties are better off than before. This is contrasted with a response to conflict by force that does not require the consideration of each other's well-being. The fundamental nature of social conflict focuses on the social norms and political processes in question beyond motives and other psychological environments. In fact, conflict in a given system cannot be resolved without changes in institutional processes and structures required for responding to the root causes of problems such as forced annexation of territories, denial of rights to use an ethnic language, confiscation of land and other properties, random abduction and torture of opposing group members, etc. The sources of marginalization need to be identified to explore strategies for changes in the system.

Successful conditions for conflict resolution

Besides the commitment of parties to problem solving, susceptibility to a win–win solution is contingent on the constellation of interests and the availability of alternative options. The mechanisms of reducing structural inequalities create a more tolerant social environment. The improved inter-group relations could not emerge in an insecure social, economic, political, and military environment which creates uncertainty.

When competitive interests have a high win–lose component, one or both sides feel threatened by the other. The term "interests" has been employed generically to cover all motivations, including the fulfillment of one's needs and realization of values and ideals. In general, however, economic aspirations can alter with circumstances and be negotiated. In fact, competition over material goods and role occupancy tends to be transitory as long as it does not entail components of food, shelter, freedom, and inherent human needs for physical and psychological well-being (Burton, 2001).

Not every contentious issue is subject to compromise, especially when it is related to fundamental rights to freedom and autonomy (related to control the destiny of one's own life). It is also difficult to reconcile differences in value-oriented conflicts over abortion rights opposed by Catholic church hierarchies or the appointment of gay bishops within the Anglican churches, since passions are attached to what people believe. Differences in approaches to population control between environmental groups and conservative religious leaders have been the most acute to reconcile at various global events which discuss the future health of this planet. While the control of rapid population growth is critically needed for the mitigation of ecological destruction, fundamental Christian and Islamic groups have been adamantly opposing any birth control measures by invoking their rigid religious doctrines. The demand for the recognition of political independence or self-rule is yet another example of a serious trigger for conflicts, for instance, in such places as Kosovo and Kashmir.

Differences over material interests need to be separated from highly emotional and value-oriented issues that do not easily succumb to trade. Externally imposed decisions do not quell

the yearnings for freedom and self-rule, but only aggravate the sufferings of civilian populations as is evidenced in Russian military campaigns against the Chechens. The conditions for
the realization of human dignity and self-fulfillment should be recognized in addressing the
discontent originating from discrimination and other sources of social inequality.

Most importantly, the premise of conflict resolution has been based on the understanding that differences in nonnegotiable needs and cultural values are not something to be
divided but have to be accommodated (Burton, 1997; Kelman, 2008; Mitchell, 2002). In
return for the satisfaction of one's own essential concerns, the other party's freedom,
autonomy, and other vital needs ought to be respected in formulating non-zero sum,
win–win solutions. Perceptional changes can lead to redefining shared needs and interests
instead of making an attempt to gain bigger concessions from opponents. Instead of being
judgmental about the adversary's demand, a collaborative process promotes understanding
of each other's anxiety and fears about security. Mutual accommodations can bring net
advantages to all through the art of collaborative problem solving.

Structural approaches to conflict resolution

In a long-lasting conflict, it is not always clear how to predict when resolution can be
achieved. In addition, questions linger as to whether agreement on contentious issues at
hand is sufficient to prevent future hostilities. The perceptions of a desirable outcome at an
acceptable cost diverge among parties according to the nature of their goals and issues. In
general, "any initial agreement on different aspects of problems which have arisen from a
broad conflict relationship is most likely to be partial" (Jeong, 1999, p. 15).

An agreed settlement may not be favored any more if the changing circumstances controlled by either party demand renegotiation. For instance, global warming is most likely to
generate a contentious process to renegotiate various terms in the existing Antarctic treaty
which bans mineral exploration. Owing to new internal or external circumstances faced by
each party, the necessity for adjustment to original agreements arises, demanding renegotiation of implementation terms. In post-conflict transitions in Mozambique, El Salvador, and
other places, rebel leadership often refused to proceed to full disarmament and demobilization of their fighters as scheduled when there was a delay in electoral reform.

The integration of reconciliation and reconstruction of social fabric in a continuing
spectrum of conflict resolution is necessary due to various challenges in establishing the
foundation of stable relationships. Even if reaching agreements on basic principles after a
long period of hostilities leads to the acceptance of new conditions for resolving future differences, it does not necessarily mean the immediate end of adversarial relationships. If
negotiated settlements break down, adversaries are more eager to revert back to costly
struggles. Worthless peace treaties and off-again-on-again civil wars have been character-
izing conflicts in Burundi, the Democratic Republic of the Congo, and other African countries, as well as Sri Lanka and Colombia. The end state of negotiated settlement can be
unpredictable until the successful establishment of a political framework that can put
together fragmented social structures.

In general, conflict resolution needs to be assessed in terms of an outcome as well as a
process which can enhance a prospect for warring parties to abide by their agreements. In
ending civil wars, thus, peace treaties have often included political or economic incentives
for laying down arms. In addition, the reintegration of the population as well as the return
of refugees and rebuilding the economy, especially in such cases as Bosnia-Herzegovina,
can still remain a vital task even a decade after the conclusion of a peace treaty.

The nature of post-conflict institutional building is likely to be affected by the means adopted for a struggle. In general, nonviolence minimizes the lasting effects of adversarial struggle. The process of achieving independence through armed struggles in Angola and Mozambique resulted in two to three decades of internal warfare between rival factions over the control of the newly created state after the colonial power Portugal left voluntarily in 1974. This is contrasted with India which nurtured stable democratic institutions after gaining independence in 1947 by nonviolent struggle.

The process of conflict resolution is supposed to reconstitute and recreate a democratic public domain through empowerment of those whose voice has been marginalized. Thus a response to deeper sources of social disintegration entails more substantive efforts than self-control of anger and frustration.

Preventive management of conflict does not need to wait until popular discontent and mobilization turn into violent confrontation. The longer the grievance remains, the more intense tensions are likely to be built up. The suppression of negative feelings or other expressions by force or co-optation can simply postpone the inevitable explosion. Existing relationships can be renegotiated to eliminate economic disparities and political discrimination which serve as a source of resentment and grievances.

Methods for dealing with conflict

Depending on the nature and sources of conflict, there are different ways to deal with conflict. In many contemporary conflicts, official and unofficial conflict management methods have been utilized in support of communication functions or improvement in relations designed to create a favorable atmosphere for a negotiated solution. As part of official diplomacy, governments can be engaged in sending special envoys for negotiation while international organizations may dispatch fact-finding missions to investigate cease-fire or human rights violations. Other formal activities range from good offices to conciliation to mediation aimed at diffusing a crisis. The scope of conflict management covers informal meetings through back channels of communication as well as unofficial contacts through intermediaries.

The failure of negotiation is often attributed to a contest of will that leads to a refusal to make concessions needed to reach a compromise. When one side is forced to accept the other's position, resentment emerges as its own concerns go unaddressed. In order to avoid military confrontations, adversaries must engage in a search for mutual solutions that meet the goals of both sides. When 15 British sailors were seized off the Iranian coast in April 2007, intensive diplomatic moves were taken to diffuse the crisis. Eventually, Iran freed the sailors in return for the apologies by British officials in tandem with the release of an Iranian diplomat held by the Iraqi intelligence forces under the US military command.

The settlement process of an inter-state conflict may combine threats and coercion with persuasion to break each other's intransigent positions. While Britain attempted to put pressure on Iran by seeking the UN Security Council resolution to condemn the act, British Prime Minister Tony Blair highly praised the Iranian civilization in his statement addressed to the Iranian people. The Iranian President described the sailors' eventual release as an Easter gift to the British people, a gracious act, rather than a concession made under international pressure. In order not to appear to be formally conceding, both governments referred their goodwill gestures or intentions to the other countries' populace, not government.

In negotiation, parties can reach an agreement through a compromise formulated by the trade-off of different priorities. Negotiations are needed in a variety of settings not just being limited to resolving contentious issues between adversaries. In an organizational setting, NATO members negotiated on the number of troops each country had to contribute to military operations in Afghanistan. In spite of their asymmetrical relationships, the Bush administration could not dictate its own terms in negotiation with the Iraqi government on the time limits of US troop presence, facing stiff resistance. Even in adversarial relationships, compromise is less costly than the pursuit of economic sanctions, other punitive methods or military actions designed to force one's own solutions. In order to achieve a successfully negotiated outcome, both parties must feel that the end result is the best they could accomplish and that it is worth accepting and supporting.

In contentious bargaining, the adoption of win–lose strategies tends to produce an outcome that is likely to reflect power differentials. The involvement of a third party often helps forge mutually satisfying outcomes through a free flow of information and open exchanges of ideas which assist in discovering common interests. The degrees of the intervener's decision-making power, types of responsibilities, and their relationships with contestants can have a significant impact on the process of settling contentious issues.

The types of required communication functions depend not only on the sources of conflict but also the nature of the existing relationship between the parties. In general, hostage negotiations are conducted under very unusual elements of surprise, urgency, mistrust, and the importance of confidential and indirect channels. In such cases as arguments between close allies, sorting out factual differences and clearing misperceptions may be sufficient enough. In mediation, the quality of communication between protagonists and the acceptance of a final deal by each party reflect on an intermediary capacity to convince, cajole, or induce a reluctant party and eventually change their perceptions.

Court procedures and arbitration fit in a conventional framework that is managed within the boundaries of existing laws and norms. Territorial or other types of disputes between two states can be referred to the International Court of Justice. Although their verdict is supposed to be final, sometimes it continues to generate tension when one of the contending parties is reluctant to accept the verdicts. In situations where minority or other dissident groups develop nonconformity with state institutions, domestic courts, lawyers, and public officials tend to treat the conflict in a superficial way often by disregarding deep grievance attributed to social injustice. In addition, decisions on constitutional issues by a judicial body can further politicize the conflict and widen distance between opposing social forces, as is illustrated by the Turkish court verdict on the dissolution of legitimate Islamic political parties.

In judicial settlements and arbitration, the imposition of a third-party decision quickly determines the fate of disputes. A direct form of communication between protagonists is not necessary in a judicial setting. Adjudication is an adversarial process since the outcome often reflects a win–lose zero-sum solution to the problem. Arbitration is not successful when value differences of participants create difficulties in the development of objective criteria applied to the verdict. The World Trade Organization's arbitration panels award decisions based on existing treaties and generally accepted practice. Facts and laws are not suitable means to sort out emotional problems or incompatible values, limiting their utility to fact-based disputes or legal rights issues. In a nutshell, an authoritative third-party decision does not take socio-psychological issues seriously even though they can be a source of contention.

While mediation often helps communication between parties, a focus on the settlement of narrow issues would not delve into the analysis of deeper sources of exploitative social and economic conditions. Dialogue or other interactive processes of conflict resolution utilize a collaborative method to explore the root causes of conflict and conditions for satisfying vital needs of adversaries. When official negotiating channels are closed or dysfunctional, citizen groups can play an important role in nurturing a climate of trust and even develop proposals to be delivered to their own governments. In 2006, unofficial contacts between Israeli and Syrian advocacy groups yielded an informal agreement on the conditions for the Israeli return of the Golan Heights to Syria.

Themes and agendas

This book examines diverse types of conflict at various levels of complexity, and discusses practices and concepts applied in mitigating hostilities needed to settle differences between adversaries. The strategies and methods for the control of antagonistic behavior need to be adaptable to specific conflict dynamics. In identifying strategies to remove or at least mitigate conditions for a protracted conflict, a suitable starting point is to identify the causes of conflict and control escalation processes. The movement from mere disagreement to more polarized, extreme positions narrows the application of options based on a nondestructive, collaborative process.

A settlement process hinges either directly or indirectly upon the nature and causes of conflict. It is not often orderly due to the involvement of distorted psychological attributions leading to misjudgments and inaccurate assumptions about the events and behavior. Various noncoercive intervention methods based on persuasion and other collaborative efforts may have to overcome the psychological hindrances associated with mental anguish in decision making, cognitive inconsistency as well as a group process which reinforces stereotypical enemy images. A positive relationship can be cultivated through empathy and increased interdependence between opposing parties.

One of the main aims of this book project is to illuminate the processes and methods of turning contentious battles into collaborative process. The practice of conflict resolution has been emphasizing integrative outcomes with a paradigm shift from adversarial (win–lose) to positive sum (win–win) solutions; the willingness to address each other's concerns for mutual coexistence stimulates a search for joint benefits.

In response to the above challenges, this volume highlights the underlying dynamics of social and psychological relations involved in the process of conflict resolution. While the first half of the book covers various issues related to transforming conflict relationships, the second half focuses on negotiation, mediation, facilitation, and methods of reconciliation.

Following this introductory chapter, the next chapter discusses the quality of relationship, behavioral, and attitudinal changes in managing conflict dynamics. Chapter 3 examines multiple dimensions of conflict transformation after pointing out the shortcomings of a conflict management approach. After investigating various types of direct and indirect relationships between identity and conflict, Chapter 4 looks at the conditions for reconstruction of social identities. Chapter 5 illustrates different degrees of power asymmetry along such dimensions as both physical and psychological endurance in absorbing the cost of struggles as well as resource mobilization capabilities. Chapter 6 highlights the role of structural sources of discontent, including alienation from institutions and practices of governance as well as their impact on conflict resolution efforts.

Chapter 7 sheds light on ethical issues, questions of justice and neutrality after providing comparative perspectives of how judicial settlement and arbitration differ from negotiation, mediation, facilitation, and other collaborative methods. In understanding a negotiation process, Chapter 8 reviews bargaining strategies (related to compromise and concession making) and elements to influence them. Chapter 9 examines models of mediation practiced in international diplomacy with the provision of typologies of mediators and their characteristics. In Chapter 10, in general, facilitative methods illustrate the nature of communication oriented toward attitudinal and cognitive changes. In Chapter 11, successful reconciliation consists of apologies for atrocious acts, recognition of sufferings, expression of mercy and forgiveness, healing and the cultivation of mutual respect and security.

Further reading

Anderson, M. (2004) *Cultural Shaping of Violence: Victimization, Escalation, Response*, West Lafayette, IN: Purdue University Press.

Burton, J. W. (1997) *Violence Explained: The Sources of Conflict, Violence and Crime and Their Prevention*, Manchester: Manchester University Press.

Byrne, S. and Irvin, C. (2002) "A Shared Common Sense: Perceptions of the Material Effects and Impacts of Economic Growth in Northern Ireland," *Civil Wars*, 5 (1): 55–86.

Jeong, H. W. (2008) *Understanding Conflict and Conflict Analysis*, Thousand Oaks, CA: Sage Publications.

Kriesberg, L. (1998) *Constructive Conflicts*, Lanham, MD: Rowman & Littlefield Publishers.

Miall, H. *et al.* (1999) *Contemporary Conflict Resolution: The Prevention, Management and Transformation of Deadly Conflicts*, Malden, MA: Blackwell Publishers.

Mitchell, C. (2002) "Beyond Resolution: What Does Conflict Transformation Actually Transform?" *Peace and Conflict Studies*, 9 (1): 1–24.

Rubin, J. *et al.* (1994) *Social Conflict: Escalation, Stalemate, and Settlement*, Boston: McGraw-Hill.

2 Managing intractable conflict

One of the main issues (which partisans face in a protracted conflict) is how to overcome the debacle and move on to solutions which are acceptable to them. In a continuing struggle such as a long-term civil war, waiting for fighting to subside naturally is too costly, further contributing to the intractability. Efforts can be made to mitigate a conflict prior to seeking settlement. Diverse methods and strategies can be adopted to control various types of escalation and entrapment. Long-term entrapment (such as US–Soviet relations during the Cold War period) was structurally managed by regular communication and other crisis management mechanisms.

This chapter reviews actor behavior and decision making from the perspective of managing the adversarial relationships and dynamics involved in the resolution of differences. Though many conflicts may seemingly look chaotic, they can be characterized by a series of moves and countermoves. A conflict management and resolution process needs to focus on the behavior of parties, relationships, and institutions (which regulate the choices of individual actors) beyond the immediate issues under dispute. Peace building has become an essential task for a transition from conflict to the establishment of stable interactions between former adversaries in the process of reconstructing violence-torn societies. Given the costs of violence, conflict prevention has been promoted to respond to the surge of ethnic struggles in the post-Cold War era.

Conflict evolution

Despite differences in the number of phases of conflict, there is a commonly identifiable sequence of behavior that ignites and perpetuates confrontation. In large part, conflict can be characterized by the emergence of antagonistic positions and their eventual settlement through engagement in problem solving (Jeong, 2008; Kriesberg, 1998; Mitchell, 2002; Rubin *et al.*, 1994). In negotiated settlement, different positions need to be integrated or aggregated to explore mutually compatible solutions with the adoption of cooperative tactics.

In spite of variations, a sequence of behavior is likely to unfold over time along semi-predictable phases of conflict. After a latent phase turns into a manifest conflict, threats and forces might be exhibited in an attempt to get one's own way. In a series of events preceding the violent Palestinian uprising and heavy Israeli military response in the early 2000s, violent tactics were driving each other's actions to a higher level of casualties and destruction. The exchange of adversarial moves diminishes the hope of amicable solutions through negotiation. When cooperation is perceived to yield the lowest outcomes, incentives for preemptive attacks are high in order to demoralize the opponent.

Once conflict is accelerated, it runs its own course in the absence of countervailing forces which can reverse the continuing patterns of retaliatory responses to each other's punitive actions. After a round or two of escalation, a runaway spiral can expand in the absence of self-restraint or successful external intervention, either diplomatic or military, to cool down intensifying violence. In an internal conflict, an initially peaceful protest can be switched to mass violence or armed campaigns by militant groups due to government oppression of unarmed opposition movements. The origins of civil wars in Sri Lanka, Guatemala, El Salvador, Colombia, Algeria, and elsewhere can be traced back to bloody oppression of mass protests and the arrest of opposition leaders. In a long-term struggle, balance of power on the battlefield normally sustains fighting until unregulated confrontation subsides. In such internal warfare as experienced in Angola, El Salvador, Guatemala, and Mozambique, it may take more than a decade to enter the stage of de-escalation needed for a settlement (Jeong, 2008).

It is a very difficult task to change the dynamics of conflict especially when it is seen as a struggle for survival. Negative inter-group interaction entails an ontological character by denying each other's identity and security. Cognitive rigidity as well as such affective factors as feelings of anger, fear, and hatred have a negative impact on the transition to de-escalation. Intentions to harm the other party derive from dehumanization. The cessation of communication intensifies perceptual distortion. Each party believes that they have no or fewer options than fighting owing to the hostility. The rise of hard-line factions may even stiffen antagonistic positions along with the support of external allies. The political rise of Hamas among Palestinians has weakened the capacity and credibility of the moderate Fatah government based in the West Bank to negotiate with the Israelis.

To move from a contest of coercive power to win–win solutions is, therefore, complicated in a deep-rooted conflict. Due to negative energy and its behavioral manifestations embedded in social interaction, intractable conflict is not easily amenable to resolution. Escalatory behavior is normally mirrored by the other side, affecting the conflict as a whole. Unless one party overwhelms an opponent quickly and easily, the tide of every struggle either continues with varying degrees of intensity or ebbs to a dormant stage awaiting another surge of violence. Irregular intervals intervene after a finite cycle of confrontation, as each side prepares for the next round of fighting in seeking a final victory through military superiority.

Although some conflicts are more resistant to changes in the patterns of adversarial interaction, each component of conflict dynamics can be modified to bring an end to fighting. In moving toward de-escalation, an all-out struggle begins to subdue in such a way as to enhance the prospect for dialogue or negotiation. If negotiated settlement ought to be achieved, a wide range of cooperative activities are needed to overcome the legacy of an atrocious act committed during the armed struggle.

A series of conciliatory events can mitigate the destructive aspects of struggles while creating a positive environment for talks. In preparing for peace talks in Northern Ireland, meetings between the political representatives of adversarial communities, including the exchange of views between the leader of the moderate Unionist Social Democratic and Labour Party (SDLP) John Hume and the IRA-affiliated Sinn Fein's Gerry Adams, paved the way for an all-inclusive conference that started in 1996. The momentum for inter-communal dialogue was initially created by the 1985 Anglo-Irish Agreement which confirmed the necessity of the consent of the majority of Unionists in any change in the status of Northern Ireland.

The varying duration and patterns of a struggle shape the nature of conflict dynamics. The process of a protracted conflict is likely to alter the initial conditions for conflict with the creation of an emotional residue attached to loss in the struggle. Long-lasting conflict reinforces militant social elements, and a return to the previous relationship may not be possible or desirable. The end of a civil war may mean the adaptation of insurgent organizations to political parties which can compete in an electoral cycle. In inter-state conflict, the restoration of occupied territory may have to be accompanied by the emergence of new security arrangements as well as the renegotiation of political relationships. At the end of the conflict process, even in fortunate situations, the protagonists may find only partial satisfaction with what they originally desired.

The Sahrawi quest for independence

The indigenous Sahrawi population in the former Spanish colony of Western Sahara has been engaged in a multi-decade struggle with Spain, followed by Morocco and Mauritania. The conflict's long history is full of armed fighting between the indigenous population and their different occupiers over a century. Even though the conflict has been de-escalated and managed without major warfare since 1991, the situation has not yet been resolved due to the failure to hold a promised referendum on independence.

The uprising in Spanish Western Sahara started in the early twentieth century, but the armed conflict was more effectively organized after the formation of the Sahrawi rebel Polisario Front in May 1973. Even though armed rebellions and raids successfully pushed the Spanish forces out of much of the territory, the goal of independence was not achieved. The Spanish retreat in 1975 only meant the division and transfer of the Sahrawi homeland to Morocco and Mauritania. Thus the Polisario Front continued to wage guerrilla-style hit-and-run attacks against Morocco and Mauritania along with the declaration of the Sahrawi Arab Democratic Republic.

The continued armed struggle induced Mauritanian retreat from Rio de Oro with the acceptance of Sahrawi rights to Western Sahara. A comprehensive peace treaty (August 1979) was accompanied by the formal recognition of the Sahrawi Arab Democracy. Right after this event, Morocco militarily annexed the newly independent southern half of Rio de Oro. Thus the armed resistance kept going in Western Sahara occupied by Morocco as well as the new area evacuated by Mauritania. From the mid-1980s, there was military stalemate between the Moroccan and Polisario troops. No side obtained decisive gains in spite of continued artillery strikes and sniper attacks by the guerrillas.

The war eventually became difficult for Morocco to sustain due to the economic and political strain. In September 1991, both sides agreed to a cease-fire observed by UN peacekeeping forces with the promise of a referendum on independence. The referendum did not take place the following year, as agreed, stumbling over differences in voter rights. Whereas the process was stalled, the prolonged cease-fire has been held. Many attempts, including the 2003 Baker plan, have not yet yielded a final breakthrough.

Degeneration from a peace process to war: the Israeli–Palestinian conflict

In the long history of the Israeli–Palestinian conflict, the Oslo Peace Accord (1993) was a groundbreaking event to offer a real possibility for a negotiated settlement. Yet the failure to determine the future status of Palestinians living under Israeli occupation had eventually slid into violence. By summer 2000, both sides were quite frustrated with the peace process. The Palestinians never did get close to a clear path toward the creation of a sovereign state, an end to continuing Jewish settlement in the West Bank, or economic improvement. The Israelis did not feel a real guarantee of security against terrorism and violence by Palestinian extremists. The early stage of the peace process was full of good intentions and rational bargains, but it regressed to the gradual path of building animosities with growing frustration and support for hard-line positions within Israel. The second intifada by Palestinians in September 2000 completely shattered the foundation of hopes for lasting security which both sides originally wanted to obtain through mutual collaboration.

The new cycle of conflict between the Palestinians and Israel was provoked by the Israeli right-wing politician Ariel Sharon's visit to the Muslim shrines on the Temple Mount and the al Aqsa Mosque in Jerusalem. The Israeli–Palestinian relations were already on shaky ground after the failure of the Camp David summit attended by both Israeli Prime Minister Ehud Barak and Palestinian Authority head Yasser Arafat in July 2000. US President Bill Clinton's mediation did not narrow the gap between the widely different positions held by both sides. The post-Camp David negotiation process was rocked by violent clashes between the Israelis and Palestinians which wrecked confidence.

As Table 2.1 (pp. 22–23) presents, the intense scale of violence sparked on September 28 ended with the complete loss of any future hope for peaceful relations between the Israelis and Palestinians after the election of hard-line Likud party leader Ariel Sharon on February 6, 2001. Even high-level summit diplomacy (e.g. the October 16–17 Sharm el-Sheikh summit meeting attended by Arafat, Barak, Clinton, Egyptian President Mubarak, and Jordan's King Abdullah) failed to turn the tide of violent reprisals. Palestinian cross-border and drive-by shootings, and other attacks against Israeli communities alternated with the Israeli assassinations of suspected radical group leaders, violent settler vigilante action in tandem with the closures of Palestinian towns and villages, and destruction of Palestinian houses. The Israeli use of helicopter gunships and F-16 air attacks prompted accusations of "inappropriate" and "excessive" use of force. Although some grotesque killings were committed by extreme Palestinian groups (e.g. the murder of two Israeli soldiers by a Palestinian mob on October 12), excessive Israeli military counterattacks were often indiscriminately targeted toward civilians.

Mitigation of protracted conflict

A multi-step conflict resolution process aims to identify types of contentious issues, discover underlying causes and develop a process to remove them. Along with the analysis of a system of interaction and its surrounding environment, negative perceptions need to be changed to bring about attitudinal changes. The negative forms of change within a conflict system have to be reversed by a shift in interaction patterns from demonization to humanization, from stereotypes to empathy. The intensity of conflict can be moderated with the removal of incompatibilities by means of conjunction with a search for a formula to increase compatibilities between different positions related to each party's goals.

A different internal and external environment needs to emerge in the transition toward conciliation. The weak abilities of adversaries to manage their relationships may demand the support of external allies and also the invitation of an intermediary to narrow emotional, psychological gaps between antagonists. Psychological changes may come along with readiness for concession making that is necessary for a compromised solution. In order to accommodate each other's needs, parties need to abandon the contentious tactics associated with achieving unilateral gains. Decision making for de-escalation needs to be adjusted by the necessity for mutual concessions. New views about adversaries shape different understandings about conflict.

As a result of conflict, partisans tend to go through the transformation of their organizational structures and identity. The cessation or reduction of hostilities may come from changes in personal motivations and social context following watershed events. Dramatic events can reshape our view about a conflict, eventually preparing psychologically for disengagement. The My Lai Massacre proved to be a turning point toward de-escalation in the Vietnam War. On March 16, 1968, the killing of as many as 504 villagers (nearly all of whom were children, women, and the elderly) in My Lai by the US army unit Charlie Company badly undercut support for the war, demoralizing US war efforts.

In peaceful resolution, goals are pursued by means other than threats and actual use of violence. In managing ethnic relations, coercive approaches often produce a backlash by generating further resentment and violent resistance. The maintenance of the status quo by force is no longer feasible, or too costly to one's international reputation (or the maintenance of domestic support). The right circumstances for successful de-escalation (to break a costly impasse) can be discovered by a careful analysis of conflict situations. Prior to de-escalatory moves, parties acknowledge a stalemate situation; the parties themselves are not able to envision a way out of the conflict with dreadful costs whereas neither side is likely to win or lose in the short term. The futility of efforts to impose unilateral solutions can be realized after the recognition of the limited capacity to push for any gains along with an adversary's resistance. In the absence of palatable options, pressures of time and other elements of a crisis create pessimistic views about conflict.

Conciliatory dynamics

The withdrawal of negative sanctions (such as a trade embargo) as well as an offer of new rewards (such as economic assistance) are normally employed in an attempt to initiate positive interaction. The exchange of rewards can set off a series of events in support of mutual cooperation. The modes of behavior, strategies, and tactics are influenced by different motivations. In negotiation with the US during the Vietnam War era, North Vietnam released some US prisoners of war as a goodwill gesture. In order to obtain cooperation from the Chinese government in putting pressure on North Korea and Iran to end their nuclear programs, the Bush administration removed China from the State Department list of the worst human rights abusers in the world along with ceasing to request the release of key political prisoners.

In a successful conciliatory process, the reciprocal actions can amplify positive changes. Each party is more likely to reciprocate conciliatory gestures when their offer of a counter-reward (such as the removal of restrictions on the movement of monetary assets) does not involve a high cost to them. The US government unfroze North Korean financial assets upon Pyongyang's agreement to cease its plutonium processing programs in 2007. Given that it may take time to overcome the legacy of animosities created by punitive measures, incremental processes (e.g., the exchange of mutual visits by orchestras or sports teams) may be adopted to thaw relations (for example, US–China relations in the 1970s). The messages of compromise or conciliation (that signal reversing negative attitudes) may precede the cessation of violent tactics.

Even if parties agree to negotiate, it is often a long, tumultuous process to reach a settlement. Balancing opposing interests or values in an acceptable manner to all sides is a real test to ending intractable conflict. In meeting the other's concerns, it might be necessary to offer concessions on the issues an adversary considers crucial. Most importantly, a balanced exchange of concessions is more likely to create a high potential for a successful deal making.

Table 2.1 Escalation of Israeli–Palestinian violence, September 28, 2000 to February 2, 2001

	Israeli action/reaction	Palestinian action/reaction
9/28–30	*A provocative visit to the Muslim shrines on the Temple Mount and the al Aqsa Mosque by right-wing politician Ariel Sharon*	*The beginning of mass riots*
9/29	The Israeli security forces opening fire in the al Aqsa Mosque compound in Jerusalem's walled Old City	Six Palestinians dead and close to 200 wounded
9/30	*The first major armed clashes*	Spread of violence to the Gaza Strip and West Bank; 14 Palestinians dead, including a 12-year-old boy
10/1–2	*Cease-fire agreement but quick collapse*	
	The death of an Israeli border policeman	30 deaths
	Solidarity protest by Israeli Arabs	
10/3	*Another cease-fire agreement but immediate resumption of clashes*	Six deaths
10/4–6		20 deaths
10/5	*Israeli closure of the West Bank and Gaza for the first time*	
10/8	The first death of a Jewish settler; death of one Arab Israeli	Two deaths
10/12		A Palestinian mob's killing of two Israeli soldiers
10/12	The first helicopter attacks on Arafat's compound and Palestinian Authority security forces	
10/16	A summit meeting in Sharm el-Sheikh, Egypt, designed to halt violence	Agreement on inquiry into the causes of violence and a return to negotiation
10/20	Israeli threat to suspend a peace process	14 Palestinian deaths, including a 14-year-old boy
10/23	The first large-scale attempt to blockade a Palestinian town Beit Jalla	
10/26		*The first major suicide bombing attack on an Israeli post by the Islamic Jihad*

10/28	The continuation of sporadic fighting with heavier fighting near Beit Jalla	
10/30	*The first efforts to create physical barriers* between the Israelis and Palestinians	
11/1	The death of three Israeli soldiers	
11/2	Two Israeli deaths by Palestinian car bombing	The Palestinian explosion of a car bomb in the Jerusalem marketplace
11/3–	Gradual decline in the number of clashes	
11/15	Israeli helicopter attacks resulting in four Palestinian deaths	
11/17		Arafat call for the cessation of shooting in the Palestinian controlled areas
11/20–	Israeli killing of Palestinian gunmen	Continuing car and roadside bombing
11/21	The missile strikes	The escalation of gunfire
11/21–	Israeli military targeting armed group members	The *persistence of unchecked violence* with continuing casualties
12/19	Israeli–Palestinian meeting to discuss prospect for peace	
12/23	Clinton proposal for resuming negotiations	
1/21/2001	Beginning of a new round of Israeli–Palestinian talks in the Egyptian Red Sea resort of Taba	Progress made despite some deadlocked issues
2/6/2001	The electoral victory of conservative Likud party	The end of the peace process

Note
Although frustration and anger ran deep especially on the Palestinian side prior to the end of September 2000, a provocative visit to the Muslim shrines by Ariel Sharon unleashed the entire cycle of mob violence, military retaliation, cease-fire, renewed violence. Violence took place alongside an attempt to reign in uncontrolled fighting and to reach a durable solution. The italicized acts and events in the above table indicate each step toward a further heightened level of hostility.

Post-conflict transformation

Even if the main issues may have been resolved, lingering doubts and suspicion continue due to the uncertainty of future interactions. The emergence of new relationships ought to focus on future expectations beyond present interaction patterns as well as past memories of atrocities and victimization. Institutional restructuring (needed to tackle a source of grievances) brings about new ways issues are to be addressed in the future. In the failure of continuing to deal with root causes, a post-conflict process can be derailed only to see the return of more contentious battles (Jeong, 2005).

Thus the process to bring about a negotiated solution needs to be linked to incorporating post-conflict peace building efforts. In the case of Angola and Mozambique, in spite of control of violence as well as political stability, economic and social progress has been lagging. While economic rewards and government posts were offered to the former leaders of rebel forces in Angola, ordinary combatants and refugees faced numerous economic challenges. In Guatemala and other poor countries emerging from civil wars, a high level of economic insecurity (as related to unemployment, etc.) has created social uncertainty. To keep a low level of violence, Australian peacekeepers have occasionally intervened in East Timor to prevent political instability from becoming out of control.

Once parties agree to the cessation of violence at the negotiating table, it is accompanied by the longer term challenges of land, electoral, constitutional, or security sector reform. Thus, transformation can broadly touch not only psychological relationships of overcoming victim–offender relationships but also institutional reform. Ethnic pluralism can be institutionalized by power-sharing mechanisms (based on the acknowledgment of ethnic differences and veto power on matters vital to each group) along with economic opportunities and the respect for cultural traditions of diverse groups.

In the process from settlement to reconstruction, democratic institutions nurture a foundation for human rights and reconciliation. Synergies for transforming adversarial relationships can be created by the recognition of the suffering and trauma from past atrocities and prioritization in healing social wounds. The cessation of violence and intimidation is an essential condition in the empowerment of victims and restoration of their social status.

Approaches to conflict prevention

Prevention is more effective and less costly than handling a crisis after the eruption of a violent conflict. The initial focus of prevention sheds light on controlling behavioral dynamics created by a catalyst of violence in a polarized society. Fear and mistrust lay the groundwork for the recurrence of contentious fights. In the escalation of existing tensions into violence, prevention may focus on containing the spread of fighting. A violence-control mechanism such as peacekeeping creates safe space for addressing the root causes of intractable conflicts. The ultimate goal of conflict prevention can be achieved through institutional arrangements designed for the mitigation of inequality and other sources of grievances.

Once a manifest conflict starts, prevention may focus on a destructive aspect of adversarial relationships. The rules and dynamics of struggle need to be established in the way resolution of differences does not require a violent contest of will. The efforts to promote nonviolent competition support the control of escalatory force. The destructive elements of conflict need to be replaced by a struggle which does not depend on mass violence. Beyond political intervention, civilian peace monitors (dispatched to observe and report any incidence of human rights violations) and humanitarian aid can serve as tools to mitigate violence inflicted upon civilians.

As a matter of fact, violence control, as an initial step of prevention, is essential to engendering a hospitable environment for negotiation. In addition, it is more difficult to handle a conflict once the escalation of initial confrontation generates more issues to be handled. The mere containment of violence may produce freezing effects in intense fighting, not paving a road for problem solving in itself. A multitude of negotiation forums can be designed for active search for transforming the roots of a conflict.

The nature of intervention differs in varying crisis situations. As happened in Macedonia (during the mid-1990s) after the eruption of Albanian ethnic violence, preventive diplomacy initially consists of the dispatch of a special envoy in conjunction with a human rights monitoring team. In the immediate aftermath of the 1993 assassination of the Burundi president, James Jonah (the UN Undersecretary General for Africa) departed for Bujumbura as part of a fact-finding mission. Instead of providing the international military protection requested by Prime Minister Kinigi, the UN Secretary General's special envoy for Burundi, Ahmedou Ould-Abudallah brokered political settlement via mediation in an attempt to bring stability to the crisis situation (Maundi, 2003).

In a humanitarian crisis characterized by uncontrolled violence and starvation, coercive intervention is necessary, as seen in Somalia. As French and British forces did in the internal conflicts of Western African countries, forceful intervention can restrain horrific acts by undisciplined militia forces. The British sent troops to quell indiscriminate attacks on civilians by the rebel forces during the civil war of Sierra Leone in the mid-1990s. The French military intervened in an effort to calm a civil war which broke out in 2002 and divided Côte d'Ivoire into a rebel-held north and a government-controlled south. In addressing atrocities in gross power asymmetry, external parties may have to depend on coercive forces for the cessation of further human suffering. In response to the Haiti military dictatorship's abuse of their population, the Clinton administration restored democracy on the island by the dispatch of armed contingents in 1994.

Both overt and covert coercion, ranging from economic sanctions to military intervention, is adopted as conflict regulation strategies. As part of the pressure on the military government to seek negotiated settlement in the Sudanese civil war, its neighboring countries (Uganda, Ethiopia, Eritrea) imposed economic sanctions. Various approaches to conflict prevention and mitigation fall in a continuum between short-term intervention such as peacekeeping or enforcement and long-term security promotion (oriented toward the protection of human rights and economic well-being) and institutional change. The "minimum" condition for peace is the absence of overt physical violence through the immediate cessation of uncontrolled violence. The establishment of conditions for the safety of civilian populations can be supported by the surveillance of warlords and militia activities, and the restriction of troop movements as well as protection of refugees.

Management approaches are oriented toward handling an imminent crisis within a framework of humanitarian intervention. Preventive measures may emphasize the control of significant armed violence or its spread, but at the same time they need to pay attention to humanitarian crisis. International intervention can be designed to mitigate a negative impact of social chaos or the lack of order on direct threats to civilian populations. Coercive diplomacy might be needed in reversing an escalatory motion, but the restoration of order through military force needs to be linked to long-term planning to change the conditions for the causes of violence. Political and economic solutions are necessary to avoid continued dependence on outside assistance (Boutros-Ghali, 1995).

Early warning has been a main pillar of the UNDP Ferghana Valley Preventative Development Program and OSCE CONFLICT monitoring in Kyrgyzstan. In particular, preventive diplomacy by OSCE has allowed Kyrgyzstan to buttress social relations especially because a status quo can be challenged by weakening states and erosion of social structures. As the increased tensions in the Ferghana Valley region exposed vulnerability to violent conflict, the Kyrgyz–Tajik Conflict Prevention Project, carried out with the assistance of two regional NGOs, was aimed at the peaceful coexistence of different ethnic groups in both countries in tandem with restored social infrastructure. The program targeted border areas vulnerable to violent conflict due to inter-group tension ascribed to competition over resources on disputed borders. The conflict prevention project has been built into public awareness, education on inter-ethnic tolerance, and community mediation.

Behavioral and structural dimensions of preventive approaches

A focus on proximate causes of an unstable conflict situation might be oriented toward preventing the translation of triggering events (coups, electoral fraud) toward full-blown hostilities. Violence needs to be controlled before the achievement of any kind of agreement by a negotiation or facilitation process. On the other hand, a frequent resort to threats (intended to curb warring parties' behavior) is incompatible with building trust in a search for a more effective, long-term response to the causes of internal civil war. Long-term visions need to be developed to allay underlying stress (associated with poverty, ethnic, racial and religious differences, weak state capacity to manage tensions and power inequalities).

Prevention may shed light on the transformation of preconditions for the emergence of a conflict originating from the administrative and political incapacities of the government to produce effective policy responses, and consequently loss of authority. It can also respond to both behavioral and structural factors which drive partisans to contend with each other as well as conditions behind the formulation of antagonistic goals. In the long run, escalation to a deadly conflict can be prevented with a structural or attitudinal adjustment.

Various settings of conflict prevention demand actions to avoid the recurrence of violent incidents of antagonistic confrontations. Residual antagonism provides a fertile ground to nourish future hostilities. In terms of prevention, long-term efforts (including track II diplomacy based on sustained informal communication and contact) can be made to allay the deep emotional hostilities and negotiate a political arrangement which is more compatible with each other's needs and interests. In addition, development assistance can be reformulated in transforming a wider context of conflict by supporting regional integration along with support for good governance and civil society support. Infrastructure development linking countries of the southern Caucasus was supported by the European Union, UNDP, USAID, Oxfam, Save the Children, and ICRC with the broad aim of poverty eradication in mind.

Context of conflict regulation

In general, an indirect and regulated competition (for instance, sales in an open market) is less likely to generate adversarial relationships than class or racial conflict. In malignant social processes, however, competitive orientations make it difficult to forge common interests. In fact, direct interference with the other's preference has a high potential for producing enmity. On the other hand, adversarial competition can be prevented from turning into hostile confrontations by regulations based on the adherence to rules and the imposition of sanctions against rule violations.

When it is difficult to resolve or even reach a short-term settlement, it becomes important to control a negative orientation toward violent conflict which perpetuates long-standing cycles of hurting and destruction. Once conflict is formed, peacekeeping and other methods can be introduced to contain and reduce aggressive acts. When the accommodation of different values and needs are difficult to achieve in the short term, priority may fall to the control and mitigation of violence prior to the creation of a durable peace structure. Reaching an agreement on the cessation of armed hostilities enables warring parties to exit from the violent phase of a conflict. If adversaries fail to find a formula to address the core underlying causes of conflicts, old attitudes and structural contradictions can easily pave the way for conflict recurrence.

The necessity to control violent confrontations has led to the development of appropriate forms of third-party intervention. These entail the development of a buffer zone between warring factions and surveillance of troop movements. Peacekeeping operations have been dispatched to numerous conflict zones to hold a fragile cease-fire agreement between belligerent parties. In a comparable manner to international peacekeeping, community policing has been utilized for lessening bloodshed among gang or militia group members.

Peace enforcement and humanitarian intervention would be required in civil war situations, as is exemplified by the 1994 US-led intervention to stop warlord violence and mass starvation in Somalia. In a chaotic humanitarian situation, urgent relief work and other immediate assistance are needed to contain and control explosive situations. A crisis-driven response to violent conflicts often includes not only military but also civilian components such as provision of health care, prevention of widespread disease, and supply of food and other basic necessities for refugees.

Coercive diplomacy may be effective in the restoration of order prior to the application of mediation and other methods of bringing settlement. The intervention of West African Economic Union forces cooled down chaotic fighting among rival factions in Liberia between 1994 and 1996, eventually facilitating negotiations on the political transition. In the Nigerian civil war in the mid-1960s, intermediaries dispatched by the British government and the secretariat of the British Commonwealth attempted to convince both the government and Ibo rebel commanders to cease fighting.

Mitigating tension does not deal directly with the sources of deep divisions, but only buries the crisis. As is illustrated by the Israeli occupation of the Golan Heights in Syria since the Six Day War in 1966, contentious issues can be frozen to await future resolution for a prolonged period. The principles and activities involved in management are different from those of resolution.

Conflict management strategies

Strategies of conflict response are diverse, ranging from standing firm, negotiation, and disengagement, to submission. These choices have implications for balancing the pursuit of one's interests and relationship management. Standing firm with principle may be necessary to signal an adversary regarding a commitment to block excessive and unreasonable demands. It is likely to serve as a communication means to let opponents know one's own uncompromising priorities beforehand to prevent an unnecessary test of will. Those who have higher stakes in the issue are likely to take more confrontational strategies although that can be moderated by an imbalance in power and weaker capabilities to confront an adversary.

The parties may have opposing objectives, but they can agree on the means to settle differences. Principles on fairness in competition can be established in making decisions on the distribution of goods and resources. In employment or other contract relationships, reward systems can be accepted by regular bargaining. Excessive expectations can be contained or controlled by the creation of a negotiation culture which supports collaboration in search of acceptable options to all parties. Negotiated settlement becomes difficult if discussion about substantive issues translates into differences in principles, hence making any concession appear like a defeat. When functional problems turn into matters of control and power, it is more difficult to focus on the original concerns.

In cultural settings oriented toward collectivist values, avoidance and yielding are common methods of nonconfrontational conflict management. In a culture where survival traditionally depends on close cooperation among family and community members, the overt expression of hostile feelings is regarded as a threat to the group unity. The suppression of individual desires is highly valued in collaborative cultures oriented toward preserving harmony. In most affectionate relationships, yielding can be based on sacrifice to meet a close group member's needs, as is the case with women in Africa who give up food for their children in the case of starvation.

By conceding, one party accepts their loss in favor of the other's gain, but it can be the quickest way to contain, regulate, and end conflict by satisfying the demand of an adversary. It is easier to give up part of one's wants if the existence of multi-faceted issues furnishes a substitute for the concession or lends priority to other issues. The availability of alternative paths to satisfying one's objectives reduces the necessity for a contentious engagement. In a closely integrated relationship, yielding on one issue is not necessarily a loss in the long run if a future reward is likely to come.

If relationship maintenance brings about overall benefits, either tangible or intangible (for example, affection or prestige), conceding is more desirable than insisting on narrow gains. Preventing damage to the existing relationships can be a main objective when beneficial transactions exist. It is less costly to manage all the contentious issues within agreeable boundaries. A party, which regards the relationship as more beneficial than the other, is more likely to acquiesce. On the other hand, continuous submission is detrimental if the other party takes advantage of goodwill, not valuing the importance of concessions, and disregards the conceding party's concerns or needs.

As a method of conflict management, the avoidance of contentious issues can take various forms, ranging from the denial of existence of a problem to disengagement. Stepping back from a conflict may be preferred under varying circumstances from a low stake in the fight to little chance of achieving the goals and a dim hope for a solution (ascribed to the complexity of the situation).

If the fighting is not worth risking full-scale war, conflict can eventually subside by withdrawing from contentious engagement. In cases where the risk of escalation is too high, parties may be willing to scale down their demand and shy away from escalatory tactics. In a series of wars in Kashmir, both India and Pakistan carefully avoided expanding the armed confrontations to their main territories. In the 1998 Kagli conflict which was the first incident after the possession of nuclear weapons by both sides, India chose disengagement strategies not to escalate the conflict after repelling the Pakistani-backed incursions.

In the absence of perceived significance of the issues, diplomatic or military clashes can remain a one-time fiasco or episode which does not merit time or attention. The Colombian army's entry into Ecuador's territory in spring 2008 produced uproar among Ecuador and its allies in Latin America, but it ended without a serious escalation because of the Colombian government's apology. The preservation of the status quo can be the main motivation behind the desire not to enlarge the scope of the fight, but it may work for a short-lived, minor conflict.

Even though too great a gap in substantive interests and needs as well as capacities (to pursue them) may force any of the adversaries to give in, balanced outcomes can still be sought by a creative use of avoidance and compromise. In the failure to attain integrative solutions that permit both parties to obtain what they want, the identification of commonly held principles or values can contribute to the establishment of the basis for fair decision making. The rulings by the International Court of Justice may serve as a better venue for a conflict between states whose relationships are characterized by power or status asymmetry.

Even in zero-sum situations of competition, the relationships can be preserved if the rules are considered agreeable and if the loser has a future opportunity to compete again for the prize. Before emotions flare up, thus competing parties may agree to refer to an acceptable set of values and principles as a basis for managing their conflicts. The decision-making rules may need to be occasionally reaffirmed or refined according to changing circumstances.

The acceptance of mutually agreeable, established procedures to settle differences helps avoid resistance against yielding to a person. The unfavorable decision made by a judge or panel can be more easily swallowed when the process is institutionalized (in such situations as trade disputes handled by the WTO). Indeed, deference to shared norms and values saves one's face, neutralizing emotional attachment to a win or loss.

Asymmetry in conflict styles

Trust-based relationships can be further strengthened by the reciprocation of yielding. At the same time, the strategies adopted by opposing parties can be imbalanced or diametrically opposed. Even though one party wants to avoid conflict, the other party may choose confrontational approaches by taking provocative actions to extract a response to their demand. In other situations, one of the opponents seeks mutual accommodation, but the other party may take an uncompromising position.

Most importantly, waging conflict takes a different path, depending on the extent of asymmetry in issue salience as well as power differentials among parties. A weaker side is likely to seek avoiding a major confrontation with a stronger opponent since the costs of action are perceived greater than any possible returns. In response to Israeli air strikes on a suspected nuclear laboratory in September 2007, Syria chose to limit its reaction only to verbal condemnation owing to its clear military inferiority and the lack of a good prospect to get compensation for the destroyed facilities. By forcing a weaker party to abandon their objectives or give in, a stronger party may be able to maintain control and domination.

On the other hand, issue salience may push even a subordinate party to organize protests despite fear of torture, arrest, or other harm. In unfortunate circumstances such as Tibet under Chinese occupation since 1950, very few choices exist for the marginalized party in that ascent to an oppressive rule means the acceptance of the dominant party's total control over cultural and religious life as well as the deprivation of freedom and civic rights. In such situations that gross injustice is inevitably embedded in an oppressive relationship, a weaker party can be morally or politically supported by advocacy groups.

Theories on decision making

Although a coherent body of knowledge on conflict has yet to emerge, diverse theoretical perspectives have offered an explanation about the causes of violent behavior and its control. The roots of social conflict are connected to the struggle for the imposition of a hierarchical system and the denial of dignity through institutional control of religious, social, and economic aspirations. A variety of theoretical explanation seems to be necessary due to difficulties in capturing multiple dimensions of conflict behavior and attitudes under one gigantic umbrella theory. As conflict is considered innate in human interactions, research on conflict resolution should pay more attention to decision making in broad social relationships.

Rationality and decision-making behavior

In "rational choice" theory perspectives, optimal decisions satisfy a set of calculations which serve cost–benefit analysis based on the principles of minimizing losses and maximizing gains; therefore, weighing rewards and costs of various courses of action is guided by the single criterion of self-interest. The utilitarian principles are often either implicitly or explicitly applied to decision making on initiating or ending a fight as well as negotiation strategies. Israel could have directly invaded Gaza to stop rocket fire by Palestinian militants, but given its expected heavy casualties, in June 2008, the Israeli government chose to agree to relax the economic blockade of Gaza in return for the cessation of further attacks originating from the Hamas-controlled territory.

In "rationalist" thinking, the motivations for the termination of conflict are ascribed to decreasing chances for gains through continued fighting and the availability of less costly options of settlement. In order to recover the Sinai, the Egyptian President Anwar Saddat decided to negotiate instead of preparing for yet another war after the American-sponsored truce in October 1973. In a rational choice paradigm, thus, conflict behavior is adapted to a changing balance between different interests embedded in continued fighting versus early settlement. In zero-sum situations, one's gain is diametrically opposed to an adversary's loss.

Negotiated settlement is aimed at converting a zero-sum game situation into win–win outcomes. By agreeing to return the Sinai occupied during the Six Day War, Israel was able to enhance security since the deal eliminated any possible future attacks by an alliance of Arabic states. Although Egypt became the first Arabic state which recognized Israel and gave up some other territories, Cairo was able to reclaim a vital part of its territory without shedding any blood.

In many real world situations, individual actors seek competitive strategies to maximize short-term, narrow self-interests, but cooperative moves are often necessary to yield a better long-term outcome in a highly interdependent relationship. For instance, unregulated pollution may increase one country's economic competitiveness in international trade due to cheaper production costs, but it eventually hurts the country's own long-term well-being through the negative effects of global warming. Thus multinational cooperation is essential to obtain public goods (the prevention of climate change) by regulating each state's polluting activities.

The rules of a game can create incentives and disincentives for certain behavior. Because the outcome is in the hands of more than one player, structural features of the game itself (manifested in gains and losses associated with different moves) are key concerns in decision making. In considering that an adversary's response changes the outcome matrix of one's choice of actions, as in a prisoner's dilemma games, the expected utility is closely related to the effects of each other's strategic choices. The dramatic increase in Chinese and Indian emissions of greenhouse gases can easily outstrip reduction in the emission level of carbon dioxide by Western Europe. The overall reversal in global warming trends cannot be achieved without collective actions which prevent a "free rider" who wants to shoulder less than a fair share of costs needed to fix the problem.

One's welfare can be increased only by cooperation with adversaries. As exemplified by the arms race, one country's attempt to maximize unilateral gains (military superiority) would lead a rival state to do the same thing since unconditional cooperation (unilateral disarmament) in this situation generates the worst outcome (insecurity). In the absence of trust and agreement on coordinated actions, the most rational strategy is to persist with a competitive strategy (an arms race) to avoid an undesirable result of unilateral disarmament. Gains achieved by seeking exclusive self-interests are only shortlived, since the other party is most likely to reverse its own course of action even if they might have initially taken a cooperative move.

The pursuit of self-interest by each party yields an outcome that is far less attractive than is produced by mutual cooperation. When achieving unilateral gains is a dominant strategy for each player, mutual defection (competition for superior arms capabilities) produces a less desirable outcome (decreased economic growth in combination with growth in destructive military capabilities by an adversary) than joint cooperation (disarmament and devotion of financial and technological capabilities to economic prosperity and social welfare).

The dilemma in a collective bargaining situation is that cooperation produces a better outcome than competitive strategies, producing the greatest benefit for all. Yet competition remains as a dominant strategy owing to a suspicion of an adversary's motives (for unilateral advantage at the expense of one's loss). Given a lack of trust in most conflict situations, a tit-for-tat strategy has been presented as a solution to this dilemma with stress on the norm of reciprocity. One party may start with a cooperative move on the basis of an expectation of an opponent's reciprocal action. In the event of defection by an adversary, the party can quickly switch to a competitive game with a retaliatory move. However, once the other party opts to choose a cooperative strategy, the party will forgive and return to a reciprocal exchange of cooperation. In the end, cooperation can be institutionalized to develop predictable patterns of transactions.

Despite its great heuristic (conceptual) value, the application of utilitarian perspectives is often limited in managing adverse relationships. The outcome of conflict may not be evaluated from universalistic assumptions about an individual actor's calculations about utility values if differences in psychological or other personal characteristics (such as emotional arousals and willingness to take a higher risk for bigger political gains) play a more important role in determining ultimate decisions. The decision-making choices can also be circumscribed by organizational constraints as well as the group psychology of a policy-making body. Internal divisions complicate the choice of actions by a group in that discussion about the stakes in conflict is likely to involve power struggles reflecting different factional interests. In addition, rational choice theories are more suitable for assessing purely interest-based bargaining structures than value-based, multicultural conflict settings.

Cognitive and perceptual limitations

People do not always choose decisions on the basis of maximum interests. Prospect theory suggests that most people can settle less with more certain outcomes than seeking higher benefits that are less likely to be gained with more effort. Indeed, time pressure and complexity of data drive many decision makers to choose the most minimally acceptable alternative (encountered first) as opposed to exhaustively gathering information in a search for the maximum.

According to bounded rationality defined by Herbert Simon (1996), humans are not being fully informed to make the most suitable decisions in many given situations due to difficulties in the management of information overload. Individual cognitive functions are programmed differently to process most information which we encounter. It is often the context of an individual's experience that orders perceptions according to preset belief systems, theories, or images.

In many socio-psychological theories of conflict behavior, perceived threats are attributed to a lack of trust and misinterpretation of intentions. A high level of threat causes stress to decision makers, producing cognitive biases. As is most clearly illustrated by the Bush administration's decision on going to war in Iraq, both the limited ability to consider various options and the misrepresentation or distortion of data can be factors which contribute to the initiation of a conflict. Collective misjudgment and risk-taking behavior result from a small group decision-making environment which encourages a tendency to seek conformity, prohibiting questions about each other's reasoning and confidence in the success of aggressive actions. In ethnic warfare in Bosnia-Herzegovina and Rwanda, group dynamics are affected by stereotyped images of enemies and the dehumanization of competing out-groups.

In general, psychological challenges to conflict resolution are, to a great extent, derived from rigid perceptions and cognitive inflexibility. In fact, pessimistic attitudes toward the cessation of a struggle produce perceptional limitation on any initiatives to bring about conciliation along with a lack of knowledge about each other's true intentions and necessities. Sustainable peace might be difficult due to long-held attitudes especially hardened after the experience of atrocities. Exclusive values and ideological commitments put cognitive limitations on the recognition of an adversary's rights, needs, and interests. Orthodox Jews are making historic, biblical claims to land with expanded settlement, while Hamas denies the existing state of Israel that cannot be reversed. The dim prospect for a negotiated settlement is ascribed to rigid belief systems deduced from a blind loyalty to a group and a continued commitment to its extreme values.

Culture and social behavior

Resolving conflicts that include such dimensions as ethnic claims to territories and political autonomy often requires negotiation of incompatible values beyond material interests. In cross-cultural perspectives, an overall process of conflict and its resolution is not separable from complex systems of meaning that prescribe rules about mutual interaction, verbal interpretation, and management of expectations. Most importantly, cultural norms provide a point of reference for communication and acceptable patterns of behavior. Collective sentiments are represented in a diverse set of understandings about the outside world.

The social world is fragmented into a multitude of cultural meanings which advocate particular moral visions and knowledge bases. The articulation of issues and expectations regarding desirable forms of agreement are heavily influenced by our understandings of the self and the world. In conflict resolution, the mediation of different social worlds is derived from the interpretation of alien cultures. Meanings attached to conflict by individuals and groups are revealed through different concepts of social life which in turn affect behavioral manifestations. In a Western dispute resolution model, the conceptions of a person prescribe the control of emotion, measured behavior and logical calculations. To be successful in interest-based bargaining, we have to adopt rational narratives.

Recurring cultural patterns and underlying principles emerge from particular social settings and institutions that facilitate the internalization of beliefs and attitudes about the establishment of our relations with an external world. A cultural scheme of reference can be utilized for understanding the identity and behavior of a social group. As people do not share the same value judgments about each other's behavior as well as assumptions about conflict processes, interaction patterns between adversaries can be relegated to differences in cultural norms about honor, respect, and trust (Faure, 2003). From the perspectives of culture, conflict resolution is considered in terms of the unique patterns of relations embodied in specific time and space.

Negotiation between North Korean and US government officials has been full of suspicion and mistrust often associated with different interpretations of each other's behavior. In arguing over the responsibility for the collapse of the 1994 landmark agreement to freeze Pyongyang's nuclear programs, the Bush administration officials focused on a specific set of issues (such as uranium enrichment programs). On the other hand, the North Koreans accused Washington of a lack of commitment to improving bilateral relations which is, in their view, essential to trust building that would in turn let them fully proceed to the abandonment of their nuclear programs without a fear of future US attacks. Insulting words (such as "tyrant" and "pygmy") and other statements disparaging the North Korean leadership by President Bush (such as "loathing" President Kim Jong-Il as well as categorizing North Korea as one of the "axes of evil") were taken far more seriously in Pyongyang than US government officials imagined. An extreme sense of humiliation, contempt, and insecurity provoked the North Koreans to take highly provocative actions that culminated in the testing of nuclear bombs in the fall of 2006, even further risking their isolation from the outside world.

In a high-context culture, the issues are not distinctively separated from the relationship or person. It is contrasted with a low-context culture which does regard the sources of contention as separate from the protagonists (Avruch, 2002). In particular, conflict in industrial societies is interpreted from an impersonal, instrumental, solution-oriented stance, but affective, relational, personal issues such as respect and shame are inevitably crucial in a traditional culture which emphasizes communal links. Thus individualistic, low-context cultures shed light on competitive bargaining strategies without much consideration of the implications for future relationships. The adoption of collaborative strategies is encouraged in collectivistic, high-context cultures that stress inclusion and association.

In many high-context cultures, "face" is viewed as a psychological-affective construct closely connected to the notions of disgrace, honor, and obligation, along with its contribution to the maintenance of mutual obligations of group members. Indeed, these relational qualities "are reciprocal forces that serve to unite groups, police the boundaries, define who is included or excluded, and enforce conformity" (Augsburger, 1992, p. 103). While "face" needs to be respected, face saving can be manipulated in international conflicts for political gains.

China is known to aggressively defend its self-image and skillfully uses face-saving devices to fend off foreign pressure to improve human rights conditions or demand balanced trade. The Chinese government successfully convinced US policy makers that pressure tactics would not encourage them, for instance, to deregulate their currency values in an international market, effectively taking the issues off official negotiation agendas. In authoritarian Asian countries, any foreign scrutiny of human rights violations has been countered under the name of "Asian values" oriented toward a collective cultural context.

This notion has been effectively challenged by former South Korean President and Nobel laureate Kim Dae-Jung who illustrated that there is no such thing as human rights abuses in Asian values.

Face saving can be applied to the promotion of the reputation and values of one's own community, but paradoxically it can lead to ignorance of the collective interests of a larger community. Japan is known for highly regarding social obligations, honor, and shame for a wrongful deed and policing its own members' behavior. For instance, when some Japanese tourists scribbled on the Italian historic monuments, they were socially ostracized in their own society, and the Japanese voluntarily offered Italy payment and other compensation with their sincere apology. However, on the issues of whaling, the Japanese government has been adamant about its violation of the international whaling ban and even attempted to sabotage and derail the long-established international policies. In spite of a widespread international outcry and condemnation, the Japanese have defended their position on whaling by referring to their "cultural tradition."

The role of power in conflict process and outcome

Power relations as well as different psychological and cultural attributes play an important role in a conflict process. In the paradigm of *realpolitik* one country's ability to affect the outcome of an international conflict is reflected in the parties' power status vis-à-vis their opponent's. In a relational context, power yields the capability to force another to act in one's own desires or wishes by changing the party's future welfare conditions (Blalock, 1989). Thus power superiority puts one group in a position to either dictate or influence another group's behavior via the control of a reward or punishment system.

The impact of power distribution on a conflict outcome can be mitigated by a range of political and psychological factors such as national unity, ideological commitment, morale, etc. While there are quantitative indicators to measure the amount of power such as economic, technological, and physical capabilities, these elements do not directly translate into specific effects. Each party certainly has different capabilities to mobilize resources to effectively resist a rival's attempt to force their own way. In direct military clashes with Israel, such antagonists as Hezbollah are likely to have more ability and determination to provide sustained resistance than the standing armies of Syria.

In understanding contemporary political realities, some argue that power struggles remain as the genesis of human conflict, since those dissatisfied with the status quo inevitably challenge dominant group positions (Darhendorf, 1959). As represented by protracted political battles in Lebanon for the last 18 months, political landscapes were redrawn by the mobilization and counter-mobilization of opposing groups in an organized campaign for challenging and defending a political status quo. In Uzbekistan and Burma, the regime's willingness to shoot unarmed civilians protesting on the streets has silenced any voice of opposition to the brutal dictatorships, but a highly oppressive state apparatus cannot be sustained for ever, and will eventually have to come to an end.

The existence of power asymmetry seems to be ubiquitous in most contentious struggles, ranging from labor strikes to competition for scarce water and land in Africa. Racial and ethnic tension arises from the superimposition of power relations on major social cleavages along with political and economic disparities. The power of a majority government can be a source for social injustice when it suppresses minority group rights to survival. The deconstruction of dominant power relations may come from the transformation of social values and institutions which permit their justification.

Further reading

Boutros-Ghali, B. (1995) *Agenda for Peace*, New York: United Nations.

Burton, J. W. (2001) "Conflict Prevention as a Political System," *International Journal of Peace Studies*, 6 (1): 23–32.

Byrne, S. (2001) "Consociational and Civic Society Approaches to Peacebuilding in Northern Ireland," *Journal of Peace Research*, 38 (3): 327–352.

Conteh-Morgan, E. (2004) *Collective Political Violence*, New York: Routledge.

Franke, Volker (2006) "The Peacebuilding Dilemma: Civil–Military Cooperation in Stability Operations," *International Journal of Peace Studies*, 11 (2): 5–24.

Galtung, J. (2007) "Conflict Formation and Transformations: Deep Culture and Structure," in C. P. Webel and J. Galtung (eds) *Handbook of Peace and Conflict Studies*, New York: Routledge.

Lee, H. (2001) "Cultural Confrontation and Compromise: The Response of Non-Western Societies to Western Political Ideas," *International Journal of Peace Studies*, 6 (2): 53–74.

Sandole, D. (1998) "A Comprehensive Mapping of Conflict and Conflict Resolution: A Three Pillar Approach," *Peace and Conflict Studies*, 5 (2): 1–30.

Singer, J. D. and Small, M. (1972) *The Wages of War, 1816–1965: A Statistical Handbook*, NJ: John Wiley & Sons.

3   Conflict transformation

Since conflict can be very destructive, how to wind down the rage of violence and bring normalcy to inter-personal, inter-group, inter-state relations has become an important concern. Various efforts can be made to promote conflict prevention, to bring about the de-escalation of an unending struggle and eventually the building of peace. In particular, long-term relations are also affected by structural, institutional, and cultural dimensions of conflict. In an attempt to bring an end to a conflict peacefully, it is key to understand various aspects of conflict transformation that constitute the essential conditions for resolution.

This chapter reviews different types and categories of conflict relations and various processes that alter conditions for violent struggle. The movements of protracted conflict, for instance, in Bosnia-Herzegovina, Iraq, Afghanistan, and Palestine are organic, not static and often amorphous. The maintenance of oppressive relations by torture, killing, and other abuses as well as uncontrolled violence draws a cloud over the prospect for peace.

Meanings of transformation

There are certainly desirable directions of change to open a collaborative road to conflict resolution along with the cessation of activities organized to inflict atrocious acts upon an adversary. Most clearly, actors' capacity changes during the multiple stages of conflict from emergence, escalation, entrapment, de-escalation to termination. In power imbalanced situations, a superior party is not likely to have much incentive to make compromise, since it can push its own way to end the conflict. Thus each adversary attempts to prevail in a quest for victory and to bring about favorable changes in strengthening their positions. The attempts to impose one's own views or values on an opponent can unavoidably involve a costly contest and struggle.

As part of a natural conflict process, both the internal and external conditions faced by each adversary continue to alter regardless of our efforts to resolve them. Various dimensions of conflict have evolving characteristics, owing to the addition of new issues or the decreasing salience of existing issues as well as changes in tactics to pursue one's pivotal goals. The participation of new actors in a polarized conflict may create unexpected turns in a struggle. Rules of engagement in the fight may evolve along with changes in the expectations and norms that the actors follow in their interactions with each other.

In fact, the dynamics of interactions between adversaries especially in a large-scale struggle always have a potential for change, either negative or positive. In negative changes, both internal and external dynamics of conflict reinforce divisions among opposing groups for further escalation. In order to curb aggressive actions in a polarized environment, destructive forces (such as physical attacks) need to be controlled. The absence of functioning states, for instance, in Somalia and Afghanistan, has been detrimental to the development of the political capacity to overcome factional differences. In genocidal conflicts, the release of unregulated violence can be ascribed to a collapse of legal or moral codes (which define the acceptable boundaries of human behavior) as well as institutional failures to prohibit atrocious behavior.

Peaceful transformation of conflict relationships can be consigned to a conscience-driven process to reduce violence and empower a marginalized party. The positive connotations of conflict transformation are, in general, related to structural changes in support of the recognition of justice and everyone's right to survival and human dignity. In fact, durable solutions are not likely to be derived from short-term bandage approaches to political alienation or socio-economic oppression. For instance, armed opposition to the governments in the Philippines, Thailand, Morocco, Colombia, and Nigeria has persisted despite the governments' heavy investment to root out resistance movements militarily.

Some actors certainly do not have much capacity to actively change undesirable aspects of conflict conditions imposed on them. They may have no choice but to passively respond to challenges posed by powerful adversaries in a struggle for survival. In fact, weaker parties may simply have to adjust themselves to detrimental changes brought about by perpetrator parties. This has been well illustrated by the Chinese government's use of migration of Han nationalities to Tibet and Xingjian as a means to solidify their rule by rebalancing the population mix, undermining the original inhabitants' rights to their own territory.

In a lopsided relationship, even an exploitative relationship can be justified by the logic of domination. The highest ranking Chinese government official in charge of Tibet, Zhang Qingli stated in 2007: "The Communist Party is like the parent to the Tibetan people, and it is always considerate about what the children need." He even added an insult to this remark by stressing: "The Central Party Committee is the real Buddha for Tibetans" (*New York Times*, March 18, 2008). In order to justify their brutal rule in Tibet, the Chinese elite have been consistently arguing that it benefits Tibetans even though it is obvious that beneficial relationships are not imposed by oppressive force.

In oppressed regions of the world, people are deprived of economic means for improving their welfare as well as freedom to choose their political leader. Under foreign occupation, children are not allowed to learn their ancestors' history and culture. Thus the most intense repression entails the denial of a minority group's legitimate claims to self-rule and even basic rights to existence, as well as the deprivation of freedom to use and teach ethnic language and conduct religious practice and even the restriction of physical movements (e.g., the Korean peninsula under the forced annexation by Japan between 1910 and 1945, the Indonesian occupation of East Timor between 1975 and 2002 and currently Tibet and Xingjian).

In grossly power imbalanced situations, the mobilization of global public support is essential to the support of a cause for ending injustice. The transition from a white minority regime to the democratic government of the black majority was, to a great extent, facilitated by worldwide anti-apartheid protests (including divestment in the South African economy) during the 1980s. The world outcry against Chinese oppression in Tibet prior to the summer 2008 Olympics held in Beijing generated public awareness of the long forgotten issue of severe political oppression and cultural genocide: the abduction of a six-year-old boy designated as the Panchan Lama (whose status is second only to the Dalai Lama), psychological indoctrination of monks by such means as "patriotic education," the requirement of government permission to be a monk as well as the destruction of more than 6,000 precious ancient monasteries and artifacts (Beal and Khechog, 2003).

To develop a peaceful relationship, long-term transformation needs to touch upon the emotional, perceptual, and spiritual aspects of conflict as well as the emergence of new behavioral patterns. The integration of society does not emerge from the maintenance of order by means of control. In contrast with mere management approaches, resolving a deep-rooted communal conflict requires the analysis of human motivations and competitive social processes, which have led to the alienation of certain social groups in the first place (Burton, 1997).

Necessary conditions for conflict transformation

The transformation of escalation and entrapment dynamics is necessary in one way or another to resolve conflict. If conflict is ever to be resolved, protracted struggle needs to be controlled by minimizing the destructive nature of negative interactions prior to an attempt to eventually produce settlement through negotiation, either directed or assisted. The main analytical point is to discern the trend and direction of conflict movements (either retaliatory or conciliatory). It is crucial to examine how and when conflict can be reshaped to provide an opportunity for negotiated settlement instead of endless fighting.

Opportunities for communication between adversaries can bring positive changes in the relationship if conflict is interpreted as a problem to be solved. Steps toward building trust could prevent the interpretation of the situation in an extreme fashion, reversing polarization, physical violence, and rancor. The broad scope of conflict resolution seeks self-supporting and durable relationships with the realization of justice. To this end, a conflict can be reframed to examine the essential conditions for mutual coexistence and each community's prosperity. In ethnic conflict, the demand of minority groups for autonomy can be met by diverse options, ranging from independence to a high degree of self-rule to participation in power-sharing governments (Esman, 2004).

Successful negotiation is not the end of a conflict process until settlement terms have been fully implemented. In spite of an agreement on a basic framework, the continuing existence of contentious issues requires further negotiation. Even if both the white government and African National Congress had agreed to majority rule in the early 1990s, it would have taken more than three years for them to nail down details on elections which permitted the transition of power to the black majority. Preventing a return to violent confrontations is an integral part of building a new communal structure acceptable to former adversaries. These efforts are also supported by converting negative perceptions into positive attitudinal changes.

Transformation of a conflict versus a system

Mere alleviating and re-characterizing the conflict can be contrasted with the general enhancement of society as an end state of conflict resolution. The main focus can be either on the control of the conflict at hand (for the containment of violence through cessation of hostilities) or on the conversion of societies (by the initiation of institutional reform). A mere transition of conflict dynamics (from escalation to de-escalation) is often mostly concerned about the restoration of order and the mitigation of violence rather than changes in the political and economic systems which harbor a conflict.

The process of ending more than a decade of the El Salvadoran civil war during the 1990s concentrated on the abolishment or major restructuring of police and security forces (responsible for the torture and killing of civilians), new electoral systems for fair representation of those previously excluded from a political process, land reform, and the formation of the Truth and Reconciliation Commission to investigate past abuses. These measures have been aimed at the relief of economic hardships for peasants, the promotion of a freer society and the prohibition of future abuses of human rights. On the other hand, ending conflict in Cambodia by reaching the 1991 "Comprehensive Political Settlement" agreement between the government and its two opposition forces did not bring an end to, but on the contrary strengthened the authoritarian rule of Prime Minister Hunsen who maintained his grip on power through intimidation and assassination of key opposition figures after a loss in an election to his political rival.

In approaching conflict resolution, we can focus on specific incidents and related issues (for instance, the competition for government power in Kenya's post-election violence) or underlying conditions (such as long-term tribal rivalry and power disparity) that produce incompatibilities. Goal incompatibilities in competition for power can be resolved by such institutional arrangements as power sharing which allocates some key government positions to opposition parties. The conflict can be treated as either an opportunity for institutional, system changes or an unfortunate, incidental phenomenon. Repeated old tensions need to be reframed as more than simple events which occasionally surface and quickly disappear. Settlement approaches tend to be oriented toward specific issues related to conflict behavior itself rather than societal or organizational issues.

In general, recurrent struggles between opposing forces touch on more than differences in opinions and contending interests. As seen in Table 3.1 (p. 40), the denial of autonomy and self-governance to Tibetans after the Chinese occupation in 1950 has been a main source of major recurrent uprisings in 1959, 1979, 1989, and 2008. The mere reliance on surveillance, physical abuse, and other means of control cannot be the main means to quell aspirations for freedom and autonomy. It has been a global trend along with the independence of colonial territories since World War II to respect the rights of national groups under foreign occupation to self-determination. Its denial has become a deep-rooted cause of many intractable conflicts in the contemporary world.

The social and political sources of animosities may serve as a destabilizing force even being implicated in settling personal issues (such as neighborhood disputes involving whites and blacks in a divided township) which are supposed to be purely mundane matters under ordinary circumstances. A system change obviously requires long-term perspectives whereas responding to the immediate issues can be utilized to create a cumulative effect in producing larger changes. Even if conflict is built into socio-economic and political structures, superficial solutions may be deduced from trivialization or individualization of the contentious issues. In this approach, real concerns are isolated or separated from the social fabric which fuels disorder.

Long-lasting conflicts may have taken on lives of their own, almost being autonomous from the participants. In spite of changes in the personnel, each party may have reasons for persisting with the struggle with little difference in their positions. Settling disagreement on a few issues (for instance, school re-districting or the divisions of residential areas) is not the end of animosities among racial or ethnic groups if income and other socio-economic disparities hamper attitudinal and behavioral changes. The limitations of approaches to narrow issues are evident in the disregard for sources of conflict that might be relegated to one group's historical domination over another.

Transformation strategies in such places as Bosnia-Herzegovina may have to concentrate on changes not only in current antagonism but also in its surrounding environment which reinvigorates competition and disparities. Thus, the exploration of a sustainable process of conflict resolution has to consider not only imminent concerns faced by partisans

Table 3.1 Recurring conflict, Tibet

1950	**Beginning of an imposed relationship** Chinese military invasion and occupation of Tibet
1951	**Establishment of a new rule**; the forced acceptance of "Seventeen Point Agreement" The installation of Chinese civil and military headquarters in capital Lhasa Promise of Tibetan autonomy along with respect for the Buddhist religion
Mid- 1950s	**Intensification of resistance** Chinese failure to honor the Seventeen Point Agreement The outbreaks of armed resistance; mounting resentment against Chinese rule
1959 March	**Suppression of opposition** The outbreak of full-scale uprising and 87,000 of Tibetans killed in the Lhasa area alone The exile of the Dalai Lama and some 80,000 other Tibetans to northern India
1966	**Cultural genocide** Cultural revolution in China The destruction of nearly all of Tibet's 6,200 monasteries
Late 1970s	**Reinforcement of Beijing's hegemony** The continuing large-scale relocation of Han Chinese into Tibet
1987	**Gestures for conciliation** Tibetan pursuit of dialogue with Beijing for achieving genuine self-rule The Dalai Lama's call for the establishment of Tibet as a zone of peace
1988 March	**Re-imposition of harsh rule** Riots in Lhasa; the introduction of martial law in Tibet
1995	**Cultural oppression** The detention of a six-year-old boy named as the reincarnation of the Panchen Lama, the second most important figure in Tibetan Buddhism The Chinese designation of another six-year-old boy as sanctioned Panchen Lama
2006	**Further undermining of traditional Tibetan culture** A new railway linking Lhasa to the main cities of China; rapidly increasing Han Chinese influx
2008	**Re-escalation of struggle in a cycle of resistance and suppression** Monk protests spilling over into mass riots Sympathy protest around the world prior to the Beijing Olympics

Source: Freedom House, 2006; BBC, Timeline: Tibet.

but also systemic characteristics which are sources of complaint and resentment. Military assaults on civilian villages suspected of hosting Taliban forces in Afghanistan by NATO forces have been further alienating the population, as civilian casualties along with economic hardships deepen grievances against the occupation of foreign forces.

What needs to be transformed is, in large part, the feelings of powerlessness and associated structural sources of inequity. In South Africa, the shortage of electricity now causes the same inconvenience to both white neighborhoods and black residential areas. The sharing of burdens in a fair manner has certainly become a new indication of a post-apartheid democratic system. This is contrasted with the disproportionate supply of daily necessities under a racially discriminate government. Thus the unsatisfied need of the black residents is not any longer seen as a result of discriminatory policies.

Most antagonistic behavior in social conflict situations has structural origins (such as rising discontent coming from sudden change in the quality of life alongside more skewed income distribution despite new mineral wealth in Mongolia). In a situation where conflict is rooted in gross inequalities and injustice (such as monopolization of water supply through force), discussion about specific issues may need to be linked to institutional change (that can guarantee proportionate representation of opposing groups on a decision-making board responsible for water allocation).

In such places as Palestine, the life of ordinary people has become destabilized due to the structural patterns of underlying relationships. The neglect of the necessity to alter the basic patterns of adversarial relations, not only at perceptional level, but also at a structural decision-making level, can lead to the recurrence of the same type of conflict. For example, a demand for more land by Jewish settlers in the West Bank is the occasional spark that reinitiates violence between the Israeli government and Palestinians.

The process to resolve conflict can serve as a vehicle for transforming the private and public institutions (neighborhood associations and city planning board) in the creation of more participatory communities across ethnic and racial divisions. Socio-economic systems can be dysfunctional owing to violence and other costs of not changing such practices as forced confiscation of land to the benefit of greedy ranchers or dominant ethnic or racial group members. In a nutshell, the settlement of contending issues would not have lasting effects in behavior and relationships without dealing with underlying concerns (such as respect for basic needs).

As a consequence of "resolving" the issues (territorial boundaries) without touching on systemic sources, conflict "supposedly resolved" may only return in another form (Ropers, 2004). The rivalry between the antagonistic ethnic leaderships led to a border war between Ethiopia and Eritrea. Violence may eventually be reignited by either or both of the adversaries with a loss of interest in abiding by the previously agreed institutional framework. Resolution approaches seek the general improvement of society vis-à-vis merely mitigating and redefining the conflict on a surface level. Normative changes in responding to a conflict shed light on the promotion of justice.

Self-supporting "resolutions" can not be sustained without reconstitution of the social fabric (e.g., monopoly of power and wealth in the hands of one ethnic group in Rwanda). A transformative approach is necessary as a response to a recurrent conflict. If conflict is to be transformed, the surrounding structure has to be adaptable to the demand for system change. Relationship changes can be reflected in the distribution of privileges and obligations in economic, educational, and other aspects of society. For instance, the abolition of racial and gender discrimination in educational activities can affect perceptions of gender roles in societies where women and minorities have a low level of participation in the economy and politics.

In order to respond to underlying causes, transformative perspectives focus on the system from which the conflict originates. Once differences in the issues are negotiated, the development of new relationships (needed for prevention of future conflict) may derive from searches for new visions, social relations, and institutions. Since animosities can be rekindled without relationship changes, power sharing, and other types of institutional arrangements have often been employed to guarantee mutual coexistence. Despite their power-sharing deal (reflected in the presidential council, cabinet, and parliament), the May 1990 unification of North and South Yemen did not last long due to the leadership discord; the supporters of the Yemen Socialist Party fought for the south's succession between May and July 1994, but did not achieve their goal. Thus relationship changes demand more than just institutional arrangements to achieve the unity or harmony among divided groups.

From management to transformation

Transformation is distinguished from some form of management mainly oriented toward the moderation of a destructive path of an evolving conflict. The intensity of a struggle can be modified by superficial satisfaction derived from a manipulative search for agreement. However, lingering suspicion and antagonism may invite future contention in a system locked in continuing battles even though one or a few sets of issues might have been settled. In the absence of transformation, a temporary win–lose outcome of conflict is likely to be part of a long cycle of hostilities. In an undemocratic relationship, the oppressor is most likely to reproduce overt coercion in order to quell the will of the marginalized groups. The expression of differences can be suppressed or deterred due to power differentials, only waiting to see the emergence of more protests.

In a search for a mutually satisfactory solution, the major difficulty is often how to convince a more powerful party to abandon its tactics of suppression. Conflict is often protracted by a refusal to give up territorial gains achieved by a war. In return for an occupied territory, a country holding part of a rival's land after successful military ventures may set up unacceptable conditions, and the other side's rejection of such a demand sets a prolonged track of conflict (as is illustrated by the negotiation between Azerbaijan and Armenia).

In oppressive situations, reduction and complete elimination of brutality of the oppressive power need to be stressed as a means for recovering humanity. Beyond attitudinal changes, conflict transformation may also involve conversion in value systems to conform to and support undeniable conditions for human dignity. For instance, in the case of the Chinese crackdown in Tibet and Xingjian, the ultimate solution to the conflict will stem from not only the Chinese authority's abandonment of coercive strategies but also restoration of spiritual, psychological, religious as well as material conditions for the survival of the oppressed party.

It may not be very difficult to acknowledge the flaws in the existing systems and related deficiencies. These shortcomings may even be admitted occasionally by those who have a power position. Yet it can be a lot more challenging to redress these structural concerns by forging a voluntary agreement in the absence of goodwill and commitment to a long-term peace.

The cessation of protests by oppressive means destroys the very human conditions such as recognition of freedom and autonomy which conflict resolution is aimed at. The maintenance of a status quo or support of existing political order for the sake of stability may silence grievances of those who have to live under oppressive rule. State boundaries have often been treated as sacred, and the denial of minority rights to self-rule has been justified under the name of state security. The use of military tactics has been condoned in suppressing the aspirations of minority groups for autonomy in Burma, China, Indonesia, Thailand, and the Philippines under the name of war on terrorism.

Relationship transformation is essential to the empowerment of disadvantaged groups and healing of war-traumatized societies. In the case of Kenya, post-election bloodshed in February 2008 produced a rising death toll, and caused the near collapse of the economy. The political crisis eventually subsided and was settled by the mediation of the former UN Secretary General Kofi Anan. Political settlements based on power sharing provided stabilization effects, but there are still unresolved questions about socio-economic inequalities and grievances among rival tribal groups, hampering the prospect for a viable civil society at grassroots level.

Challenges to transformation: intractable conflict relationships

Various characteristics of intractable conflict can be distinguished and categorized in terms of their broad arenas for confrontation, wide scope of issues, depth of impact, and rapid speed in the development of uncontrollable events (leading to catastrophic casualties). The widening of conflict is likely to coincide with inflexibility and rigidity of adversarial positions and acceptance of violence as a main means to determine differences. Indiscriminate victimization is inflicted upon the wide population in the form of human rights abuses, creation of refugees in armed violence and other humanitarian crises. As soon as violence flares up, the conflict's stakes and expectations change, making it impossible to restore a previous status quo.

In a repeated cycle of Israeli–Palestinian conflict and fighting in Afghanistan, a new struggle has surged after a dormant period of relative calm, adding further destruction where the fighting ended previously. In conjunction with a high level of well-organized mobilization, the confrontation between Hezbollah and other factions in the Lebanese government is deeply entrenched in a power struggle where the outcome can be uncertain. In many unresolved conflicts in Cyprus, an opportunity to deal with differences has not been captured due to doubts and the refusal to abandon antagonistic attitudes (reflecting the legacy of past aggression inflicted upon each other).

The waves of violence in Georgia, Moldova, and the rest of the Transcaucasus, the Balkans, and the Great Lakes region in Africa have diminished, but continuing ethnic tensions are reminiscent of past hostilities. As is illustrated by the rivalry among Serbs, Croats, and Muslims in former Yugoslavia, protracted conflicts "typically have an extensive past, a turbulent present, and a murky future" (Coleman, 2000, p. 432). If events in past history are considered indicators for the future, a course of violence in Rwanda and Burundi is likely to resurface in the future despite the current intervals of calm.

In recurrent conflicts, the minimization of violence (via truce) can be achieved without resolution so that violence becomes less burdensome in defining each other's relationships. As negotiation processes become deadlocked, new confrontation might be agitated to return to violence. When hidden sources of competitive relationships (along with grievances against each other) stay the same, numerous broken truces may alternate with attempts to control another escalation of the same conflict (as is seen in the Israel–Hamas cease-fire). The continuation of civil wars in the Democratic Republic of Congo, Somalia, and other parts of the African continent has been an outcome of many worthless peace treaties.

The degree of difficulties in transformation is derived from the structure of the conflict, including the types and extent of incompatibilities in the objectives of the conflicting parties and the degree of willingness of each party to scale down their goals and aspirations as well as the relative balance of forces. The level of difficulties in transformation also depends on the extent to which each party perceives that the other's gains are one's own losses. Israeli–Palestinian negotiations stalled in the failure to narrow gaps between exclusive claims to the ownership of Jerusalem, refugee return and other issues considered vital to each community's future. In this situation, the prospects for settlement are dim due to fundamental value differences or entrenched political interests.

In gross power imbalance, a superior party is not eager to agree to make meaningful concessions, in the absence of external pressure, preferring to impose its own will on a weaker party. Asymmetry in vulnerability may come from a disproportionately negative impact of a conflict on each party's welfare. If one of the adversaries feels that the negative effects of a conflict are minimally disruptive, they have less incentive to wind down their efforts to achieve unilateral goal satisfaction.

The successful transformation of South Africa is contrasted with other power imbalanced conflicts that have yet to be resolved. A constructive relationship between the apartheid government and the African National Congress (ANC) was developed by the government's acceptance of the ANC as an equal partner in negotiation. This was accompanied by a decade of heavy economic sanctions and international isolation which brought about perceptional changes in the government leadership and among the public. The demonization of the Dalai Lama, and the blocking of foreign media reports about Tibet by the Chinese government promoted the polarization of views among ordinary Chinese citizens about the Tibetans' yearning for autonomy. As most Chinese are subject to government propaganda and distortion about historical facts, the issues about the future status of Tibet have become further polarized in tandem with the Chinese leadership's hard-line attitudes which have completely shut the door to any kind of conciliatory move.

Obstacles to improvement in relationships are often created by difficulties in attitudinal and motivational changes (that will be ultimately accompanied by behavioral changes). If conflict is to be properly managed and eventually resolved, it should not be seen as a problem but as an opportunity for parties to become better off. The genuine sense of conflict transformation can be accompanied by changes in the parties and their expectations. For this purpose, various socio-cultural activities (involving women, artists, and tribal leaders) were utilized to reduce a fear of war and destruction to rebuild communal relations in the Balkans, Liberia, Tajikistan, and other places.

Multiple dimensions of transforming conflict dynamics

There are diverse ways in which conflict is reconstructed along shifts in power differentials and patterns of communication in evolving intra- and inter-party relations. The transformation of deadly dynamics requires the emergence of new inter-party relationships, changes within each major adversary, and the emergence of a new external context. An actor's will, capacities, and intentions have a dialectic interaction with external force.

A series of events converge and diverge to form a stimulus for a way out of conflict. Particular incidents may invite transformation of the way conflict has been perceived or the way parties behave or interact. Even though the East Timorese guerrilla forces were fighting against the Indonesian military since 1975, their cause did not draw wide international attention until the Dili massacre by the Indonesian military. The incident drew sympathetic support from around the world along with a burgeoning solidarity movement in Portugal, Australia, and the US, boosting the cause for independence.

As patterns of interaction between adversarial groups evolve throughout the conflict cycle, parties may choose different strategies and develop new interpretations of situations. Short-term crises in inter-state relations can be managed by a smooth flow of communication, involving more private, direct communication between antagonistic countries' leaderships. During the Cuban Missile Crisis, high-level communication channels were actively engaged in delivering each other's proposals and counterproposals.

Political as well as psychological factors contribute to delays in the termination of hostilities. The support of moderate positions within each party can signal the strength of conciliatory political forces. Psychological readiness (for reversing escalatory dynamics) and its related structural conditions (such as a weakened ability to continue to fight) can open a possibility for negotiated settlement. Given that conflict is inherently a fluid phenomenon, continuously evolving, some stages should be more amenable to conflict mitigation and de-escalation.

In general, qualitative changes in one or more dimensions of conflict behavior are associated with a decrease in a number of contentious issues and a number of partisans who hold on to extreme positions. Efforts made by one party to move toward reaching agreements would not be effective without reciprocal moves from the other party. While shifting power dynamics can bring about the adoption of new strategies, a consistent move toward de-escalation is likely to coincide with the alteration of perceptions. The realization of mutual interdependence helps parties consider conflict as a shared problem. Incompatible aspects of goals pursued by adversaries can become less important or not any more mutually exclusive with the emergence of superordinate goals that allay the concerns of all the parties.

The psychological context of conflict transformation entails attitudinal, motivational, and perceptional changes that may follow continued contacts and communication even in the midst of hostilities. Motivational changes for conciliation can generate new attitudes with less hostile behavior. However, changes in one aspect of conflict dynamics do not necessarily entice changes in other aspects of hostile relationships. Partisans may reduce attacks on their opponents for tactical or pragmatic reasons for lowering costs of struggle even if they still distrust them. Most importantly, however, conciliation and negotiated talks do not need to wait until full trust is established.

Perceptional and motivational changes

Various psychological and behavioral conditions determine the dynamics of conflict escalation and de-escalation. The opportunity for the transformation of conflict dynamics could follow a coercive struggle for unilateral advantages. The signs of de-escalation might be found after the exchange of intense hostilities and violence during the escalation. A psychological condition (after military victory or failure which changes power dynamics) has different motivational effects in a desire to seek negotiated settlement. French withdrawal from former colonies such as Algeria and Vietnam in the early 1960s was accompanied by costly military campaigns and humiliating defeat on the battlefield. High fatigue levels tend to be created by public exhaustion with a long-term civil war, yet political leaders may be slow to respond to the demand for negotiated settlement.

In spite of a lack of attitudinal changes, new calculation can still emerge after experiencing mounting costs and rising risks with little prospect for victory that can be gained in a tolerable, foreseeable time frame. Multidimensional aspects of creating new psychological relations consist of a weakened motivation for continued fighting with fatigue accompanied by increasing costs, dwindling internal support, and external pressure for ending hostilities. Psychological exhaustion and economic devastation lead the parties to believe that the high costs of continuing a conflict overwhelm any gains to be achieved later. Further escalation to overwhelm an enemy would only bring about catastrophic results despite further sacrifice. Sudden changes in understanding may arise from disastrous conflict situations characterized by impending catastrophe.

The prospects for prolonged conflict may induce parties to rethink their contentious strategies. The more pessimistic views a party holds with rising costs that cannot be sustained in the long run, the more willing it is to avoid the risk of staying on the current conflict course. Motivation consists of optimism (for successful settlement) as well as pessimism (attached to a costly debacle). In a costly deadlock, motivation (to end conflict) dwells on optimism about the other party's change in behavior and conflict itself (as related to feasibility of de-escalation). Motivational change can be strengthened by the prospect for ending intractable conflict situations.

At the same time, the desire to terminate a conflict may develop new perspectives for enemies. In a perceptional mode which is the reverse of that of conflict escalation, a search for a way out of costly struggles may induce adversaries to develop a tendency to selectively choose evidence supporting the interpretation that an adversarial party is reasonable, earnest, and eager to terminate the fighting. A desperate search for not even a fully satisfactory solution may lead antagonists to spotlight any sign of improvement in their situations and downgrade indications of vulnerability to mishaps.

In psychological transformation, stronger pessimism about a continuing course of a conflict can be undermined by a high level of optimism that cooperation will help achieve each other's basic goals. In general, one party tends to be more optimistic and enthusiastic about the possibility of compromise than the other. Even though strong optimism may not exist on both sides, at least a minimum level of psychological preparedness (associated with conflict fatigue) and willingness to scale down hostile activities should suffice to enhance a prospect for de-escalation. The adversaries should be willing and ready to take a risk of making concessions and reaching settlement, while lowering the bar for the cessation of hostilities.

Readiness for de-escalation

In a deadlock, there are situations in which one party may have to make more concessions. The main question is who is willing to make concessions under what conditions. Asymmetric psychological readiness exists when one of the parties has high fatigue levels with less endurance for absorbing the cost of struggle. The eagerness to pursue negotiated settlement also, in part, depends on relative power differentials. A party facing the dire prospect for risks of defeat and total loss is likely to send concessionary signals first. Sufficient concessions by one side create interest in the other party to discuss settlement terms. Parties under heavier threats would be more likely to give in, but they are more likely to resist making unilateral concessions with the involvement of a bigger stake. The demand for concessions should be within a tolerable range of political acceptance.

Parties can move from one-sided to mutual ripeness with external intervention. The right timing may not coincide for both parties if each party has a high level of asymmetry in expectations of future outcomes as well as views about current conflict situations. If one party thinks that they can eventually prevail, attain unilateral advantage, external intervention can change these calculations. NATO served as power balancer in the Balkan conflict. When the Serbian President Slobodan Milošević refused to permit international peacekeeping forces to move in to Kosovo in 1999, opposing the Rambouillet Agreement, NATO bombed bridges and other key military and civilian infrastructure in Serbia. This created autonomous rule in Kosovo under the European Union supervision.

Mutual readiness is part of the essential conditions under which both parties are prepared for subsiding conflict. In successful conciliation, initiatives for talks are positively viewed by an adversary who is willing to make a similar move in collaboration to end stalemate. There are certain moments that benevolent actions can more easily bring about attitudinal changes.

The degree of willingness in accommodating the other party's demand depends on whether concession making falls within one's perceived bottom line as well as the probability of the other party's reciprocity for one's concessions. In the absence of a conciliatory mood between antagonists, the conditions for correct timing may be brought about by coercive means of intervention designed for the cessation of military hostilities. In addition, intermediaries may get involved to persuade a reluctant party to move to de-escalation by communicating the readiness of the other party.

Conditions for relationship change

The transformation of adversarial relationships is forged by various changes within one or both of the major adversaries, and from the struggle's external context. The process of resolving conflict can be complicated, as multiple parties hold their incompatible behavioral patterns, fighting over diverse issues often connected to each other. The existing system differences may serve as constraints to changes in the relationships. In addition, finding mutually acceptable solutions is not easy due to the difficulty in altering enemy images and misperceptions.

The improved relationship is needed for the settlement of differences in contentious issues. Sharing the same beliefs is not a precondition for meaningful changes in the nature of inter-group relationships. Most importantly, adversarial relationships need to be transformed to create conditions for sustainable conflict resolution beyond tackling specific issues.

Positive relationship change can help avoid or minimize the use of coercion without having a quest to seek an adversary's surrender. A major shift in the relationship comes from accepting the political legitimacy of an adversary's representatives as well as the acknowledgment of their grievances. A dramatic change can occur when excluded groups are recognized as legitimate parties in a conflict. The recognition of the African National Congress, the Sudanese People's Liberation Movement, the Free Aceh Movement, and Sinn Féin, a political arm of the Irish Republican Army and other resistance movements by their respective state adversaries preceded official negotiations.

The structure of inter-party relations may reflect an increasing or decreasing number of actors (as seen in Sudan, the Democratic Republic of Congo, etc.). The existence of multiple groups complicates the negotiation process, creating possibilities of reaching settlement with different adversaries separately or with a coalition of multiple groups. Preparing for international conferences to end violence in Darfur, Sudan, became complex due to the participation of multiple resistance groups which are not necessarily in communication with each other. In ending civil wars in the Democratic Republic of Congo and Burundi, the governments negotiated peace accords with multiple rebel groups simultaneously, but those who did not sign in the agreements continued to be engaged in armed struggles. Eventually they had to be defeated either militarily or be invited to join the agreed pact with some new incentives to a settlement.

In its approach to the Arabic world, Israel has developed separate negotiation tracks (setting up conditions and terms which help them counter more bitter enemies at the later stage of conciliation with the Arabic world). Israel obtained a peace agreement with Egypt (1979) and then with Jordan (1993), but relations with Syria have not improved sufficiently to start serious negotiation to return the Golan Heights occupied during the 1967 War.

Partisans are more likely to be interested in relationship changes from enemies to allies (or collaborators) under the following conditions. It may, in part, be derived from the creation of a mutually beneficial relationship in which the pursuit of one's own interests depends on the other's cooperation. Economic aid is used as a means of strengthening social interdependence in support of mechanisms to work against violence. Further escalation can be moderated by either the necessity to maintain an interdependent relationship or the existence of a common enemy. In a trust relationship, the precedent of reciprocations increases incentives to make future concessions.

Sources of relationship changes

The changes in the external environment add complexities to the inter-group relationships with more issues being drawn into the conflict. While each conflict has its own dynamics (difficult to transform), other conflicts can create an unfavorable environment for de-escalation. Diverse behavioral patterns of multiple parties may create incompatible activities along with new issues brought in by them. The involvement of neighboring countries has increased the complexities of conflict relationships due to the existence of multiple alliances compromised of not only militia groups but also their foreign backers.

Conflict in Sudan spilled over to Chad with the flow of arms, refugees, and militia movements across borders. Much burden has been put on Chad by difficulties managing a significant percentage of the 2.5 million displaced who crossed its eastern border. In February 2008, UN compounds have been broken into by armed gangs who stole trucks, forcing the international agency to scale back its services for some 30,000 refugees. Meanwhile, rebel columns armed by the Sudanese government even advanced toward the capital of Chad, N'Djamema, almost taking over the presidential palace. The success in the military attacks could have permitted the Sudanese military government to have a base within Chad to attack Darfur rebels as well as running over the refugee camps.

Given the impact of a political struggle on the dynamics of a peace process, an external actor can play a role in strengthening the moderate political forces within each party. In an effort to bring Hamas in to an official peace negotiation, former President Jimmy Carter embraced moderate Hamas political leaders despite opposition from Israel. Overall, removal of sources of grievances is more likely to produce relational changes (along with attitudinal modifications).

Fluctuation in rivalry and external alliance: Iraqi Kurdistan

A conflict episode between long-term rivals is likely to escalate and de-escalate according to changing national political climates and international alliance and vice versa. Even though they share a common cause of Kurdish autonomy, the two major Iraqi Kurdish parties, namely the Kurdish Democratic Party (KDP) and the Patriotic Union of Kurdistan (PUK), have a long history of rivalry as well as cooperation. The conflict in Kurdistan has long persisted due to divisions among tribal leaders who draw loyalty from their own group members. In fact, alliances constantly shifted due to the fact that the Kurdish groups were used as proxies by Iran, Iraq, and Syria against their neighboring rival states.

During the Iran–Iraq war in the 1980s, many Kurds fought against each other on both sides of the border until they united against the Iraqi forces in 1986. As the Kurdish population became the victims of Saddam Hussein regime's brutal gas and other military attacks, the Western powers set up a safe haven in northern Iraq in 1991. The weakened KDP in its fighting with its rival PUK invited the intervention of Saddam Hussein's government in 1996 (Helsing, 2004). After the US government successfully pressurized the Hussein government to withdraw from the Kurdish region, the Clinton administration brokered cease-fire through mediation, facilitating the emergence of a greater sense of a common community among the Kurds.

Features of actor transformation

Psychological changes can take place in a person, while institutional rearrangement can bring major changes to an organization, society, or a state. At a personal level, transformative approaches may focus on a change in the consciousness and character of the person in order to generate new attitudes and behavior. Even in a criminal justice situation, restorative justice has been adopted as a method for rebuilding relationships through the perpetrator's moral awakening. Therapeutic mediation can be intended for individual changes.

Different types of actor transformations contribute to dramatic changes in the positions of a party. Some conflicts have been resolved by internal changes such as the replacement of the leadership as well as internal political necessities. Angola and Mozambique were granted independence in 1995 after the fall of a military regime in Portugal. The military coup leaders in Portugal yielded unexpectedly to the demands of resistance groups in Mozambique and Angola.

Institutional, ideological, social, and political transformation within each party produces either a negative or positive impact on inter-party relations. The Iranian Revolution in 1979 froze the Persian Gulf State's relationship with the US. The drastic changes in South Africa's socio-political system can be attributed to a shift in power relations between blacks and whites. The reconstruction of core identities (a core sense of self) is inevitable in establishing new relationships with others. The internal changes in major parties (for instance, the demise of the Soviet Union) ended the Cold War with the US.

Internal divisions

Intra-party politics create different positions on approaches to enemies, due to the fact that most parties involved in conflict are not unitary decision-making actors. Internal divisions over alternative means (such as violent or nonviolent) can exist despite a shared consensus on the nature and extent of grievances. The impact of a political struggle on the dynamics of a peace process varies according to unique circumstances of intra-party politics. Internal fighting can be an obstacle to negotiation if it permits a hard-line faction to prevail. However, protracted internal fighting can help end the conflict rather quickly if it weakens and destroys one of the parties internally. Fighting among militias in Iraq eventually resulted in ending of internal warfare.

Internal party divisions lead various factions to argue about who is a true representative of their community and raise questions about who negotiates on whose behalf. In general, extremist armed groups favor guerrilla warfare, but moderate political leaders seek compromise. Thus conflict decisions often reflect a balance in relationships between political and military wings. Sinn Féin emerged originally as a political voice of the IRA, but the progression in peace talks let the political party eclipse the influence of the paramilitary group. The abandonment of militant tactics required in the peace accord has led to the dissolution of the IRA. Political representatives of Hezbollah reflect the military leadership's views. The organization's top leader commands both military structures as well as political strategies.

Different features of political systems (pluralistic versus authoritarian) can play a role in the outcome of internal negotiations. Though an agreement can be reached dramatically at high-level talks, key constituents may still resist a peace process. Internal politics involves the rearrangement of coalitions in support of an agreement. For instance, the 2008 nuclear deal between India and the US brought about the reshufle of the Indian government cabinet due to the withdrawal of a communist party from a coalition pact. Especially in pluralistic societies, internal negotiation among different interest groups is required for finalizing settlement terms. Issues need to be represented in a manner to be acceptable to domestic opponents. Those interested in negotiated settlement should have sufficient strength to hold firm control of extreme elements to minimize any disruption to the negotiated settlement.

Fights between hard-line and moderate factions involve a high political stake with the implication of relations with an external adversary. Both the Ulster Unionist Party and the Social Democratic and Labour Party in Northern Ireland campaigned to garner overwhelming support for the 1998 Good Friday Agreement to eventually end decades of paramilitary violence. Yet, the two moderate parties lost their majority party status, in the 2003 Assembly election, to the Democratic Unionist Party and Sinn Féin which took an uncompromising hard-line position in power-sharing arrangements between Unionist and Republican communities. Rivalry for leadership between factions complicates an inter-group conciliation process.

Strategies of transformation

The analysis of social and political sources of conflict may focus on a system of interaction and its surrounding environment. The repression of conflict contributes to concealing oppressive relations. The ability to transform conflict dynamics is linked to reconstruction of social realities with the adjustment of human institutions. At the system level, the emergence of democratic institutions and educational values have helped post-World War II Germany emerge as a symbol of peace and reconciliation in Europe.

Once we identify the goals of transformation, the question is how to achieve it. Each conflict has diverse sources of structural transformation (transition from authoritarian rule to multi-party democracy, the emergence of a leadership committed to new values, protest movements calling for change, the acceptance of new intellectual or value trends). In a power imbalanced situation, negotiation and mediation are limited in their scope to alter unjust conditions. Thus activism and advocacy can be utilized to enhance a moral and political standard for conflict resolution.

The transformation of conflict dynamics stems from a set of changing conditions as well as new policies, both short- and long-term. It is an important issue to figure out who is involved in producing changes at personal, group, and system levels. Activities at individual and group levels may focus on the ability to cultivate empathy, new understanding, and empowerment at educational and psychological levels. A range of intervention goals can cross-cut system procedures and relationship dimensions. As is illustrated by US racial relations since the civil rights movements of the 1960s, the sustenance of transformation across the affected population over a long term is necessary to bring about changes in the rigid attitudes set over a long period of time. In Pakistan, lawyers were at the forefront of forcing General Pervez Musharraf to step down from the presidency. They demanded judicial independence, but it was soon expanded to the restoration of democracy. In organizing protests, Buddhist monks have played a major role in Burma and Tibet.

Psychological, attitudinal changes

Conflict resolution ultimately rests on a reduction of the sense of threat and of the misperceptions that are caused by it. Removing stereotypes and negative images is essential in avoiding the oversimplification of the other's motives. Difficulties in harmonizing perceptions can be ascribed to distorted psychological processes. A changed sense of identity for one or both parties is often associated with overcoming the difficulty in altering enemy images and misperceptions; attitudinal changes can be attributed to new cognitive and emotional processes.

A psychological process influences how parties frame issues in conflict; the willingness to understand and acknowledge the legitimacy of the other's concerns, interests, and objectives in search for solutions involves a capacity to develop empathy with the other's grievances, traumas, and sense of injustice. The willingness to cooperate for the prevention of mutual self-destruction enhances the recognition of feasibility for bilateral solutions and confidence in negotiation with commitment to the acceptance of a durable solution for structural changes.

Self-perpetuating dynamics of conflict can be reversed by the efforts to eliminate enemy images and stereotypes. The decreased level of blaming and polarization can be achieved by exposing misperceptions derived from inaccurate attributions. A shift from threats of coercion to mutual cooperation may follow the efforts to overcome dehumanization with empathy. A psychological process to undo hostile attitudes and misperceptions is associated with the efforts to eliminate or at least diminish distrust and threats.

Conditions for empathic relations with enemies may be created by belief in the utility of cooperative relationships and a new vision of peace. Each party observes the other's principles and behaviors in one's own mirror imaging with misreading of intentions. The emergence of new attitudes requires changes in the belief that enemies are unified and thus unchangeable. An atmosphere of trust permits the interchange of a variety of issues and discussion of the options to be explored. Eradicating psychological barriers of suspicion and mistrust helps give up entrenched positions embedded in the rigid interpretation of the adversary's behavior. A relatively poor standard of mutual knowledge or understanding can be overcome by the new psychological conditions created by contact and communication.

Value transformation

In conflict transformation, the acceptance of widely acknowledged normative principles such as self-determination needs to be applied to promoting conflict resolution based on equitable and just relationships. The initiatives by the governments of Australia and New Zealand regarding the remedies for indigenous peoples have involved fostering just relationships along with bias awareness, anti-racism, and other forms of citizen education. Inter-group dialogue can be directed to healing and rebuilding wounded relationships in a reconciliation process. In the negotiation of the future South African political system, the focus was not on whether to move toward the majority political system but on how to create a power-sharing government under the black majority government (making sure that the whites' legitimate rights can be protected).

Demand for self-determination by the inhabitants of the Western Sahara under Moroccan occupation, Tibetans and Uyghurs in China can be resolved by granting the rights of self-rule. This is well illustrated by the independence of East Timor after it was occupied by the Indonesian military government in 1975 when Portugal gave up their colonial control over Timor. The long struggle eventually led to the popular referendum which approved separation from Indonesia and independence in 2002.

The consensus on the basis of public interests or highly held standards has led to treaties on ozone depletion, the ban on trading of endangered species, and preservation of habitat. These principles can be applied to negotiation on the control of greenhouse gases, discussion about the phasing out of a coal power plant, and the protection of water quality. At the negotiation table, agreed value principles can be used to repackage each stakeholder's concerns and interests.

Overcoming goal incompatibilities

A search for resolving incompatibilities in goals demands a collaborative process. Different views about meaningful accommodations have to be shared in reframing the issues so that all the concerns can be met. In resolving goal incompatibility, negotiation can be used as a means of accommodation rather than imposition of one's own will by acknowledging each other's legitimate rights and values. Resolution can be achieved especially when a superior party begins to recognize the other's demand as legitimate (as related to the solution of goal incompatibilities). The independence of India and Pakistan was more easily granted due to popular support within Britain.

Joint efforts to redefine the conflict can be made in a way to explore superordinate goals through the recognition of common interests. Integrative solutions, which are beneficial to both parties, strengthen collaborative relationships. When goals are interdependent, incompatible preferences over distributive outcomes can be converted into integrative ones. The partial attainment of goals through their subdivision may give rise to some satisfaction. Mutual concession, in conjunction with increased confidence and optimism for settlement, can be made by scaling down one's goals and aspirations.

Divergent interests have to be perceived and recognized by others in order to change the perception that the other's gains are one's own loss; the incompatibility can be removed if each party knows that the other party does not intend to obtain the same object. The perceived difference is illusory or not based on real sources with the realization that adversaries are not actually attempting to achieve the goal believed to be incompatible.

The scope of transformation

In building an infrastructure for establishing peace, transformation goes beyond mere institutional reform to overcome polarized identities, negative emotions, trauma, and grief by such means as healing, rehabilitation of victims, and restoration of justice. Not only negotiating practice among the elite but also ordinary citizen activities and contact can support reconciliation and other aspects of peace building. The quest for freedom and survival of one group should be compatible with the recognition of the same aspirations by the other group. This understanding may arise from a deeper level of attitudinal changes among the elite, organizational members, support groups, and the public at large.

Personal, relational, and systemic change occurs either directly or indirectly. Given the effects of intractable conflict among multiple constituents, it is desirable to solicit the input of large segments of the population in a peace process as well as its implementation. This would require the removal of institutional obstacles for participatory democracy and self-governance across ethnic lines. Sustainable economic development would be essential to a mutual sharing of natural resources.

While the 1979 Camp David Accord removed the possibility of any future war between Israel and Egypt, President Sadat depended on imprisonment of political opponents, intellectuals, students, and journalists for suppressing opposition to the deal (Fraser, 2008). The imposition of the treaty from the above by means of oppression in Egypt can explain the failure to invigorate voluntary activities from the population in support of expanded contact with the Israeli society despite the landmark deal obtained by the top government officials.

The transformation of social relationships is essential to the success of any sustainable conflict resolution in Northern Ireland and Israel–Palestinian relations given the fact that the daily life of adversarial communities is so tightly integrated at not only political but also economic and social levels. Since any individual incident such as stabbing or throwing rocks can easily ignite a large-scale clash, broad societal level confidence building needs to be developed by the enhancement of mutual trust. Given that it is almost impossible to divide the two communities' activities through territorial boundaries, any unilateral decision on the division of vital historic and economic assets as well as water and other natural resources will produce further hostilities and violence.

Although political division of Jerusalem was proposed by President Clinton during the Camp David negotiation in 2000, negotiating such a division (the high stake issue) may not be feasible given the near impossibility of finding a formula which can satisfy every group in the future control over the biblical city. Under these circumstances, there seems to be no alternative but accommodating each other's commercial interests as well as spiritual and religious identity since their destiny is joined together. Thus the transformation of relationships between the antagonistic communities needs to be actively sought for ultimate conflict resolution.

Quality of relationship changes

Balance in a new relationship (emerging from the process of conflict resolution) depends on how to manage value differences in the decision-making process and outcome. The quality of relationships can be assessed in terms of the degree of a shift from rivals to collaborators. Transformation effects can be manifested in multiple ways, and some are more visible than others. Relationships can be improved by the removal of the problems which have triggered the confrontational behavior in the first place. New relationships may emerge from perceptional changes and identity transformation. In addition, long-term relational aspects of conflict involve the deeper structural, cultural concerns.

In terms of the types and effects of activities, improvement in the relationship may be confined to one or two areas (e.g., security arrangement between Israel and Egypt without societal exchange). Relational changes can be limited to issues which have an immediate focus. An agreement for meaningful changes in the nature of inter-group relationships may not occur without a necessary transformation of beliefs. Although immediate short-term issues may deal with behavioral concerns (such as effective control of violence organized by extremists), deeper interests behind the current situation might involve value and structural transformation forged by power sharing and civil society activities.

Immediate behavioral changes are oriented toward the sustenance of negative peace via cessation of violence (i.e., cease-fire prior to negotiated settlement). In many post-conflict situations, despite security reform and political institutional changes (such as the reduced role of the military in political and government affairs), poverty and economic disparity have remained little changed, contributing to high crime rates, for instance, in El Salvador and Guatemala.

Views about the utility of relationships can focus on how each party feels about the continuation of their relationship and future expectations about the quality of the relationship. Ultimate success in conflict resolution depends on the transformation of the relationship from hierarchy to equality and participation; from coercion to respect. The negative aspect of relationships should become peripheral while the overall relationship needs to be based on mutually beneficial activities.

The qualities of relationships can be judged by legitimacy based on essential rightness and justice (as well as equality). Interaction should be mutually enriching and reciprocal. Non-legitimate, colonial relationships can be compared with legitimate relationships based on consent or consensus. Imposed relationships are illegitimate, especially when they involve manipulation and coercion to suppress any protest against unacceptable relationships.

The control of escalatory force (prevention of violent clashes) can be contrasted with informal facilitation and other activities designed to improve the opening of communication flows (aimed at perceptual changes in support of alterations in the adversarial relationship). Critical perspectives are necessary to investigate the nature of existing order and explore alternative strategies to respond to institutional problems. The improvement in relationships (for instance, between the Israelis and Palestinians prior to the 2000 Camp David talks) may not be sustained in the event of failed negotiations.

Depth of experience (such as healing and reconciliation) as well as institutional transformation goes beyond improved communication and the exploration of superordinate goals. A fundamental change in the relationship between parties can be derived from recognizing each other's ethnic and national aspirations. Mutual assurance for security is supported by abandoning enemy images which prolong fear, anxiety, and hostility. Transformation can go deeper to touch upon the emotional, perceptual, and spiritual aspects of conflict relationships. Parties are not any longer in contention over salient issues along with deliberate and direct efforts for reconciliation.

Sequential order

In removing the sources of conflict, a diverse context influences a sequence of necessary transitional steps toward deep transformation. A sequence of necessary transitional steps can be developed in a search for identifying and removing the underlying root causes of the conflict. Long-term efforts to increase contact and cooperation in various sectors can eventually have a cumulative effect in the relationship changes. Challenges to the status quo may be built gradually or at one dramatic moment after violence has drawn attention to it. Dramatic gestures or initiatives by leaders might bring about a sudden shift in the conflict dynamics, but they may only be short lived if they remain as symbolic gestures, creating disillusion on the other party.

The leaders of opposing communities can agree to a structural change (such as the independence of new states in the post-Soviet era) before behavioral and attitudinal changes. In South Africa, despite the new issue of income gaps between the rich and poor, the leaders of each community respect democratic principles and are committed to the newly created system which guarantees coexistence. It remains as a bastion of human rights, reconciliation with the institutionalization of democratic values. The redistribution of power through structural reform can induce economic and social changes as well as fundamental relationship changes. Institutional changes can produce a potential to encourage personal transformation.

Transformation in the attitude and behavior of the parties may eventually lead to changes in their relationship (for instance, Australian and New Zealand policies toward the Aborigines). A system level change (such as the recognition of rights of those under foreign rule to self-governance) has stemmed from the acceptance of new norms (such as anti-colonialism and anti-racism). Thus, a settlement (such as autonomy and independence) can be sought through long-term consciousness raising and public education in the absence of immediate structural changes. The agreement to immediate and shorter term issues can enhance a chance for bringing about long-term, structural changes if the process and outcome of conflict resolution influence parties, relationships, and institutions beyond the immediate issues under dispute.

Challenges to transformation

The process of conflict transformation involves not only political but also moral questions about how we treat other human beings. Peaceful resolution is not searching for outright victory or revenge as an outcome of a conflict. The replacement of ultra-nationalism by democratic principles has been essential for the Croatian government to reestablish its relations with Serb minorities and to be admitted as a member of the European Union.

It is difficult to control a variety of contexts, ranging from personal, inter-personal, and social, to industrial, in which conflict occurs. The fluid and overlapping nature of conflict activities can be characterized by their "crossing into and out of violence" (Miall, 2004, p. 161). The questions of a process for conflict transformation may focus on who is involved, and how long it will take. Interactions among various elements of conflict systems create a new impetus for conflict movements. A set of changing conditions can interact with new policies both on a long-term and short-term basis.

Power imbalanced and asymmetric relationships can be interpreted in terms of differences in status and capacities to influence conflict outcomes. De-escalation is not likely to progress smoothly to control violence if deep disparities and despair continue to feed support for hegemonic forces which reestablish order simply by relying on superior destructive capabilities. Peace cannot be simply bought by force. In Afghanistan, stability was undermined by the resurgence of insurgent movements and increase in the poppy cultivation.

New post-conflict political institutions at all levels of government are not often equipped to accommodate all the demands of new and old constituents. Gross inequalities and injustices are often deeply entrenched into the social and political institutions. Political repression remains unchanged or even strengthened after the 1995 negotiated settlement in Cambodia. Transformation is very difficult in Palestine, since Israeli blockage creates resentment along with economic hardships. An incitement to hatred excludes a possibility of reconciliation; children brought up with a culture of hatred will be more likely to turn out to be future suicide bombers.

The limited changes in actors, issues, and roles do not touch the multi-faceted aspects of conflict dynamics. While radical change is necessary to eliminate the underlying causes of conflict, it would not be feasible to remove all sources of injustice. In spite of acknowledging the grievances, the stronger parties may not be willing to rectify the conditions for injustice or bring only piecemeal changes, since the dominant party tends to resist giving up their privileges.

It is a major challenge to keep the mobilization of support for peace and to maintain the synergy of cooperation in challenging the unfavorable circumstances of adversarial relationships. Destructive energies such as displaced frustration (for aggression) need to be redirected into constructive outlets. Stability is created by the development of ties between adversaries (via geographic or economic integration) along with social bonds. By recognizing the significance of interdependence, reconciliation promotes future engagement. Northern Ireland is not likely to return to violence due to transformations of both external and internal relations. Self-supporting activities can be linked to advocacy, nonviolent activism, and education. Women's networks and self-help groups have been developed in Bosnia-Herzegovina, Bangladesh, India, Liberia and other regions of the world where solidarity and mutual support are recognized as important to collective well-being.

Further reading

Botes, J. (2003) "Conflict Transformation," *International Journal of Peace Studies*, 8 (2): 1–28.

Burton, J. W. (1997) *Violence Explained: The Sources of Conflict, Violence and Crime and Their Prevention*, Manchester: Manchester University Press.

Dedring, J. (1999) "On Peace in Times of War: Resolving Violent Conflicts by Peaceful Means," *International Journal of Peace Studies*, 4 (2): 1–21.

Esman, M. J. (2004) "Ethnic Pluralism: Strategies for Conflict Management," in A. Wimmer, R. J. Goldstone, D. L. Horowitz, U. Joras, and C. Schetter (eds) *Facing Ethnic Conflict Toward a New Realism*, Lanham, MD: Rowman and Littlefield.

Jeong, H. W. (2005) *Peacebuilding in Postconflict Societies,* Boulder: Lynne Rienner.

Lederach, J. (1997) *Building Peace – Sustainable Reconciliation in Divided Societies*, Tokyo: United Nations University Press.

Midgley, J. R. (2002) "Guests Overstaying Their Welcome: The Demise of the Peace Accord Structures in South Africa," *The International Journal of Peace Studies*, 7 (1): 77–90.

Mitchell, C. (2002) "Beyond Resolution: What does Conflict Transformation actually Transform?" *Peace and Conflict Studies*, 9 (1): 1–24.

Pruitt, D. G. (2007) "Social Conflict: Some Basic Principles," *Journal of Dispute Resolution*, 1: 151–156.

Reilly, C. A. (2008) *Peace-Building and Development in Guatemala and Northern Ireland*, New York: Palgrave.

Part II
Dimensions of conflict management

4   Identity

Many conflicts in the world have a communal nature, reflecting mutually incompatible perceptions and expressions of differences among groups with diverse ethnic and religious affiliations. Such identity bases as ethnicity, tribe, kin, class, caste, gender, and race have often contributed to the justification of inequality in resource allocation and political oppression. This has been a main source of social division and tension ranging from China to Sudan to Burma to India to Saudi Arabia to Bolivia. Identity differences in heterogeneous societies have been used as a basis for diverse types of group mobilization. As one of the most vivid examples of the manipulation of identities for political purposes, the Sudanese government has employed Arab nationalism in pitting the Janjaweed militias against ethnic African Darfurians.

In contrast with its use for agitating political violence, identity can also be invoked to call for unity and solidarity when groups go through grievances or bereavement. In fact, a sense of "we-ness" is often sought in a healing process after such tragic incidents as the terrorist bombings in New York. Thus identity tends to be strengthened in response to the loss of communal members as well as external challenges to the group's values and behavior. In the expansion of the European Union, on the other hand, a superordinate identity base of being "European" has been promoted in overcoming national, ethnic differences and advancing the common cause of democracy, social harmony, and economic prosperity.

This chapter examines the activation of identity for conflict, the formation of attitudes, and the process of social categorization. It also covers the ways in which the fluid nature of identity can be transformed by conflict resolution. Identity boundaries become more rigid with the intensification of struggles, but can be relaxed with benevolent interaction between different group members. People of diverse social categories cooperate or compete, depending on economic and political status as well as value differences.

Identity and conflict mobilization

While each conflict has different historical sources and behavioral manifestations of struggle among protagonists, adversarial relationships can be ascribed to common perceptual, cognitive, and emotional mechanisms. More specifically, divisions in a competitive setting create challenges to inter-group cooperation. Meanwhile, increased intra-group cohesiveness, morale, and conformity pressures can be accompanied by hostility toward out-groups. The content of identities is formulated by various events which shape relationships with others in a particular space and time.

The establishment of a Jewish state in Palestine has transformed the Palestinian national identity along with Palestinian anxiety and resistance against growing Jewish immigration.

The success of Zionism is attributed to Jewish emigration to the biblical and historical lands and the establishment of political, intellectual, and military capacity as well as reviving Hebrew as a functional language. Jewish identity has also evolved in a struggle with Arabs in the same land (along with such events as the annexation of East Jerusalem and the extension of Jewish settlements after the 1967 War). Zionism and Palestinian nationalism have been invoked over the right to statehood and land ownership. Palestinian resistance was the most intense under Israeli military occupation of the West Bank and Gaza in the 1980s and early 1990s.

Representing a pervasive feature of group processes, identity formation is shaped by the context of inter-group rivalry. Indeed, a strong sense of threat to one's central commitments provokes hostilities toward another group. In particular, identity can become a direct source of group mobilization with feelings of injustice and relative deprivation derived from the contest. Normative justification allows insults and attacks directed at others who are distrusted.

Not every type of social and political action is ascribed to a basis in "identity." Indeed, the variable frequency of real conflict action over time does not necessarily correlate to the content of identity but more to the context of identity mobilization. Group relations are embedded in multi-faceted layers of experiences anchored in social hierarchies (based on ethnic and other status), differences in cultural values and economic disparities. The scarcity of resources and disagreement on the distribution of power and wealth fortify socio-historical divisions.

Representing particular social characteristics, different sources of identities are important in conflict mobilization. Indeed, identity mobilization is related to how social cleavages are built and managed. In Nepal, urban/rural divisions have constituted class conflict; religious conflict in India was driven by Hindu–Muslim divisions. In Sri Lanka and Moldova, language became a marker of identity and a currency to divide the population with the disadvantage of particular linguistic–cultural groups (Russians versus Moldovan, Tamils versus Sinhalese in Sri Lanka). Identities have been further hardened as a result of conflict.

A group is necessary to develop a common goal for people who perceive their shared destiny. A strong group identity plays an important role in demonstrating a resolve to realize one's aspirations. A perception of deprivation fosters a sense of unfair treatment by others and a desire to rectify it. Cohesiveness based on common identity enables a group to develop "patterns of behavior that seem normal to members but appear contentious and polarizing to others" (Isenhart and Spangle, 2000, p. 21). In-group process contributes to stabilization of the self through reinforcement of collective values or norms.

Once collective identity is entirely seen as an end to be "defended at all costs and by all means," the eruption of large-scale conflict is difficult to control (Giannakos, 2002). Group formation is related to the fear of domination by a rival group as well as deeply held value commitments. A shared fate leads to the formation of group consciousness. Inter-group competition strengthens the awareness of intra-group cohesion and rigid group boundaries. The adoption of extreme views about enemies encourages less tolerance of intra-group differences and dissent. In the aftermath of the September 11 terrorist attacks, any political opposition to the US military invasion of Afghanistan was condemned due to the hawkish public mood.

The context of an ethnic conflict is provided by social and cultural rules and values embedded in the myths, memories, traditions, and symbols of heritages which exclusively define group characteristics. Language and other markers are invoked to establish group boundaries and determine status and social identity through inter-ethnic comparison. The basic function of shared communication is critical to the development of group consciousness. The transmission of ideas and symbols is involved in molding attitudes and behaviors separating people into antagonistic groupings. Differentiated identities are not a lone source of violence, but can lead to a deadly conflict in combination with exclusionary acts of leaders and competition for status, position, or material wealth.

Socio-historical context of antagonistic identity relationships

Political divisions among more than 250 ethnic tribes in Nigeria have been created by geographical and religious lines, largely composed of a historically Muslim north and a Christian and animist south. In general, Nigerians have recently lived in relative peace despite the mixture of the 140 million population divided between Muslims and Christians. Yet grievance occasionally arises from indigenous people's rights versus migrants as to land policies. Religion has become a proxy of many communal conflicts over political power and land. The fissures are so acute that a small tremor for an apparently peaceful community can easily open up an abyss of bloodshed.

The country's Middle Belt has traditionally constituted a hotbed of ethnic and religious violence. Its farmland and grazing pasture have attracted migrants from the more arid north for centuries. In particular, the influx of Muslim Hausa and Fulani people has created uneasy feelings among the original inhabitants of Plateau State who belong to either Christian or animist tribes. The split of political parties along religious lines has recently turned many elections into events of violence. In the December 2008 elections in Jose, the capital of Plateau State, each side charged the other for stealing their victory with cheating being accompanied by random killing and rampaging even prior to the announcement of electoral results.

Polarization of identities

The impact of social identity on inter-group interaction is manifested in the emergence of specific behavioral patterns. Identity is jointly negotiated and mutually formed in relationships through communication. In a divisive social situation, relatively uniform modes of communication and interpretation of events and behavior are accepted across group boundaries. A competitive orientation increases ineffective communication with out-groups while promoting group cohesion. A heavy investment in polarized identities becomes the principal obstacle to constructive forms of conflict engagement, since emotional attachment to one's beliefs blocks the ability to empathize with different worldviews and experiences. In fact, opposing group identities encourage the adoption of contentious tactics often justified by enemy perceptions.

Group divisions based on identity differentiation are often related to the radicalization of conflicts and extreme behavior, manifested in random killings and abusive treatment of opposing civilian populations. In a fight against "enemy" groups, identity suddenly becomes a weapon of ethnic cleansing (as seen in former Yugoslavia and Rwanda). In Croatia during the first President Franjo Tuđman era, the vigilance of the "enemy within us" (referring to Serb enclaves) increased the tendency to develop ethnocentrism in combination with authoritarianism.

Properties and attributes of identity

There are different interpretations of how identities are formed. The original discussion by primordialists highlights that an identity base is firm and stable. It emphasizes "sameness" within a group along with a foundational focus on a distinct "self." Identity is given by the outside world (such as birth and memories of shared experiences), and individuals unquestionably accept it. This view is contrasted with the notion of "fluctuating modes of the self" which entail defining a group or category from the inside out. Indeed, boundaries are created by individual will, action, and competition in the material world. In the perspectives of social interactionism, identity is a product of contingent events, reflecting the view that human agency is adapted to different situations. In a nutshell, an interactional dimension generates the perception of differences and sameness that arises from living in a multiple and fragmented world.

In general, identities are regarded as the collective phenomena of expressing group sameness. The deep and foundational forms of collective selfhood can be manifested in the great variety of distinctive cultural creativity, ranging from art to drama to literature to philosophy. Culture is an inevitable element of group distinctiveness, as social existence is tied to a particular language or a religious community associated with given social practices. The distinct memories of different collectivities are represented by histories and genealogies defined by blood and custom. The themes of homeland, founding origins, and common descent in ethnic stories foster heroism and sacrifice.

Identities are not created in a world of fantasy detached from historical reality. The institutionalization of the distinct symbols crystallizes concrete collective identities and boundaries. Various types of elites are involved in shaping the content and forms of collective identities in interaction with a broader social environment. Influential leaders activate group predispositions or propensities, aspiring for political hegemony. The political salience of identity reflects a connection to common personal experiences such as unequal treatment by other group members.

Despite the necessity for core cultural elements, identities are relational and contingent products of social action. In fact, boundaries are illustrated by the vagaries of social interaction. In developing ethnic identity, individuals "construct" their identities in an interaction process. In particular, shared rules of behavior and attitudes towards various experiences stem from knowledge of a membership in a social group with the attachment of emotional significance.

Identity can be constructed, deconstructed, and reconstructed through the reinterpretation of shared experiences, collective memories and myths in relation to those of others. Violent ethnic identification reflects the prevalence of a particular identity in an exclusive and antagonistic manner. Dangers are inscribed on the new exterior of a particular community boundary. Social identities are redefined by the inscription of new external dangers (from communists in the Cold War era to "rogue states" such as Iran and North Korea in the post-Cold War era and terrorist groups after the September 2001 terrorist attacks).

The salience of one's own group membership as opposed to homogeneous other groups is related to the manner of the creation, maintenance, or reproduction of perceptions of a social world. The question of who is and is not a member of a community depends not so much upon the content of the culture as upon the purpose for which the community acts together. There is indeed a cultural content in an ethnic community but group boundaries can be redrawn according to the purpose in hand. On the understanding that identity provides a base or motive for social action, "instrumentalism regards ethnicity as a tool to pursue self-interest or obtain material ends" (Ellis, 2006, p. 41).

Beyond serving as instrumental forms of social action, certainly various motivations are attached to a search for a group which one wants to belong to. Therefore, identity-based action is linked to not only rational–instrumental incentives but also value, beliefs, tradition, and habit. Indeed, group members are socially or psychologically interdependent in the satisfaction of needs, attainment of goals, or consensual validation of attitudes and values. An effective identity mobilization is based on beliefs and scripts for action in relation to the negative other. On the other hand, positive self-identification results from association with a group which provides emotional support and security. The need for collective as well as individual identity leads to distinguishing insiders and outsiders even when scarcity or gain is not an issue.

Different types of identities are explained by how to attain and maintain exclusionary boundaries. The salience of identities can be changeable, situational, and optional, but ethnic, religious, national, and other collective identities are more pervasive (especially when being enmeshed with memories of historical rivalry or experiences of past oppression). The proliferation of antagonistic political identities is, in part, based on the perceived need and search for security, in particular, demanded at uncertain times. Insecurity and ensuing war in Bosnia-Herzegovina comes from the collapse of stable relations along with the competition for hegemony.

A quest for self-esteem leads individuals to strive for social associations which can provide affection and boost their morale. The significance of collective identity for individuals is a desire to belong to a group in which they feel solidarity or cohesion with a *positive other*. As self-perception is connected to group membership, collective identity strengthens pride in oneself at an individual level.

"The enlargement of personal identity offers fulfillment and realization of self" (Gamson, 1992, p. 56). Identification with a larger cause and a sense of loyalty to those working for the same cause are natural to the emergence of collective identity. The emotional bonds are often formed by collective action and shared commitment to protect aims which unite those who feel grievances.

In conflict situations, identities have more or less clear boundaries well rooted in history and maintained through inner psychological cohesion. In ethno-nationalism, mass murder is ascribed to the denial of the other's existence based on the sentiments that someone else's roots distort a particular form of life. In securing identity boundaries, the violent extermination of others is seen as a matter of collective survival, as is illustrated by fascist youth violence against foreigners in Europe during the early post-Cold War period. In the absence of stable ethnic relations, threat perceptions produce the impulse to destroy the roots of other cultures as a means of constructing and maintaining one's identity.

Thus group identification results from an emotional investment and a sense of value attachment to the membership. Conformity to each other's views and perceived liking play an important role in developing a sense of a salient group membership. In general, attraction to a group and social cohesion among members are reinforced by emotional empathy and mutual regard. In addition, attitudinal and behavioral uniformity stems from perceived similarity and cooperation.

In witch-hunting, causes of distressful social events are ascribed to intentions or behavior of out-groups. During economic downturns, migrant workers in Russia, Eastern Europe, and South Africa have recently become a target of hate-motivated violence. Social chaos caused by even natural disasters can also cause brutal attacks against minorities (e.g., the massacre of Korean minorities by police and civilians alike in the aftermath of the 1923 Great Kanto earthquake in Japan).

Freudian theories explain psychological functioning by which inner aggression is displaced on an out-group (inner aggression converts into out-group hatred). According to the neo-Freudian, Erikson (1994), the ego defense is needed to protect the self from unpleasant realities. As a result, self-love associated with group narcissism facilitates antipathies and aversions toward strangers. After Serbian troops withdrew from Kosovo at the end of the NATO bombing in 1999, Albanian Kosovars shamelessly attacked gypsies who were the most marginalized group in the society, as well as civilian Serbs.

Violent ethnic mobilization is attributed to a void in identification (which produces anxiety and uncertainty) and an attempt to master the disturbing effects. Inner insecurity leads to the fear of banishment. If violence is regarded as an instrument of securing one's identity, moral constraints can be easily abandoned. The link between in-group love and ethnocentrism can be clearly made through exclusive group identification that serves as a motivational and cognitive source of hatred.

As a political identity base turns into a violent ethnic tool, the reason for and the process of a sudden move from the political realm to violence cannot be simply explained by ancient hatred or childhood trauma. The sudden eruption of violence in Rwanda, Bosnia-Herzegovina, and Algeria has turned neighbors into the objects of mass extermination and rape with the institutionalization of animistic relations. Thus violence becomes detached from its initial context along with its reproduction.

Group processes of identity formation

The formation of polarized collective identities reflects the psychological states of individuals, the structure and function of groups and the broader community in which the conflict is situated. Group boundaries are determined by issues related to relative power and status, access to resources as well as value differences. Group differences are associated with socio-economic, class distinctions, occupational groupings, gender, or cultural belongings. Most significantly, the enduring nature of identities can be explained by the convergence of language, ethnicity, religion, and other group attributes in the intensification of we-ness feeling. In multi-ethnic societies, any identifiable linguistic or other cultural properties are attributed to determining an individual's social status.

Individuals struggle either to improve low group prestige or to leave that group for one of higher status. Becoming part of a high-status group enhances self-esteem, but difficulties in changing one's identity base lead to the adoption of a strategy of degrading an out-group's image. Low-status group members may also attempt to relegate individual problems to group victimization instead of personal failings. One may strive for more positive distinctiveness by competing directly with a highly recognized group. In competition for recognition and reputation, an individual may choose a positive component of self-identity while abandoning negative ones that hold a low group image.

Socio-psychological distance is often imposed on the meanings of "border" by which the "perception of the others" characterizes interaction between the two communities. The complexities of social transition in Cyprus and their effects in bi-communal relations are related to a shift in the barriers which divide the two communities from physical to symbolic. The identity of Greek Cypriots has been transformed after they joined the European Union. Since the event, psychological distance has grown between Greek and Turkish Cypriots though the physical barrier is lower. This creates a dilemma for how to pursue peace making between the two communities. As two groups increasingly interact, symbolic borders have become a more important factor in perceptions of "others" than physical ones.

Identity strengthens cohesiveness with a shared sense of attraction, belongingness, and loyalty to the group. The significance of emotional bonds is reinforced by individual feelings about each other that arise from a positive in-group interaction. A distinct, cohesive social group bestows its members with the collective ability to act efficaciously (Simon and Klandermans, 2001). The psychological features of identity and solidarity are derived from past sufferings and present or future anxiety about group well-being and survival along with a shared meaning of the social world.

Through collective identities, group members may feel an assault on a group is an attack on one's sense of self. As individuals strive for an increasing sense of one's value by seeking collective affirmation, an identity formation process is founded on the development of a conception of self in relation to positive others along with internalization of group norms and objectives. In intense conflict situations, allegiance with group identity reinforces a positive self-concept.

A high degree of in-group identification is coupled with an intense level of outside threat which brings forth a basic impulse for self-preservation. One's own sense of security is destabilized especially in intense competition which carries a high stake. Rigid beliefs and decreased complexity in cognitive thinking can remove uncertainty and ambivalence, protecting a stable sense of self. A frozen sense of us versus them is further developed with disincentives for seeking objective information about enemies.

Connections between individual and group identity

Encounters with another group can be explained in terms of an identification process of a group membership. In politically divided societies, the self-conception of individual identity is intertwined with and often imposed by group boundaries. An increased motivation to stay in the group reflects the strengths of attractions toward the group. The uniformity and predictability of behavior are promoted by the development of cohesive group norms.

The main reference point in an inter-group interaction is based on *collective* distinctiveness marked by ethnicity or other socio-cultural elements. When individuals are regarded as merely representatives of differing groups in intense struggles such as labor negotiations or war, the most significant reference point in inter-personal interaction is based on *group* associations.

Intra-group differences are de-emphasized to strengthen internal solidarity. In violent conflict situations, a zeal to guard rigid group boundaries may lead to killing one's own group members who do not join in conformative behavior. During the Rwandan genocide, many moderate Hutus were killed because of their refusal to be part of violent campaigns against the Tutsis. While a psychological process to reduce complexity, uncertainty, and ambivalence would help sustain a continuing sense of self, a lack of an adaptive learning process (derived from the maintenance of rigid beliefs) develops a frozen sense of tight group boundaries. When one's group identity is interpreted as zero-sum in a negation with the other, stereotypical out-group images serve as disincentives for seeking new information that can change the negative, monolithic enemy perceptions. The enduring nature of self-identities is supported by a strong emotional dislike and negative images of enemy "others."

Group allegiances represent our social connections by defining, to ourselves and to others, who we are. Tensions surrounding cultural practices can be referred to broader ethnic group distinctions. In inter-personal dynamics, free of strong inter-group forces, communication functions are not handicapped by socially predetermined impediments. Thus, inter-personal dispute resolution strategies do not need to seriously consider either group or cultural influences. Interaction with other group members is not viewed as an inter-personal process once we define it in terms of heterogeneity among groups. De-individuation (by which an individual is seen as a group member rather than having their own unique values) can lead to dehumanization, eventually justifying aggression.

Interactions between inter-group and inter-personal identity are considered a continuum (Tajfel, 1981). Individuals have different levels of cognitive ability to make sense of the collective self. In fact, one does not necessarily accept all the group values, and may disagree with government policies against "enemy" others. Israeli military helicopter pilots publicly disobeyed the government order to attack civilian residents during the height of the violence in the West Bank and Gaza in the early 2000s (Chacham, 2003). A high level of cognitive complexity permits particular individuals to draw different conclusions as to the nature or significance of events from other in-group members. Social identity aligned with a particular group does not necessarily stop conscience awakening (for individual agents who abide by universal moral values rather than blind loyalty to one's own group). The Chinese dissidents wrote a letter in support of easing restrictions and harsh rules in Tibet even in the midst of the state media and Internet forums cheerleading the justification of the government's crackdown on protesters in spring 2008.

Formation of group boundaries

The construction of "similarity" of the members of any collectivity is geared toward making distinctions from other groups. Individual behavior may be attributed to "group sameness" and "foundational forms of selfhood." The sameness focuses on little variability in behavior and attitudes within each group (in a unified social category). The expression of self-identity and associated attributes is congruent with core values.

The majority of people care less morally about the welfare of people beyond their close families, community, or workplace. During an atrocious war or genocide, the notion of "the other" is particularly related to the brutal line between insiders and outsiders in the collective mind. In wholesale slaughter justified by dehumanization of outsiders, tribal sentiment is abused by moral entrepreneurs to instigate evil acts such as mass murder.

In a psychological sense, the existence of groups is not entirely attributed to member similarities. More importantly, people's realization of their shared fate increases loyalty to the group. Since group members can be similar or dissimilar in many different ways, the most critical element binding people is the interdependence of fate. The identification of common attributes reinforces the development of collective perceptions of a shared fate with the attribution of opposing features to out-groups.

Social exclusion and inclusion

The distinct manifestations of social exclusion and inclusion shape and are shaped by group boundaries. As is illustrated by the amalgamation of multinational groupings within the Austrian–Hungarian Empire and Ottoman Turkey in the eighteenth and nineteenth centuries, groups at the most general level can be largely categorized by geographical, religious, or ethnic differences, and awarded different degrees of autonomy and access to economic wealth. These transnational dividing lines have sharpened antagonistic group divisions since the departure of colonial powers and collapse of multi-ethnic federal states.

Nationalities are scattered across state border lines along with overlapping geopolitical–linguistic classifications (French versus English speaking Africa), and religious distinctions (Islam versus Christianity between the north and south of Sudan), and economic hierarchies and income disparities along ethnic and racial divisions (in Bolivia and Rwanda). Deteriorating inter-group relations, in combination with a weakened political authority, have often served as a fertile ground for the mobilization of distinctive groups with the adoption of a color-blind ideology.

The different treatment of individuals may be based on ethnic or linguistic categories whose status has been determined by political associations embedded in social–historical hierarchies. In the politicization of identity, higher levels of abstract values and ideologies often define a context for group boundaries at a more concrete level. The principled exclusion of the enemy "other" can be applied to specific settings (anyone being suspected of being tied to al-Qaeda and the Taliban) by political ideology (such as doctrines of war on terrorism) supported by legislative and institutional mechanisms. Despite worldwide condemnation, President George Bush maintained the Guantanamo Bay Detention Camp in Cuba and secret prisons for suspected terrorists in Europe only to deepen the divide between the US and the Islamic world.

The reassignment of categories is supported by a pervasive social imagery against unknown "others." Exclusion can be manifested in more specific, concrete ways through discrimination against other groups. A cognitive and emotional frame prevents an opportunity for inclusion of distinct "others" in normalized relations. A self-conception of differences between blacks and whites is anchored more to psychological and social distance than actual physical appearance.

The mechanisms of inclusion and exclusion are related to partitioning people into different social categories and its institutional legitimation (as is presented by an electoral system based on ethnic cleavages in such places as Ethiopia). For instance, identity categories in many Latin American societies have evolved out of formation of a group status in a historical process of creating social hierarchies (white, mestizos, natives, and blacks). The contentious process of social categorization often becomes a bedrock for political struggle with unequal access to valued material objects or denial of social respect. In Bolivia, provinces in low land have more income, and they have been resisting the attempt of President Morales' government at equitable wealth distribution to rectify disadvantageous treatment of indigenous people.

The rejection of an entire population becomes easier and simpler via dehumanization. The institutionalization of physical segregation is associated with political boundaries such as the apartheid system during the white minority government in South Africa or the Cold War symbolized by the Berlin Wall. Symbolic and psychological aspects of expulsion may focus on denial of prestige, recognition, respect, autonomy, and self-determination. The exclusion and inclusion of groups can be based and legitimized in linguistic, communication practice (such as the denial of minority language for an official status).

Social categorization

In-groups and out-groups are perceptually distinguished through the process of categorization which puts "self" and others into differentiated categories (Hogg, 2001). In general, social identity processes are based on the categorization of people along with exclusive preferences for one's own group relative to other groups. The categorization is likely to rely upon highly visible characteristics such as gender, ethnicity, or race. Most significantly, though, social identifications within a group are based on common attitudes and values which aggregate individual differences. The distinctive features of intra-group relations are maintained by relative uniformity and generalization of shared attributes along with reduced perceptual differences between the self and other in-group members.

In an intense conflict, multiple social categories converge. In championing the different political life of Northern Ireland, the Catholic minority pursues nationalist agendas by favoring unification with the Republic of Ireland to the south. On the other hand, the majority of Protestants remain loyal to the United Kingdom and want to keep the union. Thus unionists (also equated to loyalists) and republicans (equally known as nationalists) are divided primarily over religious fault lines. Over the decades, this main division (based on national identity and religion) has been politicized in class and other aspects of competing group identities. Many of the Catholics belong to a low-income working class, being translated into widespread segregation in housing and schools (and even social or sports club affiliations). These social differences have occasionally been manifested in the allegations of discrimination in employment practices and the legal system. Thus the single, most basic division (of being republican versus unionist) accentuates the boundaries of similarities and differences. The conversion of different identity categories along the same fault line recreates more distinctive group boundaries with a high likelihood of discrimination.

Group differentiation helps our understanding of an order in a complex world for political or social action. By defining a group from the outside in, a set of common attributes is applied to all members of a category. Distinctive characteristics of groups can be internalized as self-conception, and can be adopted for socialization. Social categorization is likely to set boundaries for the interpretation of individuals' actions and beliefs. A social context creates meaningful group boundaries in a self-categorization process (Operario and Fiske, 1999). The relationships are rendered more predictable by the construction of categories even if the categorization is based on subjective perceptions.

The membership of social categories is associated with positive or negative value connotations. The values attached to group categories define the importance of one's social identity vis-à-vis relevant others who serve as a reference group. In evaluating one's own group, individuals refer to the attitudes or behavior of another group that functions as the holder of standards for social prestige.

Social identity, as an important part of the self-concept, produces favorable in-group evaluations as distinct from other collectivities. Individuals want to enhance their own positive self-images on the basis of valued dimensions such as language and history. Positive in-group identities can be advanced by favorable comparisons with out-groups.

A strategy to seek positive group identity through the derogation of out-groups contributes to the escalation of inter-group conflict. One group's promotion of its exclusive identity is likely to generate a reciprocally negative response of ethnocentrism from the other side. Morale can be enhanced by unquestioned loyalty to a group and call for sacrifice. Yet this process can negatively reinforce exaggerated threat and blind enemy images in self-fulfilling prophecies.

Self-categories are activated in specific situations, but they can be institutionalized in a continuing relationship. Different social and political institutions have an ability to select their own criteria for inclusion and exclusion. In Ethiopia, major ethnic groups are represented in a political process by registration according to their ethnic origins. Subjective categories can be objectified in the political evaluation process of granting or denying available rewards. In constituting the core of socio-political relations, ethnic and racial identity is reflected in establishing the dominant or subordinate positions of individuals or groups (Simon and Klandermans, 2001).

Identity politics revolve around who controls the process to define communal boundaries. Political entities mobilize resources and people behind institutionalized symbols.

Identity formation can be colonized by hegemonic relations which allow the appropriation of linguistic, social, and cultural resources in the production of marginality. Local and particular claims to separate identities over general ones are asserted in the struggle to establish new terms of relationship. In ethno-politics (for instance, Palestinians living in Israel), power differentials shape the nature of balance between pressure on a marginalized group to accommodate the outside world (being an Israeli citizen) and resistance against dominant relations (maintenance of Arab identity). This contradiction is especially intense during the height of violent confrontations. The sympathy protests in Israeli–Palestinian villages during the early period of the second intifada (which started in September 2000) created mutual suspicion between the Israeli state and its Arab populations. The government dispatch of tanks to Arab villages generated a sentiment of being treated as marginalized "others" among the minority population.

Cognitive representation of identity

The construction of collective identities is supported by societal beliefs of common roots in history or other shared group distinctiveness. More precisely, a subjective psychological process interacts with common group cultures in digesting external influences and experiences. The established categories have a filtering effect on people's perceptions of events and objects. The social representation of experience, knowledge, and action is managed by cognitive systems.

The mere perception of being a member of two distinct groups is sufficient enough to develop an orientation toward favorable judgments about in-group members' behavior and abilities. Individuals may construct images about their groups and others through a cognitive process. The increased perceptions of distance in interests, roles, and other easily identifiable properties between in-groups and out-groups lead to an emphasis on in-group similarity. The adopted categories relevant to the conflict create group boundaries (along such social divisions as nationality, ethnicity, religion, and language). The polarized identities support monolithic and exclusive in-group discourse and further widen inter-group divisions in the intensification of a conflict.

This is well represented by the Chinese leadership's psychological attitude toward the Tibetan uprising in spring 2008. The highest ranking Chinese official in charge of Tibet, Zhang Qingli emphasized: "We are now engaged in a fierce blood-and-fire battle with the Dalai clique, a life-and-death battle between us and the enemy." The hostile sentiment was further echoed by his other remark as "The Dalai is a wolf in monk's robes, a devil with a human face but the heart of a beast" (The Associated Press, April, 1, 2008). In general, demonized views about an adversary signal hardened identity positions and refusal to take any kind of conciliatory move toward amicable solutions to a conflict.

The motive for self-esteem leads to social differentiation in conjunction with positive valuation of in-group characteristics. A process of group differentiation results in an emphasis on the positive aspects of one's social identity with in-group favoritism. In the construction of collective identity, a sense of in-group superiority is often linked to repudiation and vilification of out-group properties.

The accentuation of intra-group similarities and inter-category differences may shed light on racial, ethnic, religious, and cultural divisions. Even if the differences are not objectively meaningful, the perceptual act of group categorization in a competitive context can produce discrimination along with the development of stereotypes and bias.

In-group standards of desirable behavior justify the discriminatory behavior against out-groups. Middle-class professionals in India have prejudicial views about their servants being dishonest, and they are often suspected of any theft. In one recent incident involving the murder of a small girl, a Nepalese servant was automatically accused of the murder, but later he was also found killed in the same manner that the girl was murdered. In a conflict setting, one's own group is evaluated with a reference to specific other groups to which a low prestige is generally attached. The existence of strong, rigid group boundaries reinforces the attribution of negative individual behavior to out-group characteristics. A shared identity base permits the behaviors of in-group members to be more forgiving relative to out-group members. Attributional bias is more likely to be involved in stressful interactions. In emotionally charged conflicts, the behavior of other group members is considered destructive, while one's own tactics are portrayed as cooperative.

Competition for higher status between roughly equal groups is likely to invoke a negative reference to rival groups. In-group bias in support of pride results in over-evaluating the virtues of one's own group members. Perceived intra-group similarity and liking tend to ignore even detrimental behavior of the same group members. Rigid categorization leads to conformity to a group's behavioral norm as well as collective views about an enemy group. Diverse options are not seriously considered due to conformity pressures.

Interacting with members of different social groups generates the awareness of a group membership. Engagement in social competition leads to efforts to protect self-images, rights, and privileges. The boundary lines of societies and groups are affirmed by conflicts. In-group favoritism is associated with the process of social identity formation in conflict settings. An inherent drive to establish a positive social identity contributes to the formation of affirmative views about one's group. The image of one's own group member is regarded as trustable, whereas members of the opposing group are often described as aggressive. Increased hostilities are supported by the rigid group boundaries in conjunction with negative patterns of communication confirming biased perception.

Different sets of information are activated to produce stereotypical effects in a different context. More favorable information is selected in the process of self-affirmation of in-group qualities. The homogenization and depersonalization of out-group members are an inevitable result of stereotyping, being solidified by category-based attributions (of "not being trusted" or other negative qualities). In fact, stereotypes foster bias-confirming communication in support of self-fulfilling prophecies (Gudykunst and Mody, 1989).

When differences are perceived as threatening to the identity or well-being of the group, a competitive context is likely to further widen psychological distance and biases against opposing group members. Beyond objective differences in interests, it is a group process which contributes to the categorization of individuals. Inferences about distinctive group features can be made deductively via category-based stereotypes (Abrams and Hogg, 2001). Conforming to a positive in-group image is combined with the avoidance of a negative self-image.

Negative others can be demonized, through image distortions, to improve self-esteem and provide positive in-group valuation. Negative ethnocentric or racial attributions produce a strong dislike and the negation of others. The exaggeration of in-group qualities is associated with denigrating out-group performance. In a zero-sum struggle, negative, stereotypical out-group images are necessary for preserving one's own identity. Frustration experienced by competition with an out-group is linked to the development and expression of the out-group hostility.

The impact of social indentification on inter-group action

Through political mobilization, groups or individuals are incited to kill or die in order to "preserve, maintain or acquire their identities." Ethnocentrism is based on the glorification of in-group properties, and derogation of out-group aspirations and values. This may be fueled by competitive interactions based on incompatible interests; perceived threat to one's goals augments in-group solidarity and heightens out-group hostility, supported by a history of antagonism. In ethnocentrism, in-group love is reciprocally connected to out-group rejection and hate.

In crisis situations, in-group unity and common bonds are reassured by the collective identity. On the other hand, in-group glorification helps sustain authoritarian submission as well as ethnocentrism, as is illustrated by Nazi Germany under Hitler. The obedience to authority is emphasized in highly cohesive groups often in combination with autocratic leadership which defines and enforces individual conformity with collective norms. Whereas group cohesion provides collective self-esteem and satisfaction with the leader, cohesiveness produces conformity pressures on decisions. More extreme behaviors may occur in the group context than if the individuals were acting separately.

Bridging in-group and out-group differences

Intolerance is most likely to prescribe individuals to act and react towards opposing group members according to their social identification rather than individual qualities. The exaggeration of between-group differences can be minimized by stressing the uniqueness of individual out-group members as well as equating them as part of a larger human community. In addition, the inclusiveness of group boundaries can be expanded by the transfer of in-group favoritism to out-groups.

Positive inter-group relations are facilitated by the improvement in attitudes and behavior toward out-group members. Group biases can be more easily reduced by a history of successful cooperation in inter-group relations. The absence of contact often contributes to a poor standard of knowledge about each other and misreading of intentions. Extended interaction between group members emerges from functional cooperation which will eventually lead to the development of common goals. As is presented by the contact hypothesis (Allport and Pettigrew, 1998), group boundaries can be narrowed by the development of increased inter-group interaction on the basis of a strong norm of equality.

In-group identification does not necessarily produce negative attitudes toward out-groups in a non-competitive setting. The existence of common goals helps groups cooperate rather than be engaged in competition. Increased contact can develop benevolent effects only if groups have equal status to avoid one party's domination. A narrow group identity base can be diluted by positive experiences of contact with out-group members whose characteristics disprove stereotypes. Personalized information about an out-group member in repeated interactions can over time erode the stereotypical enemy images.

New information gained through personalized interaction helps replace existing categories which form the basis of classifying each other. In the long run, the inter-group contact is expected to produce a change in the attitude toward a group beyond immediate individual encounters. Opportunities for personal acquaintance between group members can be expanded with the support of authorities within and outside of the contact situation (e.g., education and cultural exchanges such as the Fulbright programs sponsored by the US government).

As groups cooperatively work to develop a common goal, inter-group bias can decrease along with an increased contact supported by institutional or social forces. The recognition of inter-group similarities and common interests helps members of both groups acknowledge the strengths of the other group as well as their own for improved inter-group relations. The newly created bond can be vulnerable to conflict re-escalation, as is exhibited by various peace camps which brought Israeli and Palestinian youths to friendship prior to the exchange of violent assault in the early 2000s. Inter-personal acquaintances developed through "Seeds for Peace" and other programs were easily replaced by antagonistic behavior in the midst of flaring violence. A common fate or shared threat has more lasting effects in forming activities than positive images of the other group developed by inter-personal attractions.

Thus the contact hypothesis needs to be complementary to or reinforced by other intergroup cooperative phenomena. Out-group bias and discrimination can be minimized by crosscutting social categories among multi-group membership. Multiple exposure helps avoid the over-generalized experience based on the negative encounters. The patterns of conflict regulation can be socially institutionalized by the development of cross-cutting ties which promote cooperation among multiple functions and roles of various groups. The existence of multiple identities reduces dependence on a single, concentric identity for the search for meaning.

Less inter-group conflict has been ascribed to the existence of multiple reference groups (e.g., kinship, age, ritual) vis-à-vis the organization of societies around a single axis (Ross, 2006). Thus internal heterogeneity (rather than homogeneity) is helpful to the development of cross-cutting ties among diverse communal members. According to anthropological studies of tribes in southern Zambia, Tonga kinship groups are dispersed across many settlements, helping to develop close relationships with their neighbors through cooperation in herding, farming, and communal rituals. The coexistence of diverse cultures has been effective in promoting tribal ties. In another example, joint economic and social activities among the youth and women have been promoted in developing cross-cutting ties in the peace-making process in Northern Ireland.

In general, the recognition of the necessity for cooperation and common bonds can emerge from the development of superordinate goals. Inter-group boundaries are deemphasized with the promotion of common interests of both groups. Superordinate identity can be anchored to higher level categories (e.g., nations) which are more inclusive than ethnic, kin, or other lower level ones (Gaertner and Dovidio, 2000). Some sort of identity widening by a new self-categorization is designed to induce inter-group cooperation through the construction of interdependent goals and superordinate group memberships. It evolves out of the expansion of identity circles with shared experiences and beliefs, as represented by the experience of the European Union.

A perceiver's goals, motives, and recollection of past experiences can be modified to develop a more encompassing and inclusive category in a given context. Group differences become a less important issue if the strengths of two groups are not concentrated in the pursuit of competing interests. A mutual respect for each other's skills can be complementary, not hampering harmonious inter-group relations. Personalized interactions can eliminate a category-based bias with the existance of common interests in shared categories.

Crossed categorization

The inter-category differences can be weakened by crossed group boundaries and encouragement of divergence within each category. Even when "others" are classified as outgroup members on one dimension, they can still be regarded as an in-group member on another dimension. Various reconciliation organizations in Northern Ireland (e.g., Women Together for Peace founded in 1970) attempted to tackle a rise in sectarian intimidation and violence by focusing on empathy built on the shared experience of being subject to indiscriminate violence. In order to develop a bridge among sectarian groups, direct-action movement has confronted the incidents of violence within the interface areas. They were engaged in clearing up the ruins of bombing and preventing rival youth gangs' stone throwing. In Bosnia-Herzegovina, women's groups emerged from the bond centered on the experience of victimhood despite their ethnic differences.

De-categorization and re-categorization

Qualitative change in the core sense of self may come from de-categorization and re-categorization. Through de-categorization, group boundaries can be redefined in the manner that opposing group members are encouraged to recognize similarities and differences on an individual basis. In addition, divergent group members can adopt a superordinate group identity through re-categorization that results from a change in their classification of out-group members. The frameworks of de-categorization and re-categorization are complementary to each other in improving inter-group relations by bias reduction. In a nutshell, intra-group identity becomes less salient in tandem with the promotion of diverse identities between groups as well as the reduced significance of the boundary distinction in managing inter-group relations.

De-categorization

The members of different groups conceive themselves and others no longer as separate individuals by ceasing to see each other from the standpoint of distinctive group properties. Out-group members' behavior is attributed to common individualized characteristics instead of being category-based (Davidio, 2005, p. 248). Information about group categories provides a less useful basis for classifying each other than individual characteristics. In degrading exclusive group boundaries, thus, de-categorization sheds light on the attributes of separate individuals rather than properties of group members. The decrease in the salience of the original inclusive–exclusive boundaries produces less inter-group bias.

Interactions based purely on personal qualities (such as intimate relationships and close friendships across group boundaries) are not based on qualitative inter-group differences. Individual recognition and rewards are related to personal abilities that are not part of group affiliations (as is the case with affirmative action). The base of personal identity can be separated from an inter-group exchange derived from different group attributes. Inter-personal differences are ascribed to unique personalities or individual qualities rather than group associations. Individualized conflict, expressed almost entirely in inter-personal terms, can be handled precisely as a personal matter.

An emphasis on more personalized interactions promotes separate individual identities with the erosion and de-categorization of group boundaries. Improved inter-personal relations are eventually expected to avoid over-generalization of out-group members in general. The personalization of out-group members helps de-activate the undesirable images of an out-group in reducing group hostilities. The reduced salience of the original inclusive–exclusive group boundaries is expected to decrease inter-group bias. Inter-personal similarities can undermine the basis of identification that focuses on group differences.

Inter-group trust can be built by informal contacts at an inter-personal level. For instance, unofficial diplomacy has been utilized in de-freezing conflict relationships by expanding informal contacts among members of enemy societies. In the US–Soviet relations during the Cold War era, a multitude of networks and contacts among professional groups were developed to narrow wide gaps between the two societies. The main objective was to develop personalized contact and ultimately promote changes in public perceptions in their home countries. By switching a focus from the inter-societal differences to the inter-personal level of intimacy and common interests, the group members could more easily cultivate shared human values. Many experts believe that these contacts influenced the Soviet leadership's thinking about their system and necessity for reform (which brought down the bureaucratic socialist system).

Improvement in race relations can be followed by desegregating the school system and other types of social and educational activities which have individualized orientations. One of the major challenges in Bosnia-Herzegovina is that each ethnic group is engaged in separate economic, cultural, and educational activities, being deprived of an opportunity to develop individualized contact across group boundaries.

Re-categorization

Re-categorization redefines group categorization at a higher level of inclusiveness without diminishing or abolishing existing social categories. Two groups can be conceived of being distinct sub-units within the context of a superordinate identity. For instance, a sub-unit membership within a corporation or governmental agency is compatible with a large organizational representation. Re-categorization can be achieved by identification with a single superordinate identity with reduced salience of sub-group identities, or by the development of a dual identity in which both superordinate and sub-group identities are granted legitimate. In the Netherlands and Switzerland, ethnic language, customs, and other aspects of communal life have primary significance in identifying groups, but they have joined together to maintain a multi-ethnic, pluralistic society.

In the post-apartheid South Africa, unity has been achieved by a shift from racial differentiation to recreate national identity. In this incidence, re-categorization was achieved by a shift in the main basis of group differentiation to a new superordinate category which embraces all different racial groups. Reduced inter-group bias stems from the decreased salience of original group boundaries. In particular, the increased inclusiveness of group boundaries can bring about compatibility with various out-group characteristics in combination with the minimization of unique aspects of in-group identity.

The concentric circles expand with the extension and enlargement of one's identity, feelings and experiences to contain more people and diverse ideas. Higher level categories (such as nations) are more inclusive and embracive than lower level ones such as family or neighbors. In a re-categorization process, the cognitive representation of multiple sub-groups expands the circle of inclusion with enlarged common boundaries. Superordinate identity may emerge from the attributes of new categories with which rival groups have not been associated. Alternatively, it can also be derived from amalgamating different types of organized categories. As is illustrated by the process of creating an economic union in Western Europe since World War II, the perceptions of past experiences and future expectations can be modified by changes in goals and motives. In enhancing environmental consciousness, the level of category inclusiveness (such as eco-centric identity) can be broadened to incorporate diverse heterogeneous groups (characterized by race and gender differences).

In various arrangements for maintaining dual identity, superordinate and sub-group identities can be simultaneously salient. The application of favorable attitudes to additional out-group members coincides with the introduction of a cooperative relationship between groups. Diverse representations within the same superordinate group permit a dual ownership of superordinate and sub-group identities. A dual identity has been sought in easing inter-racial and inter-ethnic tensions in national integration. In general, strong allegiances to their sub-groups should not undermine a newly emerging in-group identity of a superordinate entity given that they are based on different levels of categorization. As is illustrated by the evolution of the European Union, therefore, the development of a common identity does not necessarily demand that each group abandon its less inclusive group identity.

Sub-group identities can be managed in diverse ways within the context of dual identity representation. The sub-groups can develop identity representation in an organizational context which allows for the coexistence of different group members as part of the same superordinate entity. For instance, a more cosmopolitan Bosnian identity can be adopted as a superordinate identity for Croatians, Serbians, or Muslims in order to create a functioning federal political entity. Sub-group identities can have an equal status to each other under a rubric of superordinate identity which does not degrade the original in-group versus out-group categorization scheme. New overarching identities may not be complementary to existing in-group identities if the superordinate identity interferes in maintaining the core values of separate identities. Accepting a superordinate identity does not deny individuals simultaneously carrying multiple identity group memberships. A more inclusive, common identity does not need to suppress the sustenance of salient sub-group identities.

Identity relations can therefore be more easily managed by the establishment of common identity than an attempt to abolish or modify feelings of attachment to sub-groups. In considering the permanent reality of enduring ethnic solidarities, it is not desirable or feasible to force sub-group members to relinquish identities highly central to them (Davidio, 2005). The simultaneous possession of multiple identities permits minority group members to keep their salient ethnic and cultural features.

In curbing ethno-nationalism in multinational states, supranational identity can be promoted in conjunction with power sharing and other political or social arrangements which grant a unique role to minority groups. People in Quebec have the dual identities of being a Canadian and French-speaking national group. Separatist elements in Quebec have been controlled by the institutional accommodation which entails an advantageous political status, privileges for the minority language as well as economic benefit of being part of Canada.

While connections can be developed through superordinate group identity, difference may remain strong with the longevity of original sub-group identity. In spite of all the positive effects of identity restructuring, the tension created by the pursuit of competing goals may trigger greater inter-group conflict in the process of social disintegration and political instability. As national crises in the former Yugoslavia suggest, separate group identities become more salient, refueling inter-group conflict at the times of unusual competition which generates feelings of threat to each group's security.

From de-categorization to re-categorization

People may like each other as individuals, but they can still harbor negative attitudes toward the other group as a whole. The shortcoming can be overcome by a sense of common collectivity derived from a shared superordinate identity. This is a reverse process of accentuation of intra-group similarities and inter-category differences. The commitment to a new superordinate national identity decreases the salience of disparate group boundaries so that they can become less obvious to insiders and outsiders.

Gaining new multiple sub-group identities dilutes the intensity of attachment to a narrow existing identity base with the creation of crisscrossing category memberships. Crossed-categorization can reduce bias in line with a decrease in the salience of original group membership. Striving for self-esteem can be satisfied by at least some multiple sub-group memberships, eliminating the necessity to depend on negative attitudes toward others for promotion of the self.

In post-conflict reconciliation, the process of apology and forgiveness is part of the rituals to rediscover each other's humanities as a shared identity base. The experience of atrocities deeply touches upon human existence beyond ethnic or national divisions or any other group boundaries. The emphasis on shared humanity permits individuals to be seen as either victims (whose dignity should be restored) or perpetrators (who are responsible for their own acts).

Renegotiation of identities

Identity can be renegotiated in the process of conflict resolution and establishment of new relationships. Inter-group relations are formed and sustained by physical proximity, psychological needs, and social reciprocity. Group boundaries can be rearranged (to create psychological distance or proximate relationships). Polarized identities can be reconstructed to curtail animosities and reconcile past histories of violence with current necessities for coexistence and mutual prosperity. In the rapprochement between France and Germany after World War II, antagonistic identities have no longer been put in the context of exclusive ethno-nationalism but in the future vision of peaceful, economically prosperous Europe.

In discursive terms, de-escalation would accompany the creation of a more inclusive narrative practice. A new discursive structure could bring about the renegotiation of identities of the self and others. Identity can be reinterpreted by the necessity for coexistence through development of new relationships. Reconciliation can lead to the transformation of a collective identity by supporting changes in the perceptions of negative others.

The reconstruction of identities reflects qualitative changes in the communicative, social-psychological nature of human relations. Not only differing interests and incompatible values but also rigid perceptions of self in relation to the rest of the world are obstacles to communication. The win–lose perceptions can be overcome by the accommodation of values embedded in the core identities of opposing groups (that can be supported by various methods of contact and communication developed in unofficial diplomacy).

Negotiation of identity means more than a trade-off of different priorities or the search for a common interest. Resolving differences within an interest bargaining framework does not create conditions for understanding values and identities. A context of meaning changes due to the emergence of different frames of references over time. Social differences and ambiguities can be negotiated by translating the unfamiliar to the familiar. The exhibition of multiple meanings of a social world can expand tolerance and legitimate differences.

It would be difficult to establish a discursive process for conflict resolution without finding a set of principles, values, or reasons which create the basis of different subject positions. A new form of discourse has to be constructed for establishing a collaborative relationship between self and others beyond a limited set of negotiable interests. The conditions for security can be negotiated through a shared understanding. New expectations about the self can be created without causing threats to the enemy other. The identity of the self could be ingrained in the perceptions of peaceful relations with others.

As is evidenced by the division of Eastern and Western Europe during the Cold War period, the exclusivity of identity boundaries discourages cross-group interactions. In identity conflict, especially, differences are often constructed in negative terms. Identity transformation requires a capacity to project a new way of life as well as the willingness to reason from another's point of view. Images attached to adversarial relationships could be decoded with the changes of old boundary functions.

Prevailing identities may lose their appeal in competing with other established identities or newly emerging identities which can meet psychological needs of the collectivities better. For instance, the influence of Pan-Arab nationalism was diminished with the failed attempt to create a new state comprised of Egypt, Libya, and Syria in the mid-1960s. Its appeal further declined after the coalition of Arabic countries which fought together against Israel in 1966 and in 1973 began to split after Egypt and Jordan concluded a peace accord with Israel.

The demand for redrawing identity boundaries can be ascribed to power and status reversals that result from social, political changes or severe economic competition. Intergroup conflict tends to be less intense if group boundaries become less salient (in the management of one's expectations about security and well-being). In the relaxation of identity boundaries, it is important to change the circumstances of identity rigidification such as constant threats and danger as well as discrimination. Rigid identity boundaries based on stereotyped images create difficulties in collaborative discussion and an attitudinal change.

The dynamics of inclusion versus exclusion change according to political necessity. As diverse religious groups in the Middle East have built different alliance systems, identity boundaries have been reshaped along with the location of conflict. The superordinate Arab identity appealed to ordinary people on the street from the capital of Tunisia to that of Saudi Arabia during a war between Israel and Hezbollah in the summer of 2006. However, the Shi'ite–Sunnis rivalry has replaced superordinate Islamic or Arab identity in shaping the geopolitical map in the Middle East. Psychological boundaries can be hardened or crystallized by homogenization and depersonalization of out-group members. This process is not constant, but fluid in that identity is often manipulated for political interests.

The possibility of renegotiating identities depends on the permeability (or penetrability) of identity boundaries. The degree of fluidity of identity relates to the extent of difficulties to change its core beliefs. Strong beliefs generate uncompromising positions, since they constitute a sense of self attached to the very roots of our being. Social inclusion and exclusion can be embodied in religious doctrine or in law. The suppression and intolerance of differences by the imposition of monolithic identities often lead to denial of autonomous group rights and inequality.

In a conflict setting, individual motivations and interaction patterns tend to be shaped by macro social structures. The perceptions of a lower status may come from exclusion often manifested in social disadvantage in such areas as education, health, and housing as well as the unequal access to power. Imposed identities (often manifested in the illegalization of cultural and social practice of minority groups) justify illegitimate and unstable relations. Positive ethnic identity affirmation is necessary for the self-preservation of minority groups which have been disempowered by discrimination.

The salience of racial and ethnic identities differs among majority and underprivileged minority group members. Minority groups in a multicultural society face the incompatible demand of assimilation into the dominant society and preservation of their own cultural/ethnic identity. By assimilation, "individuals are induced (or coerced) into abandoning their original identity, accepting membership in the dominant community and adopting its culture" (Esman, 2004, p. 204). Minority group members are naturally concerned about assimilation that devalues their ethnic traditions, pride, customs, and rituals.

The politics of identity hinges on the balance of assimilation–accommodation. The termination of ethnic violence, from Northern Ireland to Bosnia, can be institutionally supported by power sharing or other means of accommodation. The demand of ethnic minorities can be met by ethnic pluralism which legitimizes dual identities. The learning and adaptation process in identity development involves assimilation and accommodation in social interaction. Democratic institution building should contribute to an increase in inclusiveness.

The successful accommodation of pluralistic identities can be undermined by a disproportionate level of poverty, relative deprivation based on ethnic, religious, or racial differences, weak capacity to manage tensions, and power inequalities. In the lack of upward social mobility, disadvantaged groups perceive inter-group boundaries to be impermeable. The perceived lack of accessibility to power within a society induces minority groups to resist the dominant power-holder groups by attacking the symbols of identity boundaries. The boycott of restaurants and buses (adopting segregation policies) had ignited widespread protests in the US civil rights movements during the 1960s.

Management of identity differences: institutional arrangements

The management of identity differences can be based on either reduction in the salience of existing identity boundaries or their relaxation. Various identities can be malleable or even completely abandoned (exemplified by the transition in Eastern Europe after the fall of communist regimes). The creation of a new, more embracing identity can be based on democratic principles (European Union). The switch from Warsaw Pact to NATO membership by Eastern European countries represents the abandonment of the old and joining the new.

Identity differences can be managed by the division of states, as seen in such instances as Czechoslovakia. The recognition of differences and dissolution of a state into two ethnic homelands (Czech and Slovakia) did not produce animosities, but they are still part of and share a common identity in the European Union (EU). Thus each group's national loyalty coexists under the EU superordinate identity through re-categorization.

The collapse of the Soviet Union into ethnically controlled states illustrates a reverse process of creating a superordinate identity. This process has produced a lot of uncertainty given the competition among ethnic groups vying for the control of the newly created states. The formation of new sub-groups in the absence of legitimized central authority provoked civil wars in Tajikistan, Georgia, etc., since new state building has led to the imposition of one group's power over another, instead of developing superordiante or cross-cutting identities among multiple ethnic groups.

The coexistence of identities through harmonization between primary and superordinate identities is evident in the association of Wales to the United Kingdom. The British Commonwealth identity is weak compared with a desire to seek European Union membership. Yet cultural and historical proximity often influences the degree of loyalty. Great Britain supported Canada (a British Commonwealth member) in its dispute with Spain (an EU member) about over-fishing near Newfoundland. On the other hand, Spain blocked the strong EU condemnation of the Argentine during the Falklands War due to its past colonial links to Latin America.

In a new state-building process, social, cultural, and linguistic tools can be applied to persuade diverse groups to form a newly shared community. The new articulations of identities (differentiating "us" and "them") have to be an integral part of a transformed relationship. Managing identity conflicts at all levels may require a structural change designed to create an organizational culture that embraces diversity. Realistic attempts to resolve ethnic conflicts demand an appreciation of contingent origins of values and identities in understanding the emotional and illusory nature of homeland psychology.

Further reading

Abrams, D. and Hogg, M. A. (2001) "Collective Identity: Group Membership and Self-Conceptions," in M. Hogg and R. Tindale (eds) *Blackwell Handbook of Social Psychology: Group Processes*, Malden, MA and Oxford: Blackwell, pp. 425–460.

Davidio, J. F. (2005) "Social Inclusion and Exclusion: Recategorization and the Perception of Intergroup Boundaries," in D. Abrams, M. Hogg, and J. Marques, *The Social Psychology of Inclusion and Exclusion*, New York: Psychology Press.

Forbes, H. D. (1997) *Ethnic Conflict: Commerce, Culture, and the Contact Hypothesis*, New Haven: Yale University Press.

Hogg, M. A. (2001) "Social Categorization, Depersonalization, and Group Behavior," in A. M. Hogg and R. S. Tindale (eds) *Blackwell Handbook of Social Psychology: Group Processes*, Malden, MA: Blackwell Publishers.

Kellet, P. M. and Dalton, D. G. (2001) *Managing Conflict in a Negotiated World: a Narrative Approach to Achieving Dialogue and Change*, Thousand Oaks, CA: Sage Publications.

Schlee, G. (2008) *How Enemies are Made*, New York: Berghahn Books.

Simon, B. and Klandermans, B. (2001) "Politicized Collective Identity," *American Psychologist*, 56: 319–331.

5   Power

Power is an essential ingredient in understanding conflict relationships and behavior along with identity. In general, power can be defined in terms of what one party can either coerce or persuade the other to give up. Power is characterized by an ability to hurt each other economically, physically, and psychologically when actions and counter-actions are mutually opposed in direct confrontation. The outcome of a power struggle often results in the substitution of old relationships (e.g., the emergence of a new black majority government in South Africa and the independence of Namibia, E. Timor, etc.) as well as the creation of new conditions for future interactions (such as the power-sharing government in Northern Ireland).

As power emerges from a wide range of social relationships, it is embedded in the diverse context of inter-group struggles. In asymmetric relationships, power can be used to impose and justify discrimination against another group. Power has not only physical effects (such as the control of bodies of adversarial group members through torture or killing) but also effects in an individual actor's perceptions. The exercise of power varies according to the nature and nuances of inter-group relationships and social settings.

This chapter discusses how to understand power in conflict analysis and resolution and examines cognitive, affective, and behavioral dimensions of power relations. It also investigates various sources of limiting the use of power, ranging from the benefit of interdependent relationships to contextual or cultural norms restricting coercive force to personal and group values as opposed to violence. It can generally be said that different degrees of power asymmetry present diverse prospects for conflict resolution. Given the almost inevitability of power imbalance in many conflict relations, it is important to discuss power asymmetry in a diverse context of managing human relations as juxtaposed by such factors as moral asymmetry.

The context of a power relationship

In a general context, power can be defined as "a capacity to realize goals ... by making particular things happen" (Haugaard, 1997, p. 119). In conflict situations, power provides an actor with the capabilities to control the others' preferences and opportunities in one's own quest to achieve desired conditions. One party has a greater control over an outcome than the other party by enforcing change in the other party's behavior. In producing the intended effects of power, one's action gets the other to behave in the way one wants. In relational terms, power functions as a concept of measuring the psychological and behavioral effects of one's action in another. Power can be exercised by using threat or actual coercion as well as control of reward and punishment.

The effects of power are based on not only the physical but also the psychological aspects of relationships. Power is aimed at influencing human behavior by manipulating motivations and perceptions and other psychological orientations via the adoption of diverse means. Each party attempts to control the expectations of another party by influencing their judgments. The perception of capability and intent of a hostile action are often not considered completely separated from each other. The increase in military capabilities of a competitor state is likely to be seen as evidence of probable intent to take aggressive actions. This is especially so under such circumstances that ideological and regime differences intensify incompatible beliefs about a rival country and that the suspicion is inferred from its past and present behavior. Perception about either peaceful or aggressive intent reflects images about a particular country. The excessive use of force against their militarily inferior enemies, as illustrated by the Israeli assault in Gaza in December 2008–January 2009, has contributed to the rise of Israel's aggressive image.

As has been presented by more than a year-long struggle between Hezbollah and the Sunni-led government in Lebanon (2007–2008), the process of competition is often managed by power relations in the absence of weakness in institutional rules of decision making. As is often the case with conflict between equals and unequals in international conflict, power differentials (symmetry/asymmetry) matter especially when the issues are zero-sum and when the stakes are very high, involving even one's own survival. In zero-sum conflict relationships, one party's gain is achieved at the other's expense. "The distribution of power between or among parties has a significant impact on the course and conduct of a conflict" (Northrup, 1989, p. 61).

A power struggle emerges from incompatible positions ascribed to scarcity and resource control, both actual and perceived, as well as opposing values. Most importantly, disparities in economic benefits and social recognition as well as a lack of sufficient decision-making power generate the feelings of dissatisfaction and powerlessness. Due to oppression and gross power asymmetry, many conflicts may not even be initiated, and stay latent for a long time, erupting only occasionally. The involvement of real action (as a condition for manifest conflict) is derived from an ability to mobilize a significant number of people in a visible manner despite the fear of loss and physical harm to be absorbed by an adversary's retaliatory actions. Given its ability to impose coercive measures and punishment, oppressive power is used to prevent any visible expression of grievances or protest against unjust treatment.

Power is frequently imposed to maintain or reinforce non-reciprocal arrangements and interactions (which generate feelings of grievances). The coercive use of power is not needed in reciprocal relations that yield mutually beneficial transactions, typically among allies such as the US and Canada. Threats and other attempts to alter or constrain the other's behavior are counterproductive in the symbiotic, organic relationships that are mutually interdependent and favorable. Power becomes almost an irrelevant factor in disputes between countries such as Belgium and Germany which have interdependent and democratic relationships in the larger governance structure of the European Union.

Non-reciprocal, forced relations are imposed upon marginalized groups by such coercive arrangements as forced annexation of territories or slave systems. A lack of legitimate rules exacerbates resistance from those marginalized. In imbalanced relationships, claims to rights and obligations are largely determined by power differentials. An expressed struggle often results from exploitative, asymmetric relationships.

As exemplified by the Chinese government's policy toward minorities in a country dominated by the Han nationality, one of the most common strategies adopted by a powerful party in an asymmetric, undemocratic relationship is to control, silence, or remove incompatible views, interests, and values through the unilateral imposition of one's own decision. It is contrasted with a collaborative process of communication by which differences are recognized for accommodation (for instance, the Canadian government's accommodation of Quebec's demand for decision-making power in immigration and other key policy areas). In an internal conflict, ethnic differences are often denied or suppressed within a state in the process of obtaining a more homogeneous society. The method of control is associated with the systematic exclusion of a minority from political and/or economic power for the purpose of safeguarding a dominant position in society.

Power can erode over time, especially when it is not institutionalized or legitimized. Since particular types of relationships such as colonial rule cannot be sustained permanently, the European powers most often voluntarily ceded independence to former colonies since World War II. Foreign occupation and annexation of neighboring territories have also been ruled as illegitimate by the international legal communities. The military or one-man rule, not restrained by the popular will, cannot be legitimized. As happened in Pakistan and other places, military generals eventually had to transfer their power to popularly elected politicians in order to restore stability.

The authoritarian government's capacity to control diverse dissenting groups can be weakened under economic hardships (triggering revolts or other open challenges to the elite) or reduced revenue for the regime. The violent expression of grievances and increased challenge of minority groups to the unjust rule (such as foreign occupation) represent the regime's declining grip on the population through the police and army. Repressive measures have not prevented or stopped secessionist movements and colonial struggles seeking self-autonomy (e.g., Kurdistan, Burma).

In multi-ethnic societies, relative power differences do not remove challenges to the idea of unqualified majority government. In Thailand's Pattani, Yala, and other southernmost provinces, Muslim rebels have been waging a low-intensity conflict in the predominantly Buddhist country. The region's Muslim residents (who are ethnic Malays) belonged to a sultanate until the Thai annexation in the early 1900s. The insurgents have been terrorizing Buddhists entering the region with the ultimate goal of establishing a separate Islamic state, relying on the support of the Muslim population disenchanted by decades of misrule and discrimination by the central government. The recent government crackdown and other hard-line approaches only accelerated bombing and violence despite a heavy police and military presence.

Power distribution and behavioral effects

Power relations have an impact on the conflict styles of each party (aggressive, assertive, competitive versus passive, accommodating, compliant). In power asymmetry, a weaker party has the choice of disengagement, negotiation, resistance, standing firm, or subordination. The adoption of avoidance or yielding may stem from the fear of defeat, reflecting the perception of a large power imbalance. The weaker party is not likely to risk fighting, owing to little chance of winning. Low self-esteem also contributes to an orientation toward the sacrifice of one's own interests. The process of yielding is likely to involve obedience or deference to those in power along with a desire not to damage the relationship.

While power can be the main determining factor in the outcome of many conflicts, its real exercise bears both long-term and short-term costs and other consequences. A weaker party can adopt passive, subtle resistance to undermine the interests of the superior. In response to exploitation and physical oppression of landlords in the 1970s, peasants in

Southeast Asian countries adopted various forms of sabotage (i.e. causing damage to properties, petty theft, the killing of animals, etc.) as resistance beneath the surface of compliance (Scott, 1985). The overt mechanisms of physical repression (relationships between landlords and peasants) did not completely deny an ability of a weaker party to hurt the interests of a superior party. The coercive forms of power are less effective and more costly than persuasive influence in garnering voluntary cooperation.

Power as a means of influence

Influence strategies can be carried out by either an explicit or implicit threat of violence or promises of various kinds of rewards (diplomatic recognition, food assistance, energy supply, military aid, technical or financial support). In fact, psychological effects such as fear relate to human motivation and action. The means to extract compliance with specific demands are not necessarily limited to anticipated coercive action and its punitive effects. In fact, persuasion can be used through high-level emissaries (respected by the opponents) or informal dialogue processes. Persuasion will be effective especially if the adversary cares about their image of being reasonable. Moral, spiritual power depends on inspirational dimensions of human relations.

Parties are "relatively advantaged in different forms of power" aimed at influencing the other side's motivation (Tillett and French, 2006, p. 88). The structures of power relations are defined in terms of not one-dimensional strength but a variety of qualities related to the mobilization of material, financial, normative, and human resources. Multidimensional structures of coercive mechanisms are supported by not only military technology oriented toward improvement in offensive weapons and ally relationships but also economic incentives coming from a benefit of trade. As Russia's relations with Ukraine, Belorussia, and its other neighbors indicate, various types of rewards (such as the supply of cheaper oil and gas) help to build positive relationships while threats tend to generate resentment and resistance as well as fear.

Potential power can be translated into different forms of actual power through diverse psychological effects. In terms of effectiveness, some actions (for example, military attacks) can bring about immediate consequences. The effects of economic embargoes are indirect, and slow. Other actions such as a boycott of the Olympic Games (for instance, the US boycott of the 1980 Moscow Olympic Games in the aftermath of the Soviet invasion of Afghanistan) can have less tangible effects but nonetheless they are seen as important symbolically.

Power relations in conflict process and outcome

The distribution of power between groups is an important element which affects the dynamics and outcome of a social conflict as well as the parties' approaches to the conflict (Blalock, 1989). Power relations determine a range of behavioral options available to the parties. In conflict situations, coercive elements are involved in controlling the other's actions against their wishes, forcing them to abandon or modify their objectives (with a threat, either physical or psychological). Thus, relative strength is critical in measuring the ability of each party to achieve their aspirations. If goal incompatibilities between parties are not great, there is less necessity for the use of power. In the sense that power needs to be understood in relational terms, the context of exercising power is also crucial in analyzing the impact of power on behavior.

The exercise of power by one party often generates resistance from the other party in a show of the will of determination. In a coercive struggle, a conflict outcome is often derived from the degree of balance between the ability to inflict injury on an enemy and the capability to endure the attacks. Israeli and Palestinian conflict can be characterized by a history of imposing one's will on the adversary and endurance of costly loss of lives and destruction. Israel has a capacity to restrict the movements of Palestinians and their activities which gives the Israeli's more leverage over the outcome of each of many struggles. Palestinian resistance against the Israeli expansion of settlement and housing projects as well as a harsh external rule has been organized by unconventional militant groups.

Various dimensions of power, psychological, physical, and organizational, are linked to an attempt to control conflict processes and their effects in human behavior. Rough power parity is likely to engender more severe competition, hampering settlement, in that more or less equal power relations lead to continued deadlock or protracted struggle without external shocks or pressure. The fear of imbalanced military capabilities often leads to a competitive arms race, creating a prisoner's dilemma in which aspiring for a superior destructive capability hurts each other's welfare without guaranteeing more security. The efforts to change the status quo may involve an even further escalation of conflict.

Power asymmetry has an immense impact on the course and likely outcome of conflict as well as conditions for resolution. In fact, power advantage makes clear who has to make concessions. With other conditions being equal, power imbalance is less likely to induce a dominant party to develop compromised positions given its ability to impose its own desires on the weaker party (without negative repercussions). A highly unbalanced conflict is characterized by the suppression of any reasonable demand. A unilateral concession can be forced upon a weaker party, leaving hard feelings. Superior power positions encourage uncooperative behavior in satisfying one's own interests at the expense of the others. Faced with the other party's resistance, a stronger party may adopt bullying tactics when they do not fear they have anything to lose by pushing.

Even though competitive, aggressive behavior may win an immediate contest at a particular time, it produces resentment over the long haul, undermining the dominant party's future chances for obtaining voluntary cooperation. Since no single party can control every aspect of a relationship, the solicitation of goodwill and cooperation serves the best interests of every party.

The dominant party may resist changes in existing norms and rules despite their illegitimacy. Even though other countries accepted a new international agreement to put their peacekeeping soldiers under international criminal judicial jurisdictions, the US government rejected the treaty's legal enforcement. In general, the asymmetry inherent in unbalanced power relations hinders equitable solutions in a dispute. In unjust relationships, power balance is needed for conflict settlement via the equalization of capabilities by diverse means. "In some conflict resolution processes, attempts are made to use power balancing techniques to redress an unhelpful power imbalance between the parties" (Tillett and French, 2006, p. 88). External support (either moral, political, and even military) might be needed for conflict resolution initiatives (for instance, Syrian withdrawal from Lebanon, in 2006, under heavy pressure from Western powers).

External actors, including patrons, allies, intermediaries, and a relevant audience (the concerned public), can affect the conflict in such a way as to support an underdog. Such interventions can be based on serious ethical and practical considerations of conflict transformation. NGO communities and activist movements were mobilized against Chinese support for the Sudanese government involved in the Darfur genocide. An economic boycott and other international campaigns were organized against the military dictatorship in Burma and President Mugabe's one-man rule in Zimbabwe.

The outcome of power struggles

The outcome of power struggles produces conditions for the creation of new norms and expectations. Power relations evolve following each set of conflicts, leading to a new equilibrium. Each conflict, for instance, a labor strike, has an impact on the next series of conflicts. Technological and economic changes undermine the bargaining power of each party (especially in such cases as a new method of industrial production or the introduction of weapons with more destructive capabilities to an international conflict). Most importantly, differences in the established rules of a game determine the outcomes of a struggle.

Lacking a history of institutionalized democracy relying on stable expectations, elections are often used as a means to establish one group's privilege over another. Power relations among major tribal groups in Kenya have been balanced and rebalanced through political changes sometimes mired in violence. The Kikuyu (that has formed the core elite since the British colonial rule) has long been resented by other tribes. Independent Kenya's first president, Jomo Kenyatta, sealed his tribe Kikuyu's dominance in politics and commerce. His successor Daniel arap Moi, a Kalenjin, counterbalanced the privileged status of Kikuyu during his 24-year rule. However, the victory of Mwai Kibaki in the 2002 elections reinstated Kikuyu power. The incumbent's victory in the close 2008 elections was tarnished by a charge of the vote being rigged by the Luo, Kalenjin, and other tribes. The intense post-election violence eventually subsided with the introduction of a settlement agreement which struck a new balance in sharing government decision-making power and positions.

The perceptions of asymmetry in power relations generate different expectations about conflict outcomes. In asymmetric guerrilla warfare, the goal of insurgents is often not to bring astounding defeat to regular armies but to increase the vulnerability of a stronger opponent with the injection of heavier costs. Successful resistance can indeed contribute to a new rule of the game in future fighting. For instance, Israel's failure to wipe out the Hezbollah forces in the 2006 Lebanon war has reshaped the role of the Israeli military's omnipresent power, at least at a perceptional level, in future conflicts especially with the well-organized guerrilla forces.

Contingencies in the exercise of power

In influencing the behavioral style, the effect of power is deflected by such socio-psychological variables as issue salience to the party, contextual or cultural norms in the conduct of conflict, and one's expectation of the other's reaction. Despite partial satisfaction of interests, compromise (and concessions by every party) might be reached under such conditions as limited time and the requirement for a quick resolution of issues after initial contending and power contest.

Power is likely to be employed for confrontational strategies under varying circumstances (low cost of fighting, the high likelihood of winning, and high commitment and salient values attached to the struggle). Issue salience (along with psychological intransigence associated with a strong will) is likely to fuel assertive behavior by an underdog in spite of power asymmetry. Under power parity, in particular, the personality of the leader can play a key role in determining the outcome of a contest in a conflict situation characterized by a game of chicken such as the Cuban Missile Crisis in October 1962. The high costs of fighting along with the low significance of the issues at stake can reversely affect the contest of power. The re-emergence of antagonistic interests (creating new frustration) may make the relative power positions become suddenly important.

The effectiveness of power depends on the types of capabilities utilized for given strategies and external contingencies. Power (related to waging conflict) consists of commitment to goals, morale, and organizational unity (that prevents the diversion of commitments to fighting with external enemies and promotes mobilization capabilities). The exercise of power is either constrained or maximized by both the external and internal conditions of each contestant party. Group mobilization under various conditions (e.g. the split within a resistance group; development of links with ethnic kin in neighboring states) can influence power relations in a civil war. The exercise of physical force can be constrained by cognitive and societal limitations (derived, for instance, from Quaker, Buddhist, or other religious traditions). Institutional norms (such as the prevention of participation in war stipulated in the post-Word War II German constitution) impede the mobilization of latent power resources for destruction.

Power can be legitimized on a normative basis to bring about consent. Voluntary acceptance of values or principles is less costly than the actual exercise of coercive force. The employment of power needs to be justified by a wider community's norm (e.g., international laws in support of peace enforcement or humanitarian intervention to stop massacres). Just war theories have been developed to provide legal guidelines about warfare. The UN Charter has been emphasizing the settlement of disputes through negotiation. In engagement in war, normative judgments have been provided by just war theory which puts great restraints on attacks on unarmed civilians as well as hospitals, schools, and other targets. The International Court and Prosecutors Office have played an important role in establishing legally and morally acceptable boundaries in the conduct of civil wars in the case of Bosnia-Herzegovina, Darfur, etc.

Effectiveness of coercive power

Behavioral aspects of conflict can be manifested in a power struggle that translates into the context of exchanges of negative sanctions or their threats. In social–psychological terms, it is the perception of power, rather than the actual possession of coercive forces, which is important. When competitions, whether defined in military, economic, or political terms, are perceived as zero-sum, coercive forms of power are most likely to get involved in escalating the adversarial relationships. However, if the conditions for a conflict and their perception can be shifted from competitive win–lose struggles to a search for a mutually beneficial outcome, then the options for conflict management are greatly augmented by promoting bargaining, exchange relationships.

The influence relations can be measured by voluntary compliance or acceptance of the demand under pressure. The effectiveness in the exercise of power lies in the comparative ability to employ force for domination or resistance. To exercise power over the other, one party should have an ability to make a difference in the other party's present and future welfare conditions. The mutual exchange of punitive sanctions can be accompanied by the reduction or the withholding of a reward. The relative magnitudes of differences in power need to bring about perceptual relationships for real effects.

The effectiveness of coercive power can be determined by such factors as the credibility of the threat of punishment. The attractiveness in the adoption of force (as a means of influence) is undermined by the possibility of being retaliated against, the enemy's determination, and the moral vulnerability as well as financial burden and human sacrifice associated with the use of force. The strategy of inflicting actual pain can be strengthened by little real cost to the sanctioning party, being combined with high real cost to the target. A low net cost to the inflictor is based on differentials between the price to pay for carrying out the punishment and any specific benefit gained by force. The failure of demonstration effects is exemplified by the US invasions of Iraq, North Korea, and Iran (all three of them declared an axis of evil in President Bush's State of the Union Address in January 2002). The ineffective attempt to exercise coercive force leads to the deflation of power, reducing the credibility of future threats.

Power relationships can be assessed by the relative strength of each party as regards the specific issues in contention. The success in exercising coercion depends on the degree of the other side's capacity and determination to resist. Exercising force against another party or even organizing to do so carries not only material but also symbolic and political implications. The costs incurred from the actual use of force (for instance, the invasion of Iraq) need to be compared with other means of influence (e.g., the maintenance of international sanctions on Saddam Hussein's government). The costs of exercising power will increase when the adversary has a higher capacity to endure (or absorb the effects of) coercive measures.

Sources of power

The methods or strategies to employ power as well as its distribution among the parties strongly influence conflict dynamics. The basis for the mobilization of power – not only physical, material, organizational but also informational and symbolic – shapes relationships. The sources of power and powerlessness differ in particular conflict settings. In fact, different types of resources are needed for the exercise of power in diverse issue areas. In general, however, the conceptions of power as a quantifiable mass have largely given way to the notions of power which stress an influence relationship in an attempt to shed light on a "behavioral result" (Sprout and Sprout, 1971, p. 167).

The endowment of power can be personal, positional, or situational. The charismatic, personal charms or political skills of control and manipulation (exhibited by Stalin) can render individual leaders' power unchallenged even by institutional norms and procedures. The position held by individuals can also permit the establishment of subordinate–dominant relationships (Bourdieu, 1991). Power can be exercised on the basis of institutionalized roles and functions or possession of strategic resources needed by others. Power can be understood in social structural terms beyond the ability to manage inter-personal or inter-organizational relations. Given that the expression of conflict can be suppressed by various cultural and social instruments, the absence of conflict does not necessarily mean the existence of social harmony.

Power can be associated with status, competence, or resources that carry political influence in decision making. As an undeniable element which governs human relations, power is often disguised especially in the absence of its physical exercise. Even if some laws or regulations benefit only a few, legislative power is based on normative standards and values accepted by the public as well as key socio-economic institutions. A pervasive quality of power runs through the relationship of authority, influence, manipulation, or force.

As power is diffuse at every level of society, domination is based on a normalized structure and social practice related to generating controlled and predictable behavior of individuals (Foucault, 1977). Not being limited to one particular kind of source, power entails a pervasive quality of force penetrated through statecraft in the maintenance of unequal political and economic relations. A normative structure of expectations is created to control behavior that does not conform to the norms and rules of society. Since a coercive base of power alone may not always be effective, power imbalance has been institutionalized by national ideologies or religious values (involved, for instance, in the interpretation of the role of women in society in Islam, etc.).

Diverse forms of power relationships

In understanding social dynamics, many different forms of power can be exhibited by bargaining or authoritative as well as coercive contexts of relationships. A particular type of influence is suitable for different kinds of relations – family, religious organizations, big corporations, or state institutions. The coercive exercise of power is wielded through credibility of threats and their possible effects on the target's well-being. Power exercised in authoritative relationships reflects the party's status. The effects of power can also be generated by rational persuasion in a bargaining situation. In bargaining relationships, one's power depends on whether they have a capability to offer highly valued resources desired by their opponents in return for meeting one's own needs.

The exchange relationship is permeated by social bargaining power that promises rewards in return for loyalty to the authority as illustrated by Peter Blau (1964). Warlord politics in Afghanistan indicate that multi-faceted motivations and incentives sustain the grip of militia group leaders over their followers. In fact, the relationship between local tribal or military leaders and their followers relies on more than coercive means, in that free-wheeling elements are not tightly managed by military leaders (who are detached from the field-based carders). In order to keep their control, group leaders have to supply security, financial means or other support for fighters and their families.

The sources of legitimacy become an important matter in maintaining stable authority relations. The general tendency in affectionate types of interactions, for instance, in a family or kinship society, is devoid of physical coercion, contributing to mutually compatible expectations of continuing relationships. Power and authority relations in tribal or kinship societies emerge from the necessity to keep communal bonds and solidarity.

The fulfillment of one's obligations can be based on normative rules and agreements especially in the relationship devoid of physical enforcement. In the struggle between the World Bank and Chad, the main focus was on the use of oil revenue. World Bank loans for building oil production and export infrastructure in Chad were granted under the conditions that the oil revenue would be devoted to improvement in welfare of the impoverished, not for military equipment. However, Chad broke the agreement, and the unilateral action by the Chadian government generated confrontation with the World Bank. In invoking normative values, the World Bank advocated humanitarian concerns while Chad was arguing about sovereignty.

Interaction between actors is rarely manifested as a pure interplay of one kind of power; the sources of power in bargaining and other types of contest are inextricably embedded in a given situation, for example, parents asking children to do homework may involve various means of inducement as well as punitive measures. Punitive action can be supported by rules and regulations derived from norms (e.g., sanctions against the government of President Mugabe in Zimbabwe by the European Union). Different combinations of persuasive, bargaining, manipulative and coercive relations are manifested in an adversarial relationship. The employment of reward or punishment can be used in this way to affect the other party's desire, want, and behavior.

Multiple dimensions of ethnic power relations

Power disparity is created by balances and imbalances among different types and dimensions of power resources. Political and economic power differentials are generally translated into racial and ethnic tension. One group may have economic wealth but lack access to majority political power (as seen by Indians in Fiji, the whites in South Africa, Chinese in Indonesia and Malaysia, and Indians in Kenya). Economic and political power relations can be negotiated along the way to permit mutual interdependence. For instance, in South Africa, economic wealth of the whites is protected while government power is held by the leaders of the black majority.

Disparities in economic benefits and social recognition as well as a lack of sufficient decision-making power on important political matters reflect rank order in a hierarchical relationship (which also often shapes group identity). Many dimensions of asymmetric relations can be superimposed on major social cleavages. Some groups do not have both economic wealth and political power (in such cases as native inhabitants in El Salvador, Nicaragua, and Guatemala). In a hierarchical system, prevailing groups tend to play down and even refuse to recognize the conflict's existence. Conflict can be kept less visible or invisible so that suppression is accepted as a normal state of human affairs.

The sustenance of asymmetrical relationships can be based on the claims of moral and normative legitimacy of the rule. The empowerment of a weaker party is essential to transforming a highly imbalanced adversarial relationship where justice cannot be achieved without the recognition of moral and normative values. Along with overcoming imbalanced capabilities, confrontation is necessary for the recognition of key issues.

Rebalancing ethnic power: Fiji

In multi-ethnic societies, disruption in the existing balance in ethnic privileges and power often provokes conflict which indicates that a social contract of coexistence is broken. In Fiji, the tension between the indigenous Fijians and the Indians was wrought with inequalities between the ethnically diverse communities around the contest over political representation, the distribution of public service jobs, and the ownership and leasing of land. The divisive nature of multi-ethnic politics was reinforced by linguistic and other cultural separation between Indians and Fijians as well as living apart in segregated residential and farming areas. The persistence of confrontation has often been manifested in the breakdown of communication and low-level violence. The discontinuation of constitutional order was eventually accompanied by the failure of communal leaders to accommodate each section's interests through the informal, consultative devices.

The delicate divisions and "balance" were kept by each community's different advantages in both politics and economy prior to the 1993 election whose outcome was nullified by the 1995 military coup. Traditionally, the Fijian superiority in politics was maintained by the control of the prime minister's office and the public bureaucracy as well as the Fiji Defense Force. Economically, the Indians controlled the lucrative sugar industry as well as the ownership of small and intermediate-size commercial operations. Despite a high percentage of land ownership, Fijians were left with the least lucrative part of the agricultural sectors of economy (Premdas, 2003). Thus the Fijian economic disparity vis-à-vis the Indian community was compensated by their advantageous political status.

The defeat of the ruling Alliance Party in 1987 in the hands of a political alliance (which includes a predominantly Indian constituency) set off massive protests that eventually led to a military coup. The series of political events further strengthened Fijian supremacy in politics, later being reflected in the 1997 constitution designed to create a new democratic order. In fact, the 1997 constitution became the third balancing and rebalancing act to manage the divergent interests and claims of Fiji citizens in the aftermath of failure to do so in the first (1970) and the second (1990) constitution. In the constitutional amendments, various social forces have been pressuring for change, sometimes being met by such setbacks as a military coup (e.g., the May 2000 Defense Force's intervention staged by General George Speight).

Quest for power and anarchy

The preoccupation with power reflects an anarchical system composed of sovereign states. Owing to the absence of a central authority at the world stage, many decisions are not binding or enforced on states. It has been a predominant tradition that states resort to the threats of force or its actual employment in influencing another. International conflicts have traditionally been featured by military capabilities as an instrument of achieving national objectives. International diplomacy and conflict management has been conducted, historically, within the shades of threats of war and the application of coercive force.

The realist school of international relations describes conflict as a result of a shift in power and the display of relative strength. Power struggles have been considered omnipresent, unending, even the innate part of an anarchic world order. Power and conflict cannot be avoided in an anarchic system which generates endless competition for relative gains. From a realist perspective, it is not poor communication or cultural differences but competing interests that are the irreconcilable sources of conflict. States have a power-seeking tendency owing to competition for security especially in an anarchic system. Thus "the chief regularities of the system is the struggle for power among states" (Cashman, 2000, p. 238).

States in an anarchic international system have similar motives, norms, and institutions in regulating internal structures and also establishing relations with other states. Given constant suspicion and perceptions of insecurity (derived from the absence of a centralized power system which provides stability in inter-state relations), each constituent unit in the international system is motivated to seek power. In this Hobbesian tradition, power justifies everything in the formation of political order with the notion of survival of the fittest.

In *realpolitik* perspectives, inter-state conflict will not be resolvable (since competition for power often leads to coercion and violence). Negotiated agreements are not adequate to fix the inherently irresolvable situation of a power struggle. In an anarchic political system, a sovereign unit is not compelled to constrain their actions or cooperate toward a common goal. By pursuing their own interests, states are engaged in self-help. It is very difficult to achieve satisfactory arrangements for all the parties in inter-state relations. For neo-realists, rational actions emerge from adjustment to the structure of international anarchy and the operation of a given system (Waltz, 2001).

The analysis of international conflict is intimately linked to assessing the realignment of military capabilities and the possible use of force as an instrument of influence as well as its psychological effects in adversaries' strategies. The increasing arms race in many parts of the world (despite the demise of socialist systems in the early 1990s) reflects competition as a dominant state strategy. Each opponent attempts to increase the level of ally support while trying to divide and co-opt enemies. Concessions and reward are regarded as a game of maneuvering in re-establishing one's positions vis-à-vis another.

"If power is quantifiable and essentially military, the power of a state can be expressed as its war-winning ability" (Sprout and Sprout, 1971, pp. 165–166). During the Cold War period, the status of power was recognized by the balance of terror known for the super-powers' capacity for overkill. If power is to serve as a means to have deterrence effects in constraining an adversary's action, it has to be perceived by not only allies but also enemies. Yet the very concept of power itself changes radically because of the advancement of destructive technology and introduction of new methods of violence (illustrated by suicide bombings, etc.).

In realist perspectives, parameters of conflict are drawn by the role of power along with the recognition of state supremacy in an international system. The system of conflict management based on deterrence and fear is quite vulnerable to miscalculations and misperceptions. In fact, "international conflict is a process driven by collective needs and fears, rather than entirely a product of rational calculation of objective national interests on the part of political decision makers" (Kelman, 2004, p. 59).

The control of violence would become easier under a hegemonic world state (such as the Roman and other historical empires) that has an ability to deter individual states' aggression. On the other hand, transition toward a unipolar or hegemonic international system can be highly unstable or violent, because the establishment of a more centralized order may come after wars between competing powers (except the example of a transition toward the post-Cold War order). If states have an ability to destroy each other with the ownership of nuclear weapons, the horror of mutual destruction can create a universal deterrence system (Kaplan, 1957).

Examining international order from the perspective of power allocation among states takes away the opportunity to fully consider the causes of war and, furthermore, strategies to remove those causes. Mutual accommodation can be derived from the replacement of coercive tactics with persuasion. In *realpolitik* perspectives, there is very little room for conflict transformation given its neglect of noncoercive means for managing relations; the emergence of post-World War II order in Western Europe (indicated by Franco-German relations) suggests that the guarantee of justice as well as the healing of past wounds can transform centuries of military rivalry.

Patterns of power alliance and conflict management

The number of alliances correlates positively to the chances of more conflicts but on a smaller scale, reducing the chances of major system wars (Singer and Small, 1972). Increased cross-pressure comes from the existence of a multiple number of alliances with more interaction opportunities. On the other hand, rigid alliance creates a deeply polarized dyad around which most conflicts are likely to break out. Because the spread of antagonism among multiple actors decreases pressure for conflict built on any single relationship, a multi-polar system has a less serious potential for major power confrontations than a bipolar one.

A pluralistic system of complex relationships avoids rigid cleavages and polarization due to the existence of diverse interests and demands crisscrossing with each other. Thus, opposition to one actor on one issue does not necessarily lead to opposition to the same actor on other issues. Therefore, behavior in multi-polarity is modified by cross-pressure, crosscutting loyalties among actors. By utilizing its unique position of close ties to Europe and Islamic countries, Turkey has been playing a mediating role between Israel and Syria; it has also offered help to diffuse tension between Iran and the West.

An increased number of actors in a multi-polar system does not allow entire preoccupation with any single opponent. In a tightly organized bipolar system, on the other hand, a regional conflict can escalate into global confrontation given the superpowers' involvement around the globe. The high stakes of superpower conflicts and the potential danger of escalation into global war resulted in arms control negotiations and the development of other power-stabilizing mechanisms during the Cold War (Cashman, 2000).

The role of multi-polarity in the promotion of system stability is both positive and negative. The increased number of actors provides not only more potential for conflict as well as greater opportunities for cooperation. The increased number of actors means greater flexibility in alignment. The enlarged number of alliances crisscrossing with each other's conflict systems diminishes the potentiality of bipolarization. In multi-polarity, more mediators should be available to arbitrate (temper or restrain) conflict that might explode into armed clashes. In Latin America, Brazil has been alleviating tension between pro-American Colombia versus anti-American bloc countries led by Venezuela which are allied with Ecuador and Bolivia.

The crosscutting alliance systems create challenges to predicting precise divisions between allies and enemies. In fact, difficulties in managing multi-polarity power alliances can be related to ambiguity and uncertainty that arise from the large number of major actors and the complex linkage between them. In the absence of hegemonic power or a stable balance of power (perceived by major actors), misperception and miscalculation generate a greater probability of provocative behavior by aggressors such as attacks on Iran and the invasion of Kuwait by Iraq's Saddam Hussein in August 1990. These mishaps are attributed to the risk-taking behavior of a ruthless leader who has expansionist motives.

In a nutshell, the degree of power concentration (unipolar, bipolar, multipolar) influences risk-taking or risk-averse behavior, creating different calculations along with power alliance patterns. It is generally believed that the more ambiguous and uncertain power alignments are, the more likelihood of misperception and miscalculations exists, encouraging risk-taking behavior. Dissatisfaction with the status quo along with perceptions about their rival's declining power is likely to encourage provocative actions that challenge the existing system. Despite its relative military inferiority, Pakistan triggered the Kashmir wars with India in 1964 and 1979. The 1964 war took place after India's military defeat by China over a border dispute while the 1979 war was waged after Pakistan's development of nuclear arms following India's example. Expansionistic states (such as Japan and Nazi Germany prior to World War II) are more willing to challenge the existing status quo.

The geostrategic map in the Middle East is characterized by complex patterns of both cooperation and conflict. In a polarized system (exemplified by the Middle East), war might break out across loose alliance structures and multiple dyads. Either explicit or implicit patterns of cooperation do not guarantee lasting alliance, while the necessity of survival or desire for domination is likely to produce coalition among unlikely allies.

During the two decades of the Lebanese civil war, Christian militia groups were aided militarily by not only the Israelis but also the Syrians. The Syrian supply of arms and military assistance to a major Christian political faction in 1974 led to mass killings of Palestinians, provoking the condemnation of Damascus in the Arabic world. To establish its hegemony, Syrian troops eventually drove Palestinian forces out of Lebanon with implicit approval of the US and Israel.

The mass casualties of the Palestinians were the result of the Israeli supported attacks. Palestinian refugee camps turned into sites of indiscriminate killing fields, being attacked by Christian militias who were armed and transported by the Israeli army with the approval of Defense Minister Ariel Sharon. Being occasionally allied with and supported by the

Israelis and Syrians, Palestinian, Christian, Shi'ite, and Sunni Muslim militia groups cooperated and then betrayed each other at least once according to the evolving logic of a power game which ended with the 1989 Taif Peace Accord (Helsing, 2004).

Power symmetry

Power symmetry exists in multiple patterns of relations among interacting units. In an anarchic system, it is best illustrated by a balance of power that prohibits the domination of a single powerful state or combination of powers. The collapse of balanced power relations and emergence of a superior power is interpreted as a major cause of threat to the security of the rest since military superiority is likely to produce a desire to dominate others. Thus shifting alliances and countervailing pressures are necessary to keep any single power from gaining disproportionate military strength beyond the tolerable limit of an equilibrium. The successful management of conflict by balance of power inherently depends on a mutual threat of destruction. Indeed, alliance building or other means are geared toward increasing retaliatory capabilities and readiness for fighting if necessary to oppose hegemony.

As a method of preserving a status quo, the balance of power can be attained by either a bipolar or multi-polar system. Power alliance in the nineteenth-century European security regime is widely known for contributing to successfully managing stability among rival states in multi-polarity. The loose balance of power has also been advocated for structural arrangements to deter a war based on the efforts to match up each other's military strength and diplomatic maneuvers. In a loose bipolar power game, each actor is supposed to flexibly switch their alliance in rallying against any militarily superior states. On the other hand, the tight bipolar system, as illustrated by the US–Soviet rivalry during the Cold War period, has clear boundaries between enemies and allies especially due to the absence of neutral powers and inflexibility in power realignments.

According to realists, stability can be undermined by any attempt to upset or tip the balance of power. The interests of every actor reside in prohibiting disturbance in the balance (Cashman, 2000). The maintenance of stable relations between major powers is based on deterrence, but major powers may occasionally adopt coercive force to control smaller states. Each major power tolerates its rival's engagement in wars with smaller states as well as proxy wars on the periphery. The US involvement in the 1950 Korean War helped the Soviet Union consolidate its grip over Eastern Europe which fell under their influence after World War II. Opposing factions in the Angolan civil war were supported by not only the US and South Africa but also Soviet bloc countries, including Cuba which dispatched troops.

If power differences do not exist or are small, adversaries may be able to deter each other by dependence on mutual threats. When threats used against an equal power adversary are expected to be reciprocated by retaliation, small margins in the military capabilities are not likely to produce confidence in risk-taking actions because of the prospects of facing severe mutual destruction. However, a marginal advantage can be misjudged and misperceived to provoke a preemptive strike. Even though the occurrence of violence is affected by different patterns of power allocation, the outcome of a power game is likely to be unpredictable due to diverse perceptions of power relations by key decision makers as well as miscalculations of an adversary's response to the other's actions (as vividly demonstrated by the beginning of World Wars I and II).

Dyadic relationships

Long-term enduring rivalries with the legacy of mutual mistrust and pain involve a conflict-prone dyad in an international system. Rivalries in power symmetry since World War II include the US–Soviet Union (1945–1991); Greece–Turkey (1964–present); Syria–Israel (1948–present); India–Pakistan (1946–present); Eritrea–Ethiopia (1979–present). In these situations, mutually destructive capabilities have been taken seriously to restrict a full-scale military confrontation to a limited area.

Greece avoided their counter-military action in response to the Turkish invasion of Cyprus in July 1974. The past wars between India and Pakistan were contained in Kashmir, not targeting the rival's main territories. In the Six Day War of June 1967, Israel did not advance beyond the Golan Heights to the main part of Syria. The Eritrea/Ethiopian wars and military skirmishes mostly centered on border regions. The US kept its pledge not to attack Cuba in return for Soviet missile withdrawal.

Conflict has occasionally been managed with a manifest expression of cautious intentions. In the 1961 Berlin Wall crisis, the US sent a signal to the Soviet Union that it would accept the erection of the barrier. On the other hand, the Kremlin instructed their soldiers not to shoot even in the event of any provocation. In addition, the superpowers pressured their more radical allies to curb provocative behavior. Moscow refused to supply advanced offensive weapons for Egypt which intended to prepare for another war in the early 1970s.

Ethnic rivalry

Power struggles among ethnic groups are essentially unstable with the declining state capacity to manage ethnic rivalry. The weakened functions of state institutions create anarchy often in the aftermath of one-man rule. Somalia and Liberia experienced chaotic fighting among militia groups after autocratic rulers were gone. As is illustrated by the unexpected collapse of multi-ethnic states (such as the former Yugoslavia and the Soviet Union), the sudden transition increases ethnic rivalry. Greater uncertainty produces greater likelihood of a civil war in the absence of an institutionalized process to manage differences and build consensus. Groups competing for power develop great mistrust and challenge each other's political and social status.

Ethnic balance of power or its absence has repercussions for competition in the reallocation of territories, economic wealth, and production facilities. The income disparity between Hutus and Tutsis in Rwanda and Burundi translated into ethnic military and political power imbalance. Institutional distribution of power among ethnic groups can also be negotiated instead of being determined by armed struggles. Not just armed mobilization but also capabilities to control a political process are involved in asserting hegemonic power. Ethnic majorities in Estonia, Lithuania, and Latvia reestablished their superior status over the Russians who constituted close to one-third of the population after their independence in 1991 by requiring stringent conditions for citizenship qualification. Newly emerging groups tend to marginalize other groups in the ethnic power struggle derived from new state formation.

A high level of hostility in a polarized system is most likely to provoke intense armed struggles as seen in Rwanda, Chechnya, Northern Ireland, and Bosnia-Herzegovina. Any hostile incident can (for example, the assassination of the Hutu president in Rwanda in 1993) trigger mass mobilization leading to protracted confrontations. The assassination of President Melchior Ndadaye's Frodebu (who won multi-party polls) by Tutsi soldiers in

1993 threw Burundi into ethnic warfare which claimed some 300,000 lives. The crisis management capabilities virtually do not exist at low-level institutionalization of managing ethnic rivalry. The reciprocation of hostilities by rival groups creates a zero-sum game in which even small gains made by one side are perceived as a great potential loss or a grave threat to the other.

In internal conflicts, eventually victors emerge to establish hegemonic power in the country by means of either military success or post-conflict national elections. In Angola, Mozambique, Tajikistan, and the majority of countries (which ended civil wars) except the noticeable example of Nicaragua, the incumbent presidents have been able to reestablish their rule in their countries through elections. The degree of stability can be transitory or relative until all the armed groups accept a reestablished state. Even though he won the presidential election arranged through a peace accord in 1996, the arbitrary use of power by Charles Taylor in Liberia provoked another civil war in 1999–2003, ousting him. Warlord politics eventually ended with the election of Ellen Johnson-Sirleaf, the former World Bank official and finance minister in 2005 after an internationally sponsored peace arrangement.

In contrast with Liberia, the Democratic Republic of Congo has continued to experience instability after Mobuto was overthrown militarily in 1993 by rebel forces. After major civil wars in the late 1990s and early 2000s, the power-sharing government (installed by the 2003 peace accord) has not yet established full control over the territory due to continuing resistance of some armed groups organized by Tutsis on the country's eastern border with Rwanda. Owing to volatile political, military relations among multiple ethnic factions in African civil wars, peace agreements between the government and rebel groups have frequently proved to be a paper exercise.

Ethnic rivalry with the mixture of multiple groups can end with de facto partition. In Bosnia-Herzegovina, Croats and Muslims have created an alliance against Serbs. The partition of territories along ethnic divisions stem from the massive movement of the populations during the civil war. Despite the creation of a federal government (where presidency rotates among three ethnic groups), different cantons and municipalities have been geographically designated exclusively for each ethnic group.

Some countries such as Somalia and Afghanistan have been, for a long period of time, experiencing anarchy which resembles an international system. Afghanistan and Somalia have not yet reestablished stable central state functions. In Afghanistan, despite Taliban challenges, the current status quo has been maintained by the US and NATO backing of the central government, while most provinces are controlled by various political factions.

Beyond the overall struggle between the Karzai regime in Kabul and the Taliban, regional alliance in Afghanistan has been reflected in clashes among warlords in the south and west. This factionalism has been cultivated by regional powers which support proxies to advance their economic interests and security. While Russians have expanded their sphere of influence by supporting Fahim in the north, Iranian armed support was offered to Ismael Khan in the west. The existence of unique social alliances and political mobilization processes can explain a different path to restore a new hegemonic order in an anarchic society.

Balance of power in protracted internal conflicts

A status quo based on balance of power can produce predictable patterns of interaction. The leverage of minority groups can be measured by their population size, territorial compactness, and external military support (Stetter, 2007). Shift in population balance in Lebanon has led to demand of Shi'ite groups to increase their representational power in the government vis-à-vis Christians and Sunnis. Hezbollah has built its own military strength, establishing credible fighting capabilities against Israel. Hezbollah has occasionally fought with its rivals to reaffirm its status of power when they were challenged (they routed rival ethnic militia forces in May 2008). It also attracted concessions from the government headed by a Sunni prime minister after the Hezbollah leadership successfully blocked government attempts to reassert its power over them by preventing the removal of their favored military commander in charge of security near Beirut airport.

Internal wars were protracted due to a balance of military capabilities over a long period of time (as is experienced by El Salvador, Colombia, Guatemala, Mozambique, Angola, and Rwanda). The existence of multi-polar alliances produced divisions within the same ethnic groups and religious sects. In Burundi, several Hutu groups agreed with their main Tutsi rival to join a power-sharing government while one of the major Hutu militia groups was fighting the Hutu–Tutsi coalition until spring 2008.

Power balance is likely to be tipped eventually due to the growing strength of one protagonist over another via an increase in fighting capabilities sometimes associated with foreign military aid or an adversary's loss of major patrons. The significant military assistance to the Colombian government by the US helped marginalize fighting capabilities of rebel forces. Peace accords in the Mozambique and Central American civil wars were accomplished after the collapse of communist bloc countries (which supported leftist insurgent movements around the world) in the early 1990s.

Ethnic hegemony

The degree of unequal distribution of power represents relationships between a hegemonic ethnic group and its primary challenger (in multi-ethnic societies). In order to gain autonomy or independence, the minority may fight against the government run by antagonistic groups; minority challenges may be suppressed militarily (as is seen by Karen in Burma) or settle with limited or full autonomy (Aceh in Indonesia, Miskitos in Nicaragua, and Chittagong hill people in Bangladesh). Uighur uprising in 1980 and 2009, and Tibetan mass protests in 1959, 1988, and 2008 were all suppressed by the Chinese police and military. De facto partition from Azerbaijan allowed Nagorno-Karabakh to join Armenia after Armenian military forces successfully occupied a corridor linking the ethnic enclave within Azerbaijan to Armenia (1992).

Occasionally the majority fights against the government controlled by a minority group. The native populations (constituting the majority in Bolivia) were long deprived, but their conditions were improving after the election of an indigenous president in 2004. In South Africa and Zimbabwe, the white minority gave up their political power through negotiated settlements. The minority's bargaining power and position reflect their relative prestige and ability to develop effective political groupings.

As illustrated by the collapse of colonial power in Angola and Mozambique, a chaotic process of independence has led to rival competition among militia groups. As ethnic rivalry predates back to colonial rule, a post-colonial state becomes a prize to be seized upon. In Rwanda, Tutsis have been able to establish hegemonic relations with the majority of Hutus through their advantages in commerce and control of institutional power of the state. Indeed, Tutsis have monopolized strategic positions within the military and police in conjunction with their newly crafted state ideology that helps legitimize their domination over state institutions.

Hegemony over the state is established by not only the control of police and military apparatus but also a patronage of junior political partners for power sharing. In the long run, the uneven rates of income growth, decreasing level of education, and division within a hegemonic power group produce the erosion of a power resource base along with the diffusion of arms. The relative position of each group evolves according to changes in power distribution. In the absence of a power-sharing government (complemented by a minority veto power), a dominant group reestablishes hegemonic power through majority rule in elections. The marginalization of minorities through an electoral process can provoke discontent and violent confrontations.

Ethnic power struggle and anarchy

In Kenya, Nigeria, and other multi-ethnic societies, conflict can flare up and subside in the cycle of relative power balance reset by either elections or military coups. The status quo can be maintained by the preponderance of one group over others in the exercise of state power. The decline in the hegemonic roles of states (as a sole source of legitimacy) initiates a period of increasing military and economic competition among groups (e.g., former Soviet republics). The successive Islamic factions opposing each other in Somalia have moved in and out of capital Mogadishu without fully monopolizing their power over state institutions and government infrastructure.

The decline of the hegemonic group can be attributed to the challenge to its rule's legitimacy along with the rise of the challenger's power. Hegemonic decline leads to a call for systemic changes (toward greater multi-polarity). As each ethnic entity declared independence, the domino effect completely broke up the Socialist Federal Republic of Yugoslavia (composed of Slovenia, Croatia, Bosnia and Herzegovina, Macedonia, Serbia, and Montenegro) from 1992 and then came the further split of Serbia with the demand of independence by Kosovo. The decline in the capacity of American descendants to control a multi-tribal society eventually generated a vacuum in state power in Liberia.

Highly unstable structures of a state are ascribed to the absence of gravity toward core values and institutions which hold diverse groups together. That becomes more visible after the demise of a long dictatorship (Somalia, Liberia in the 1990s) or a military coup. The absence of central power in Somalia was followed by the death of a dictatorship. Anarchy can be created by a military coup that causes the collapse of a coalition government.

Protracted civil wars produce a collapse of centralized order, but the degree of anarchy varies, depending on the nature of governance. Extreme anarchy in civil war situations is featured by various conditions (created after the collapse of the central government) such as warlord rivalry in Liberia in the early 1990s and civil war prior to Taliban rule in Afghanistan between 1996 and 2001. This situation is contrasted with organized anarchy among states in which dominant power provides some kind of stability and order whilst acting according to their interests.

Power transition

A deep sense of uncertainty, in tandem with changes in the perceived degree of security, is created by a shift in balance between dominant power and a set of its rivals. The shift in a power hierarchy most likely leads to the demand to establish new relations along status disequilibria. The emergence of new power balance or imbalance can be represented by a rise in the capacity of funding militia forces (e.g., the accumulation of revenue coming from oil or other types of mineral resources), demographic growth, etc. Despite their smaller population size, Tutsi wealth supported their armaments that in turn provided superior fighting capabilities against the Hutus. The reason that Angolan rebel forces sustained their war against the government for more than two decades was their control over some of the country's diamond mines and oil fields.

In a multi-ethnic society, power transitions underway are likely to create conditions for conflict. Rising and declining power groups develop different levels of anxiety and expectation. A decreasing power gap is perceived as threatening by a superior group, while increasing ambiguity about relative power relations emboldens a lower rank group to claim rights to ascendance (Dahrendorf, 1959). Newly gained power is likely to contribute to demanding a new status or bigger share of wealth or resources (as illustrated by the Kurds in Iraq since Saddam Hussein's fall). In the absence of any reliable mechanisms to negotiate power sharing, fighting is a more likely means to determine the power status for both the challenger and higher status group.

A superior group may have a temptation for preventive aggression to preserve its status and block its further decline. An unfavorable shift in relative power balance may induce the declining power to initiate preemptive attacks in an attempt to halt a further decline in their status. Pakistan attacked India in 1971 prior to the loss of East Pakistan which was heavily populated by the Bengalis, after they accused India of supporting the ethnic population's demand for independence. On the other hand, a clearer sense of transition in power relations may encourage a declining power to be more willing to negotiate after their initial resistance against any compromise. Owing to difficulties in maintaining the apartheid rule, the white minority government in South Africa graciously transferred their long-held power to the African National Congress by permitting the majority rule while keeping their superior economic status.

The relative power of the parties can be rearranged by granting veto power to groups on the issues which are of grave concern to them. The relationship can be aggravated if the dominant group is too inflexible to agree to new relations, refusing to make concessions. In particular, power shifts contribute to the escalation of conflict if the surge of an ethnic challenger is unpredicted and rapid (such as the rise of the Tamil Tigers and Chechen rebels in the 1990s). The Iraqi internal fighting reflects Sunni resistance against a transition to the Shi'ite-dominated government.

The likelihood of a conflict between two parties may be affected not only by their relative power at a given point in time but also by any changes in their relative power over time. Prior to more than a year-long street protest and violent clashes with the supporters of the Sunni–Christian coalition government in 2008, Shi'ite leaders in Lebanon had long demanded their veto power as well as a greater share in cabinet positions in proportion to changes in population ratios favoring them. The declines in the dominant economic and military positions of a reigning group create incongruence with the existing distribution of political power and prestige.

Civil wars are often fought to control a state in the affirmation of ethnic or other group power (e.g. Afghanistan, Somalia). The establishment of Hutu governments by the majority votes in Burundi and Rwanda in the early 1990s was met by the Tutsi-dominated military's violent tactics to undermine the stability of the newly established governments (e.g., the assassination of two Hutu presidents in Burundi within the span of a year). Rwandan Tutsis regained control over state institutions after the Hutu government collapsed in the ensuing renewed civil war. The resurgent civil war in Burundi ended with the agreement to a power-sharing government in 2001.

In ending ethnic war, even a negotiation process may prove to be another means to dominate each other, as seen in the long, protracted stalemate in decisions over a new government structure. After a civil war, new power relations are established to signal the emergence of a new equilibrium and stability. In Kazakhstan and the Baltic states, a hegemonic system has been recreated by the emergence of a new ethnic majority along with new political boundaries. Negotiated settlement (based on mutual recognition of each other's power and status) can provide a more stable transition than all-out war.

Rank discrepancy

Stratification is created by a hierarchy of positions that are unequal with regard to military power, diplomatic reputation, economic growth, industrial capacity, and social prestige. In a stratified social system, power distribution, actual or felt, creates conditions for conflict. Dissatisfaction with inferior treatment not matched by actual achievement produces discontent of a minority group. Perceived rank discrepancy results in challenges to the existing hierarchy with a motivation for upward mobility.

The initiation of attempted changes is likely to come from those who are motivated by aspirations for prestige as well as frustration. In general, a superior group has little desire to change the system while completely disenchanted groups have neither the material resources nor the inspiration for change. India and Brazil feel improvement in their international status and prestige after rapid economic growth, seeking permanent UN Security Council membership. The Indian middle class was angered by President Bush's remarks about linking the global food crisis in spring 2008, in part, to growing demand for consumption created by the increased standard living of India and other newly industrializing countries. Rank discrepancy groups refer to the next highly ranked status group for their comparison and aspire to emulate them. In the midst of declining US power, polarity is expected to be accelerated due to global financial crisis and severe economic downturns.

Imbalanced status can be created by strength in the military realm, but a lack of economic progress. A discrepancy (between high or low ranks) in different arenas creates imbalance in the group's influence. During the Cold War period, the leading military contenders (Russia) and economic contenders (Japan) did not have status consistency across the arenas of influence (Cashman, 2000). A system with a high level rank consistency is more stable than an imbalanced system. At the end of the Cold War, Russia lost its superpower status, while the US has remained as the sole superpower. As they seek UN Security Council permanent seats with its improved economic status, both India and Brazil have been seeking to display their global military reach. Despite the global economic recession, Brazil has decided to build its advanced naval forces with global reach by relying on the military–industrial technology of France.

Aspirations for a higher status are felt more keenly by status discrepancy groups during rapid social change. Pressure for upward mobility can be destabilizing if peaceful channels are not available. In a quest to improve their status, rank discrepancy states tend to initiate more conflicts with the promotion of nationalism. The upward mobility may be carried out through violent aggression in response to frustration. In fact, strong frustration might be felt if political and diplomatic status lags behind the military or economic one.

The impact of asymmetry on behavior

In general, the strategies adopted by each party and the outcome of the struggle are influenced by different degrees of power asymmetry, from high, moderate to low. In a high level of power asymmetry such as slavery, a subordinate party may give up resistance if the other party is too overwhelming, and submission may be the only way to guarantee their own survival. However, various mechanisms of nonviolent resistance may still be used to maintain a continuing struggle against the imposition of unjustified rule.

Whereas power asymmetry is common, especially on the international scene, it is not simply a matter of the extent of power differentials that determines individual actors' behavior. The costs in the exercise of coercion become high with fierce resistance from the other party. The translation of power relations into real action is affected by motivations to change the status quo as well as the degree of balance in the destructive capabilities of each actor. Psychological dimensions of power asymmetry are characterized in terms of differentials in will, intentions, and resolve.

In power asymmetry, subordinate parties have fewer options because more powerful parties can simply impose their will on them. However, attempts to dominate tend to prolong a struggle especially in a situation when power differences are not likely to reduce the determination of the oppressed group to achieve freedom and autonomy. Russian military abuse in Chechnya has been successful in quelling guerrilla resistance, but it is not considered a permanent solution to the conflict. Even though power asymmetry allows one party to dominate the relationship, it can increase the will of the subordinate group to resist an unacceptable order. The widows of victims of the Russian military assault carried out attacks on a Moscow theater in 2002. In response to continuing resistance, a superior party may try to find ways to increase costs to a subordinate group to further skew conflict relations with torture or even killings of civilian sympathizers. This policy is often based on the belief that there is a limit on what the weaker party is capable of paying, but the oppressive party's calculations may need to be altered by an international moral outcry and public pressure.

Power dynamics evolve along with a rapid rate of unexpected social change, involving the modes of economic, industrial development, and population growth. Anticipated changes in the relative size of various racial, ethnic, or religious groups within a society can have profound effects on the course of a conflict among the groups. The strength of each party can be modified over time in response to changes in the level of determination and capacity.

In a highly asymmetric conflict (for example, relations between China and Taiwan), the superior party often uses a high level of psychological pressure through military intimidation and diplomatic isolation. Power differentials are used as leverage for prevalence in the relationship of mistrust and suspicion. The psychological dimensions of power relations have been heavily embedded in political, diplomatic struggles in an attempt to resolve differences over North Korean and Iranian nuclear programs. Each party may use psychological pressure to gain an edge even though they prefer settlement.

Moral, normative asymmetry

Many conflicts (involving a series of struggles over a suspended period of time) are characterized by power asymmetry between multiple actors as well as the interlocking nature of their relationships. Types of asymmetry can also be manifested in high moral, ethical imbalance. The examples of moral asymmetry include the suppression of minority rights in China, imprisonment and torture of political activists in Burma, the Amazon rainforest struggles between ranchers and tribal inhabitants, and pollution of indigenous people's land by mining industries. In these conflicts, moral persuasion or pressure may serve as a potent means to influence the powerful party's behavior with the support of a larger global audience.

Table 5.1 Power/moral asymmetry

	Moral justification of acts	
	H	L
H	Humanitarian intervention	Invasion and occupation of another country by a stronger party
Power status of an actor	(US intervention in Haiti and Somalia)	(China's suppression of Tibet)
L	Nonviolent resistance by a weaker party (Tibetan protest)	Terrorism and guerrilla attacks as a means of resistance (Iraqi insurgents)

Table 5.1 illustrates that moral justification can be made in terms of both the causes and means adopted to achieve them. Nonviolent protests aimed at achieving autonomy for one's own rule (as presented by India's nonviolent resistance under the British colonial rule in the 1930s and 1940s; Tibetan nonviolent struggle against China since 1950) carry high moral justification even though their military power (or capacity to induce physical coercion) is nonexistent. The US-led humanitarian intervention saved many lives threatened by starvation caused by the militia group violence and thefts in Somalia; another intervention in Haiti brought an end to the abusive military dictatorship committed to massive human rights violations. These types of acts by a powerful actor can easily be justified on a high moral ground. On the other hand, it is highly immoral to maintain physical domination over the population after military occupation of another territory by a powerful party (Indonesia's invasion and occupation of East Timor between 1975 and 1990 and Chinese continuing oppression of Tibet after their invasion in 1950). The attacks of the civilian populations by insurgent forces in Iraq and Afghanistan are immoral, while they are militarily fighting against superior foreign forces.

In overcoming underdog status, moral legitimacy becomes an important means to rally supporters. A moral high ground can carry persuasive power. Moral superiority can be used to reshape the nature of conflict discourse with a focus on universal human values. The acknowledgment of racial injustice and atrocities and the offer of apologies have been an essential condition for the reestablishment of new relationships in societies which went through gross violation of basic rights of many individuals that occurred during the period of violent conflict.

The effectiveness of moral authority is derived from the support of public opinion both within and outside of perpetrator countries. In the case of Gandhi's resistance against the British colonial rule, a significant section of British intellectuals was sympathetic to the nonviolent causes for Indian independence. It is contrasted with the Chinese government's suppression of dissident intellectuals. Anti-racist movements symbolized by Nelson Mandela broadly appealed to the world public, inciting an economic boycott of South African businesses and isolating white South Africans from various world events. The success of the anti-apartheid coalition suggests that it is important to broaden moral appeal by exposing the symbols of injustice.

The subjective and objective dimensions of moral claims may not always be congruent. One's own moral justification may differ from the moral perspectives and judgments of others. Israel–Palestine conflicts illustrate perceptional gaps in moral claims between the two sides and political legitimacy of such claims. While Israeli assault on civilian targets might be justified in a response to suicide bombings, the excessive use of force has generated sympathy for the Palestinian cause among many neutral observers. Even though all types of violence are essentially inhumane and should be condemned, violent forces exerted by a dominant party in oppressive relations particularly tend to draw criticism.

The structure of normative expectations can differ according to the actor's political values. In terms of moral judgments, US armies are more vulnerable to accusations of torture than the Iraqi insurgents due to the former's proclaimed values of democracy and obligation to respect human rights. Terrorist organizations are not bound by normative or legal considerations, since they seek a total warfare by any means.

Even though moral judgments can be based on subjective values and feelings, more objective criteria such as universal human rights standards can be used to develop common understanding. International norms have not been established yet to put a strong moral responsibility on stronger parties. For instance, civilian deaths and other consequences of NATO bombings in Afghanistan have been neglected under the name of war against terrorism, but a lack of humanitarian consideration has undermined a broad goal of obtaining the support of the local populace needed for political stability.

Rebalancing power asymmetry

Because of differences in the social context of each conflict, an embedded power structure could have different implications in resolving a specific type of conflict. Mediation may not be effective in relationship asymmetry composed of power imbalance combined with social injustice that an oppressive party is not willing to admit. If political oppression and economic exploitation exist, escalation is often necessary in order to transform the nature of conflict. In this situation, changes in the attitude and negotiation positions of the dominant party are an essential condition for conflict resolution which guarantees justice. Perceptions of fierce resistance and political costs may sway the powerful party's decision to negotiate.

Especially when faced with the oppressor party's attempt to impose their values and beliefs, overcoming mental depression and dependence on one's own culture and identity for empowerment become important for the oppressed groups. Solidarity within one's own group or community is essential to overcome the coercive structure which deprives the marginalized of their status and material well-being. In the late 1960s, indigenous awakening helped the movements of the Amazonian people spread from Ecuador to Bolivia in resisting the encroachment of foreign oil companies and the arrival of a wave of colonialists. The federation of indigenous organizations (e.g., the Shuar Federation in Ecuador) was aided by segments of the Catholic Church and human rights lawyers in an attempt to stave off invasions and occupations of native lands by undertaking legal actions (Mauceri, 2004). The Katarista Movement formed by various Aymara groups in La Paz and Oruro in 1968 adopted the name of a leader of the indigenous rebellion of 1780–1781 in order to boost the spirits of their resistance.

Mobilization of the oppressed

In an asymmetric conflict, the main concern is how to transform unjust social relationships (Miall *et al.*, 1999). In power-balancing acts, transforming asymmetric relationships is an ultimate condition for conflict resolution demanded by many groups ranging from the indigenous people's rebellion led by Zapatistas guerrillas in Mexico's Chiapas to Hill people

Hmong in Laos. In resistance against South Africa's white minority regime, the African National Congress adopted both nonviolent and violent strategies with a campaign for creating ungovernable conditions in black townships. The underground campaign for ungovernability was more effective than guerrilla warfare. The equalization of capacity by nonviolent mobilizations or guerrilla tactics is essential to effectively confront an imposed order in a one-sided struggle (as seen in the colonial struggles of the Vietnamese and Algerians in the 1950s and 1960s).

Increased awareness and higher confidence levels (that come with new knowledge and access to social participation) strengthen positions of a weaker party prior to the negotiation of a new relationship, enhancing self-esteem and self-efficacy. The political movements supported by wider sectors of society contribute to public awareness and pressure on government officials. In overcoming the opposition of a dominant party, weaker parties can also be empowered by both technical assistance and moral support. During the Bosnian civil war (that ended in 1995), NATO permitted leaks in the embargo for Bosnian Muslims given their military inferiority to Croats and Serbs. Success in the South African struggle is attributed to diplomatic and economic sanctions, international isolation of the minority regime as well as intensive mobilization of the resistance movement's large constituents.

Even though it may not produce visible, immediate effects, nonviolent struggle can be adopted as a main strategy to address the intransigence of a powerful party. In a confrontation with the stronger party, nonviolence can serve as a viable alternative to armed struggles especially for extremely disadvantaged minorities or indigenous peoples. Marginalized parties may use nonviolent tactics to communicate their intentions, educate and persuade adversaries as well as to draw sympathy from actors outside of the conflict. The capacity and will to resist by a weak party increases the cost to a more powerful party with the consequence of prolonging the conflict. The system of social relations within which adversaries interact can be altered by nonviolent strategies especially if the dominant party can be persuaded to look at the sources of injustice. In response to the other party's coercive tactics, nonviolent strategies have been advocated for providing moral superiority to redress power asymmetry.

Further reading

Blau, P. (1964) *Exchange and Power in Social Life*, Edison, NJ: Transaction Publishers.

Bourdieu, P. (1991) *Language and Symbolic Power*, Cambridge, MA: Harvard University Press.

Cashman, C. (2000) *What Causes War?: Introduction to Theories of International Conflict*, Lanham, MD, and Cumnor Hill: Lexington Books.

Dahrendorf, R. (1959) *Class and Class Conflict in Industrial Society*, Stanford, CA: Stanford University Press.

Foucault, M. (1977) *Politics, Philosophy, Culture, Interviews and Other Writings, 1977–1984*, UK: Routledge.

Freire, P. (1970) *Pedagogy of the Oppressed*, New York: Continuum Publishing Co.

Scott, J. C. (1985) *Weapons of the Weak: Everyday Forms of Peasant Resistance*, New Haven, CT: Yale University Press.

Tillet, G. and French, B. (2006) *Resolving Conflict: a Practical Approach*, Oxford: Oxford University Press.

Womack, B. (2006) *China and Vietnam: the Politics of Asymmetry*, New York: Cambridge University Press.

6 Structure

While there has been sufficient emphasis on research and practice on cultural and psychological issues, adequate attention has not been paid to questions of social justice and economic inequality as sources of conflict and problems to be resolved. In most analysis, structure has been considered as given rather than conditions to be rectified (a parameter rather than a variable). The role of conflict management has been oriented toward how to maintain or restore order. In the Hobbes' tradition, human beings are assumed to be inherently aggressive, and thus behavioral control becomes a main concern of conflict management mechanisms. However, diverse structural concerns need to be understood in the examination of overall conditions of group behavior and social processes relevant to managing tensions and animosities. In fact, violent protests in Kenya, frequent social unrest in Nigeria, and Hindu–Muslim violence in India are in one way or another connected to ethnic rivalry and resistance against the hegemony established by state institutions.

This chapter discusses the ways in which structural concerns are important for understanding conflict and its resolution. In Burma, Uzbekistan, Sudan, and other undemocratic societies, the deeper causes of conflict can be relegated to the structural features of antagonistic relationships arising from illegitimate institutions (that prohibit fair distribution of power and wealth), but also a lack of mechanisms and processes that rectify systemic failure in conjunction with severe oppression. In this chapter, various types of conflict relationships are interpreted from systems and field theory perspectives. If conflict is considered innate in society, research on conflict resolution should pay more attention to conditions which regenerate animosities and hostilities. Conflicts need to be tackled at source by an adequate understanding of how human behavior is related to social and political processes.

Structural conditions for conflict resolution

One of the main puzzles in examining the failure to end a protracted conflict is why conflict does last so long in some countries (e.g., Sudan and Colombia) without any prospect of ending, despite the existence of negotiated settlement in other comparable cases (illustrated by Aceh, East Timor, El Salvador, Guatemala, and Nicaragua to name a few). Even though each conflict may develop its own dynamics over a long period of time, the manifestation and resolution of conflict are embedded in certain structural conditions which inhibit new political arrangements. Most importantly, each society manages social–structural divisions differently; in fact, some governments are more accommodating to an ethnic demand for autonomy (regional political representation in Spain's Basque region). The organizational characteristics of opposition groups are also related to the feasibility of negotiated settlement within the existing state.

In managing either rivalry or asymmetric relations, conflict is part of an inescapable process and outcome of any contentious interactions in the absence of universally accepted laws and abidance by them. Often one group desires to control the destiny of the other group in pursuit of one's quest for political domination and economic benefit. The marginalized group's language, customs, religion, and other aspects of distinctive identities are often suppressed to deny the group's rights to autonomy and political independence.

In addition, the motives of domination come from not only territorial expansion but also economic advantages. Incompatible interests may stem from conditions of scarcity (whether it is related to shrinking supply of resources or rapid increase in the demand of the same resources). Thus inherent competition for limited resources is a pervasive aspect of contentious politics in a world of inequality and disorder. The questions about how to respond to the scarcity is likely to be affected by the nature of inter-group relations. A disproportionate control of decision making over the allocation of shrinking resources (e.g., water in Africa) creates feelings of inequity and disparity. Inter-group clashes are often expressed in either war or other types of violence.

The paths of large-scale conflicts are profoundly shaped by the structure of overall relationships between the opposing collectivities (e.g., symmetric versus asymmetric) and by how various agents interpret those structures (beneficial or exploitative). The structural character of the relationships is attributed to different coercive and material capabilities of each party as well as valued cultures. The extent of adversarial competition in economic, social, and cultural arenas presents the overall relationship quality.

The nature of inter-group dynamics as well as underlying conflict conditions can be attributed to particular system features which might severely restrict an individual human agency's capacity to effect their acts, as they intended. As superior actors have a capacity to bring undesirable changes to other actors, marginalized parties may have to be forced to accept the unforeseen social and economic arrangements that they neither planned nor could avoid. Political oppression, population transfer, barriers to economic and educational opportunities have been some common tools used to sustain hegemonic rule in minority regions (e.g., Chinese occupation of Tibet).

Thus it can be claimed that conflict relationships are formed and cemented in a wider political, economic, and socio-cultural environment (that permits one group's advantage over others). Group autonomy and social justice are affected by structural conditions that privilege particular social forces through educational and economic opportunities. Broadly speaking, most internal conflicts in the modern state system arise from the monopoly of power in the hands of one or a few groups which represent particular sectors or regions of a country to the exclusion of others. The paradigms of conflict resolution have been focusing on the removal of socio-economic conditions that regenerate oppressive relationships by emphasizing human needs perspectives (Burton, 1997; Kelman, 2002).

System change and adjustment

In the absence of democratic relations, the repression of conflict contributes to concealing oppressive relations while avoiding the adjustment of human institutions to the need for changes in the system of distribution of power and resources. In an authoritarian regime, lack of change leads to the system's rigidification. The forced integration of minority territories and denial of basic rights cannot be justified by the fear of disintegration. In fact, self-rule for minority groups has been recognized as a principle to govern inter-group relations since World War I.

When mistrust among groups is derived from system domination and insecurity felt by marginalized groups, structural change is essential for the constructive accommodation of conflict (as illustrated by power sharing in Northern Ireland; a shift to a majority rule in South Africa). The premise of conflict resolution is based on the fact that a powerful party needs to be convinced of the cost of not changing a system of alienation (Burton, 2001). Then the task of conflict resolution is to explore strategies to respond to institutional problems based on an understanding of social fabric which fuels disorder by creating imbalances between social and economic forces.

In fact, system changes can stem from a search for new relationships between the parties to the conflict. The transition to a peace system entails various steps to prepare for small or large changes (such as removal of prejudices, educational reform, for instance, in Bosnia-Herzegovina as well as a new electoral system). In an asymmetric conflict, transforming systems might involve persistent activities and vision (e.g., independence of East Timor and transition to democratic rule in Liberia after civil wars). Interdependent relationships can be created by the pursuit of shared values and mutually beneficial economic arrangements.

An atomized process (such as a coercive response to a particular ethnic riot) seeks superficial solutions with the individualization of problems that leads to an isolationist approach (Botes, 2003). In many intractable conflict situations, the removal of institutional obstacles for participation in self-governance is considered a key in allaying the discontent of a disenfranchised segment of the population. In ending several decades of the Indonesian military's oppression in Aceh and armed resistance, the negotiated settlement guaranteed the right of the residents of Aceh to independently represent their interests by creating their own political party.

Systemic change beyond perceptual modifications often focuses on the restructuring of social institutions (as seen in post-communist transition in Eastern Europe and Russia) as well as a redistribution of power (between different sectors of society and even generations). The correction of inequities and injustice along with social and political adjustments is necessary to provide all groups with their vital human needs. The failure to guarantee economic fairness has been manifested in street riots in the Baltic states such as Latvia and Lithuania. A change in the relationship between parties can certainly be accompanied by a perceptional change in the recognition of each other's legitimate needs. In general, however, changes in individual perceptions are not sufficient to prevent future conflict without responding to the root causes of injustice attributed to social institutions. In the post-civil war period of El Salvador and Guatemala, most notorious military, security institutions had to be either abolished or completely reformed due to their involvement in massive abuse of civilian rights and killing of political opponents.

When asymmetric, imbalanced relationships have been rectified, crosscutting ties serve the development of bonding between former adversarial groups. The post-apartheid South Africa has been devoted to conciliation between former white rulers and the majority black population in a joint quest for the continued realization of democratic principles and shared economic prosperity. Violent conflict leads to the destruction of valuable economic and social interdependence, thus raising the cost of conflict significantly. Building or restoring crosscutting ties between potential adversaries is imperative for addressing and preventing the process of social polarization. In Northern Ireland, youth education and local development programs have been carefully cultivated to interconnect both Republican and Unionist communities which have been divided for many decades.

Ideally, all conflicts in a social system should be resolved in such a way as to create a conflict-free society. Conflict will remain inherent in a system that entails competing demands and inadequate procedures to allocate resources. System adjustment is a never ending, open process beyond a specific agreement to end a dispute. Beyond settlement of short-term manifest disputes, sustained conflict resolution practice needs to be designed to prepare parties to be ready to embark on long-term structural transformation. In addition, a process to remove the main sources of contention demands continuing adaptations to a new external environment that challenges the newly established relationships (e.g., the management of ethnic relations in Lebanon through power-sharing deals which permitted the constitution of a new government in 2008).

The management of conflict in various social settings

Differences within an existing system can be easily settled by reference to established rules and institutional processes if they have been accepted by all the disputants. The provocations (attributed to inadequate knowledge, misperceptions, and differences in preferences) are managed within ordinary social and organizational relationships. In fact, complaints can be aired and resolved by an ombudsman and other assisted communication that leads to the exposure of government abuse of power. The remedies for damage are sought through arbitration or other authoritative judgments. Most importantly, differences can be easily managed via organized discussion when the sources of the problem are found within the system. Thus in pluralistic democratic societies, in general, conflict regulation mechanisms include mediation and arbitration guided by value consensus that is acceptable to various members of the society.

Institutionalized approaches to mediation in the US originate from grassroots efforts to bring social harmony and empower the urban poor in the 1960s and 1970s. However, it has evolved into a system management tool after professionalized practice took over the movement. Mediation was encouraged by the established legal arrangement to mitigate the burden of a court system. In some states, for instance, divorce mediation is mandatory prior to any court procedures. It is seen as a cheaper, more efficient and convenient means for settling differences among individuals. Thus, professional mediation has been adopted as a functional tool to be complementary to existing institutions.

Social structures create mechanisms that help control or channel conflicts through normative regulation, but the degree of their institutionalization differs. In kinship and tribal societies, informal traditional social practice is used to handle group conflicts without dependence on modern legal systems. A sense of justice emerges from the intrinsic values of society. Often religious functions are combined with communal cultural practice which has a wider acceptance in societies. There exists a wide range of conflict management procedures and styles, reflecting socio-cultural variations. Ridicule, reprimand, and ostracism are part of the diverse informal mechanisms in some indigenous tribal communities in Canada which emphasize rehabilitation of perpetrators as well as restitution and compensation. As a method of rehabilitation, youth (responsible for causing harm) might be abandoned in a remote wilderness until after the period of remorse is over. The process of handling conflict (i.e., the role of culture in the choice of conflict management methods) has been designed for preserving or even strengthening the relationship among communal members.

Arguments and disputes are inherent in any type of relationship, either traditional or modern. In a kinship society, arguments or disputes with neighbors are handled by elders and religious leaders who have good insight, wisdom, and intuition. In a small community bonded by blood, and closely knit social networks, written legal codes are not necessary to make decisions on who is right or wrong. Contrary to that, regulating conflict has become institutionalized with an increase in the complexities of modern societies which are ripped by multi-layers of interests. In some societies, traditional norms (collectivist over individualistic) have been adopted for retributive justice. In Saudi Arabia, any killer's life can be saved as long as their family and community members bring a large sum of money set by the victim's family. Sometimes emissaries have to get involved in communication between the two families to lower the amount of money which the offender's family cannot raise. The whole process puts the approaches to crime and punishment in a collectivist communal perspective.

Functionalist perspectives

In the functionalist interpretation of a social system, each action is viewed as a consequence of complex inter-working relationships. In an analogous manner to biology, system theories explain society and organizational function as if they were part of internal organisms of living systems that survive in a larger environment. The concept of an organic system provides a point for the analysis of maintenance of a stable structure and orderly processes of social life. Various events and activities need to be incorporated or fitted into larger social processes. In structural functionalist views, conflict needs to be properly controlled to keep an existing system stable.

In defining system characteristics, an entire whole is composed of relationships among interdependent parts. The properties and functions of an entity have characteristics that are distinctive from individual components. A network of relationships among interacting parts (e.g., political–administrative regulatory policies designed to restore confidence of the financial market) can determine the quality of the system's operation. System stability is derived from sufficient redundancy to keep the regulated interaction on track through a set of self-organizing forces.

Whereas a system is made up of parts, the operation of a whole social system cannot be reducible to activities of its parts and proprieties. In fact, interrelated wholes (as exemplified by socio-cultural systems which govern clan relationships in Somalia) represent social realities better than individual acts; a whole exists prior to the parts. As the interdependent components characterize the overall system attributes, individual parts or individual incidents need to be understood in the context of dynamics operating in the whole system (Singer, 1971).

In failed states such as Somalia, political order is not provided by a functioning government but by the balance of relationships among diverse social forces, including warlord factions. The economic activities of Somalia are thus adjusted to "a shadow economy" which fills in the vacuum caused by a lack of established political order. The interdependent components of the overall system explain the recurring patterns within and beyond the conflict system. Negative dynamics in a conflict-prone system (e.g., ethnic rivalry) are manifested in certain types of persistent behavior such as clan warfare.

In order to constitute a persistent order, the system must perform certain functions; for instance, the economy should generate enough income for the majority of people in society to meet their basic daily necessities. The equilibrium point of a system can be achieved through proper coordination among its components, political–administrative, economic, and cultural. As illustrated by many societies emerging from long-term civil wars in Angola and Bosnia-Herzegovina, certain functional prerequisites such as security need to be fulfilled to maintain the preservation of political order and elimination of threats to system maintenance.

In a faltering economy, political–administrative measures step in to compensate for the functions that have not been successfully fulfilled (Habermas, 1987). For instance, the US government has devoted public money to rescuing Wall Street investment firms and mortgage giants. A government is not supposed to regulate the operation of a free market, but in a response to the major economic crisis, it has become common for political and administrative decisions to get involved in resource allocation.

In contrast with advanced Western democratic societies, some states do not have the administrative capacity to cope with economic crisis, causing regime collapse or social chaos. In weak states, disorder and militia violence may start with mutinies by some military units which were not paid due to financial difficulties ascribed to reduced government revenue. A political aspect of a social act is judged in terms of its relevance to the authoritative allocation of values for a society. The absence of respected rules or established principles is more visibly exposed during a crisis, often causing system collapse.

Interdependence between different sub-systems (e.g., economic and political subsystems) can be manifested in different ways. For instance, in Saudi Arabia, the royal family tightly controls the government and economic wealth coming from oil revenues. They depend on secret police forces for rooting out opposition to the power of monarchic rule, undermining the notion of autonomous civil society. In China, while the government is not popularly mandated, it has maintained its grip on power by pursuing rapid economic growth and controlling educational systems and media to block any external information considered to be threatening to their legitimacy. In these systems, conflict is managed by the oppressive means of injecting fear and imposing coercive order rather than dialogue or other means of improving understanding of diverse perspectives among members of society.

The behavior and pattern of culture and religion need to be supportive of the functional prerequisites for system maintenance. Religion often does provide certain rituals to endow the existing political rule with symbols of legitimacy. After the demise of communism, Russian orthodox churches have replaced the old socialist ideology in supporting state legitimacy. A sufficient proportion of component actors ought to be motivated to satisfy their required roles in a given system. Cultural patterns should be compatible with the minimum conditions of stability or orderly development of social values. The continued patterns of inter-group interactions can be explained by an integrated set of interests and meanings derived from values and norms. In multi-ethnic societies, the failure to develop shared value and identity weakens social integration, often creating political crisis.

System maintenance functions

The adaptation or adjustment of a given system can be accompanied by evolving functions of components. Dysfunctions of any crucial system component lessen the whole system's ability for adaptation. The basic reality is based on interrelated elements of the whole that constrain negative effects of individual acts on other part of the system. Each organization has functions to regulate the deviant behavior of individual members unless it faces institutional deficiencies.

In functionalist perspectives, conflicts are not considered dysfunctional as long as they serve the maintenance of the social structure. If existing norms of interaction between political opponents are upheld, the intended changes (such as reform of electoral systems) may aim at adjustment rather than a total replacement of the system. Opposing roles (merchants versus buyers) produce mutually incompatible interests (over price). However, this kind of a role conflict is managed by mutually recognized bargaining cultures. On the contrary, a high level of tension is created especially when the values of actors contradict the fundamental assumptions upon which the relationships are founded. Whether imposed or indoctrinated by dominant ideologies or co-opted by economic incentives, the prevention of serious dissension is necessary to sustain an existing social structure.

If conflict is seen as dysfunctional, relationships need to be renegotiated to develop new system features that accommodate opposing members of a society. Conflict, regarded as an opportunity for the removal of an oppressive relationship, can contribute to the establishment of a more egalitarian, symmetric relationship. The active avoidance and suppression of conflict may come from a dominant group's desire for system management. However, this kind of system is likely to generate more conflict along with greater pressure for change than consensus-based systems. Frequent riots in China are more likely to produce pressure for system change (from one party rule to a democratic government embracing diverse groups).

In fact, different models of governance (pluralistic political systems versus authoritarian ones) fit in diverse modes of conflict management and resolution (via bargaining among diverse interest groups versus the state control of disenchanted groups). It is related to how each society sees dissent and challenges of conflict to the system maintenance. Many governments have different levels of confidence in the assimilation of opposing perspectives in forging political consensus. When a system cannot be normatively justifiable, authoritarian regimes rely on coercion and force for their maintenance (as seen in China's minority policies) instead of accommodation.

Political instability and conflict

In system perspectives, the continuance of the system is synonymous with the maintenance of the accepted order and successful control of disruptive deviant behavior challenging political authority. While maintaining a body of rules and a normative order, political systems arbitrate jurisdictional disputes between disharmonious elements of the society. In some political systems, a peaceful process to regulate the clashes between possible winners and losers is not sufficiently developed in redistributing political and economic power; state authority has been dissolved and taken over by 2008 military coups in Guinea and Mauritania.

In these countries, political instability feeds a cycle of a long-term dictatorship, elections, political squabbles among the political elite, and military coups. Since its independence from France in 1960, the political history of deeply poor, mostly desert country of Mauritania has been engulfed by about a dozen attempts to topple sitting governments. The 2008 military coup was staged by the top four military leaders whom the president, Sidi Mohamed Ould Cheikh Abdallahi, fired. The president's infighting with the 95-member National Assembly coincided with the legislature's criticism of the government's ineptitude in preparing for rising food prices and declining oil revenues as well as corruption. Whereas the military ceased a constitutional order this time, they ended the 21-year corrupt and repressive rule of Maaoya Sid'Ahmed Ould Taya in 2005. The new government established by free elections in 2007 did not last longer than a year. Either military intervention or ethnic war ensues often due to various combinations of poverty, corruption, oppressive rule, and political infighting which produce deep public despair and volatile social atmosphere.

The killing of Burundi's Hutu President Cyprien Ntaryamira along with his Rwandan counterpart (by shooting down the plane carrying them over the Rwandan capital Kigali) in

1994 plunged Burundi into yet more ethnic violence, sparking a series of political crises. In the political vacuum, the Tutsi military coup toppled the government of the newly appointed president, Sylvestre Ntibantunganya, who was parliamentary speaker prior to 2003. In turn, Hutu opponents initiated a civil war that lasted until a power-sharing deal was reached in 2001. A low level of institutionalization and absence of political culture of compromise, and bargaining have been a fertile ground for military coups or civil wars in many unstable countries.

In overcoming political crises challenging the state identity in 2008, the constitutional courts in Thailand and Turkey have played a pivotal role in determining the losers and winners after the existing process had only deepened the distance between opposing political forces. Proving the system's democratic maturity, all the parties in Turkey and Thailand accepted the rulings of the constitutional court. The stabilizing role of the highest court authority in the two countries can be compared with the mistrust of the Kenyan court by the opposition party in Kenya. As the Kenyan court was believed to be biased against the opposition, no institutional arbiter existed to settle the post-election disputes. The contentious battles between the two main political foes in presidential elections turned into mass violence. In the absence of stable institutional functions, inter-group violence (often erupting after elections) exposes traditional ethnic rivalry.

The loss of equilibrium (such as loss of capacity to maintain social order with existing laws and coercive instruments) means that the system does not have any more capacity to regulate tensions arising from incompatibilities between opposing forces despite their threat to the system. This can be followed by such extreme types of interactions as revolution or war resulting in riots. The disintegration of the system by such means as violent revolution or mass protests (i.e., the weakened monarchic rule in Nepal by weeks of protests in 2006 and its eventual abolishment in 2008) results from the loss of old equilibrium in the absence of the homeostatic mechanism (such as restoration of order via constitutional means), which continues to readjust various functions in keeping deviance (created by social disturbances) within given limits. Such events as the Russian Bolshevik revolution in 1917 or the Iranian Islamic revolution in 1979 abandoned political processes and values that sustained the power of old political elites.

Turkey's struggle between secularism and political Islam

In many politically divided societies, conflict management is an important function for system survival. Political entities have different degrees of institutionalization to manage constitutional and other types of crisis that threaten state unity. Since Turkey's founding in 1923, military generals, lawyers, and their secular supporters have successfully deposed elected governments (run by Islamic parties) four times in Turkish history. In fact, Islamist parties (popularly mandated to govern through elections) were even overthrown by the intervention of the military closely allied with secularist elements.

Following the 2008 court decision, Turkey's ruling party Justice and Development (AKP) has been permitted to operate (ruled as not being unconstitutional), but the court imposed a penalty on the party by verdict which cut part of the funding to the party (with a minor effect in the party's operation). As the system matures, the judicial system has to find a delicate balance between opposing political factions which represent religious and secular values. Institutional arbiters are often essential to overcome a system crisis which entails opposing values (a more openly religious society versus fear about political Islam's influence in secular lifestyles).

Response to system stress

Rules of action have to be justified by particular forms and types of resource mobilization as well as symbolic meanings (Giddens, 1986). Our judgments about social order are often forged by values and procedures that are fundamental to shared political culture. In recently independent states such as Kazakhstan, state educational systems and propaganda have been mobilized to restore traditional ethnic rituals and language or create new state symbols.

The functional integration of interacting parts is necessary to respond to challenges from external system boundaries (for instance, existential threats from adversaries). Often past memories are invoked to develop unity within a nation, as exemplified by trips of Israeli students to holocaust sites in Poland as part of their school activities. Internal cohesion is important in producing the effective response to external conflict (Coser, 1956). However, reduced food production along with dramatic shortage of arable land (famine in Africa) can put pressure on the society beyond their stress managing capacity.

In general, stability can be threatened by either excessive external pressure (i.e., financial crisis or economic sanctions) beyond the society's coping capabilities or the failure to manage even ordinary internal tension attributed to rapidly declining system capabilities. The collapse of former Yugoslavia in the early 1990s reflects the failure of the federalist system to manage tension among diverse ethnic regions created by financial crisis in transition from a socialist economic system and weakened coercive capabilities to control the local ethnic leaders' campaign for creating a separate state. The disintegration of a system can be ascribed to a breakdown in organizational ability to provide a response to challenges by failing to maintain harmony among component structures.

During conflict escalation, significant armed violence produces such consequential effects as humanitarian disasters. The flow of refugees, human rights abuses, and casualties test a stable system's ability to manage and control stress. Pathological aspects of a conflict add complexities to the perpetuation of violence with the involvement of warlord insurgencies, unlawful mineral exploitation, and illegal smuggling activities by organized criminal groups. The ability to mobilize crucial resource bases to alleviate conflict does not exist when the key actors (who can hold the system together) seek their own exclusive interests.

System stress can be managed by government oppression, but is eventually exposed to collapse when a conflict trigger (such as coups or electoral fraud) exacerbates a high degree of structural tension. In understanding a potential conflict, underlying stress (poverty, ethnic, racial, and religious differences, a weak state capacity to manage tensions, and power inequalities) represents system weakness. The comparison of one's status in power, wealth, and prestige with others can result in increasing levels of aspiration as well as feelings of deprivation, questioning the legitimacy of the existing system. The agitation of apprehension about economic, cultural, and even political survival may produce frustration that can in turn be expressed through ethno-nationalism. In a collapsing state or other dysfunctional systems, groups mobilize physical violence as a main means for either defending or claiming their political status (for example the atrocious civil war in Bosnia-Herzegovina between 1992 and 1995).

In a system perspective, conflict is ascribed to the disruption of the existing status quo in the system (Rummel, 1976). A confrontation over core issues of a society (such as the legitimacy of group rights) can translate into system failures if they cannot be settled within the accepted boundaries of relationship among the constituent members. The imposition of Islamic law and customs marginalized the Christian population of south-eastern Nigeria, eventually provoking a civil war. As a political conflict, the Nigerian–Biafran War (July 1967–January 1970) started from the attempted secession of the south-eastern provinces which proclaimed themselves Republic of Biafra. The government military victory re-affirmed the state hegemony over the rebellious region, restoring the status quo.

A settlement may bring about a new balance of power or reaffirm the existing hegemony of one group institutionalized in the political system. In post-civil war situations in El Salvador, Tajikistan, Mozambique, Angola, Guatemala, and other places, the ruling party has been successful in the reaffirmation and legitimization of their rule through elections. The regular electoral cycles often balance and rebalance power relations between the government and opposition groups in an orderly manner.

Violence structure in a failed state

Even though different criteria for good governance can be developed, a state's legitimacy can be supported when the population is a benefactor of public good such as orderly functions of society and the guarantee of a fair distribution of wealth. Institutional legitimacy needs to be based on agreeable norms, as state authority has to be acceptable to the population. Most conflict-prone states are predatory instead of providing public service. Thus institutional insufficiencies and inadequacies contribute to conflict. There are different types of pathological states, depending on the level of repression and exploitation of the marginalized.

The vulnerability of weak states comes not only from globalization and transnational economic activities (above) but also from the pursuit of exclusive self-interests by certain cities and violence by militant groups (below). In many dysfunctional states, patrimonialism is bred by personalized patronage politics that hijack functional state operations. Thus, state institutions exist to serve parochial interests in the absence of neutral administrative functions. The failed state often provides an opportunity for various armed factions to profit from instability along with the control of the population.

As was most vividly illustrated by the prolonged conditions of anarchy in Somalia (since the removal of dictator Siad Barre in 1991), state failure constitutes a particular type of structural deficiency, creating permissive conditions for a perpetual cycle of violence. The state loses its national identity and character, opening wide competition among private actors who seek to control properties and functions of public institutions. The capture or colonization of a state by particular groups (tied to tribal or ethnic origins) deprives state legitimacy further, as the state does not represent the entire population politically nor carries out revenue-generating functions independently to sustain itself and provide welfare service.

In Liberia (1989–1996) and Somalia (1990–present), the chaotic political struggle was touched off by overthrowing one man's rule which put state administrative functions under private control. In other situations seen in Uganda (during Idi Amin's rule from 1971–1979) and currently in Zimbabwe (under the atrocious rule of Robert Mugabe), the state may nominally exist, but ceases to carry out official functions. State institutions prey on the population instead of serving them, creating a dismal economy (several thousand percent of inflation in Zimbabwe). The government is operating in accordance with formality, but the autocratic rule by one man does not draw any support from the majority of society. The chaotic climate generally creates conditions for humanitarian intervention. Idi Amin's regime in Uganda was toppled by the Tanzanian military intervention which led to the election of a new government. In the case of Zimbabwe, out of old loyalty and reward for the past support of ANC's struggle during the apartheid period, the South African government provided continued support for the Zimbabwean president Mugabe despite the atrocious killings of political opponents and many civilians by his armed gangs. The state functions go through further decay every continuing day of Mugabe's rule in the midst of the deepening miseries of the population.

There are different degrees of state failure: 1) complete failure exemplified by Somalia (with the absence of institutionalized, central political authority); 2) a semi-failed state still remaining de jure; 3) the existence of a de facto state without international legitimacy; 4) transitional state toward failure. In the first category, the Soviet withdrawal from Afghanistan after almost nine years of occupation and war with Mujahadin guerrillas left a big political vacuum which allowed intense factional fighting. The Afghan state did not exist either de jure or de facto to provide normal government functions. As the most common among the four categories (e.g., the Democratic Republic of Congo), a semi-failed state maintains different degrees of authority over the population. The state may have lost part of its territorial control while keeping loosely aligned groups as a coalition to govern the country. They are constantly challenged or threatened by military insurgencies. The dependence on foreign forces (NATO in the current Afghan state; UN peacekeeping in the Democratic Republic of Congo) is inevitable to keep the governments alive. In the current state of Afghanistan, authority is limited to the capital city and surrounding areas. It is recognized de jure (as it was set up by the Western government) but does not actually function as a de facto state.

As a contrast with this example, Somaliland exists de facto, but not de jure (since other countries have yet to agree with its independent international legal status). The Taliban rule (1996–2001) was recognized only by Saudi Arabia and Pakistan despite its total control over Afghanistan's territory and population. By losing its legitimacy with bad governance, an existing state can degenerate into failure (e.g., Uganda's Idi Amin government, the current Mugabe regime). As they abuse their own populations, foreign governments withdraw their approval; the failure of governance is visible in an autocratic rule.

The fragmentation of political authority is one of the main characteristics of state collapse; quasi-governmental structures emerge outside of the state with significant proportions of the population under various factional control. Yet the loose control of the competing elite over their constituencies does not create sustained loyalty or help warlords deliver promises made in public. In the absence of mediating social institutions, mutually opposing militia forces prohibit any efforts to re-create new state institutions. In addition, protracted conflict in failed states is sustained by abnormal economic transactions. In a combat economy, conflict entrepreneurs search for resources in order to effectively wage

Table 6.1 The status of the Afghan state

	de facto control of territory and population by one group	*de jure (international recognition)*
Soviet military occupation (1979–1989)	No	No
Fighting among rival militia groups (1989–1995)	No	No
Taliban rule (1996–2001)	Yes	No
The Karzai government (since 2001)	No	Yes

war, while the majority of the population depends on a coping economy for survival. In conflict-torn societies (e.g., the Bosnian economy during the civil war in the early 1990s), a shadow economy is constituted by illicit activities.

Therefore, in general, failed states are characterized by structural vulnerability to violence often instigated by political tensions and inequality. Even though the majority of conflicts may have started with grievances originating from poverty and repression, the emergence of predator groups leads to rent-seeking or profit-taking activities involving corruption. In Afghanistan, the drug economy has continued to support the Taliban and warlords taking advantage of geographical isolation and political/social exclusion of the population.

The nature of civil war or other types of protracted violence is thus often molded by structural tensions within a state; order can be restored after regional or international intervention has brought about the cessation of fighting and disorder. The anarchy caused by fighting among several militia factions in Liberia (between 1989–1996) was ended by a joint military intervention force, the Economic Community Monitoring Group (sponsored by the 16-member Economic Community of West African States), opening the path for electoral competition and restoration of government services. On the contrary, the UN intervention in Somalia failed despite the existence of a peacekeeping operation; in addition, numerous conflict resolution attempts have not been successful, representing one of the most prolonged failed states in modern history.

Quasi-state

Even though their official political representation is not recognized internationally, some non-state political entities effectively control a significant proportion of territories and populations, setting up de facto administrative functions such as policing and taxation. Their rules are generally either tolerated, accepted or even actively endorsed due to the limits of existing state authority. In the absence of formalized official status, governance functions depend on informal networks of revenue generation and political support. Even though their international legal status has not been recognized by the UN or other international organizations, Somaliland has been successfully carved out of the chaotic process of state collapse in Somalia. In contrast with the almost anarchic state of their neighbor, Somaliland has proved to be a politically functioning entity with the established government structures run with a certain level of professionalism.

The north-western part of Sri Lanka, long occupied by Tamil Tiger forces, also established semi-government functions, including taxation, medical service, education and even issuance of passports. The region was constantly under pressure by the Sri Lankan military forces until the summer of 2009 when the Tamil Tigers were routed; thus their final official status was determined by a defeat on the battlefield instead of some kind of negotiated settlement. The long-term civil war in Sudan ended with the establishment of self-governance in southern Sudan where arrangements were made by a peace accord.

During the decades of civil war in Mozambique, Angola, El Salvador, and Guatemala, opposition forces maintained administrative rule in territories under their military control prior to their participation in an official political process after signing a peace accord. This is compared with more predatory relationships between warlord factions and the populations in Sierra Leone. The rebel groups in the Eastern Congo have occupied a large swath of territory, militarily pushing the government forces out of the region. The military strength of these groups has been boosted by neighboring countries (such as Rwanda) which support their kin groups on the other side of their border.

Hamas has provided all the ordinary government services in Gaza since 2006 despite the economic blockade by the Israeli government while the Fatah government maintains the official Palestinian government status in the West Bank. While they do not seek a politically and territorially independent status over the state of Lebanon, Hezbollah has run de facto administrative functions (supported by welfare service and armed capabilities). They have even proven militarily more capable of waging a war against Israel than the Lebanese armed forces. Ethiopia, Rwanda, and other cases demonstrate that well-organized rebel forces have a capacity to establish themselves to counter and eventually take over governing power.

Even though territorial annexation through war is not approved internationally, the victory in a short war (in 1993–1994) virtually enabled the Armenian enclave Nagorno-Karabakh within Azerbaijan to set up their own autonomous region (with a narrow corridor linked to Armenia). Since no state recognized the annexation, the enclave survives with various types of informal transactions with Armenia proper. On the contrary, Kosovo has maintained a quasi-state status under the UN administration, prior to the declaration of independence in 2008. The UN governance permitted Albanian Kosovars to elect government officials and run their own government with new legal codes separate from Serbia.

The unofficial status of these territories is characterized by their informal political, economic, or even military links to other groups or states. Semi-official political entities have sprung from a legitimacy crisis of existing states along with their weakening administrative capacity and absence of unifying identity. Nonofficial political territories develop even an implicit social contract between non-state actors and the populations. The informal ruling elite forge a dialectical relationship with their constituencies until their final political status is determined by the evolution of a conflict.

Extra-system environment

In addition to the interrelations of its elements, the system's operations (i.e., the maintenance of harmony in multi-ethnic societies) are bound by the extra-systemic input (such as agitation by kin groups in a neighboring state or the influx of refugees). For example, the long-term struggle of the Democratic Republic of Congo to restore order stems from the perpetuation of civil wars originating from the influx of Hutu refugees after the 1994 Rwandan civil war, the neighboring states' military intervention. Most civil wars and political instability in Burundi, Rwanda, Uganda, Sudan, Chad, the Democratic Republic of Congo, and elsewhere in Africa have been perpetuated by the external system pressure which preyed on the weak internal state capabilities to maintain order and unity.

In a broad sense, a system environment is constituted by "spatial, temporal, and sometimes symbolic space or set of conditions" (Littlejohn and Domenici, 2001, p. 125). The system's action affects its subsequent actions through the continuing feedback loop between the environment and system operations. In their mutual interaction, the operations of a system are linked to the environment through a more complex feedback process. In a two-way interaction of cybernetic control mechanisms, an action of the system may contribute to changes in the extra-system environment, while the environmental input sets parameters on the system's subsequent actions. In many weakly integrated societies, there is a great imbalance between intra-system's adaptation capabilities and external pressure (that often leads to disorder or civil war). On the other hand, stronger actors (e.g., the US) have a greater ability to control the input of the system or create a new system environment that changes behavior of other actors.

In cybernetics theories, self-guiding feedback loops are needed for the operation of systems through adaptive or learning behavior required for a response to input from its environment. Each system has to be constantly adjusted to new challenges arising from the environment. In this process, deviation from accepted standards is controlled and contained, contributing to a steady modification of the system. The abilities to overcome such challenges as refugee and militia flows from conflicts in neighboring countries are essential to prohibiting spillover effects. The close links between conflicts, for instance, in the Great Lakes region of Africa, expose a weak, vulnerable state capacity to external stress, thus requiring UN peacekeeping or other types of internal or regional support in compensation for weak internal conflict management mechanisms. Successful feedback through adjustment depends on a balance between the level of demand from the environment and the system's coping capabilities. The absence of internal abilities to prevent genocide or other types of mass violence has often called for humanitarian intervention.

Through feedback loops, negative influence needs to be self-corrected to perpetuate a steady state. Thus, adaptation is an essential function for system survival in a dynamic environment. Being faced with ethnic or racial violence, various legal and administrative mechanisms can be adopted to guarantee the promotion of diverse groups into leadership roles. Intra-organizational complaint procedures help manage grievances within institutional structures. These procedures and mechanisms can be further bound by labor laws or government regulations. The properly managed complaint systems can protect the company from such external intervention as expensive law suits and damage to its reputation. The social, economic, and political dynamics of an external system bring about changes in the actors' behavior and their interests over time through adaptive learning.

The functions of system boundaries can be featured by "the degree to which a society is open or closed to new groups, traditions and ideas" (Opotow, 2000, p. 409). Each system has different abilities to respond to a larger context of prevailing political, economic conditions through various methods of mobilization of available resources. For instance, Vietnam's socialist economy was gradually converted to a capitalist economic system by courting foreign investment and cultivating export market for its manufacturing goods.

A closed system is designed to minimize external pressure by blocking any information which threatens the system's core characteristics instead of permitting internal mechanisms to be adjusted to new or existing problems. North Korea is less vulnerable to external economic shocks since their "self-reliant" economic system is not closely connected to a free market economy (although a certain level of input is necessary such as importing oil and food). Their populations are adjusted to poverty and scarcity and have low expectations. However, once the system is opened up to outside contact and exchanges, its system can become suddenly vulnerable to the demand of more rapid and dramatic changes than can be handled by its existing capacity.

Some societies, the best example being China, open up their economic systems to the world economy while tightly controlling any information and demand which can potentially challenge the monopoly of power held by the communist party elite who do not any longer believe in socialism or state ownership of properties. Despite international sanctions, Burma, Sudan, and other autocratic countries (accused of gross human rights violations) are exposed partially to extra-system input by maintaining economic and diplomatic links with China and a few other countries which do not abide by international human rights norms. In general, a system based on oppression is less likely to respond to external shocks than a consent-based system, eventually exposing its weakness. In the case of Cuba, its system boundaries have been involuntarily restricted from the outside by the US long-term economic blockade.

Linkage politics

Various types of international system are associated with different conditions for intense violent struggles among state actors. The internal characteristics of societies prone to be engaged in external wars can be related to the emergence of aggressive government leaders (i.e., Saddam Hussein), the prominence of a military–industrial complex, a lack of socialization, and education promoting peacefulness. The examination by British economist John A. Hobson and Russian revolutionary Vladimir Lenin of the economic attributes of capitalist states at the turn of the past century uncovered crucial linkages between domestic interests and policies abroad. From Hobson's perspectives, expanding forces of modern capitalism fueled by rapid industrialization promote competition for resources and market, provoking imperialist wars. It is widely expected that the dwindling resource base in the future could create volatile conditions for competition among states over minerals in Antarctica and other parts of the world.

In neo-liberalist perspectives, the external and internal boundaries of a unit can be murky due to interconnected processes within and between the societies that underlie state action. International conflict is conceived of nonstatic nature of influence relationships. A dynamic process of international politics is shaped by changing realities and interests. In managing tensions in intra-state rivalry, "coalition across party lines" has been encouraged as a means for building support for conflict resolution. As the conflict is driven by domestic factors as much as the patterns of interaction between the two countries, the dynamics of conflict (composed of relationships between two societies) are dependent upon what is happening within each society.

In general, foreign policy behavior can be attributed to domestic interests and politics since a state is not a unitary actor (Wittkopf and McCormick, 2008). Internal divisions within each society put constraints on political leaders. The US position on the conflicts between Israelis and Palestinians has been, to a great extent, attributed to internal politics such as the influence of conservative Jewish lobbyist groups.

The conflict behavior of an internally repressive state is more oriented toward assuring power of the ruling elite. In particular, unpopular regimes may initiate provocative actions to diminish opposition (Argentina's initiation of the Falklands War in 1982). In the case of Iran, nuclear confrontation diverts pressure for domestic reform to the struggle with the West and Israel. Politicians even in democratic societies sometimes are likely to take hardline postures to build strong leader images as well as garnering popular support.

System and sub-systems

System level characteristics can be applied to diverse types of conflicts, ranging from intra- and inter-communal divisions (race, clan, class, sex, and religion) to regional hostilities, and international relations. In isolated, mountainous areas of Kurdistan (which is territorially divided among Turkey, Syria, Iran, and Iraq), the estimated 30 million Kurds have developed a common sense of ethnic identity through their struggle for autonomy and independence, but they are further divided along clan ties. Their tribal way of life has often hindered building greater unity since most Kurds are loyal to their tribal leaders who are often fighting among themselves (Helsing, 2004).

The disintegration of the Soviet Union has produced many ethnic conflicts in almost every newly independent state (i.e., Tajikistan, Kazakhstan, Moldova, Georgia, etc.) which include minority groups. The boundaries of a sub-system's activities can be determined by its interaction patterns with other sub-systems and the main system. Adversarial relationships at a sub-system level such as ethnic conflict may arise from various state characteristics (e.g., cultural exclusion, ideological differences, concentration of political power, and national rivalries).

The current world system is composed of a global capitalist economic system and loose international political order (Wallerstein, 1980). There are also overlapping sub-system boundaries (such as ethnic, bio-region, and state sovereignty boundaries). A hegemonic empire in past centuries embraced diverse ethnic groups and regions of the world under one system; war occurred less frequently within the empire even though occasional revolts were suppressed to maintain dominant rule within the system.

A conflict system may represent linkages and a web of overall relationships among the parties, illustrating each actor's behavior within more specific political, ideological, strategic, and economic arenas of sub-systems. The overall relationship between two actors can be constrained by an international system (for instance, Eastern and Western Europe during the Cold War period) which puts each actor's behavior and policy in opposing positions. Various features of a larger international system shape the relations between conflicting states whose effectiveness is associated with differential levels of military capabilities, internal political stability, technological advances, economic size, trade surplus, and national wealth. Specific conflict relationships may reflect large patterns of historical, social interactions over time. The decline in the US economic power has various ramifications, for instance, for the regional political economy of Latin America.

Component parts of international systems by themselves constitute their own systems in the sense that they, too, are made up of subordinate elements. The operations in the whole international system can be composed of the procedures and activities of international sub-systems ranging from regional economic and security arrangements (for example, the European Union, the OSCE, African Union, Western African Union), national systems, and national sub-systems. National dynamics (China's success in export and huge trade surplus) give rise to different patterns in global trade relations. At the same time, state behavior (for example, trade policies) is also shaped and constrained by forces below (supply of labor and wage levels) and above the national level (WTO rules).

The control of a conflict can be based on both the intra- and extra-system ability to put limits on escalatory dynamics. Intra-system limitations on conflict escalation include such inhibiting factors as institutionalized procedures and rules that manage communication in a crisis that can trigger an unwanted warfare. The crisscrossing of various exchange relations reduces the potentiality for bipolarization and enlargement of opposing groups focused on a single, superordinate conflict system.

A fragile international system of political and economic asymmetry has spawned much violence and terrorism. Intra-state conflicts are often molded by conditions that are external to the state. Many intractable conflicts are derived from a fragile international system which entails ambiguous roles and responsibilities of each state and uncertain power relations. The Western-backed Palestinian Fatah government's struggle with anti-Western Hamas in control of Gaza maintains its own dynamics, but at the same time it is influenced by the events and issues in a regional and international system that involves the US, Israel, Iran, and Egypt.

Within the current international system, many protracted conflicts involve civil wars, frequently being regionalized, as is the case with Darfur in Sudan. In Colombia, the informal economy run by drug cartels constitutes a sub-system of the overall conflict system. The local political economy of diamond and timber trade in Liberia, Sierra Leone, and Angola fueled ethnic warfare in the 1990s with revenue generation, but its operations were supported by international criminal economic interests.

Intra-state conflicts often spill over to an external environment. At the same time, internal conflicts can be intensified by external events. The Ferghana Valley in southern Kyrgyzstan bordering on Uzbekistan has been an incubator of multiple sources of conflicts, ranging from control over water resources and land to border tension along with inter-ethnic tensions. North–south political conflicts have also evolved over the control of Islamic radicals and criminal activities such as drugs and human trafficking. Political and social tensions in the south of Kyrgyzstan have been intensified by the displacement of Uzbeks across the border after the brutal oppression of an uprising in neighboring Uzbekistan's Andijan. The Uzbek dictator suppressed mass protest against flawed presidential elections in 2005 with many deaths and injuries as well as imprisonment. However, the 2005 defunct parliamentary elections in Kyrgyzstan resulted in ousting President Akaev through the Tulip revolution.

Various characteristics of regional sub-systems can be illustrated in terms of internal cohesiveness and stability of a power structure. For instance, the elites in control of Arabic states have diverse relationships to their populations with different means to maintain their power. The Arab sub-system is not cohesive, since Jordan, Egypt, Saudi Arabia, and other moderate states are closely linked to the West politically, and economically, while Iran and Syria take an anti-Western stance.

Different types of extra-system elements can either enhance or inhibit the possibilities of a conflict settlement. Such factors as US military aid to the Colombian government may influence a sustained armed conflict, since the aid reduces government incentives for negotiated settlements with its strengthened military capabilities. The US support for the Ethiopian military operation in Somalia legitimized external invasion, generating further animosities among local inhabitants. The outside pressure has inhibited the Sudanese government's ability to further justify atrocities in Darfur. The conflict-inhibiting external pressure has been balanced by conflict-enhancing factors such as the availability of oil export revenues used for the maintenance of government control over society.

De-escalation moves toward an eventual cessation of hostilities come from overcoming unregulated competitive relationships. Quite often external parameters can have a decisive impact on intervention actions and the course of a conflict. In the event of insufficient local initiatives, the incentives for continued fighting have to be created by the external, regional security systems such as the Organization of Security and Collaboration in Europe (OSCE). The level of capacity and commitment to enforcement actions, and the quality of decision-making institutions affect the outcome of any intervention. A lack of international intervention in the atrocities committed in Burma and Sudan is ascribed to either explicit or implicit opposition of such international actors as China and India to US and European efforts to the mandatory imposition of sanctions on the military governments. The international system has yet to establish a decisive authority committed to taking actions against killings and other types of human abuses.

Sub-system level conflict in Kashmir

The 1999 Kashmir insurgency and Pakistani incursion initiated a short civil war in the Vale region of the Indian states of Jammu and Kashmir. Pakistan dispatched hundreds of militants, Afghan Taliban volunteers and Islamic activists as well as troops to the Kargil area controlled by India in May 1999. India pushed them back, and Pakistan withdrew its contingents under US pressure. In July Pakistani prime minister Nawaz Sharif eventually accepted and expressed respect for the dividing line in Kashmir (Kalpakian, 2004).

This incident represents a complex ethno-political landscape composed of different alliances, often tacit, in Kashmir. Among 36 armed Kashmiri paramilitaries, 30 were supported by Pakistan and the remaining six had various arrangements with India. The insurgents themselves fought each other over whether Kashmir should join Pakistan or choose independence. Many Kashmir Muslims fear union with Pakistan in favor of independence for the Vale of Kashmir while other groups such as Ladakh preferred staying with India.

Muslims, including the Jammu and Kashmir Liberation Front (JKLF), wanted independent Kashmir since Islam practiced in Kashmir is overwhelmingly Sufi and anti-fundamentalist, differing from the varieties in Pakistan. JKLF was opposed by pro-Pakistani Kashmiri organizations, Pakistan, and India. Whereas JKLF and its rival Hizb-ul Mujahedin served as the main movement, they were challenged by numerous newly emerging organizations which varied in their numbers and scope of military operations.

Various groups developed tacit truce and outright cooperation with Indian and Pakistani forces. JKLF developed an implicit understanding with India but was rhetorically engaged in attacking India while organizing a few hostile incidents (such as kidnapping soldiers, though, quickly to be released) to retain its credibility with the Kashmiri public.

Boundaries between states and ethnic identity

Each society has diverse fault lines along ethnicity, class, religion, and language demarcations. The urban–rural tension in Thailand masks or is reinforced by other forms of cultural, religious, and economic division. The epicenters of conflict are isolated, poor regions of the country long neglected by the government in competition for resources. In Nepal, the aspirations of the rural educated middle and working classes were not met by an elite pact between the royalists and the urban middle class of the Congress Party which has brought about the democratic transition. In Afghanistan, religion has served as a powerful force for mobilizing and radicalizing groups; the Taliban recruited their support from those excluded from economic and political transitions.

In fact, groups can be motivated and mobilized by ideological convictions, political, and economic interests. In multi-ethnic states, internal homogeneity is measured in terms of size and degree of fragmentation of ethnic, religious groups. Depending on a focal point of a conflict, groups can be classified according to diverse social, cultural divisions such as race, class, sex, ethnicity, religion, occupation, generational differences, and wealth.

Structural sources of conflict in multi-ethnic societies can be attributed to incompatible system boundaries between states and ethnic groupings reinforced by differences in religion, language, customs, and income levels. In fact, many of these fault lines originate from the legacy of colonial rule and the creation of a modern state. Power relations can have historical origins; the British put a Sunni Arab from Arabia in charge of the majority population of Shi'ites. The current divisions between Sunnis and Shi'ites in Iraq may even be traced back to the British colonial period when Sunni Arabs were brought in to rule the Shi'ites.

Most importantly, cultural boundaries have often been ignored in the creation of a modern state (for instance, the collapse of the Austrian–Hungarian empire and Ottoman Turkey after World War I; independence of European colonial territories in Africa and Asia since World War II; disintegration of the Soviet Union and Yugoslavia; the territorial annexation of Tibet and East Turkestan to China after the civil war's ending in 1950). Consequently, ethnic rights to self-determination have collided with political control claimed by state sovereignty.

Hegemonic nation-building strategies in many newly independent states have resulted in inhibiting cultural autonomy of minority groups by imposing a dominant group language and religion on the entire population. The state formation of Tajikistan evolved over competition for expanded power and coalition building among clans and religious factions intermingled with traditional regional rivalries. During their independence talks, the English-speaking part of the population in Cameroon decided not to join Nigeria, but preferred being united with French-speaking Cameroon. Even though Nigeria uses English as the official common language, the English-speaking Cameroon population was fearful of their being subjugated to Nigeria's strict Muslim laws.

Insurgencies may pursue secession or some form of autonomous status, seeking new political order through regime changes. Eritrea became independent after a long Ethiopian civil war ended in May 1991. Bangladesh achieved its independence after India's military intervention in March 1971. Greater autonomy was granted to Aceh along with the first local elections introduced by a peace accord in 2005. There are countries where central governments do not fully control all the territories, exemplified by self-declared autonomous regions of South Ossetia and Abkhazia in Georgia, Transnistria in Moldova, and Sudan's southern autonomous government as well as tribal regions in the north-western regions of Pakistan bordering Afghanistan.

Different properties of a system characterize the sources of conflict, creating complex interrelationships. The sources of identity may consist of language, religion, etc., but different elements can be emphasized in a nation-state building process. To prevent intra-state conflict, the relations between majority and minority groups need to become fluid, in the long run, with a shift in political arrangements and toleration of diverse cultural identities as well as the promotion of equitable economic development.

The imposition of state hegemony: Bangladesh

Despite noticeable exceptions such as Switzerland, Belgium, the Netherlands, Canada, and other Western pluralistic democracies, the hegemonic nature of a modern state structure (reflected in constitutions and institutions) in many multi-ethnic states has not been equipped to embrace all the groups in society. The state institutions and constitutions of the newly born state of Bangladesh (after its independence from Pakistan in 1970) have embodied the hegemony of the Bengali "nation" over the non-Bengalis. As the newly born state of Bangladesh emphasizes unity and solidarity of the Bengali nation, religion, culture, and language often serve as the instruments of domination and assimilation. The superimposed identity derived from its dominant language and culture has put other groups in a marginalized position (Moshin, 2005).

Even though Bangladesh contains 45 different ethnic communities, the constitution and state institutions (based on the notion of a homogeneous Bengali state) have failed to recognize the political and cultural diversity of the newly born state. In fact, this is a reflection of the hegemonic idea of power embedded in the creation of a modern state. Whereas the Chittagong Hills and other tribal areas have demanded constitutional safeguards such as political and economic autonomy for their protection as a separate community, the government has insisted on only one state identity, "Bengali nationalism." The political elite representing the dominant "Bengali" population solidified hegemonic rule imposed on "separate communities" within the state of Bangladesh by adopting the 1972 Bangladesh constitution that recognizes only one official language and culture to the resentment of the marginalized other.

Separatism in Moldova

As Moldova became independent after the collapse of the Soviet Union in 2001, major political parties (representing the majority of the population) wanted to impose their ethnic language Moldovan (a dialect of Romanian) on the Russian enclave "Transdnestra." This attempt was vehemently resisted by the dominant Russian-speaking population in the enclave. Even though Moldova was annexed to Russia as part of treaty prior to World War II, the boundaries have not been clear due to the influx of large numbers of workers to man the industries of Transdnestra as well as ties created between Moldova and Russia.

An even bigger concern was the reunion with Romania proposed by one of the main political parties. In addition, the central government proposed broadening the industrial base geographically by relocating industrial plant in Transdnestra. The concerns about the nature of governance was even strengthened by the Moldovans' desire to move closer to a European market economy. On the other hand, Transdnestra wanted to remain closer to the Commonwealth of Independent States (led by Russia). These concerns and anxieties led Transdnestrans to declare independence, provoking a civil war in 1992. Even though their de jure statehood was not recognized internationally, Transdnestra has maintained de facto independence.

Network analysis

The structure of a multitude of conflict relationships can be illuminated from the network analysis framework. As a principal unit of analysis, a network provides the links that tie together actors or agents. The ties between units can represent various types of relationships. Relational ties can be described by density and proximity of activities based on shared meanings and understanding among actors. An alteration in actor activities or behavioral interactions can stimulate changes in other parts of a network structure such as a flow of resources, material transactions, or patterns of alliance. In civil war situations, the effects of military and quasi-military activities are manifested in political alliance building, war financing efforts or even negotiations to end the war.

The nature of actors involved in a conflict has become more amorphous along with the fluid boundaries of activities; the expanded social networks (with the addition of splinter groups) sway each actor's behavior. There are diverse types of anti-system groups, ranging from Zapatistas (which led the rebellion in Mexico to demand indigenous people's rights) to global social and environmental movements in Brazil and other nonviolent anti-globalization movements. Protest groups promote interests, values, and identities that have not been favored by the existing order. In considering that dynamic interconnectedness is crucial for empowerment and solidarity building, network mapping has been utilized to identify the emergence and disappearance of conflict groups.

The external and internal boundaries of cross-border networks are connected through ethnic, political, or economic links. Conflict boundaries cut across the regional networks of war. As seen in Sudan, multiple internal insurgencies can be organized around competing agendas, being supported by foreign sponsors. By claiming security threats, various coalitions of states joined the Second Congolese War (1998–2003) in support of local militias. Realignments among the numerous state and non-state actors emerge with varying degrees of mutual support and mobilization.

Opposing network structures stimulate competition among armed groups mobilized by diverse motivations ranging from political grievances to economic interests. Pathological network structures of militia organizations in Uganda and the Democratic Republic of Congo have been responsible for the terrorization of local populations by systematic murder, rape, and forced labor. Destructive warfare is supported by "the extraction of natural resources and the exploitation of civilians for self-financing wars." The instruments of violence promote "private interests for control over valuable resources" despite a dismal economic condition of a war-torn society (Carayannis, 2005, p. 85). A personal fiefdom of warlord insurgencies weakens state institutions and control. In conflict situations (along with institutional decay or malfunctioning), the development of informal, influence networks (e.g., smuggling, logging, etc.) contributes to the creation of lawless conditions.

Formal and informal network structures

Networks can be compared in terms of governance structures, adaptations of goals, core values, decision-making procedures, and mobilization capacities (funding and identification of member interests) as well as information and action flows. Decentralized, flat and fluid organizational structures develop open boundaries; on the other hand, hierarchical control is often maintained by bureaucratic structures. Networks (involved in the promotion of peace) have inclusive boundaries as seen by the activities of Green Peace, Friends of the Earth, etc.

In conflict escalation, radical groups with rigid boundaries often exacerbate violent situations; hate groups withdraw from a wider community, enforcing violence on a society with terrorism. Violent conflict networks exemplified by al-Qaeda, the Irish Republican Army (IRA), and the Basque terrorist group ETA, are exclusive and secret, being maintained by cell structures. The IRA attempted to maintain a strict discipline through secret executions of internal informers.

While some networks have a high degree of factionalism, others are relatively harmonious or unified. Networks (created for particular issues) may disappear after a certain period, while others may last longer with ambitious ideological or political aims. Given the inevitability of different degrees of participation in network operations, some play a more prominent role in setting general aims. In a hierarchical coalition, patrons provide resources for fighting and lay down specific goals for their subordinates' activities. Even though Hezbollah was created by Iran after the Lebanese War in 1982, it developed a significant level of capability to fight on its own.

A network's scope can be global or regional, differing in the degree of specialization and the level of control and impermeability in decision making. The functions of networks are shaped by internal decision-making structures. Small and egalitarian network structures encourage equal participation of members in decision making with shared costs and benefits. On the other hand, hierarchically organized decision-making structures are likely to emerge from the necessity to manage a high level of functional differentiation and specialization.

Network structures are characterized by a shared common purpose, rules of conduct, self-organizing responses to constituents' needs, and capacity building. Voluntary and equal relationships for organizing joint activities lead to the development of coordinating networks. The range of interdependent relationships can be expanded to much larger, more fluid and anonymous communities through shared value systems.

Central network nodes are involved in goal clarifications, development of structures and norms. Broadening contacts and activities may result in a shift in interests in tandem with the diversification of resource and knowledge bases. While new networks emerge, old networks can be transformed to cope with different tasks (from nonviolent protest to guerrilla warfare). The Tamil Tiger forces (fighting against the Sri Lankan government) initially started with protest student movements and switched to terrorist attacks and then fully armed military resistance. Some networks evolve into formal organizational structures and even take over government functions after military victory over their adversary or a peace accord (e.g., rebel movements in Ethiopia and Sudan). Thus structure changes along with the evolution of conflict from military struggle to governance. Organizational changes (from hierarchically organized guerrilla groups to democratic political parties) occur in a post-conflict settlement. For instance, Mozambican National Resistance (RENAMO) in Mozambique and Farabundo Martí National Liberation Front (FNLM) in El Salvador participated in post-civil war elections, taking parliamentary seats representing their own constituents. This type of transition is often supported by foreign donors who have sponsored a peace process.

Field theory and conflict

In field theory (Lewin, 1997), the existence of contending social and psychological forces (defined as various movement vectors) shapes individual behavior in the world of human interaction. In delineating latent and manifest patterns of interactions, field theory develops a general framework that links behavior to the basis of actor characteristics. Thus the behavior of actors and their mutual influence are projected on the basis of their attribute properties (van Atta, 1973). The distance between two or more actors in rank-ordered sets of positions is created by relative power, value differences, and economic status inequality. Both the magnitude and direction of social distance are significant to the analysis of actor relationships. The relative distance between social units on attribute dimensions (e.g., economic wealth, etc.) can reflect their attitudes and behavior toward each other.

The social distance between poor and rich countries at international meetings of debt relief can be perceived in terms of the participants' economic status, ideologies (state controlled versus free market), and post-colonial trade linkages. The social, psychological distance between the US and Canada is different from the relationships between the US and Mexico, reflecting diverging political history, economic status, and cultural values. This distance generates different structures of expectations regarding the levels of capabilities, power, and interests.

The concept of "a field" illustrates a mutual influence of social units irreducible to an individual organization's rules, goals, rewards, and sanctions. Society is conceived of as a field of tension, conflict, and power struggles between different social roles and segments. The field contains diverse vehicles manifesting our values and norms in correspondence with our interpretation of a socio-cultural world. Each reality is endowed with different meanings attached to dichotomous value judgments such as good and bad, strong and weak.

Field theory can illustrate such actor dispositions as power and role differentials which have an impact on the formation of each party's goals, motives, and attitudes. Interaction patterns between individual actors are explained by a distance vector on such attributes as wealth and prestige. The distance vectors in inter-group relationships reflect various features of socio-cultural space (composed of differences in language, religion, ethics, law, power, and class). Threat perceptions are formed by the awareness of opposing relationships (originating from incompatible values, unequal power distribution, and access to resources) over time.

Field forces (indicative of different capabilities, interests, and will) can explain the inter-action of multiple actors. In competition for power and status, a variety of pulling and pushing forces eventually have to be balanced with the creation of different rules represent-ing a new status quo. Human decision-making processes are associated with expectations that arise from diverse status and positions (for instance, different bargaining positions of buyers and sellers in a housing market).

For instance, competing attitudes toward free trade and currency manipulation held by the US and China stem from impulses behind a commitment to antagonistic interests and opposing values. As different psychological forces (embedded in organizational and social contexts) motivate or inhibit particular types of behaviors, "people are passive in one setting but aggressive in other settings" (Heitler, 1990, p. 5). If the perceived threats at work encourage the adoption of a competitive tactic, a person, seen as collaborative by friends or family members, can become assertive in a hostile organizational setting. In this situation, identifying systemic forces affecting organizations is essential to conflict man-agement so that any dispute is not interpreted in the context of enemy relationships with co-workers.

Psychological dispositions and behavioral manifestation

According to Lewin and other social psychologists, a psychological field consists of stimuli and their effects in social relations, often being characterized by the amount of friction (such as tension). The psychological climate supports or inhibits certain attitudes by creat-ing trust or mistrust as well as promoting open or closed communication. A behavioral dimension can be attributed to the interests, needs, goals, and capabilities of actors relative to others.

In mutually oriented interactions, one's behavior can be intended to influence another's subjective experiences, but it may not bring about the intended outcomes. Behavior explains goal-oriented activities but at the same time is bound by rules, norms, or habits. Psychological dispositions reflect, in part, shared subjective universes (such as identity). If our misperception of others leads to conflict, it can be settled by either corrected percep-tions or restoration of a balance enabling both parties to accommodate diverse viewpoints embedded in the multiplicity of structures of expectations.

In fact, different kinds of behavior are mainly associated with diverse structures of expectations. The bonding relationships of families (based on love and affection in a parent/child relationship) are manifested in selfless behavior directed toward the protection of each other's welfare and aid. The shared sense of destiny and affection can also be found in feelings of ethnic and other types of group loyalty along with a mutual and total involve-ment of interests, concerns, and empathy. At the same time, the relationship can change over time with the development of new expectations.

Socio-psychological space and conflict

The incongruence between a structure of expectations and existing power relations pro-duces a pressure for rebalancing through manifestation of conflict. All interaction is either a struggle for rebalancing (conflict behavior) or cooperative interaction reaffirming a stable structure of expectations. A mismatch between structures of power relations and values for their justification produces a demand for change.

National self-images are represented in the conceptions of one's status and role in the international system. The new structure of expectations (accompanied by material and social changes) may be inconsistent with old values or norms. It is visibly expressed in the reactions of fundamentalist Islam to modernizing forces that promote the equal economic and political status of women. The disruptions in structures of stable expectations are often manifested in war, revolution, or other types of violence.

Global communication, intellectual innovations, new ideas, and technological developments create a constant need for adjustment between values, institutions, and the environment. Inconsistencies (in religious beliefs, ideology, institutions) produce social tension, and its solution might be imposed by military or other forms of force (as illustrated by the Algerian military's veto of an election result won by an Islamic party in 1993). The established structure of expectations supports the legitimization of the existing distribution of rights and privileges.

The likelihood of a demand for a change (such as income redistribution through changes in tax laws or revenue sharing of mineral export) reflects the incongruence between new value expectations and the existing power structure. The active pursuit of a new status by an emerging group generates direct confrontation with other groups which have equal determination to protect their status. Social order is recreated by the acceptance of new rules, agreements, and contracts following changes in the structure of expectations over time. Despite strong interests and wants, the party may not have sufficient capabilities to pursue their goals (Marcus, 2000). Different structures of expectations need to be readjusted through bargaining.

Field forces and change

As a recursive patterning of human behavior in time–space, structure is not static, creating new rules and conditions that will have to be eventually changed. Values are formed in justifying certain types of the structure/agent relationship. Structures can be inter-subjectively understood, reproduced, or transformed by the practice of constituting agents who have different degrees of capacity and commitment to institutional changes (Giddens, 1986).

In social transformative perspectives, conflict resolution may aim to disturb the dominant understanding that functions to perpetuate social and political hierarchies by uncovering their historically contingent origin and political role. In doing so, it can contribute to exploring a social space that favors autonomy and tolerance of differences. Identities and interests are interpreted in a specific social space in which symbols and meanings represent reality.

Conflict is essential to unfreezing the status quo by overcoming the forces of resistance by those who have the greatest interest in preserving the system (Marcus, 2000). If there is a high level of tension (for instance, being associated with such system failures as inflation, unemployment, or the rise of authoritarian leaders), a particular event can more easily turn into conflict. In bringing about change, the forces which drive an anti-status quo have to be relatively stronger than the resisting forces.

Envisioning a desired future state is essential to the establishment of a goal and purpose of unfreezing, as well as being open to something different. If human action is regarded as part of the continuous flow of causation toward an envisioned future, the creation of a transition state (designed to obtain a desirable outcome) should be based on the assessment of the current state. Learning involves understanding differences and similarities between current and past experiences as well as interpretation of their context.

Further reading

Giddens, A. (1986) *The Constitution of Society*, Berkeley: University of California Press.

Legro, J. W. (2005) *Rethinking the World: Great Power Strategies and International Order*, Ithaca, NY: Cornell University Press.

Lewin, K. (1997) *Resolving Social Conflict, and Field Theory in Social Science*, Washington, DC: American Psychological Association.

Marcus, E. C. (2000) "Change Processes and Conflict," in D. Morton and C. Peter (eds) *The Handbook of Conflict Resolution*, San Francisco: Jossey-Bass Publications.

Rummel, R. J. (1976) *Understanding Conflict and War*, Beverly Hills: Sage Publications.

Part III

Settlement and resolution procedures

7   Conceptions and practice

Diverse procedures exist to respond to various types of problems at personal, communal, and international levels. Disagreements over responsibility and liability (arising, for instance, from ordinary social settings) can be overcome by direct negotiation, mediation, or law suits with the application of established rules and regulations. In the international arena, governments can refer their territorial disputes to an international court system instead of fighting if direct negotiation or mediation fails. However, these formal methods (confined to handling "pure" interests-based disputes) have not proven adequate to balance the diverse needs of partisans in ethnic or class conflicts that tend to easily ignite violence.

This chapter examines diverse ways to manage and resolve issues emerging from adversarial engagement in the pursuit of incompatible goals. Given the costs of destructive conflicts in the contemporary world, a creative approach to problem solving is essential. Keeping that in mind, we need to approach a wide range of theories and practices involved in the development of conflict regulation mechanisms. In managing a conflict process and determining its outcome, various approaches can be compared in terms of decision-making power, institutional roles, communication patterns, etc. In particular, the chapter will examine different intermediary roles (from fact finding to enforcement) and the context of intervention. These functions and activities will be covered in a discussion about adjudication, arbitration, mediation, negotiated rule making, and facilitated group processes.

Principles

In responding to conflict, parties may take different approaches to problems. Whereas fights over land use among neighbors and complaints about late payment of rent can be handled within the existing contract system, serious communal conflicts resist settlement within the existing channels of dispute resolution. Economic and environmental policies may invite resistance from those who are negatively affected, sometimes pitting the government against their constituents. If established institutional mechanisms are available to protect a weaker side, decisions on the award can be rendered in compensation for a legal or contractual violation of rights.

An interest-based framework can be applied to settling price differences or land disputes. It encourages a compromise based on the division of loss and gains. The use of a stakeholder approach is applied widely to community problem solving which requires the cooperation of all parties involved. A needs-based approach seeks coexistence based on the agreement of the removal of exploitative and oppressive relationships (Bingham and Nabatchi, 2003). Symmetric relationships can be sought by recognizing different identities and respecting each other's dignity.

Protection of rights

The protection of rights can be a main goal in the restoration of justice. Rights-based approaches range from a court verdict and arbitration to grievance procedures. The violation of rights or harm caused by governments, corporations, or other individuals can be rectified by a series of measures comprised of the recognition of past abuses, apologies, compensation, and the reinstitution of the victim's dignity. Often confrontational strategies need to be adopted if the abusers deny past injustices and continue to harbor antagonistic attitudes toward victims. Support groups can be formed to provide advocacy in defending the legal, moral, and political rights of the abused.

Depending on the goals of the parties and nature of issues, arbitration, litigation, and victim–offender mediation can be utilized. If the fairness of judges is guaranteed, the ruling of court procedures can provide remedies for a weaker party. The verdicts on war criminals in former Yugoslavia and Rwanda as well as Liberia have brought justice to those who are responsible for genocidal acts. International Criminal Court prosecutors also issued charges against the Sudanese leader who ordered the attacks which caused the death of many civilians as well as some international peacekeeping soldiers.

The context of the application of rights approaches through a judicial process is widely different between domestic and international conflicts. International systems do not have strong legal mechanisms in the protection of victims (in such areas as human rights). In particular, legal settlement is not always easy given the insufficient enforcement power of a supranational authority. The support from relevant governments has been necessary in indicting those responsible for genocidal acts in Bosnia and Rwanda by the International Courts of Justice. Under the condition that the law is based on the equal treatment of every disputant, a court system protects the rights of individuals. The European Court of Human Rights (established by the European Convention on Human Rights of 1950) protects individual citizens' civil rights by allowing them to sue their own government.

In domestic arenas, the application of rights-based approaches to justice through adjudication also has to overcome many obstacles. Institutional deficiency and gross power imbalance between perpetrators and victims permit the powerful to manipulate the justice system. The judgment can be skewed due to a lack of judicial independence when the fairness of the process is subject to political authority. Thus, the victims of injustice and abuses (by military or police forces) may not always be able to have access to or afford to have competent representation to challenge institutional power. For instance, activist lawyers in China were barred from defending Tibetan protesters at court. In Colombia, powerful paramilitary groups confiscated the land of peasants in tandem with widespread abuse and killing in the last decade, but the persecution of paramilitary warlords has been sabotaged due to their close connections to key figures in the government and judicial system.

Given the insufficient institutionalization of legal mechanisms (related to resistance of powerful abusers), some processes are limited to fact finding in support of exploring truth and making policy recommendations. Fact finding (for instance, being conducted by OSCE) has been widely used to detect the violation of minority rights in preventing the eruption of conflicts. Past abuses cannot be simply ignored, and many post-conflict societies have established the Truth and Reconciliation Commission (TRC). Whereas the South African Commission played a powerful role in the country's transition to a post-apartheid democracy, institutional power can obstruct the process by using intimidation. In

Guatemala and El Salvador, some panel members were even subjected to personal threats by the military who were engaged in mass killings. Respect for institutionalized norms and authority (which guarantee an objective process of judgment and decision-making power) by all parties is essential to the success of a rights-based approach.

Interests

Interests-based bargaining models are suitable for organizational, industrial, matrimonial, and other types of dispute that do not involve widespread violence, confrontations with authorities, or defiance of legal norms. According to some negotiation models (Fisher and Ury, 1983), interest bargaining is favored over contests of power in conjunction with the discouragement of emotions. A compromise (which entails a division of losses and gains) can be obtained either by negotiation or mediation. Issues are framed in terms of manifest interests, but the process is not appropriate when responding to underlying grievances and deeper concerns or needs.

Effective negotiation skills or adequate representation of interests in a bargaining process are essential to guaranteeing a fair outcome. The adequate protection of a weaker party's interests can help avoid the domination of most powerful parties in bargaining. In a hierarchical relationship, mediation can serve the purpose of co-optation by powerful groups which want to manage conflicts to their advantage, restricting the political agenda (Amy, 1987).

The "utilitarian value of the greatest good to the greatest number" is applied to interest-based approaches. In particular, non-judicial alternative dispute resolution methods such as mediation have been advocated for being cost-efficient in settling disputes which might have otherwise been protracted by involving unnecessary emotions and power struggles. It is speedy given that it is not being affected by court case loads. Non-judicial settlement is known for informality, because private arrangements are not governed by official rules. Its private and personal nature is characterized by the fact that parties develop their own rules and guidelines. It offers a more relaxed atmosphere than a full adversarial trial.

Needs-based approach

Less tangible issues of self-esteem and respect are often enmeshed with territorial or other types of tangible objects that antagonists fight over. In the Israel–Palestinian conflict, for example, interests (tangible, such as land and water) are associated with identity (intangible). Some issues such as the protection of marginalized parties' essential needs for survival cannot be compromised, while the control of global warming and other environmental issues is essential to the well-being of the current and future generations of humans. The significance of these issues needs to be recognized rather than being compromised for powerful interests or sustenance of the status quo in an existing system.

Coexistence is feasible only through the recognition of inviolable human conditions for survival and well-being. Thus facilitation can often play an educational role in engaging parties in a dialogue to recognize the necessity of changes in behavior or policies. The accommodation of a weaker party's needs by a powerful party lies, in part, in the realization of self-interests embedded in a shared future. For instance, the white minority regime in South Africa voluntarily gave up their power for the sake of long-term stability and continuing economic prosperity. This was the same principle behind the Oslo Peace Accord although the Palestinian–Israeli peace process was derailed because of prevalence of hawkish factions within each party which refused to see the benefit of mutual coexistence in favor of an attempt to dominate.

The need for structural change can become part of the conflict resolution process. The analysis of needs to be satisfied is necessary for the resolution of protracted conflict between hostile ethnic and racial groups. In contrast with labor–management or other types of interest-based disputes, ethnic struggles or other identity-based conflict cannot be managed by a focus on contractual relationships. More specifically, ethnic struggles or other identity-based conflict often demand changes in laws or other political arrangements.

Settlement activities

There are a range of approaches to handling conflict from passive avoidance to active engagement. A diverse spectrum of conflict management methods is represented by inaction, informal discussion, negotiation, mediation, arbitration, administrative rules, judicial decision, legislative vote, nonviolent protest, and other direct action. Inaction via avoidance leaves decisions to chance (Sidaway, 2005). While avoidance has low assertiveness, it entails low cooperation. In the event of the existence of rights violations, such formal procedures as fact-finding missions can be designed to detect the problem and to produce an early response to a potential for escalation. Direct, representative, or facilitated negotiations can be conducted to bring about voluntary settlement after the mitigation of hostilities.

Self-control over the outcome decreases when settling differences between the parties is left with a third-party judgment. Through arbitration or judicial trial, authoritative judgments can be made to award one of the disputants. A win–lose struggle does not become destructive if the rules are fair, acceptable and applied to everyone. In this case, an official decision-making body (such as a government arbitration board or court) is recognized as a neutral referee. Legislative and administrative decisions often reflect the nature of the power balance and imbalance among various interest groups in society. The failure of existing institutional mechanisms to meet the salient interests or needs of key social groups may lead to either nonviolent or violent protests.

Mechanisms to manage conflict have a wide variety of formality (from institutionalized procedures sanctioned by law to facilitated dialogue among various types of stakeholders). Formal procedures are firmly backed by existing laws and administrative power, whereas informal settlement depends on goodwill and trust among the disputants. In mediation and facilitation, power to settle the conflict is ultimately in the hands of the disputants, since both the settlement process and outcome should be acceptable to them. A more complex process involves multiple participants in a public setting (e.g., the 1991 Madrid conference which searched for international consensus on resolving the Arab–Israeli conflict).

Depending on the circumstances (a breakdown of communication or difficulties in reaching an agreement), the assistance of a third party is essential in ending disputes. They can help straighten distorted facts, deliver a message or propose terms for a negotiated settlement. Building sustainable relationships is important in many pre-negotiation interventions. Facilitation helps eliminate misperceptions generated by a lack of communication. When the agreement is tenuous or the situation is volatile, intervention can be geared toward guaranteeing the implementation of settlement or supporting the rules.

The adoption of specific skills depends not only on the context of dispute but also the nature of the existing relationships between the parties as well as the goals of conflict resolution. Some methods would support quick settlement or prevention of escalation by engaging each party in dialogue or even by force. It can be complicated to negotiate opposing interests originating from deeply divided social structures (e.g., Sri Lanka and

Colombia). In resolving differences, the replacement of coercive tactics with persuasion is the most democratic and sustainable way of responding to a conflict. Many conflict resolution methods are geared toward the cultivation of the atmosphere of trust, understanding, and exchange of views that will ultimately lead to an agreement. This process may require a problem solving spirit as well as collaborative communication.

Types of settlement methods

Diverse procedural means favor varied modes of decision making and related attributes. The adequacy of each procedure depends on the conflict's psychological orientations as well as its substantive characteristics. Voluntary settlement activities such as negotiation and mediation are oriented toward a compromise of interests, but the main tasks of arbitration and litigation are related to the production of fair judgments about the rights and entitlement of disputants. Approaches vary in terms of whether the primary focus will be on resolving substantive issues or managing a relationship. In settling differences in interdependent (intimate or ally) relationships, a power contest can be substituted for a desire to preserve harmony.

Settlement methods are compared more specifically in terms of various degrees of formality, favored communication patterns, as well as types of pursued outcomes. In mediation and other facilitated processes, an intermediary has no decision-making authority to impose settlement. Thus, the qualities of negotiated settlements depend very much on effective communication between primary disputants. However, there is no direct interaction between protagonists in arbitration or judicial proceedings except an attempt to convince judges or juries to believe in the validity of exclusive claims. In judicial procedures, the imposition of a third-party decision eliminates the necessity for a direct form of communication between protagonists.

Judicial settlement is oriented toward delivering decisions without any concern about relationship consequences, but in facilitative methods, the settlement of issues is pursued by the creation of a non-adversarial atmosphere and trust relationships. The inadequacies of formal decision-making mechanisms are ascribed to a lack of control over both the process and outcome by disputants. The development of informal procedures is based on a necessity to seek non-adversarial, collaborative solutions to the problems.

The process of conflict settlement is molded by the different roles of the intervening parties, means of influence, and time constraints. When parties are collaborative, amicable solutions can be deduced from open discussion in tandem with the communication aid of facilitators. The clarification of issues along with reduced tension is necessary before the parties are ready to talk at formal mediation. Low levels of collaboration in a highly competitive situation create an obstacle to the search for a mutually satisfactory outcome. In general, arbitration is more suitable for sorting out issues which have a clear definition and a high demand for fairness.

One method does not need to be incompatible with other methods in its application. For instance, mediation can turn into direct negotiation between the two sides if trust is built during the initial stage of assisted contacts. In divorce or other types of inter-personal disputes, parties feel more pressure in compulsory mediation ordered by courts than in voluntary settings (Spencer and Brogen, 2006). The failure of mediation can lead to arbitration or judicial decision making.

The types of decision-making authority and roles held by a third party shape a settlement process and its outcomes. By moving "from negotiation to judicial processes, the choices become more formal, more costly, more distributive than integrative in outcome and more adversarial" (Isenhart and Spangle, 2000, p. 24). Neutral observers, process managers, and judges have different responsibilities for the final outcomes. Parties have more power to control the content of final settlement in negotiation, mediation, and facilitation vis-à-vis arbitration and judicial processes.

Evaluative decision making

Judicial and arbitration processes are characterized by making an award based on the rules of evidence and supporting facts in conjunction with the evaluation of the merit of the claims made by each of the adversaries. Thus evidence/fact-based cases are more susceptible to decision-making modes dominated by a judge or arbitrator. Decision-making rules and procedures are more easily relaxed and informal in a quasi-judicial process. If disputants are allowed to choose their own judges or arbitrators, it can greatly reduce a lot of uncertainties. A decision regarding material interests can be made by arbitration, but a third-party decision is not effective in dealing with the issues of feelings. In addition, legal proceedings and arbitration do not provide an appropriate format to discuss value differences. They do not prevent an irreconcilable breakdown in the relationship between the parties, since facts and laws cannot deal with emotional problems and incompatible values.

Judicial decisions

In judicial decision making, parties in disputes have little control over not only the process but also outcomes. They cannot choose a judge or jury who delivers a verdict on their cases. Court arguments are guided by precedents and legal norms rather than an analysis of the values and needs of the disputants. The decisions by judicial authorities are generally binding and enforceable. As a formal legal process, adjudication can handle disputes in the areas of property rights between individuals, an election result and territorial disputes between states.

The heart of the legal system is the hierarchical relationship between the judge and all other actors in the courtroom drama (Lynch, 2005). As a controlled process, litigation involves proof before judges. Given that their primary purpose is to efficiently produce a decision outcome, a judicial process is not an effective means of exploring the root causes of problems. Formal and binding decisions of the court do not always reflect immediate social concerns and human well-being. As a traditional method, court settlements are oriented toward the maintenance of the status quo.

To predict formal court decisions, parties may utilize a mini-trial where private judges make nonbinding decisions after hearing the evidence and arguments. Through informal procedures, disputants can observe how their presentations will be accepted in front of a panel presided over by a neutral judge. The predicted outcome assists disputants in reaching a reasonable settlement without being exposed to the disadvantages of formal judicial decision-making mechanisms (such as high expenses and publicity). Thus the whole objective of mini-trials and summary jury trials is education about a specific case's relative strengths. Mini-trial agreement allows for frank, open, and confidential discussion without the fear of backlash or retribution (Ross and Conlon, 2000).

The International Court of Justice (ICJ) provides verdicts on a wide range of issues from territorial sovereignty, land and maritime boundaries, and nationality to economic rights (Merrills, 2005). Since the Corfu Channel (involving the United Kingdom versus Albania) was submitted in May 1947, 140 cases were considered by October 2008. Only sovereign states can submit their cases, in general, with the consent of the other country. The court holds compulsory jurisdiction over cases stipulated by bilateral and multilateral treaties as well as those submitted by states. In the above case, the court ruled that Albania should compensate for the loss of crew members of British naval vessels caused by the Albanian maritime mines. Some other well-known cases include the harmful effects of French nuclear tests submitted separately by Australia and New Zealand (1973) and disputes over fisheries' jurisdiction in the North Atlantic filed against Iceland by Germany and the United Kingdom (1972).

Even though the court itself has no enforcement power, their decisions are binding. The failure to satisfy the obligations can lead to recourse at the UN Security Council. Most states have carried out the court's decisions, but one of notable exception is the United States' refusal to pay reparations to the Sandinista government of Nicaragua in 1986. The court's decisions are regarded as legitimate by the international community. The ICJ also provided an advisory opinion submitted by United Nations organs and specialized agencies regarding admission to the UN and the territorial status of South West Africa (Namibia) and the Western Sahara. They are only consultative, but are taken seriously. In its July 2004 decision on the Israeli security fence (requested by the UN General Assembly), the ICJ called on Israel to dismantle sections built in the West Bank and East Jerusalem by citing Israel's violation of international law.

Arbitration

The arbitrator provides disputants with an opportunity to be heard and considers all the presented claims with supporting facts and evidence prior to rendering an award which is final. Communication patterns are characterized by the procedures in which both parties make arguments, respond to the other side, and answer arbitrators' questions at a hearing. Since participants have to assent to accept the outcome, goodwill, trust, and cooperation between parties are not required. Impartial judgment is the most important reference point of arbitration.

In weighing the merits of a case, arbitrators consider objective factual matters. The major concerns for arbitrators ought to be fairness, impartiality, equity, good conscience, and natural justice. Expert arbitration examines complex questions of fact which are central to the dispute in terms of objective criteria. A question of legal interpretation or technical assessment of practical problems can be more easily applied to such areas as property or other material damages as well as different interpretations of commercial contracts. In international trade disputes, the World Trade Organization has a wide range of authority to hear complaints and provide rulings for binding decisions.

Most importantly, the Permanent Court of Arbitration has been involved in managing border disputes and other international conflicts. The Permanent Court of Arbitration (PCA) established in 1899 has responded to international dispute resolution needs of states, state entities, inter-governmental organizations, and private parties. Tribunals and commissions under the auspices of the PCA have examined not only territorial and human rights disputes between states but also commercial and investment disputes (e.g., gold mine companies versus Krygyz Republic after the mid-2000s). Parties can select their own arbitrators, but the PCA can be called upon to designate or appoint them. In the aftermath of armed conflict in Abyei, the government of Sudan and the Sudan People's Liberation Movement/Army submitted their dispute to arbitration in July 2008.

In settling a territorial dispute between Eritrea and Ethiopia over a border town (submitted after the Agreement signed in Algiers on December 12, 2000), an arbitration commission (composed of two members appointed by each country as well as a chair) delivered a binding decision on its transfer to Ethiopia in April 2002. In consultation with both parties, the commission adopted procedures regarding not only the analysis of the initial findings but also the determination of the priorities and sequence for its work.

In a response to war damages, the second panel (Eritrea–Ethiopia Claims Commission) has separately been delivering decisions on all the claims for loss, damage, or injury according to violations of international humanitarian law, including the 1949 Geneva Conventions (December 2002–May 2008). The Commission reviewed the two parties' claims alleging mistreatment of their respective prisoners of war, diplomatic immunities, claims of misconduct of military operations in the front zones, and allegations of mistreatment of civilians. Opinions and expertise from officials of the International Committee of the Red Cross and the International Organization on Migration were solicited in reviewing the treatment of POWs and of civilians and their property.

As an informal category of adjudication, arbitration thus exists as a quasi-judicial process within a legal system. In contrast with litigation, the merit of arbitration permits private arrangements as well as a certain level of informality and flexibility. The advantage of a quasi-judicial mechanism vis-à-vis formal adjudication is less costly, and more convenient, while the arbitrator's decisions have binding effects as legal proceedings. It can be more predictable than a courtroom trial that can be determined by a gamble on the emotions of a jury. In arbitration, the disputants can flexibly agree to arrange and modify forms and schedules.

While some decisions may have an advisory effect only, parties tend to sign a formal agreement to accept binding decisions with legal implications. As seen in the Sudanese and Eritrea–Ethiopian cases, formal agreements or rules can be developed, in advance, to accept the arbitrator's award decisions. The procedures of binding arbitration are normally supported by existing laws and norms. The purpose of nonbinding arbitration is "a sort of 'dry run' to measure the strength of its case and its appeal to a neutral, informed, tribunal" (Lynch, 2005, p. 425). The nonbinding judgment can clarify a basis of suspicion about the inflation of the other's claims.

The arbitrators should be experts in the subject matter of contention as well as having the ability to make an impartial judgment. Given their involvement in the design of decision-making procedures, adversaries possess more control over a process in arbitration than a judicial system. Disputants can appoint the same number of arbitrators who choose the chair of a commission. Otherwise the authority of the system (which appoints the arbitrators) should be acceptable.

Ombudsmanry

In many institutional settings, the protection of individuals against possible government abuse of public trust is an important priority in a democratically functioning society. The modern practice of ombudsman has its roots in the traditions of Africa and Scandinavia related to receiving and investigating complaints against government bureaucratic actions or corruption and making suggestions for appropriate solutions. The ombudsmanry system protects individuals against possible institutional failures and abuse of public trust. The practice is based on the notion that elected officials and public institutions should be subject to public scrutiny and evaluation, in that all power is accountable to the public.

More empowered ombudsmen are tasked to propose changes to policies and practices, as well as monitoring and upward referral of trends.

The bulk of ombudsmen's work comes from individual citizen complaints about administrative decisions made by public agencies. Investigating the sources of a complaint and looking into rights abuses have been main features of the ombudsmanry. The procedure is normally objective, confidential, neutral, informal, inexpensive, and quick. The role of ombudsmen's public advocacy work can be designated in a particular field or a specific geographical area. The majority of Canadian provinces have a classical Ombudsman's office with legislative mandates besides reporting procedures. Formal statutory powers grant them jurisdiction to examine any aspect of governmental administration. Despite their power to recommend, they cannot mandate implementation. At a national level, Canada's Official Languages Commissioner is endowed with wide-ranging investigative power under the Official Languages Act and makes recommendations based on their findings to the Speaker of the House of Commons.

In fulfilling their functions of guarding individual rights from abuse by authorities, the political independence of an ombudsman is important in investigating complaints and preparing a report. The reliability of the process is guaranteed by the involvement of an independent agent, ranging from a nonpartisan investigative committee or team to an ombudsman. Reforms in policy and practice can be generated by the hearings of grievances related to a pattern of neglect, incompetence, or inadequate implementation of policies and procedures. As a result of the investigation, efforts can be made to find remedies within established procedures and systems.

Functions similar to those of an ombudsman can be found in some newspaper sections, and television and radio programs that deal with individual complaints. The threats of large-scale publicity about an institution's failures have a compelling impact on the immediate corrections of problems. Whereas the ombudsman may suggest new policy-making procedures and recommendations as well as making legislative recommendations, they are not in a position to make changes in laws or policies by themselves; thus their power is indirect.

The main concerns originating within wider organizational settings are the protection of the rights of clients such as children, college students, employees, prisoners, and health care patients. In some workplaces, the grievance-handling process (originating from the harassment of employees, verbal offense, physical and sexual assault) is incorporated into the management system. Some conflict at the workplace results from discrimination on the basis of race, sex, marital status, and physical impairment. In most cases, problems might be presented, as an initial step, to the head of the department or agency with responsibility and power to respond to the complaint.

In resolving disputes, the ombudsmen serve as communication channels by handling complaints or providing information, reframing issues/developing options, and looking into a problem. In fulfilling their mandate to informally resolve internal work-related complaints, some corporate ombudsmen support low-level negotiation, advice/coaching, education, and assisting the complainant to develop options besides referral to formal mediation. Ombudsmen in an organizational setting do not have formal power except making a report to the upper echelon of organizational hierarchies.

Collaborative problem solving

Interest in negotiation, mediation, and facilitation can be ascribed to values attached to collaboration. In negotiation, the perception and understanding of the situation are affected by the degree and quality of communication between negotiators. Disputes over material interests can be managed by clarifying the facts or by collaborative efforts to expand the resources. In some cases, improved communication and clarification of some factual matters may be sufficient to manage conflict. The existence of a contentious relationship hampers the analytical process of problem solving.

In contrast with authoritative decision making by a judge or arbitrator, a collaborative process is often facilitative, nondirective and informal. One common function of intermediaries is opening up blocked communication created by a deteriorating relationship. The concerned parties can move toward direct interaction in handling their differences after a trusted third party opens communication links. An agreement can be derived from separate consultation with disputants organized as part of an informal facilitation process. Facilitation can be used to characterize not only a process of mediation but also a large group process oriented toward problem solving. There are wide differences in formality and group dynamics, since facilitation is sufficiently flexible to permit an intermediary and disputing parties to design the process of interaction.

A variety of assisted and unassisted approaches to resolving conflict stress a collaborative perspective. As part of informal, noncoercive interventions, good offices and conciliation are designed for the support of communication between adversaries. Intermediaries may serve as a go-between, make proposals if the contestants are eager to find a compromise. Fact-finding can proceed to clarify differences in support of a settlement. The good offices of the UN have assisted in managing complex political situations such as Afghanistan's complaint about Pakistani border crossings, cross-border firings, rocket attacks, and restrictions placed on refugees in 1998–1999.

Various types of communication needed for a conflict resolution attempt to influence mutual perceptions by changes in narrative processes. In fact, settlement mechanisms can provide contingent strategies in moderating and peacefully ending a protracted conflict situation. Pre-negotiation contact can be made by a nonofficial intermediary before the emergence of a formal negotiation stage (for example, the termination of civil wars in Tajikistan, Burundi, and Mozambique). In the early 1990s, the UN special envoys mediated between opposing parties in El Salvador and Guatemala to end civil wars.

Stalled negotiations often generate the necessity for various types of facilitation by neutral third parties. Assisted negotiation can be attempted to help two countries fighting over territories stop a war (e.g., proposals developed by Saudi Arabia and other states to end a protracted war between Iran and Iraq during the 1980s). In the absence of trust, an informed consensus can be forged through dialogue between influential figures in a nonofficial setting. The process is generally seen as nonconfrontational and nonadversarial to enhance understanding of each other's deep concerns and explore the possibilities of coexistence.

Facilitated discussion is supposed to provide support for a process to reach agreement. Reasonable compromises can be made through the cultivation of goodwill and mutual confidence. The third party would create good faith and confidence by assisting their communication. Parties are allowed to express their concerns and feelings directly or indirectly at meetings facilitated by mediators. A third party is mostly concerned with the process rather than content of disputes.

Protagonists may jointly investigate strategies of transition from confrontation to collaborative problem solving in tandem with face-to-face exploration of perceptions. Managing group dynamics demands the skills of a trustworthy nonpartisan who can guide the process of issue clarification, progressive mutual acceptance, acknowledgment of each group's real goals, and an eventual move from a tentative compromise to a more lasting settlement. Prior to the emergence of shared perceptions about the full cost of fighting, participants representing adversarial groups should be allowed to have emotional as well as intellectual interactions.

Negotiated agreements

Depending on the nature and sources of conflict, negotiation can be conducted in different ways. The major issues can be identified directly by the antagonists who are willing to get engaged in the process of lowering tension. Activities to search for settlement terms may involve canvassing possible solutions, examining all the possible consequences, and communication of preferences. Decision making is supported by agreements on factual matters, reasonable overall objectives held by disputants, clear definition of issues or concerns.

In negotiation, parties can reach an agreement through compromise. If negotiations between two parties are not possible, third parties can be involved to promote communication, make proposals for solutions in assisted decision making. In multilateral conference (on treaty making), consensus among multiple interest groups can be forged through technical analysis of problems and trade-offs of priorities (Menkel-Meadow, 2003). In ethnic conflict, facilitators may assist adversaries in exploring options that can satisfy their desire for identity and other basic needs. Conflict resolution is sought by agreement based on shared understanding and mutual accommodation.

Negotiation stages, in general, move from defining agendas to clarifying bargaining positions. Final bargaining is preceded by a search for a bargaining range and exploration of trading possibilities. The exchange of specific, substantive proposals may entail demand, offer, bid and their counters. The ritualization of outcomes can be followed by formal affirmation, public announcement, or official recognition. Negotiated outcomes need to be affirmed and executed through the allocation and administration of rights and resources. One set of negotiations is accompanied by another series of discussions about the formal agreement terms. Therefore, more than a series of negotiating sessions constitute a complex settlement process, as is seen in Israeli–Palestinian negotiations.

By relying on goodwill rather than threats, parties to a dispute can settle their differences via compromise. When parties have enough confidence and are strongly committed to settlement, third-party intervention may not be needed (e.g., the exclusion of mediators in negotiations on the transition to majority rule in South Africa). On the other hand, third-party involvement is inevitable under circumstances of a high level of continuing uncertainty surrounding distrust and power imbalance as well as a lack of efficient, direct communication channels (e.g., Israeli–Palestinian peace negotiations for the determination of borders and the future of Jerusalem). The intervention of multiple intermediaries is common in complex conflicts.

Mediation

Mediation is often advocated as a more amicable way of ending conflict than adversarial bargaining. The achievement of mutually satisfactory outcomes in an efficient manner is derived from the opponents' willingness to be open to meeting the other's needs and interests. Mediation is more suitable than arbitration when emotions drive misperceptions and stereotypes, being deepened by poor communication or miscommunication. Since people do not see the issues in contention the same way and do not make the same assumptions, mediated communication is an effective means in clearing misunderstanding.

Active mediators tend to interpret information, make tentative suggestions (even at a limited level), inject opinions, make recommendations, evaluate preferences and demands of the parties and propose solutions and modifications. In fact, a powerful mediator may adopt active strategies to twist the arms of adversaries if the settlement is seen as essential to ending the protracted conflict situation. In ending the civil war in Bosnia-Herzegovina, US mediation efforts led to a forced settlement. If an intervener has a fair sense of justice and does not have to appease one of the disputants, an intermediary can bring about a more balanced settlement.

One of the most important aspects of mediation is that the disputants make final decisions on the issue along with a commitment to implementation. They are not, in principle, forced to accept or reject the negotiated outcome from a fear of threats or force. Thus consent to a mediation process is voluntary and can be withdrawn if participants feel the process unfair to them. In addition, parties have a great degree of freedom to reject undesirable outcomes.

Since voluntary agreement is necessary for a settlement, all forms of mediation are more democratic in their nature than judicial or arbitration processes. Mediation has become more popular than the legal system due to the latter's deficiencies which lack flexibility. As people are supposed to learn a new process of resolving their own disputes, the new knowledge is considered self-empowering. All that is necessary is to interact in good faith and confidence. Mediation would not be suitable in the event of a potential for violence, abuse, or similar unacceptable behavioral conduct by one of the partisans (Stitt, 2004).

Group facilitation

In facilitation, a third party may have the minimal involvement in problem solving as an observer instead of directing the process or making suggestions regarding desirable outcomes. In collective decision making (for example, community development), an informal consultation process is the first step toward convincing the stakeholders to commit themselves to a consensus-building process. In a similar manner to mediators, facilitators keep order, suggest a procedure, set up a schedule, manage meetings, and reiterate points of agreement. In general, however, group facilitators are less involved in discussion about substantive issues than mediators. When groups need particular skills to manage meetings, facilitators can be invited to offer training instead of being an integral part of the whole process.

Various steps often need to be taken to minimize tension prior to getting the parties talking by adopting social methods of influence. An intermediary may initiate a process to reach an agreement through a range of intervention activities such as consultation. Dialogue is designed to improve relationships among adversaries via increased contacts. By overcoming differences in opinions, adversaries will be able to explore the mutual accommodation of different needs. It is a process of jointly seeking an outcome satisfactory or at least acceptable for all the partisans. As dialogue progresses, opponents can define and redefine the terms of relationships.

Negotiated rule making is more suitable for handling policy disputes which implicate multiple stakeholders in setting global trade policies or international environmental standards. A non-authoritarian and non-judgmental mode of decision-making is more helpful for reaching consensus. Mutual satisfaction arises from innovative and flexible solutions made by the maximum involvement of participants. New relationships among opposing forces within a community can emerge from building a broad level of consensus in key public policy arenas.

Assessing decision-making modes

A settlement process can end by either judicial decision, arbitration, or agreements forged by mediation, conciliation, and facilitative methods. The quality of a settlement can be judged by both substantive and procedural terms along with the different costs and lengths of time required to reach a particular settlement. The voluntary acceptance of nonbinding settlement terms in mediation or other types of collaborative process stems from the participant's satisfaction with the outcome's substantive nature. On the other hand, litigation and arbitration often involve a high stakes win–lose situation. A high level of emotional anxiety is generated by an unpredictable outcome, as the partisans have no control over the final verdict.

Fact-finding is considered effective in cases involving different assessment of relevant information as well as clarification of misinformation and misinterpretation. External expert opinion can be used for breaking deadlocks in negotiations or mediations as well as jury decisions of arbitration or legal proceedings. Arbitrations and judicial proceedings are generally concerned with the factual content of the conflict; presentations at a hearing are made in a context to prove the validity of one's arguments. Given a zero-sum solution to the problem, litigation and arbitration are an adversarial process.

Border disputes even between friendly states are often referred to judicial mechanisms rather than bilateral negotiations due to the domestic political constraints of making concessions. In resolving a dispute regarding sovereignty over the small islands and rocks of the Ecrehos and Minquier groups, the International Court of Justice recognized, in November 1953, the British sovereignty of this small territory between the British Channel Island of Jersey and the French coast. While both the UK and France made serious attempts to win by invoking historical facts tracing back to the eleventh century, the ruling helped the French government give up their claims more easily than protracted bilateral negotiations.

On the other hand, binding decisions imposed by a judge or arbitration panel can deepen continuing animosities between rival states. A border dispute between Thailand and Cambodia over the Temple of Preah Vihear was settled by the International Court of Justice decision in 1959, but conflict flared up again when a group of agitated nationalists in Thailand brought up the issue in spring 2008, resulting in the dispatch of troops by both countries. While this incident calmed down without any military clashes, the Ethiopian–Eritrea border dispute remains tense owing to the former's refusal to accept the 2002 verdicts by the international arbitration commission. Stable and long-term relations will not emerge from a decision in favor of one party, but a third-party evaluation of each party's claims is a far better way to settle differences than resorting to a war.

Some issues are easier to settle or resolve through institutionalized frameworks. Organizational disputes can be professionally handled by administrators, managers, or industrial arbitrators who are familiar with the issues at stake. In advanced democratic countries, the modern practice of ombudsmanry performs investigative functions in response to the violation of minority rights and other matters. These methods contribute to the prevention of serious escalation of social discontent by providing a recourse for complaints. Peer or voluntary mediators have been institutionalized to handle arguments between people at many school settings. Mediation, court procedures, and arbitration can fit in a conventional framework of dispute settlement. In situations where a minority group develops non-conformity with the dominant values, on the other hand, courts, lawyers, public officials, and mediators are not adapted to in-depth analysis of the conflict.

In a collaborative process, shared power replaces each party's attempt to impose one's own will on the other. It is contrasted with litigation which is, in essence, an adversarial process where parties are forced to oppose each other without direct communication. The partisans have more control over the process, in that decisions are not imposed on them by judges or arbitrators. Opponents attempt to learn more from each other at facilitation sessions which they join voluntarily. Since facilitators do not have any authoritative decision-making power (and do not make rulings or impose an agreement), neutral third-party assistance is restricted to support a negotiation or dialogue process. Overall, settlement is to discover "the art of the possible"; developing a sense of "what is probable" is needed to "help bring the parties to a mutually acceptable and accepted position" (Lynch, 2005, p. 561).

Collaborative approaches to conflict resolution are characterized by relationship building in the exploration of strategies to pursue mutual goals. Joint gains emerge from power sharing in decision making. Empathy leads to improved understanding and valuing the merit of each other's claims along with information sharing. This is contrasted with a power bargaining process which generates discontent. The dissatisfied party wants to change the settlement terms in the future. In adversarial bargaining relationships, win–lose attitudes often lead to devaluing others by promoting self-interest; bluff and intimidation as well as information withholding are used as an attempt to hold power over others.

Power versus collaborative problem solving

Power-based approaches are contrasted with the collaborative process which searches for amicable solutions. Each partisan tries to exert strategic influence either via coercive methods or persuasion. A power-based approach relies on an attempt to force the other to give in by intensifying damage to an adversary (e.g., strikes or lockouts in labor disputes). Power-based decision making can also be based on the imposition of one's own privileges or preferences on others either with legislative, legal, or political procedures.

In a response to conflict, partisans may push their own ideas to demand the capitulation of an adversary. In considering that decisions are made in the way to determine winners and losers, there is little room for dialogue. The capacity to influence a situation depends on proving who is more powerful. Even though it may keep negative peace through control, a solution based on power differentials can be tenuous, as is the nature of power relations. Given the zero-sum nature of a fight, a loser is likely to feel a lack of satisfaction.

The uneven distribution of power (a power imbalanced situation) allows high-power persons to be engaged in the manipulative tactics of pseudo-collaboration as well as domination. A power-based solution and its tactics (such as threats and intimidation) are costly in the long run, because coercive approaches invite further resentment and more forceful resistance. Even if coercive tactics are successful in the short term, they can generate long-term grievances. The maintenance of the status quo based on fear is no longer feasible in a functional relationship. It is more costly especially when the relationships are supposed to be communal and symbiotic (parent/child, and ally relationships).

In an ethnic struggle (embedded in long historical animosities), "win–lose conceptions may be self-destructive," contributing to a protracted struggle; this realization may bring about "a window of opportunity for introducing possible 'win–win' strategies" and for co-existence based on mutual respect. The maintenance of the status quo is not any more feasible, or it is too costly in terms of one's own reputation or financial burden. Coercive approaches produce only a backlash by creating further resentment and violent resistance. Given the costs, a protracted conflict's outcome is likely to be negative-sum even if victory is achieved. It may lead to the gradual understanding that the pursuit of one's own interests depends on the other's cooperation.

A voluntary form of cooperation is derived from an emphasis on rationality. In an interdependence relationship, self-interest can not be pursued successfully by coercion. The methods of persuasion have been utilized to substitute coercive approaches to resolving disputes. Given the costs of adversarial struggles, rational individuals should be able to resolve their differences without depending on coercive means.

Rationalist/utilitarian perspectives

Rational conflict management is based on the assumption that parties know their best interests. When conflict arises from illusory grounds due to misinterpretations of proposals or circumstances, clear communication for better understanding of each other's interests and intentions may be able to eliminate problems. Thus rational decisions can be reached, in part, by removing misunderstanding that emerges from stereotypical perceptions. Third parties help identify issues, control each party's aspirations, remove misunderstandings of each other's goals, analyze interests, formulate proposals, and suggest alternatives.

It is based on the assumption that as long as rules are fair and voluntarily accepted, desirable conditions or outcomes can naturally be achieved by the efficiency of practice. In addition, negotiators are assumed to have equal ability to bargain over their interests. Rival positions may be deduced from disagreement over scientific and technical aspects of the issues. The value of direct contact lies in its possible contribution to rectifying misconceived enemy images. Conflict can be managed and controlled by setting up rules and norms for competition.

In a search for a formula to satisfy mutual interests, emotion and anger have to be controlled for rational calculations of objective interests. Problem solving is designed for the discovery or creation of mutually beneficial choices by sorting out conflicting interests and exploring an optimal method which satisfies everyone. Examining underlying concerns with particular issues in a negotiation process leads to the expanding resources available for the satisfaction of both parties' needs and exchanging concessions on matters with different priorities to each party. The efficient, mutually acceptable solution is found in a win–win method equated with "the greatest joint benefit" to all parties.

Interest-based bargaining is more easily applied to a "dispute" characterized as problems which can be managed within an existing system through compromise or other methods (Burton, 1997). When diverse interests are articulated and institutionalized in a contractual relationship, the existing agreement on the rules and norms helps guide a process to solve differences stemming from the pursuit of competing interests. Such methods as mediation are helpful in resolving disputes arising from misunderstanding and conflicting interests, but are not suitable for responding to issues related to basic principles (such as human rights, protection of endangered species, or preservation of land).

Depending on whether we see particular issues as matters of interest or principles of public interests to be protected, the solutions and approaches are different. "Negotiations cannot and should not compromise nonnegotiable principles which are based on deeply held values or beliefs concerning the way society should function" (Amy, 1987). Principled matters (environmental laws) are generally handled in more traditional institutions such as a court or political process in the event that these are not successfully handled by facilitated dialogue.

The role of culture

Cultural differences play an important role in developing resolution modalities. A Western mediation model is more "structured, task oriented, directed towards agreement." On the other hand, collectivist cultures focus on a "dynamic directed to resolving tension in community" with an "emphasis on responsibilities of disputing parties and reconciliation" (Sidaway, 2005, p. 89). In rigid organizational cultures, a mediator controls the formal process via ground rules. Formality in discussing volatile issues supports security and stability.

Non-assertive cultures adopt indirect means of communication (e.g., a go-between) supported by the involvement of recognized leaders. This reduces perceptions of threat with face saving, balances power and equalizes verbal skills. In linear Western models of mediation, one thing at a time is discussed within a defined schedule of discrete sessions. On the contrary, issues and relationships are interwoven, while tasks and schedules are secondary to relationships and social ritual in community-oriented cultures.

In promoting communal links through various development projects, antagonistic tribal groups have been brought together to elicit cooperation. The assistance of various kinds of third-party settlement can be adaptable to particular cultures. Mediation and arbitration have more often been adopted in many horticultural and pastoral societies, replacing aggressive self-help initiatives.

In an egalitarian social organization (hunter–gatherer societies), due to lack of positions of higher authority, friendly mediation is more suitable than arbitration or adjudication. Peace making is easier in cultural settings which encourage toleration but discourage aggressive behavior. In traditional cultures, a clan resolution process can be sponsored by political brokers, local or regional headmen, or religious leaders.

Impartiality and neutrality

Most conflict settlement models emphasize the importance of impartiality and neutrality, both perceived and actual. If the process and outcome of intermediary intervention are perceived as fair, there is a high likelihood of satisfaction with conflict settlement. Nonjudgmental attitudes of intermediaries toward not only the conflict but also the parties permit them to take an "inclusive and even handed approach with regard to" the issues and process. An intervener's opinions about the outcome should not interfere in the desires of the disputants so that the parties can make their own decisions. Indeed, mediators are more likely to be free from bias toward the parties when they do not have any stake in the settlement's outcome.

In arbitration and adjudication, neutrality and impartiality are more crucial than mediation since the final decision making is not subject to amendment. The independence of judges and arbitrators needs to be guaranteed for fair and unbiased decision making. Autonomy is also critical in any procedures involving fact-finding in order not to compromise the process of investigating complaints and preparing a report. Discriminating against none means avoiding prejudicial opinions or unduly favoring any disputant. In fact, "impartiality" represents a "commitment to serve all parties" as opposed to a single party by being free from favoritism either by action or by word. Given the necessity of a mediator to have balanced concerns with all the disputants' well-being, "a preference or liking for one party over the other" is not considered desirable (McCorkle and Reese, 2005, p. 15). The attitude of the intervener should reflect unbiased opinion.

In general, neutrality relates to the relationship between the intervener and disputants as well as attitudes and behavior. Neutrality can be guarded by the exclusion of values of mediators in an intervention process. The principles of neutrality have been modified by some humanitarian organizations. The International Committee of the Red Cross have a long established policy of no discrimination in endeavors to relieve the suffering of individuals, while not taking sides in hostilities. Their actions are solely committed to the needs of victims. More of an advocacy stance has been taken by Doctors without Borders which prioritizes the welfare of victims in conflict zones such as Chechnya over political/religious neutrality. Doctors without Borders was created in opposition to the Red Cross which insisted on neutrality regardless of circumstances such as attacks on civilians, medical personnel and hospitals and mass starvation caused by the Nigerian army during the Biafran war (1967–1970).

Pure noninterventionist approaches to impartiality and neutrality do not explain power asymmetry as well as ethical standards about conflict outcomes. In social conflict, due to the unequal distribution of power instituted by various social arrangements, neutrality is skewed toward favoring compromise within existing values and status quo. That leaves mediators in no position to rectify power distribution by regarding justice as part of the role of political process.

If a basic concern is settlement of the dispute itself, an intermediary should not be an advocate for either side of a dispute. Impartiality is important in prohibiting the implication of bias in any forum which puts blame on one side or seeks to apply social norms in an arbitrary manner. The quality of conflict resolution is certainly improved by process-oriented fairness. Yet sustainable peace cannot be achieved by neglecting such concerns as abuse in power asymmetry and ignorance of common good for the community.

Thus impartiality should not necessarily mean a lack of care or interest in substantive outcomes. In fact, effective resolution may not be achieved by a value-free intervener who is devoid of opinions. In particular, deficiencies with a neutral, noninterventionist third party are clear when one party has low self-esteem, status, and power, or is lacking personal confidence. A submissive personality combined with poor verbal and personal skills is likely to presage an unfair outcome for a party which has nonassertive bargaining strategies. This kind of situation raises questions about strict neutrality.

Regardless of being nominally committed to impartiality, interveners unavoidably play more than neutral facilitator roles of eliciting information, asking questions or determining agenda. An intervener's knowledge, values, and expertise are important in assisting "disputants in identifying concerns that affect them and exploring the specific needs that must be addressed in any outcome." While conflict resolution practitioners should "strategically use … skills to keep the communication process balanced, fair, and productive," their conscience should not be closed to injustice. Especially in power asymmetry, an intervener may need to be engaged in diverse subtle methods of addressing issues of justice.

In order to push for a negotiated settlement, an intermediary can express their views about undesirable actions by one of the parties even though they do not take any punitive measures. The US government reiterated that Israeli settlement activities and expansion in the West Bank are not consistent with Middle East peace road map obligations; even though a lack of sanctions did not have much effect on Israeli actions, this might have helped the Palestinian side feel moral support from the US (considered a staunch Israeli ally).

Indeed, subjective judgment and feelings are likely to get involved in determining the extent to which neutrality is respected. There are circumstances under which a certain degree of intermediary partiality is acceptable to the adversaries. In a losing war, intermediary intervention can save one party's total defeat by forging negotiated solutions. If the mediation offer is rejected, intermediaries may even pose a threat to support the other party's efforts. Neutral (agreement–settlement oriented) versus non-neutral (advocacy) third-party intervention has different implications for conflict management and resolution.

Non-neutral intervention

Interveners can provide advice or consultation for one of the parties in support of their efforts to obtain fair conflict settlement. Sometimes they can serve as a pressure group to weaken an unyielding party's positions. Whereas consultants suggest alternatives or plans of action for consideration, advisors recommend solutions for particular problems or areas of concern. Consulting roles entail the offer of analysis about options as well as ideas about improvement of their client's positions. Consultants can also help parties identify and order agenda items prior to negotiations.

Through their direct involvement in negotiation or other representational roles, advocates champion the cause of a client. Cases involving the violation of rights can be represented by an advocacy or representative group such as trade unions on behalf of individuals. In such areas as environmental and industrial conflicts where power imbalance is prevalent, advocacy plays an important role in providing an input to achieve a fair outcome.

In addition, the role of advocate is needed especially in such cases as sexual harassment and child abuse that need to go to court since seeking justice is an important issue. Emotional problems and personality conflicts may require the expert knowledge of social workers and psychiatrists. Intervention in violent conflict requires sensitivity to the needs of victims as well as validating the experiences of victims from their own frame of reference.

Questions of justice

The field of conflict resolution has long grappled with such questions as when and how justice can be addressed (for instance, the distribution of goods at a specific time). Many different interpretations of justice are related to how we assess different claims. While distributive justice concentrates on egalitarianism, procedural justice is derived from unbiased, fair processes in the administration of law. Distributive justice entails concerns with what is right as to the allocation of wealth, income, jobs, welfare, and opportunities. Famine and poverty (attributed to wealth disparity) at the global level can be interpreted in terms of distributive justice. The subsidies to ethanol production in the US have created further difficulties for people who suffer from shortage of food in poor countries by using corn or soybeans for making fuel.

In seeking distributive justice, conflict resolution activities can focus on the development of the criteria which guarantee fair outcomes. Palestinian–Israeli negotiation essentially delves into the issues of distributive justice (the division of Jerusalem, Jewish settlement in the West Bank, refugee return, access to water). Distributive principles in resource allocation can be based on the dialogue of what people deserve and the basis for their claims. Individual merits or needs often serve as a basis to assess the fairness and effects of the division of objects and conditions which each party desires.

Restorative versus retributive justice

Repairing relationships has been the main focus of restorative justice. It is designed to seek healing by looking into the deeper meanings of atrocious acts through a face-to-face meeting between offenders and victims. Transformative justice seeks to identify the root causes of crime, and treats a criminal offense as an opportunity for not only offenders but also all other members of the affected community. It is aimed at meeting the needs to preserve the dignity and safety for those harmed, perpetrators and their communities of care. People harmed by wrongdoing receive some type of restitution from an offender while offering forgiveness.

In institutionalized healing, restorative justice can be manifested in reparation and apologies. Since the 1970s, victim offender mediation was initially applied to a vandalism case and minor juvenile crimes in North America, Britain, New Zealand, and Australia but was later expanded to sex and other offenses. Restorative justice promotes healing by encouraging a perpetrator to take responsibility for their own deed. Innovations within a criminal justice system have been growingly applied to post-conflict settings, for instance, in East Timor.

Restorative justice can be compared with retributive justice in which proportionate punishment is a morally acceptable response to crime with little consideration of the punishment's effects on the person and society. Penalty should be reasonably proportional to the severity of the infraction. Revenge motives or desire of punishment are often justified by the notion of retributive justice on the basis of the punishments of "a life for a life, an eye for an eye." In conflict situations, this notion is illustrated by the US attacks on Afghanistan after the terrorist attacks in September 2001 and Israeli retaliatory attacks on Lebanon in 2006. In a more strict interpretation of retributive justice, the level of punishment should be scaled in relation to the severity of the offending behavior. The amount of punishment ought to be proportional to the amount of harm caused by the offense or the amount of unfair advantage gained by the perpetrator.

Ethical issues

The initiatives to transform conflict involves ethical questions such as when and how to stop atrocities. These questions may need to be answered prior to taking initiatives of mediation or other types of negotiated settlement. In venturing to transform individuals, relationships, or societies of which they are not a part, outsiders need to examine the moral and ethical foundations related to the terms of intervention. While US intervention in Haiti was related to the practical political concerns of an increasing number of refugees (combined with human rights abuse) in 1995, the invasion of Panama in 1988 was motivated by American domestic political interests. One of the most important criteria for intervention is respect for human rights along with the requirement of saving innocent civilians from atrocities (e.g., the case of US intervention in Somalia). The new type of intervention is represented by the blend of both military and humanitarian work.

Ethical issues center on the circumstances of intervention in humanitarian situations (such as the worsening refugee situation's effect in deteriorating political instability and requirements for more costly future intervention). At the same time, ethical considerations cannot avoid an entangled web of power, truth, justice, and healing. There is contradiction between the logic of power politics versus universal conscience (Wilson, 2003). It is well illustrated by comparison between the lack of action in the Rwanda genocide and the NATO bombing of Serbia to press the Milošović government to accept international peacekeeping.

There are always lingering questions regarding conditions under which amnesty can be justified for militia groups committed to atrocities. Many peace accords have an amnesty clause (e.g., Guatemala, Angola, Mozambique, El Salvador) in order to provide incentives for warring parties to lay down their arms. Warlords can be brought to justice, for instance, in Sierra Leone retroactively after cease-fire and transition arrangements were made. On the other hand, military atrocities in El Salvador and Guatemala went unanswered through amnesty agreements even though there were outcries by human rights groups and indigenous populations, many of whom were massacred by the Guatemalan armies in 1992.

It is difficult to bring justice to the perpetrators if they are still in power after the settlement (former army officers in El Salvador after the 1992 peace accord). In the case of Chile, Augusto Pinochet was extradited from Spain to his home country to stand for trial for his involvement in the torture and death of thousands of ordinary citizens. Other Argentine generals (responsible for atrocities during the military rule) were also brought back to court in the early 2000s. In South Africa, amnesty was offered in return for confession and truth telling.

Negotiation with warlords or hostage takers involves delicate ethical concerns. Negotiations on hostage swaps are often required to strike a balance between humanitarian issues and political concerns (e.g., Israel versus Hezbollah). While the French government had to negotiate with Somali pirates to seek a release of their hostages, the French eventually took military strikes against the hostage takers after the return of hostages.

UN and international aid agencies often face situations where they have to negotiate with warlords to deliver aid. Burma's military dictatorship refused to permit access of US, French, and British naval vessels carrying large quantities of relief supplies to cyclone victims. The UN Secretary General negotiated with junta leader Senior General Than Shwe to acquire a pledge to consent to more foreign access to affected regions. To draw the "concession" of getting aid to victims of the devastating May 2–3, 2008 storm, UN Secretary General Ban made no public comment on the internationally known political leader Suu Kyi being under house arrest during his two-hour meeting with the military general.

Further reading

Amy, D. (1987) *The Politics of Environmental Mediation*, New York: Columbia University Press.

Black, P. and Avruch, K. (1999) "Cultural Relativism, Conflict Resolution, Social Justice," *Peace and Conflict Studies*, 6 (2): 24–41.

Lynch, E. F. (2005) *Negotiation and Settlement*, St Paul, MN: Thomson/West.

Menkel-Meadow, C. (2003) *Dispute Processing and Conflict Resolution: Theory, Practice, and Policy*, Burlington, VT: Ashgate/Dartmouth.

Merrills, J. G. (2005) *International Dispute Settlement*, 4th edition, New York: Cambridge University Press.

Scimecca, J. A. (1993) "Theory and Alternative Dispute Resolution: A Contradiction in Terms?," in D. Sandole and H. van der Merwe (eds) *Conflict Resolution Theory and Practice: Integration and Application*, MA: Manchester University Press.

Sidaway, R. (2005) *Resolving Environmental Disputes: From Conflict to Consensus*, London: Earthscan Publications Ltd.

8   Negotiation

From ancient times, negotiation has played an important role in managing human competition in a quest for more power and wealth as an alternative means to war and conquest. Bargaining has been necessary to reach an agreement in the exchange of goods for the satisfaction of material interests as well as dividing land. In the contemporary world, negotiation has been broadly conceptualized as an inevitable part of daily life, ranging from holiday plans between spouses to making decisions on the purchase of a new car, a house or other expensive goods. Others involve collective entities (as illustrated by deals between unions and a company over severance packages, health, and other benefits; corporate takeovers and mergers, alliances between airlines or between Internet companies, etc.). Negotiation is also part of managing international relations through treaty making between two countries or on a multilateral basis.

In the broadest terms, negotiating activities entail trading of concessions and invention of options for mutual gain. Bargaining tests each other's interests and explores commonly agreeable solutions. Negotiation, as a game of influence, entails varied aspects of human interactions, the dynamics of which are affected by emotions, culture, and social environment. Mistrust and fear are an inevitable part of negotiation relationships between adversaries; owing to deep-seated hostilities, the 1993 Oslo Accord and the 1994 US–North Korean Framework Agreement have faltered even after serious progress was made in the implementation of mutual obligations. On the other hand, the agreements to end the apartheid regime in South Africa and British rule in Northern Ireland successfully brought new relations between former adversaries with the creation of alternative institutions. As demonstrated by nearly three decades of negotiation over the distribution of water between India and Bangladesh, the process of negotiation is often likely to embody fluctuations in broad political relations.

This chapter deals with the steps toward initiating negotiation, the process of reaching an agreement and its implementation. Parties to negotiation have different goals and relationships with each other. It is important to examine a bargaining context, histories of negotiating engagement, and matters of contention. The structural, strategic, psychological, and cultural dimensions of negotiations have an impact on reframing issues and the complexities of bargaining relationships. In presenting the diverse aspects of the negotiating process, the chapter also explores the factors behind failed and successful negotiation.

The essence of negotiation

Negotiation can be defined as a process to resolve differences in goals that arise from dissimilar interests and perspectives. In probing to unearth underlying concerns, negotiators share their views in order to establish the areas of common ground and agreement. Fair, efficient outcomes can emerge from the exchange of concessions in a search for creative solutions.

Cooperation and conflict are built right into negotiating relationships. The Strategic Arms Limitation Treaty (SALT) and Strategic Arms Reduction Treaties (START) between the US and the Soviet Union during the Cold War represent an attempt to control the joint vulnerability of the spiraling arms race (creating high expenditures on weapons and heightened tensions) by negotiating limits to the build up of weapons or reductions in their stockpile. Negotiation is feasible because parties have not only divergent but also shared interests. In a bargaining relationship, one party has something desired by the other. Identifying competing interests is involved in discussion about the issues.

In successful negotiation, in general, persuasion is adopted as a means of social influence to change an adversary's perceptions. The settlement of differences through accommodation stems from the recognition of the legitimacy of each other's claims. Even in friendly relationships, however, threats can be adopted if one party feels that the other side refuses to modify seemingly unfair positions in the pursuit of unilateral interests. Out of frustration with difficulties to remove obstacles for US access to the Japanese automobile market, the Clinton administration warned about doubling a surcharge on imported Japanese luxury cars at a tense moment of negotiations in June 1996.

The common understanding of sources of differences can lead to a shared framing of issues. A loss or gain can be felt more acutely in an adversarial relationship with negative involvement of emotions, creating more difficulties to making necessary concessions. The level of existing trust and past history of cooperation affect a commitment to openness and collaborative discussion. The main hurdle between Western allies and Iran in negotiations over the latter's nuclear programs has been deep mistrust as well as difficulties in gauging true intentions.

Bargaining situations

The purpose for negotiating is to achieve something by changing the status quo. "If both parties are satisfied with the way things are, there is nothing for them to negotiate about" (Kheel, 2001, p. 14). In bargaining, each party has an ability to satisfy at least part of the desires of their negotiating partner by controlling a new opportunity or creating a new relationship. If there is no immediate gain, parties should believe in potential future gains.

In coming to an agreement, parties want to improve their own situation while avoiding the worst outcome. A bargaining structure depends on whether each side has viable choices. The other party is "tempted to give as little as possible" (Kolb and Williams, 2003, p. 60). The merit of alternatives (which one can offer) strengthens one's bargaining position; multiple alternatives expand one's choice to pursue a desirable deal. Therefore the erosion of one's negotiating positions comes from having very limited options.

In asymmetric bargaining situations, one party has no alternative but "to take what is offered." There is not much room to bargain when other choices are worse than keeping the present arrangement intact. In such situations as taking less or paying more than originally expected, no deal could often be better than a bad deal that creates the worst-case scenarios. The fallback position can be to leave things as they are if negotiated settlement does not leave you any better off than the current situation and you do not lose anything.

In the situation when "one party is content to let things continue the way they are" and refuses to engage in negotiation, the opposing party may increase the stakes by escalating the costs of nonengagement to the adversary (Kolb and Williams, 2003, p. 77). North Korea and Iran would certainly want to be left alone to keep nuclear programs unchecked, but the threat of military strikes as well as economic and diplomatic sanctions forced them to negotiate with either the US or Western European powers. Expectations about settlement and the costs of non-settlement evolve during different phases of negotiation.

A stronger party may have more incentives to opt out of winning a victory by coercive means instead of negotiation. In power imbalanced negotiations, few incentives are offered, but a weaker party may have to agree to negotiate under coercion. For instance, Mexico had to cede Southern California and New Mexico to the US after its defeat in the 1846–1848 war under the terms of the Treaty of Guadalupe Hidalgo.

Negotiating relationships

The patterns of bargaining interaction depend on the extent to which each party is willing to cooperate. As is illustrated by the Israeli–Palestinian negotiations over the last 16 years, the boundaries and nature of interaction are shaped by identity and power relationships. In particular, "international negotiation can be viewed as the ultimate strategic contest" (Starkey *et al.*, 2005, p. 6). The agreement terms emerge from a series of each other's moves intended to satisfy respective interests. In a successful negotiation (most notably, between the National Party government of South Africa and African National Congress in 1991–1994), a bumpy road at the initial stage of negotiation is replaced by information sharing and commitment to the mutually satisfactory outcomes that are most likely to be forged by improved relationships.

The existence of respect and trust facilitates willingness to listen, disclose information, and commitment to a win–win outcome. In a trust relationship based on good intentions and openness, arguments and counterarguments promote collective reflection. When people share common interests and values, in particular, there is less likelihood of the adoption of divisive manipulative tactics.

The perceptions that people bring to negotiation can be changed by cultivating a climate of openness and mutual respect. Sound communication relies on the ability to listen and sort out the relevance and significance of factual information. Words and events can be interpreted in terms of outcome expectations. Most importantly, building an effective communicative relationship comes from sensitivity to other people and recognition of their needs. A lack of credibility originating from past behavior creates mistrust in the content of an adversary's presentation. Failed negotiations (ascribed to insistence on unreasonable demands) further reinforces negative perceptions.

Negotiation process

Negotiation from opening to closure is comprised of many steps and moves at each phase. Initial planning and fact-finding can be accompanied by the development of negotiating positions and exchange of information. Successful informal pre-negotiation discussion leads to direct bargaining designed to settle differences along with the exploration of each party's needs. In a tumultuous bargaining process, parties grudgingly make concessions before turning to compromise. Main activities at the proposal stage consist of information sharing, clarification of issues, and a trade-off of concessions. The exchange of concessions can be accompanied by the identification of common interests and exploration of mutual gains.

In probing the proposals, the clarification of goals precedes the examination of all possible alternatives. The advantages and disadvantages of multiple proposals need to be balanced to choose the best possible option. In closing the deal, the final stage is tasked to tie up loose ends in tandem with confirmation and summary. Negotiators check credibility and acceptability by conferring with someone else either in a higher position of authority or with the capacity to provide advice before making a final deal. Thus the whole gamut of negotiating activities is to prepare, discuss, clarify, propose, bargain, compromise, and reach agreement.

The quality of a bargaining process is improved by the exploration of each other's priorities based on information sharing. The successful settlement of differences via give-and-take is made easier by the existence of mutual respect (for example, US–Canada–Mexico trilateral negotiations for the North American Free Trade Agreement). A set of offers and counteroffers make bargaining move forward with proposals and counterproposals. In maneuvering to gain an edge, a bargainer attempts to maximize their influence on the debate over the issues along with a presentation of nonnegotiable priorities. Each side advocates their position to convince the other side to believe in what they need and deserve.

Our sense of what is negotiable and what can be achieved evolves throughout the negotiation. Mutual inquiry can influence the views about a possible outcome as well as a process to reach that. The changes in the atmosphere may create a shift from pushing to mutual exploration of acceptable deals.

We are forced to make midcourse corrections, as negotiation diverges from our expectations. In forging peace deals in the Middle East, President Carter initially promoted a multilateral process of engaging Israel's Arab rivals in a broad scheme of ending hostilities. However, Sadat's visit to Jerusalem in 1977 resulted in switching priorities to an individual bilateral peace process.

Initial assessment of negotiability of the issues can change after each party's expectations become clear. After large concessions are made, further concessions are likely to slow down especially near the settlement points. Toward closing, concessions become slimmer once settlement positions move to the near bottom of trade-off deals. Negotiators may adopt tougher bargaining positions toward a closure stage because slight changes in positioning may lead to an important shift in the dynamics.

Judgment about successfully negotiated outcomes can focus on a relational context as well as settlement of differences in substantive issues. Successful negotiation is often forged by reasonable management or transformation of adversarial relationship. In negotiations especially based on a specific fact-based approach (as exemplified by the calculation of compensation for damage or harm), objective criteria need to play a more important role in problem solving than the expression of emotions; in technical negotiations, subjective grievances are often excluded "to keep personal or emotional considerations from interfering with the building of an agreement" (Lynch, 2005, p. 392).

Northern Ireland peace process

The process of negotiation is not necessarily linear, entailing setbacks and a long hiatus. Negotiations aimed at the bringing together of parties engaged in violent conflicts are particularly challenging due to the necessity to involve confidence-building measures. In ending communal violence in Northern Ireland, the British and Irish governments played essential roles in reconciling diverse interests among the Republicans and the Unionists split into various factions. The multi-party negotiation started in 1994, but did not proceed smoothly until the 1997–1998 All-Party Talks. In particular, the IRA's violation of the 1994 paramilitary cease-fire in early 1996 resulted in a temporary exclusion of Sinn Féin closely associated with the IRA. Eventually the participants produced the Good Friday Agreement on April 10, 1998, at Stormont Castle in Belfast, outlining proposals for political relationships between the north and south of Ireland, the creation of a Northern Ireland Assembly, the introduction of new practice for security forces and policing, new human rights legislation, and the decommissioning of all paramilitary groups.

Preparation stage

At a pre-negotiation stage, each party makes determinations about the level of their commitment to negotiation, and gathers information about the negotiability of main differences. Preparation stages consist of the assessment and prioritization of issues, a glimpse into common interests or differences in goals as well as the identification of a minimally acceptable agreement. The shared definition of a problem develops room for further discussion. Framing the main agendas properly contributes to a more in-depth discussion in formal negotiation.

Negotiation setting

The creation of a comfortable climate lays the groundwork for the kind of negotiation desired by all sides. The confirmation of mutual interest in negotiation can lead to an agreement on potential agendas and ground rules. Pre-negotiation focuses on decisions on what will be on and off the table, venue, time, and structure of the meeting space (Stein, 1989). More specifically, an agreement needs to be reached on the frequency of the meetings, the length of each meeting, facilities for a caucus or private discussion, and the size and composition of negotiating teams.

Both the physical and psychological settings of a negotiation can develop awkwardness or have other subtle effects on the process. In the armistice negotiation between 1951 and 1953, the North Koreans gave the American negotiators lower chairs (when the meetings were held on their side) so that they did not need to look up at them. They were far shorter than the Americans, and they did not want to feel inferior.

A number of procedural matters (limited time and venue) as well as representation and ritual elements of doing justice (seen as being equal) can affect substantive discussion. The agreements on a protocol, agenda setting, selection of participants, decision-making procedures, and proposal making can become complicated in negotiations which accommodate the participation of many unorganized groups. In peace talks to end civil wars, insurgent groups are often too fractured to develop coordinated positions among themselves, creating questions of who represents whom and who has proper legitimacy and authority. In the event of having multiple participants, the negotiation forums can be divided into plenary sessions and committees which discuss (and are aimed at reaching agreement on) specific issues.

Formal bargaining

In general, bargaining starts with the clarification of assumptions, the exchange of each other's list of priorities and bottom lines. Issues and motivations can be revealed by assessing one's own and other's situations accurately. The construction of a bargaining formula along with the identification of a range of viable options emerges from refining persistent differences, testing trading possibilities between opposing positions. After identifying problems, parties may propose and evaluate options in an attempt to select the best ones. The exchange of proposals moves along with demands, offers, bids, compromises, and concessions.

The opening stage overviews the purpose of negotiation, sets ground rules on behavior and procedures. The norms of behaviors can implicitly emerge or be formally established to guide discussion especially in the event of having multiple participants and volatile issues. The ground rules are supposed to prevent sabotage or manipulation of discussion as well as properly defining the playing field of the negotiation. Implicit and explicit ground rules can be listening without interruption and demonstration of respect for others. These rules can be formal or informal, not necessarily being written down.

The phase of framing and setting agendas is characterized by the way we conceptualize our arguments as well as offering the context of factual information and its history. Most importantly, stories should be able to link the speakers and the listener by pointing out common concerns in the multiplicity of the issues. In fact, setting the agenda plays a crucial role in defining the objectives of negotiation. The more clearly all the objectives are presented at the beginning of negotiations, the more focused the negotiation that can take place. Negotiations may start with the analysis of problems along with discussion about the causes of conflict.

Via opening statements, each side begins to define a range of possible places for settling the negotiation. The opening statement can lead to probing problems and information gathering. Negotiators may focus on the identification of specific needs, interests, or concerns. After the opening statement, some additional preparation might be necessary by determining the other side's interests. Since interests in the opening statement can be overrated, evaluating the opponent's presentation may need to consider the possibility of presentation of incomplete information about their bottom lines. Real desires can be disguised in opening offers as part of tactical maneuvering. Negotiators are likely to ask for more than their realistic expectations.

As illustrated by the six-party talks over North Korea's nuclear programs, negotiations can be stalled at the opening stage. Instead of using the opening process as a constructive step toward discussion about disagreement, the US–North Korea contest started with attacks on each other's positions. The lengthy opening talks just served as a repetition of the already known public positions of the US and North Korean governments. The US insisted on the unconditional nuclear disarmament of North Korea while the North Koreans argued about the US hostile attempt to overthrow their regime. The initial three rounds of the six-party talks did not move on to actual negotiations, merely confirming and reconfirming the yawning gaps between opposing positions. They even failed to develop specific agendas for bargaining. According to informed observers, North Korean negotiators even felt completely bored, losing the incentive for serious negotiation (Pritchard, 2007).

Once serious bargaining starts, opening offers lead to counteroffers and a series of concessions that typically get smaller prior to getting to the no compromise zone. The initial offers need to be something for the other side to entertain and consider worth time and effort to discuss. An opening offer, far lower than the other's expectations, sets a negative tone. Unrealistic offers damage progress, since the other side would not even be willing to consider any suggestion or proposal which appears to be remote from their expectations.

Factual disagreement can be ascribed to difficulties in the verification of different interpretations that are suitable for one's goals and interests. Although Israel accepts the necessity for returning the Golan Heights (occupied after the Six Day War in June 1967) to

Syria upon its security concerns being met, there are different interpretations about the legitimate border between the two protagonists. Israel referred to the 1923 border demarcation between French Syria and mandate of British Palestine as the proper border line. However, Syria insisted on the full withdrawal and return of the border as it was just before the June 1967 war; the borderline was acquired during the 1947–1949 Arab–Israeli war. Besides historical significance, the June 4 line gives Syria unrestrained, direct access to the Sea of Galilee (Lesch, 2008). Territorial issues, especially when related to security concerns, can be a contentious bargaining point.

Negotiators may attempt to manipulate the facts of their case in order to turn discussion to their advantage. Objectively verifiable statements are not generally grounded in debatable theories. The agendas in environmental or labor–management negotiations (involving nonsecurity agendas) can be more easily clarified by factual information (for instance, the amount of polluting gases produced by one country and an appropriate level of wages and compensation packages comparable to others). The acceptance of factual matters supplied by an expert or technical committees can provide assistance in eventual agreements.

An adversarial atmosphere can be created by attacking each other's positions. Each party may attempt to persuade their opponents about the merits of their position while arguing excessive aspects of the other side's demands. Slow and reluctant concessions may come while each side overstates the values of their claims and treats an opponent's concessions as trivial. As a stalemate may arrive from rigid, inflexible positions, each side is unwilling to listen reasonably to the other. A point of deadlock in negotiation is evident when parties dig in to entrenched positions.

An impasse can stem from an unexpected or intentional standoff as well as a loss of interest in negotiation itself. In addition, resistance can also be created by unmet vital interests and needs. Negotiators may also strategically stall negotiation for bigger gains. If they have no intention of reaching an agreement, some parties use negotiation to gather information. An impasse is difficult to break in the event of the disappearance of trust in tandem with the accumulation of negative emotions.

Successful negotiation strategies focus on how to induce others to reach an agreement. Interest in negotiation becomes serious and grows with expectation of reciprocity. One's concessions reciprocated by the other help overcome rigid positions. Preoccupation with winning costs the opportunity to forge integrative solutions, since excessive demands invite the other side's strong resistance. A collaborative process emerges from the development of a common ground (Raiffa *et al.*, 2002).

Most importantly, discovery about an opponent's feelings and needs is part of constructive negotiation. Negotiation can save frustration by focusing on the right problems. The acceptance of an opponent's legitimate concerns is the key to collaborative problem solving. The more protracted the negotiation is, the more complicated the bargaining process might be due to changes in negotiators and their reassessment of interests and shift in goals. The complete derailment of the Israeli–Palestinian peace process is ascribed to the assassination of Israeli Prime Minister Rabin in 1995 and the deteriorating negotiating atmosphere being accompanied by his successor's rigid positions and resurging violence.

Bargaining strategies

Negotiations are not purely managed by "rational exercises in pursuit of self-interests or the development of creative trades" (Kolb and Williams, 2003, p. 12). Most bargaining processes begin with weariness in the absence of established relationships. If the legitimacy of the demand is not accepted by the other bargainer, what leverage one possesses in persuading the other to accept one's proposal can become a key to reaching an agreement. A bargaining atmosphere is formed in the process of testing each other's flexibility on different issues and gauging the other's feelings. As negotiation gets tougher, it is important to "deduce [an] opponent's true position and inner limits from the size and order of its concessions" (Lynch, 2005, p. 391).

In considering that adversaries have different desires for settlement and risk of failure, bargaining issues involve the management of each other's expectations. In negotiating with the Israelis, for instance, Egyptian President Anwar Sadat had more to lose in the event of failure than Israeli Prime Minister Begin (Frazer, 2008). In the end, Sadat had to be content with his less ambitious goals limited to the full return of the Sinai along with the removal of Israeli facilities while giving up a broad Arabic cause of obtaining Palestinian sovereign rights in the West Bank and Gaza (Quandt, 1986).

Variance in the types of resources and constraints among parties also creates imbalance in what one wants to achieve. In addition, external influence such as ally pressure or domestic political necessity can either increase or decrease the expectations about desirable outcomes. Memories and feelings about past experiences and outcomes can be linked to shaping negotiating positions through their cumulative effects.

Breaking an impasse

In breaking a deadlock, an impasse in one area can be bypassed by moving on to other matters or focusing on the underlying concerns. The convergence of expectations can be, in part, supported by shared interests and compatibility in preferences. The possession of similar information (as well as clarity about each other's bargaining leverages, capability, and motivation) leads to clearing ambiguity and uncertainty. The possibility of gain encourages the efforts to prevent impasse (less willing to take the risk). Persuasion can focus on an emphasis on the benefit of concessions and their inevitability.

An informal option generation session (in a noncommittal setting) can be separated from formal bargaining. Private sessions can serve as a method of covert problem solving to narrow differences. The "walk in the woods" produced agreement on the deployment of cruise missiles in Europe which was one of the most contentious issues in arms control negotiations between the US and the Soviet Union during the Reagan administration. In the 1994 US–North Korean negotiations, American negotiators effectively utilized informal tea meetings between the top negotiators to discover North Korea's bottom line that was not easily revealed in the North Korean formal session rhetoric, this being far more bellicose than their actual position (Poneman *et al.*, 2004). Indeed, opposition to concessions can be softened by the behind-the-scenes efforts or informal consultation once negotiators begin to build close working relationships.

Secret informal meetings can be made to gauge what each side may come up with. After the assassination of Yitzhak Rabin in 1995, Israeli Labor Party leader Shimon Peres' top aide Yossi Beilin secretly met with Arafat's deputy, Mahmoud Abbas, and mapped out the general outlook of a peace settlement that could have been adopted if Peres had been elected as Israeli prime minister (Quandt, 2005). The mutual exploration and understanding unfortunately was abandoned after the defeat of Peres to the conservative Likud candidate Benjamin Netanyahu in the spring 1996 election.

A more serious impasse may be overcome by having "cooling off" periods to develop better insight and maintain control over the process. In heated negotiations with strong emotions running high, unresolved anger leads to rigid positions. It is crucial to step back away from emotional entrenchment. Polarization can be minimized to concentrate on tackling issues instead of attacking the other party. If both sides recognize that an impasse is costly, they will be willing to set up rules to avoid arguing.

In fact, cooperative and competitive bargaining styles are differently applied in a wide range of settings. Negotiators may adopt distributive tactics with the involvement of vital interests at stake. It is often the case for each party to underestimate the other side's reactions to one's stiff bargaining positions. Judgment is necessary to know on what basis the other party is negotiating. In the creation of a problem-solving climate, negotiation becomes a forum to search for solutions. A win–win outcome can be achieved when parties have flexibility to explore what is feasible with an orientation toward seeking mutual advantages. Redirection of negotiation through reframing the situation is effective in countering the other's challenges.

Bargaining styles: collaborative versus contentious

In a win–lose negotiation, the structure of bargaining puts negotiators in an adversarial position, pushing each other to cut the best deal possible by staking out a specific position on an issue with demand. Especially when the resources are fixed and need to be divided, parties may push their agendas in order to leave the table with the biggest gains (for instance, territorial disputes). In arguments, questions are raised to make a point or put the other down. All sides dig in a position and argues for it, prior to reluctant concession making. Each party utilizes information about the other's needs to extract concessions.

A lack of shared information about each other's true intentions most likely breeds suspicion. In a contentious negotiation, information serves as a defense against attack or a leverage over adversaries. Power tactics such as bluff and threat are frequently adopted in tandem with holding one's own cards close to the chest. In this situation, the other party feels forced to be put in a corner with insistence on rigid agendas. The failure of the Camp David negotiations in July 2000 can be attributed, in part, to Israeli Prime Minister Ehud Barak's position that his proposal was final and the best he could offer (Dowty, 2008). As his counterpart rejected his proposal, Barak angrily charged that Arafat was not bargaining in good faith. In this kind of negotiating setting, each party guards against making all the compromising.

Techniques for contentious bargaining are comprised of a high initial demand, limited disclosure of information regarding facts and one's own preferences. Few and small concessions can be combined with threats and arguments. Negotiators should be willing to change their mind, and perceptions, but some negotiators make an open assertion about "not being negotiable" on one or more of the key issues which are essential to making or breaking a deal. In order to attain the best settlement they can get, bargainers ask for more than even they think that they are entitled to. Nonnegotiable situations are created when the motion of negotiating is meant to firmly reject any change in their position with a demand for unconditional surrender.

An unnecessary deadlock is created, hampering the atmosphere of future negotiation due to an aggressive approach which irreparably damages relationships. Once requests were rejected, the party may move to making demands. Complaints and angry statements can turn into threats, harassment and abuse. A negative conflict spiral is created by negotiators who attempt to force their way and use competitive strategies, insisting on narrowly interpreted principles. They refuse to reciprocate concessions with reference to power and rights even though the other party tries to remain interest-focused.

Much of the stalemate and occasional reversals in the efforts to denuclearize North Korea during the Bush administration (after its abandonment of the Clinton era accord in late 2002) stem from contentious attitudes held by the leadership of both sides. In response to the Bush administration's financial sanctions on North Korea with the charges of counterfeiting American dollar bills, Pyongyang was seeking information about the charges along with the request for bilateral meetings. The denial of this request and further tightening of sanctions drove North Korea to initially make complaints, demand the removal of punitive measures and eventually threatened to test its nuclear weapons. After the US government's continuing ignorance of the North Korean demand, Pyongyang carried out its threats by testing its long- and short-range missiles and then exploding its nuclear device underground in November 2006 (Pritchard, 2007). In order to bring North Korea back to the negotiating table, the Bush administration had to gradually reverse the previously imposed punitive measures.

The pursuit of one's own unilateral interests can be manifested by extreme demands and other contentious negotiating postures. In trying to force the other to make concessions, competitive bargainers do whatever is necessary to obtain the deal they want by adopting such tactics as bluffing, accusing, intimidating, creating false issues, even cheating and lying. As part of their contentious tactics, parties may release information slowly while making extreme demands to keep an opponent off balance. Naming, blaming, and claiming can be part of difficult negotiation.

Personality features, in combination with a negotiation context, affect bargaining styles and tactics. A self-centered temperament and stubborn personality is likely to favor tougher negotiating styles. In general, analytical, methodical pragmatists are more adapted to integrative bargaining. Easy emotional arousal of anger by a self-centered negotiator is a barrier to collaborative bargaining, causing difficulties in the facilitation of discussion. In addition to individual variation, goals and subject matter can contribute to intransigence. In fact, competitive relationships increase the possibility of posturing and misdirection.

Amicable negotiators, who develop empathy with others, are willing to seek joint outcomes, feeling a greater need for harmony. Even collaborative bargainers can adopt contentious tactics but are far more willing to look for an opportunity to seek mutual gains instead of seeking unilateral solutions. In comparison with his predecessors (e.g., Menachem Begin) and successors (such as Benjamin Netanyahu), Israeli Prime Minister Yitzhak Rabin can be considered one of the most pragmatic negotiators, earning high respect from his Arab counterparts such as King Hussein of Jordan as well as Yasser Arafat. Despite his previous perception of Arafat as "a leader of murderers, conniving and ruthless," Rabin was willing to move beyond his suspicion and "was able to develop agreed upon rules of engagement," for instance, in response to Palestinian terrorist attacks in Israel (Sher, 2006, p. 3).

Rabin met in secret for years with King Hussein, cultivating a high degree of mutual esteem. The negotiations between Jordan and Israel did not implicate fundamental disagreements over legitimacy and territory, but nonetheless the personal relationships between the two leaders helped a smooth negotiation of the Israel–Jordan peace treaty signed on October 26, 1994 (Quandt, 2005). Nurturing a trust relationship certainly enabled King Hussein to drop a claim to the West Bank and Jerusalem more easily.

On the contrary, Israeli Prime Minister Netanyahu's negative perceptions about Palestinians translated into highly acrimonious relationships with his counterpart. Netanyahu even refused to sign the Hebron Agreement reached with Arafat in January 1997, and American special envoy Dennis Ross had to put a "Note for the Record" to the document, indirectly confirming an Israeli commitment to further withdrawal from the occupied territories.

Those who tend to be more empathetic pay more attention to the feelings of others and have better listening skills. They are contextually better adapted, relationship oriented rather than being merely oriented toward instrumental goals. Those who are less contentious make fewer extraneous arguments, fewer degrading comments and fewer threats than those who adopt confrontational techniques.

Overcoming debacles

Low-cost trade-offs and concessions can serve as a motivator to break a stalemate. Well-regarded incentives are often able to shift the directions of negotiation. The ideal concessions carry highly symbolic values to be easily noticed by the target, but should be relatively cost free for those who offer them. In addition, the values of yielding tend to be high when none existed before. The admission of wrong or the offer of apology can become a "commodity to be traded for relationship" (Isenhart and Spangle, 2000, p. 86).

Gradual concession-making approaches can be taken in a deadlocked situation. In moving away from frozen positions, concessions can be made by one of the parties in a step-by-step manner to draw reciprocal treatment. While there is no need to concede one's own vital needs to meet the other's interests, a small reward can be offered to produce positive perceptions. In a long series of negotiations, it can be designed to reduce tension and build trust (Osgood, 1962).

If both sides are strongly committed to conciliation, the chain of reciprocal moves of accommodation can be activated by the offer made on a noncontingent and nonrevocable basis as a goodwill gesture. On the other hand, at the early stage of concession making, collaborative overtures may be misinterpreted, in adversarial relations, as signs of weakness instead of being taken as a positive move toward a fair settlement. The effectiveness in breakthrough (ice breaking) depends on how each assesses "the substantive and symbolic value of what is at stake" (Lebow, 1996, p. 69). The expectation of reciprocity can be explained by specification about concessions' objectives or value.

Progress may come with few concessions until every side is exhausted. Slow accommodations and trade-offs may eventually bring about incremental convergence if the intervention of any dramatic event can bring about a sudden leap toward a packaged settlement. It has taken more than 12 years for the Sudanese military government to engage in discussion about self-determination and secularization with the Sudan People's Liberation Movement which represented the population in the south. The change in the position came about after many years of diplomatic and economic sanctions coordinated by neighboring countries. Indeed, negotiation on substantive issues was not feasible so long as the military government headed by Omar Hassan al-Bashir insisted on the exclusion of autonomy and de-Islamization as principal agendas.

Barriers to collaborative bargaining

Incompatible values and unreasonable beliefs as well as unrealistic expectations can hinder forging a compromise. Inaccurate perception of issues may stem from difficulties in objective evaluation of an adversary's position. Obstacles to constructive discussion include emotional rage and cognitive rigidity. Negative feelings hamper the ability and willingness to listen to new evidence and jointly consider options. Negative feelings about the past and unresolved emotions might result in an attempt to get even as compensation for the past events.

Reaching an agreement can be difficult if internal politics or external pressure weigh heavily in developing compromise. The rapid decline in public support for peace negotiations forced Colombian President Pastrana to quit negotiations with the main insurgent group Fuerza Armadas Revolucionarias de Colombia (FARC) in February 2002. The negotiating environment was made tougher due to the right-wing paramilitary attacks on leftist guerrillas and the FARC demand for the government to rein in paramilitary activities.

A deadlock can be created when one or both sides adopt a "take-it-or-leave-it" position. During the 2008 World Trade Organization talks, India adamantly opposed the removal of farm subsidies. By developing a nonnegotiable stance on farm subsidies, India derailed the entire negotiation process which was so close to a package deal. Entrenched and polarized bargaining situations are created by straying away from interest-based framing to blaming mode along with the attribution of all the ills to the other side. Indeed, attacks and counter-attacks result in unproductive negotiation. Forcing tactics meet resistance rather than cooperation. If threats and coercive statements prevail, parties harden their positions with closure to new information for the exploration of solution. A sense of hopelessness prevails with fixed patterns of response (attacks and counterattacks).

The reinforcement of resistance is derived from the negative attributions and perceptions; cognitive impasses come from the failure to change the perceptions of each other. The accusation of the other party's inflexibility for the deadlock is often ascribed to the perception that they seek unfair advantage; a lack of trust leads to suspicion about hidden agendas. For instance, the North Korean intransigent position comes from the belief that the US goal is to cause the collapse of their regime instead of denuclearization of the Korean peninsula.

Refusal to move from original positions endangers an ongoing relationship while each side tries, through sheer willpower, to force the other to change its stance. The prevalence of win–lose strategies produces the outcome that reflects power differences. Power imbalance between parties leaves fewer options for a weaker party.

The failure of negotiation can often be attributed to a contest of will. In the Cyprus conflict in the 1960s, the talks between the Greeks and the Turks broke down at the pre-bargaining stage. Each of the parties had preconditions that their own draft constitution should be the basis for discussion. In this kind of bargaining environment neither side is willing to give up its position by accepting the draft of the other. As parties believe that they cannot afford to negotiate from positions of weakness, each side tries through sheer willpower to force the other to change their position. Resentment inevitably emerges in a situation where one side sees itself bending to the other side's rigid will whereas its own concerns go unaddressed.

Manipulative tactics

A frequent shift in expectations and mood (from angry to pleasant and vice versa) is designed to generate uncomfortable feelings and to keep the other off balance. A more powerful party may try to exert control over an adversary's confidence level by attacking their competence and creating doubt about their ability to protect their interests (e.g., Chinese tactics against the Tibetans). In the opposite approach, flattery can be used to "retain control over the negotiation" by appealing to the natural impulses of the other party (Kolb and Williams, 2003, p. 123).

One manipulative tactic is to elude to the main topics by concentrating on the accusation of the other side for something which is different from what should have been the main subject matter for negotiation. This is reflected in the Chinese authorities' recent negotiating strategies after reluctantly being re-engaged in talks with the Dalai Lama. After the public protest against their rule in March 2008, the Chinese leadership was under pressure from Western leaders to talk to the Tibetans. Instead of discussing self-rule and autonomy, the Chinese government blamed the Dalai Lama for sabotaging the summer Olympic Games by inciting the protest by monks in the Tibetan capital Lhasa that had already been denied several times by the Tibetans. The negotiation did not have any meaningful substantive discussion due to the Chinese leadership's mere justification of their strict rule in Tibet and legitimization of their occupation.

In contrast with good-faith negotiations, manipulative techniques (designed to fool the other side) can eventually undermine credibility. By avoiding psychological maneuverings, bargaining can switch from relational elements to the real problem. In this situation, "the best course of action is not to overreact in a negative response" (Kolb and Williams, 2003, p. 156).

As part of the pressure tactics to accept an unfair deal, a sense of urgency is deliberately created with an artificial deadline along with the deprivation of information needed to make judgments as well as denial of an opportunity for consultation with other people. People may find out later that they were cheated, feeling that they were the victims of a dirty trick. Asymmetry in bargaining styles needs to be managed by the involvement of a third party such as a mediator.

Face saving

Image protecting behavior (i.e., the main element of face saving) hinders a person's ability to make concessions in the process of reaching a final agreement, displaying their need to reconcile with the previous stand (principles, deeds, and words). The devotion of energy to the protection of their images rather than concentration on issues causes parties to get bogged down in trivial issues with irrational comments and acts. Preservation of face may motivate such negotiating behavior as digging in their heels, and stubbornly clinging to positions despite poor odds.

Face saving reflects a person's need to reconcile the stand she or he takes in a negotiation with past words, deeds, and principles. Concessions are resisted in order to preserve one's image as respected, competent, and trustworthy. In particular, personalized issues involve face saving (for instance, in defense of one's reputation of being tough). In tackling the 1962 Cuban Missile Crisis, President Kennedy's tough public stance on Soviet missiles on the island's soil, and refusal to settle the issue by negotiation in public, stem from his concern that any appearance of making concessions would brand him as being soft on communism.

It is hard to carry out constructive discussion by posing threats to the identities of the negotiating parties. The engagement in antagonistic behaviors is intensified by "fear of losing, of being perceived as weak and vulnerable, and of being undervalued" (Isenhart and Spangle, 2000, p. 132). Parties can be defensive when they sense threats to their social images. The circumstances of face threatening are created by devaluing the other's perspectives or casting doubt on their competence. By questioning motivations or truthfulness of the opponent, a negotiator may make them feel being blamed for something which they are not accountable for.

It is often a complicated task to differentiate defensive face saving from an aggressive move. By treating foreign leaders' meetings with the Dalai Lama as a slap in the face, the Chinese leadership has been attempting to suppress the international exposure of their illegitimate rule in Tibet. The French President Sarkozy's meeting with the Dalai Lama in the fall of 2008 has tested the public image of both France and China. Even though the meeting was planned several months ago with public support, the Chinese government put relentless, last-minute public pressure for its cancellation which could have been seen as a public disgrace for Sarkozy. Thus the issue became a public contest of will.

Various attempts to protect or repair the image (which others see in us) are driven by an emotional attachment to the "face" (popularized by sociologist Erving Goffman, 1963). The loss of face disrupts emotional support that needs to be protected in a social situation. Face is keeping a good image geared toward presenting one's fine qualities to the outside world. It involves such emotional content as "honor and shame." In a high-context culture, face saving serves as "reciprocal forces that serve to unite groups, police the boundaries, define who is included or excluded, and enforce conformity" (Augsburger, 1992, p. 103).

An image of the deal can be related to avoiding the loss of face which makes one of the parties look bad. When parties stick with their positions to avoid looking bad, minor concessions as well as carefully crafted statements can be used to promote the qualities the negotiators want to present to others. In order to save face, motivations or intentions can be framed in a positive manner to provide a way out with the recognition of the value in the other's perspective. In the event one's comments provoke emotional reactions, rephrasing or apologies can be made for clearing up the ill feeling while reframing one's comments in a more favorable light.

Effective negotiation

Effective negotiators consider bargaining not for domination but in the spirit of mutual respect needed to reach an agreeable outcome. A commitment to a positive, mutually beneficial solution is necessary to uncover underlying issues, and identify areas of common ground. Effective negotiators select the right starting point of bargaining with the establishment of clear communication for better understanding of each other's positions. Negotiators should refuse to yield to bullying tactics, but show readiness to change course, if necessary, as the situation dictates. A certain amount of flexibility is the key to successful negotiation.

As negotiation is both situational and relational, communication needs to be adapted to diverse situations of bargaining. When people feel vulnerable and mistrust, they refuse to share information and do not reveal their true positions. Feelings about each other and their interaction patterns affect the level of openness in discussion about issues dividing them as well as real concerns and wants. The admission of weakness in the case (rather than allowing an opponent to expose them) helps to gain credibility.

Negotiators should have skills of advocating their own interests facing a contentious bargainer who makes an unreasonable demand. In fact, advocating one's own interests is not incompatible with the efforts to accommodate the other bargainer's concerns. Full appreciation of differences is necessary to prevent sacrifice of one's own interests to satisfy the greed of another party. Making effective claims is necessary to earn credibility for one's stance; one's interests can be presented in a way for the other party to feel comfortable and willing to concede. The reciprocation of care along with candid discussion about all the issues creates a constructive atmosphere for reaching an agreement.

Communication skills

The deployment of communication skills helps assess the other's perspective, underlying interests. The articulation of ideas and listening to underlying messages are the most basic form of communication competence in negotiation. In fact, framing and active listening are key for successful exchange of information regarding the awareness of each other's priorities (needed for integrative solutions). Active listening involves the acknowledgment of feelings as well as asking questions and paraphrasing. Empowering the other party is beneficial since it helps them cooperate to share information, and express their views freely. Paraphrasing the other's statements, clarification, and further discussion are needed for checking the right message is sent out and received.

Participants should be able to talk more candidly about their needs for an inclusive discussion. Listening does not mean agreement, but is crucial to evaluation. Skilled negotiators overcome the human tendency to neglect what we are reluctant to hear or accept. The good intentions of others are often ignored along with justification of our own positions by attribution errors, contributing to self-fulfilling prophecies. Showing respect for the other's point of view by acknowledging the values of their story is a precondition for the revelation of a more complex account.

Productive mutual exchange comes from a genuine appreciation of the other's ideas and feelings beyond defensive arguments and counterarguments. Unconditional concessions can be exploited by an adversary who adopts a strategy of consistent refusal to compromise. The problem-solving phase entails non-evaluative brainstorming of potential solutions along with the creation of a climate for a free exchange of ideas. Innovative solutions can be found by bridging and linkage of different interests as well as concessions for stalemate breaking.

Inquiry can be used to develop mutual engagement beyond "trying to solicit useful information about the other party's interests or bottom line" (Kolb and Williams, 2003, p. 280). Engagement in mutual inquiry helps reevaluate each other's desires, redefining the problem itself. It is important not only to sort out what each party truly wants after getting the facts and clarifying the meaning but also to perceive the intentions and feelings behind the words. Deeper probing of the issues and shared understanding helps to convert seemingly opposing interests into mutual concerns. Moves needed to keep the negotiation on track include treating the other's resistance as an impetus for more inquiry. Mutual inquiry is based on sharing an emotional and analytical process beyond an instrumental concern related to self-interest.

Bargaining methods

In integrative bargaining, the harmonization of incompatible goals as well as unbundling interests can be an overarching strategy of negotiation. Through negotiation, common values or objectives (for example, a safer environment) can be created for the benefit of all parties. The expansion of awards for each party can be achieved by an increase in the overall amount of total goods. Individual benefit is supposed to become larger with an increase in the overall or aggregate benefit from the settlement. It can be compared with the situation where the overall amount of benefit available to all parties becomes smaller due to competition.

Even though an integrative solution increases the benefit of the settlement to all the parties, competitive situations can be created by an attempt to have a larger portion in joint gains. Not every party may be able to obtain an equal share of highly valued gains (e.g., a proposal on disproportionate sharing of oil revenue generated in a territorially disputed island and its surrounding areas between China and Japan). The overall amount of benefit can be higher for one party than the other in spite of an increase in aggregate benefit. This creates a condition under which the degree of satisfaction to each party can be disproportionate. To minimize the possibility of competition over a greater share of the increment, the adversaries may agree beforehand on terms under which the newly incremented goods or resources can be shared. The 1982 Law of Sea Treaty stipulated specific territorial boundaries permitted for the exclusive exploitation of resources as well as shared areas for mutual exploration of minerals.

Mutual interests can be satisfied by the trade-offs of priorities in different issue areas (which might have dissimilar levels of significance). In order to overcome fixed-pie orientations, negotiators may start with information sharing to learn each other's preferences and goals. Interests can be weighed with clear priorities, creating building blocks for later trade-offs with focused agendas. Trade can be made easier by redefining and unbundling the problems. Trade-off can be guided by the expectations of mutual gains, but it does not need to rely on quantitative precision.

Even though the proposal was eventually nullified by the Reagan administration, mutual understanding was reached by both the key US negotiator Paul Nitze and his Soviet counterpart in bargaining over the intermediate-range nuclear forces (INF): Moscow would give up a numerical advantage in total INF warheads in the European theater in return for the US scrapping its Pershing II ballistic missiles with quick strike times.

Trade-offs can be made easier by re-prioritization or subdivision of goals. Meta-goals can be broken down into their component parts through fractionation. Through bridging, negotiators may concede on original demands in the search for new, integrative formulations with concerted efforts to satisfy underlying interests. Via linkage, each party meets a demand from the other side in return for obtaining something that is important for them. Linkage can expand the scope of negotiation by connecting agreements of multiple bargaining issues (e.g., the US de-listing of North Korea from the status of a terrorist state in return for agreeing to the cessation of Pyongyang's nuclear programs).

In log-rolling, mutual concessions on different issues are made in the way to increase a gain on one set of issues in exchange for yielding on another which is more highly valued by an opponent. "Ideally, both are conceding points in areas that have little personal cost or importance and are gaining concessions in areas that are highly important, creating a mutually beneficial arrangement" (McCorkle and Reese, 2005, p. 149). In resolving the contentious issue of abolishing the Islamic law in Sudan, the southern insurgent forces dropped their position of secularization of the entire country in return for the law's limited application only to the Islamic north. Log-rolling becomes feasible due to the possibility of concession making based on issues of lower priority to oneself but of higher priority to the other. Given the existence of differences in priorities on issues, each party makes sure that they obtain their most valuable goals by mutual concession making.

While substitutive goods and materials can be traded off, negotiation over intangible or symbolic items (related to the recognition of identity) needs to be based on the recognition of historical meanings or intrinsic values long held by each community. The existence of only a narrow range of practical solutions leads to a settlement that is less than each party originally desired. This challenge can sometimes be overcome by a sidepayment coming from external parties.

When one party gains benefit at the expense of the other, "cost-cutting" can reduce loss to an opponent. In substitution, the loss can be compensated by alternatives of a roughly equivalent value to the material losses. In Israeli–Palestinian negotiations, discussion about land swaps has been centered around the Israeli absorption of the Jewish settlements in the West Bank in return for ceding a small piece of Israeli desert land to the Palestinians. Extra goods make up for the shortfall between their aspirations and the actual benefits. Parties gaining most goods or payments compensate the party for their loss (through repayment in unrelated areas). In addition, costs can be cancelled out rather than being offset by other types of benefit.

Motivation for reaching agreement

There are different motives involved in making concessions for settlement. Reaching agreement is desired when neither side can improve outcomes with unilateral actions. Making concessions should not be seen as damaging to one's reputation or humiliating even if they sacrifice original aspirations. In order to change the adversary's views of the situation, one party may promise rewards for concessions (e.g., the European offer of aid to Iranians for giving up nuclear programs) or reward positive actions for further concessions (economic assistance and diplomatic exchanges in return for Libya's abandonment of its nuclear programs). To influence the other party, promises ought to be relevant to achieving their goals. In power asymmetry, hints at threats and actual exercise of power might force an adversary to give up their preferences.

Bargaining range

There is a different range of deals between what one absolutely wants and the best one can get. Negotiations are successful when both sides find a compatible range of points that they are willing to agree on through compromise. In order to achieve a successfully negotiated outcome, both parties must feel that the end result is the best they could accomplish and that it is worth accepting and supporting (Lewicki *et al.*, 2001). When the needs are balanced, the outcome is more likely to produce a new level of confidence and trust.

Bargainers have their own order of priorities originating from perceptual reference points which indicate the desirability and acceptability of certain solutions. Thus, different negotiators perceptually feel a diverse range of outcomes from the most desirable to the least, as well as feasibility to achieve them. Whereas deals must be worth meeting the bottom lines, the initial bargaining position can be developed from "the most desirable outcome that could be imagined."

Several important categories of bargaining points are scattered between the spectrum of the most desirable goal and the option to walk away due to the deal's implications for the loss of wealth, pride, or status. In its dispute with Australia over sea territory, East Timor accepted sharing half the oil revenue from the disputed continental shelf while giving up their maximum desire of gaining the exclusive ownership. The compromise was acceptable since the deal improved their original situation (i.e., getting nothing).

Negotiators need to have some ideas about the price associated with making concessions in return for a particular demand met by the other side. The final settlement may fall somewhere in between the most desirable and non-negotiable. A negotiator's calculations may focus on the balance between the expected price to be paid for concession making and expected utility of one's gains.

Depending on a party's reference point, the outcome can be a success or loss. A party's opening offer and the other side's counteroffer can start from the most desirable and eventually settle somewhere before the least desirable. Negotiations most likely end around a point where each party settles for less than originally hoped. Some additional gains might be sought to "make up for the shortfall" in aspirations. The existence of more "tradable" issues makes compromise easy.

The mutually acceptable bargaining range is likely to be narrow in intractable conflict especially when one's demand is anchored in the values held most dear by the opponents. In Israel–Palestinian negotiations, territorial concessions in the West Bank and control over Jerusalem have proven a far tougher issue than the establishment of a Palestinian state or compensation for Palestinian refugees. It is due to the fact that the territories have sacred religious meanings for orthodox Jews while Arabs attach a sense of rights and pride to the recovery of land lost to Israel during the 1967 War. Pressure on a negotiator by constituents is likely to lead to the more fierce protection of margins. What most negotiators want to avoid is to give up one's essential goals by agreeing to terms which bear major loss.

Ending strategies

There are variations in the outcomes between win–win and win–lose poles. High-quality agreement can be judged in terms of maximum joint gains both sides feel satisfied about. Mutual gains (associated with win–win outcomes) can arise from accommodation of each other's essential needs. In most non-coercive negotiation settings, mixed outcomes are common; each party wins some issues, but makes concessions on other issues. One party's gains would not hurt the other party's chances of obtaining their goals. In other situations (when mutual gains are not feasible), the loss can be tolerated and turn out to be better still vis-à-vis situations to be created by the failed negotiation. In the worst asymmetric scenario, one or both parties may end up absorbing extreme loss.

The intangibles may be held to be of greater value than the tangibles. Some negotiators tend to be averse to risk in order to diminish the tension derived from uncertainties inherent in a bargaining situation. A short-term substantive benefit can be given up for positive long-term relationships. A stake at negotiation may include an opportunity, goodwill, or the quality of a relationship. In resolving their territorial disputes with Saudi Arabia in 1975, Oman retained the Buraymi oasis but ceded land with oil-producing potential with a sea corridor. The government of Oman put the deal in the context of seeking long-term, friendly relationships with its stronger neighbor. In seeking agreement, Islamic countries often justify their concessions or compromise deal by invoking the Islamic principles of "brotherhood."

Finding an appropriate strategy of ending a long, protracted negotiation can be a dilemma after so much time and energy were devoted. The longer people negotiate, the smaller the concessions they are likely to make. Yielding might be difficult and be reluctantly rolled out due to mutual hostilities and suspicion (exemplified by North Korea's negotiation with the US since 2003). In fact, a long, protracted negotiation is shaped by a shift in thinking about issues and relationships. Even though it took only a few months to reach an agreement over water distribution (that will be effective for 30 years), India and Bangladesh had spent almost two decades squabbling over a fair deal due to neither side's willingness to budge. The shift in the Indian position occurred once a new democratic government was restored in Bangladesh in 1996.

Under certain circumstances (such as battlefield loss or the emergence of a new leadership with different priorities), negotiators may lower their aspirations to find an exit from long protracted bargaining. The longer the negotiation lasts, the more likely each party seeks some kind of settlement presuming that they desire to see the fruit of invested time and efforts devoted to bargaining. It has taken more than a decade to eventually reach an agreement in Sudan; it took almost six years to reach settlement in Burundi. The persistence of neighboring countries' pressure, including economic sanctions, was necessary for breaking the impasse that stemmed from the military governments' intransigent positions and refusal to discuss key issues of autonomy and self-determination (in Sudan); power sharing (in Burundi).

Overall, the outcome must be agreeable and acceptable even if it is not fully satisfactory since it can generate long-term implications for one's well-being. Negotiated settlement produces new norms or procedures for solutions to problems of similar nature. By reaching a bilateral agreement with Israel in 1978, Sadat thought that he had created a precedent for other Arab leaders. Settlement of a specific issue may bring about a series of future changes in expectations, roles, and authority relationships. In each negotiation, "culture is formed, refined and remade" (Isenhart and Spangle, 2000, p. 6).

Negotiation is frozen if a status quo is preferred by one of the parties who holds advantage by protracting the process or not settling, being aided by power superiority. Negotiations over the return of occupied territories tend to be stalled due to difficulties in finding the balance between each other's positions. The negotiation on the return of the Golan Heights (occupied by Israel in the 1967 War) to Syria was stalled given the long political stalemate in the bilateral relationship. It is more advantageous for Armenia to hold on to its occupied territory in Azerbaijan through stalemated negotiation because the prospect of keeping control over the Armenian enclave in Azerbaijan indefinitely cannot be defended by international law.

Constituent satisfaction

Negotiations between collective entities require approval or consultation involving groups or government agencies. A negotiator in a representative capacity often does not have full capacity to make the decision final. The outcome has to be acceptable to higher authorities and the public at home; in order to satisfy constituents, negotiators attempt to leave an impression which can appeal to different audience groups by negotiating in the middle. In order to minimize the resistance of those who have stood to gain by the arms race and hard-line politicians, US–USSR arms control negotiations focused on incremental implementation (Singer, 1990).

The Clinton administration did not ratify the landmark 1994 agreement with North Korea at Congress in anticipation of difficulties in getting approval. The agreement had remained as a framework to guide a step-by-step implementation of detailed action plans until the Bush administration abandoned it in late 2002. In addition, given the difficulties to get the approval for funding, South Korea stepped in to build light water reactors to replace North Korea's nuclear facility designed to produce plutonium, thus costing the US very little.

Distributive versus integrative outcomes

Different negotiation styles produce either distributive or integrative outcomes (Lynch, 2005). Most importantly, the degree of difficulty in reaching an agreement is associated with the types and extent of goal incompatibilities. Disparity in the expectations of negotiated outcomes comes from differences in the perceptions of distribution of bargaining power (relative strength of each side's ability to achieve their objectives) as well as the degree of salient interests at stake. Power differentials are often reflected in negotiated outcomes, since in a contentious conflict situation, a stronger party is more likely to push their own way to demand concessions. Imbalanced outcomes can also be created by asymmetry in negotiating styles.

Distributive bargaining

In distributive bargaining, each side concentrates on getting the best deal for themselves giving a more visible role to tactics to promote one's own interests. In particular, negotiators who adopt more competitive orientations pursue unfair advantage with little reluctance to create impasse. Fixed-pie, win–lose attitudes drive confrontation at a negotiating table. Interests are perceived to be incompatible in zero-sum competition where each party develops their strategies on the basis of win–lose dichotomy. The entrenched positions of Iran on its nuclear programs are attributed to high stakes involved in negotiation outcomes.

In order to satisfy self-interests, contentious bargainers may get engaged in such tactics as bluff and intimidation, devaluing others and information hiding. As trust is lacking, each party demands the other's unilateral concessions and digs in rigid positions. Threats can be combined with tactics of manipulation by misleading an opponent regarding a settling point and withholding critical information and facts. In addition, losing in a struggle for power implies loss of "face."

Integrative bargaining

Integrative bargaining offers strategies for the greatest pay-offs in mixed-motive settings in which cooperation produces bigger gains for every bargainer than distributive bargaining. In a successful integrative negotiation, the parties must understand each other's true needs and objectives by creating a free flow of information and open exchanges of ideas. A high level of power sharing in negotiation leads to joint strategies to pursue integrative outcomes (such as cost sharing). Mutually beneficial solutions stem from information sharing, nurturing trust, and trade-off of interests.

In contrast with the process of distributive bargaining, integrative negotiation develops a bargaining structure which allows all sides to maximize and achieve their objectives in a collaborative manner. Goal incompatibility can be overcome by developing an outcome that bridges individual preferences in a successful search for joint gains that benefit all via trade-offs and packaging.

From adversarial to collaborative negotiating styles

Given that negotiation reflects various mixed situations of gains and losses, various circumstances dictate the adoption of different strategies of bargaining (contention versus collaboration). Since negotiation is an exercise in managing a paradoxical relationship composed of both competitive and cooperative orientations, distributive and integrative bargaining strategies may oscillate at various stages of bargaining. If a negotiating climate deteriorates, even a collaborative process can fall into a mode of distributive bargaining. Parties cooperate to search for shared interests in a complementary relationship. At the same time, a certain degree of competition is inevitable in dividing benefit and burdens.

In fact, cooperative and competitive bargaining styles tend to be differently applied in a wide range of settings. Intense competition for one's own favorable outcome creates low levels of mutual trust and induces an attempt to dominate each other, while withholding information may generate suspicious and hostile attitudes. In general, adversarial bargaining is characterized by a lack of sensitivity to the other party's interests and the use of threats in tandem with seeking power over others.

In negotiating with the president of the white South African government, F.W. de Klerk, in 1991, Nelson Mandela initially took power bargaining tactics to maximize African National Congress (ANC) control over the transition to majority rule. His intransigent positions on an elected constitutional body and veto power culminated in walking out of the multiparty Congress for a Democratic South Africa, taking the entire peace process to the brink of collapse. The ANC eventually backed down, dropping their demand on the procedural matters as a precondition for substantive negotiation in that the deadlocked stalemate produced escalating violence.

The transition from distributive to integrative bargaining is likely to emerge from enhanced relationships; the establishment of at least a minimum level of trust and cooperation is needed for progress toward agreement. The participants in the Northern Irish peace process put priority on the complete cessation of IRA and other paramilitary violence in order to cultivate confidence at the negotiation table. In a collaborative process, the parties must understand each other's genuine needs and objectives by creating a free flow of information and open exchanges of ideas focusing on their similarities in objectives.

Trusting attitudes result from a high concern for welfare of self and others as well as the readiness to resolve differences in a cooperative manner. Revealing motivations and goals can reduce the other side's fears and clear up misperceptions. Respect for opposing interests is developed by an orientation toward mutually shared power. Perceived similarity in beliefs and attitudes leads to a focus on issues.

Further reading

Bazerman, M. (2005) *Negotiation, Decision Making and Conflict Management*, MA: Edward Elgar.

Curtin, P. A. and Gaither, K. (2007) *International Public Relations: Negotiating Culture, Identity, and Power*, Thousand Oaks, CA: Sage.

Donohue, W. A. (2001) "Defining Relationships in the Negotiation Context: Features of the Negotiation Context," in W. Eadie and P. Nelson (eds) *The Language of Conflict and Resolution*, Thousand Oaks, CA: Sage Publications.

Druckman, D. (2001) "Turning Points in International Negotiation," in *Journal of Conflict Resolution*, 45 (4): 519–544.

Goodwin, D. (2002) *Negotiation in International Conflict: Understanding Persuasion*, London: Frank Cass.

Isenhart, M. W. and Spangle, M. (2000) *Collaborative Approaches to Resolving Conflict*, Thousand Oaks, CA: Sage Publications.

Lebow, R. N. (1996) *The Art of Bargaining*, Baltimore: Johns Hopkins University Press.

Quandt, W. B. (2005) *Peace Process: American Diplomacy and the Arab–Israel Conflict since 1967*, Washington, DC: Brookings Institution Press and University of California Press.

Raiffa, H. *et al.* (2002) *Negotiation Analysis: The Science and Art of Collaborative Decision Making*, Cambridge, MA: Belknap Press of Harvard University Press.

Stein, J. G. (1989) "Getting to the Table: The Triggers, Stages, Functions and Consequences of Pre-Negotiation," in G. J. Stein (ed.) *Getting to the Table*, Baltimore: Johns Hopkins Press.

Zartman, I. W. (2005) "Structures of Escalation and Negotiation," in I. W. Zartman and G. Faure (eds) *Escalation and Negotiation in International Conflicts,* New York: Cambridge University Press.

9 Mediation

In managing complex human relations, mediation has entered popular parlance from everyday life to major international arenas. Some of the well-known examples of averting and ending inter-state wars via mediation include Pope John Paul II intervention in territorial disputes between Chile and Argentina (1978–1984), Soviet premier Kosygin's sponsorship of the cease-fire between Pakistan and India in 1964, and former US Secretary of State Henry Kissinger's shuttle diplomacy achieved military disengagement agreements between Israel and its Arab adversaries (1974–1976) after the Yom Kippur War (1973). More dramatic was the Egyptian–Israeli Peace Accord that resulted from the relentless efforts of US President Jimmy Carter aided by his staff and diplomats. In fact, the 1978 Camp David Accord reshaped the perception that war was the only means to end the Arab–Israeli conflict, presenting a new model of peace diplomacy.

Although there are many forms of mediation, in general, it is widely known for "neutral" third-party assistance in reaching settlement. Theoretically, an intermediary intervention in the negotiation process is not supposed to be authoritative in the sense that mediators do not make rulings or impose an agreement. Since they are making decisions, partisans may feel it is fairer with mediation than with arbitration which they cannot control. Thus, mediation can be characterized as "a form of assisted negotiation" or at least is seen as "a catalyst for negotiation" (Touval and Zartman, 2001, p. 442). Being motivated for settlement is essential to any successful mediation not only because consent to a mediation process is voluntary but also because the disputants make final decisions on the issue.

This chapter reviews the various roles of mediators, the process of mediation and conditions for successful intermediary roles. Mediation is more easily applied to interest-specific negotiation than issues related to values or fundamental principles. However, mediation has been growingly utilized to end civil wars (e.g., Burundi, Sudan, Bosnia-Herzegovina) and other protracted violent conflicts (e.g. Northern Ireland) over the last two decades. Thus it has developed a new adaptation to different conflict situations which entail such issues as self-determination, sovereignty, and territorial disputes.

Attributes of mediation

In a classic definition, mediation is regarded as a process whereby a neutral third party, acceptable to all disputants, facilitates communication that enables parties to reach a negotiated settlement. A negotiation process can be modified or extended by the involvement of a third party. The participation of a mediator in negotiation creates dynamics which are different from straight negotiation. The assistance process helps the parties arrive at an agreement voluntarily without resorting to physical force, not invoking the authority of law

(Bercovitch and Houston, 2000). An external agent utilizes their experience and expertise in controlling fear and reducing the stereotypes and prejudices of the disputants in tandem with the supply of alternative and additional information.

In the account of one of the main participants in the 1978 Camp David Summit, the essence of a mediating role is well illustrated by President Carter's managing relations between the Israeli Prime Minister Menachem Begin and Egyptian President Anwar Sadat. In the hope of prevailing over fear and distrust, Carter put himself in the role of "psychotherapist" as well as acting as "messenger, conveying positions and impressions back and forth. On other occasions he was more the arbitrator, pressing for agreement along lines that he had determined were fair. In the end Carter tried to persuade Sadat and Begin, and through them their respective political systems, to reach a peace agreement" (Quandt, 1986, p. 5).

The most important function of a mediator is the creation of an atmosphere conducive for negotiation by the facilitation of communication that leads to loosening tensions. The assistance of a neutral third party in a negotiation is designed to support communication hampered by a conflict. The third party would create good faith and confidence in reaching reasonable compromises by aiding their communication. Parties are allowed to express their concerns and feelings directly or indirectly at meetings organized by mediators. Mediators should pay attention to issues, both hidden and overt, and be aware of how a negotiation process is affected by power and values.

The structure of interaction evolves along with changing communication patterns, exploration of different approaches to the issues, and methods for the evaluation of options. An impartial third party has no authoritative decision-making power since the disputants are supposed to be the major players. Both the process and outcome should be acceptable to the participants in that mediation is based on consent. Depending on the quality of relationships between disputants, the mediator has a different degree of controlling the process, but a final decision over acceptance or rejection of the outcome is left with disputants. No advanced commitment to the acceptance of the outcome is required to start mediation.

Given that mediation is not an institutionalized process (like arbitration or other forms of adjudication), in general, formal rules or standard procedures do not exist. In managing the communication process, mediators can be geared toward the tasks of identifying key issues rather than focusing on socio-emotional dynamics. The objective of mediation may need to be concerned about issue management instead of transforming adversarial relationships if the partisans are not committed to a search for a shared future. In general, the main activities of mediation are directed toward ending a conflict at hand rather than responding to behavioral problems.

However, mediation may improve relations via changing perceptions and behavior as a by-product of communication. In order to reach an agreement, intermediary activities may generally entail defining the areas of contention, making recommendations, and formulating mutually acceptable solutions, while endeavoring to open new possibilities. Even though some mediators may limit themselves to encouragement and advice for resumption of direct negotiation, others may advance proposals along with interpretation of each disputant's positions and persuade adversarial parties to accept compromise.

Communication links

The major mediation function is the strategic adoption of skills to keep the communication flow balanced, fair, and productive (McCorkle and Reese, 2005). The most important task is to open contact, carry messages, and clarify meanings. A mediator's job is to identify concerns that each party does not want to reveal openly. Part of communication activities is supported by the supply of missing information and the development of a rapport. The areas of agreement and disagreement can be discovered by open and sincere communication in a brainstorming process. Separate caucus sessions with each disputant are used in control or management of emotions. The chances of compromise are increased by more accurate assessment of each other's positions.

An informal communication link between the antagonists (developed by a trusted intermediary) serves the purpose of identifying the major issues. As part of informal probing, separate consultation with disputants can precede formal mediation to identify the parties' readiness to talk and probe any interest in reaching agreement. It may take many months to probe each contestant's positions on different issues, respond to their concerns, finally inducing them to agree to intensive mediation sessions. Prior to the Camp David Summit, President Carter, Secretary of State Cyrus Vance, and other American officials had been actively engaged in informal meetings and consultations as well as formal visits between February 1997 and September 1978 (Quandt, 1986). In preparatory talks, the main goals of mediation are lowering tension and clarifying issues so that the parties are prepared for negotiation. If the concerned parties are able to establish direct interaction, the disputants can be encouraged to deal with their differences by themselves.

The development of multiple communication links is necessary in complicated situations where ordinary negotiations are not feasible (e.g., hostage taking). Negotiating with an illegitimate international actor involves a lot of complexities, not only legal, political but also ethical. The release of South Korean hostages in Afghanistan resulted from multiple channels of indirect talks between the Taliban forces and the Korean government in summer 2007. The communication process was supported by Saudi Arabia, Indonesia, and other Islamic countries which had previous contacts during the Taliban's reign (1996–2001). In order to prevent public embarrassment, most governments avoid direct contact with hostage takers that might be seen as recognizing the legitimacy of hostile non-state criminal entities or groups considered terrorists. In releasing hostages held by Somali pirates, the French government kept publicity to a minimum by depending on unofficial intermediaries.

Motivations

The adversaries should believe that they need to rely on mutual cooperation to satisfy their interests in tandem with the realization that coercive approaches produce only a backlash by nourishing further resentment and retaliation. Each party might feel the necessity for a joint decision-making process through facilitation after they experience a deadlock derived from polarization in goals, methods, values, and perceptions. The maintenance of the status quo is no longer feasible, or too costly in terms of political stability or financial burdens. Mediation is often desired to break a political stalemate and improve the prospect for a negotiated settlement.

Timely initiatives for mediation may belong halfway through the conflict life cycle, not being premature or belated. The issues need to be sufficiently manifested and defined for a mediator's intervention. The adversaries should perceive negotiation as the only means to achieve their objectives due to the existing balance of power. A military stalemate between India and Pakistan in Kashmir led to the acceptance of Soviet mediation in 1965. Former UN Secretary General Kofi Annan's intervention in Kenya's post-election violence in 2008 was successful, in part, due to the urgent necessity to end the violent clashes between rival political groups which brought the Kenyan economy to the brink of collapse. In general, successful mediation is more likely to come from a strong desire for settlement (in combination with relative power parity, impasse in fighting, and external pressure to settle) as well as the absence of nonnegotiable value or principle issues and the existence of organized parties. In addition, mediation's success is likely to be enhanced by a history of cooperation or willingness to act in good faith.

In accepting mediation, each party may think that the intermediary can help influence the other party's positions. A mediation is more apt to be protracted in the event that the deep-seated interests of the disputing parties are diametrically opposed with potent policies at stake. Higher expectations about an outcome agreeable to both sides are more likely to lead to more serious talks. Prior to mediation, coercive diplomacy and an embargo on the import of military weapons might be exerted to control violence. Even though mediation ought to be voluntary, semi-coercive imposition of mediated solutions may be followed by external intervention in a deadly conflict involving atrocious killings.

The prospect for obtaining acceptable settlement in ending the Bosnian civil war emerged from the reduction of the Serb-controlled territory from 70 to 50 percent by September 1995. Bosnian and Croat military gains accrued from pounding Bosnian Serb positions with NATO air strikes and cruise missile attacks. This process paralleled US mediator Richard Holbrooke's successful attempt to convince foreign ministers of Bosnia, Croatia, and Federal Yugoslavia to accept a set of principles needed for peaceful settlement.

Roles and functions of intermediaries

As mediation is a continuing means of negotiation, a mediator should have communication skills and competence to manage adversarial relationships in order to reach an agreement. By transmitting information about possible needs and interests, a mediator assists partisans in expressing their concerns and identifying the specific needs that must be addressed. In general, mediator qualities are comprised of credibility (being trusted and respected) and empathy (related to both the feelings and ideas of the parties). By restructuring the agendas, a mediator can shape the context of negotiation; agendas should not be set in a misleading and manipulative way. A mediator develops rapport, meeting with the parties separately for a caucus.

In keeping negotiation going, a mediator can serve as a buffer as well as maintaining communication. An intermediary function can be utilized to diffuse crisis situations. The parties reduce political risks in such situations when even contact with an enemy creates uproar among their constituents and when concessions are inevitable during negotiations. Indirect talks through an intermediary help diffuse criticism of domestic opponents. In the event of failed mediation, an intermediary can be used as a scapegoat. The communication function is geared toward helping the adversaries not lose face or look weak. A conciliatory move by one party may not be seen as weakness when it is suggested by a mediator. Parties can protect their image by using an intermediary for unpopular concessions.

Depending on various settings of negotiation, intermediaries can adopt a different range of activities and leverages. In mediations on such issues as hostage release, the need for caution and confidentiality demands limited engagement; hostage takers' behavior can be unpredictable and they may not be trusted. As a channel of simple message delivery, a mediator might confine their role to the interpretation and transmission of ideas. On the contrary, some mediators have an ability to restrain more aggressive parties or make a decision on the illegitimacy of their behavior (for instance, the Western intervention in the former Yugoslavia in the mid-late 1990s). A third party may attempt to balance negotiation styles and may synchronize the sequence of movements toward eventual agreements.

Triadic dynamics

Intermediaries have diverse degrees of interest in the conflict and its outcome while utilizing different sets of knowledge, skills, and capabilities to forge an outcome. A triangular relationship is created by a mediator's role to bridge the two sides. The participants' motives for accepting or rejecting a more interventionist approach to mediation are related to the level of trust about an intermediary. Not unusually a mediator may have a close relationship with or know one party better than the other. In fact, a mediator's assumptions and biases as well as their own interests can result in favoring one of the parties.

The principles of equal distance between a mediator and each of the contestants can be modified under different conditions. The mediator's impartiality is likely to be considered less important to the adversaries' decision to accept mediation if it is not a matter of choice but of necessity (for instance, after military setbacks, etc.). Neutrality does not necessarily mean the maintenance of an unbiased position by a mediator on every issue if a mediator can bring an effective end to the fighting desired by all sides. The effectiveness of a mediator is associated with facilitating a settlement which meets at least the minimum expectations of adversaries.

As long as a mediator is believed to produce the outcome desired by all the parties, some latitude of partiality is regarded as acceptable. As the US has more capacity to alter Israel's positions than any other country, Syria accepted Secretary of State Kissinger's shuttle diplomacy aimed at bringing a lasting cease fire to the 1973 Yom Kippur war. Palestinians have no other option than accepting the US mediating role, since realistically that is the only available means to bring changes to Israeli policies. Pakistan's acceptance of the Soviet Premier Kosygin's mediation offer to end the 1965 Indo-Pakistani war was ascribed to the Kremlin's close relationship with India and ability to persuade the latter's leadership.

A mediator can have more leverage if disputants have a high expectation about an outcome and are offered future financial or political support. In 1979, the US government pressed for the Egyptian and Israeli governments to accept a negotiated deal along with its promise to provide aid. Since the US had more interest and stake in the conflict than any other countries, it was willing to provide financial and military assistance as incentives for the agreement. Indeed, after Israeli Prime Minister Begin and Egyptian President Sadat signed the formal peace treaty in March 1999, Israel was given $3 billion and a large quantity of sophisticated weapons systems while Egypt received military equipment and $1.5 billion in aid over the following three years.

Being too excessively skewed toward serving only one party's interests results in suspicion about the mediator's honesty and neutrality. As is seen in the US mediation of the Lebanese conflict in the early 1980s, the mediator's role becomes dysfunctional and can even be destructive if the intervention is seen as too partisan to serve their political objectives. The May 17 Agreement (1983) brokered and backed by the US was rejected by the majority of warring factions and Arabic states, since it was formulated to legitimize the Israelis' continued military presence in southern Lebanon. The erosion of trust was inevitable due to US attacks on Druse-Palestinian positions, raising questions about US neutrality.

Disputants may fear the interference of the mediator, and have more desire to resolve a conflict themselves or prefer impartial mediators to those who attempt to balance different power relations. As the fiasco of the Indian intervention in the Sri Lankan conflict in the late 1990s indicates, a mediating party can be easily dragged into a local conflict. In this incident, the Indians who brokered the settlement between the government and Tamil rebel forces ended up fighting the rebels to enforce the agreement. The eventual withdrawal of Indian peacekeeping forces was inevitable due to not only the military resistance by Tamil guerrillas but also the Sri Lankan society's general anxiety of a foreign troop's presence in their country. This can be contrasted with the EU's mediation and monitoring missions in bringing to conclusion the decades-old Aceh conflict in Indonesia. In this case, the EU's role was less intrusive and was welcomed by the local population as well as the government.

Small states such as Norway and Qatar were better suited for their non-intrusive style of mediation. Owing to its unique position in the Middle East, Qatar has emerged as a favorite intermediary in resolving conflict in Lebanon and elsewhere. The Emir of Qatar has managed to build friendly relations with both their two strong neighbors, Iran and Saudi Arabia. While hosting the biggest US military base in the Middle East, they supported Hezbollah's war against Israel in 2006. Since Qatar does not have serious ability to threaten any disputant, it has been accepted more easily (than Saudi Arabia and other traditionally known mediators) without fear of interference.

A rank equilibrium or disequilibrium between a mediator and disputants has a different impact on mediation success. A powerful mediator is courted by each side who wants to win their support rather than coming to terms with agreement by themselves. On the other hand, a mediator desires to avoid a sudden shift in power which can change incentives for negotiated settlement. The threat to side with another party may reduce resistance of intransigent parties against settlement. A mediator may maintain leverage by employing such means as military aid, a UN vote, diplomatic support, better future relations, and an economic down payment. Powerful mediators have resources to withhold or prevent an outcome desirable for one of the parties. Relationships between an intermediary and disputants can evolve along with changes in a mediator's bias of the disputants or changes in a mediator stance on particular issues along with the progress of negotiation.

When mediation is adopted as a means to restore regional stability, the failure of initial attempts to forge a settlement can result in dependence on coercive methods to quell disorder. Power can be adopted to put pressure on an intransigent party to change their positions, shifting a direction of mediation. In ceasing the siege of Sarajevo, NATO air strikes on Bosnian Serb positions continued for 14 days. In order to stop aggression and ethnic cleansing by Serb militias in other parts of Bosnia, NATO also depended on air strikes prior to the November 1995 Dayton Accord which finally ended military campaigns. The US officials even brokered an arrangement to prevent further fighting between Muslims and Croats, forging a coalition against more aggressive Serb militia forces in March 1994. The US special envoy, Charles Redman, successfully created a Muslim–Croat federation in Bosnia after an intensive nine days of mediation.

Diverse modes of mediation

Reflecting on different degrees of intervention, mediation can be limited purely to the support of communication with a mediator serving as a keeper of ground rules. Others may take more expanded roles by suggesting alternatives or getting involved in content-related issues beyond delivering proposals. The most active mediators are even willing to guarantee the implementation of the agreement (e.g., Israel–Egypt settlement) by putting their own resources on the table. In general, mediation (confined to communication support) generates low expectations about the outcome; bringing parties to the negotiating table itself becomes an important intermediary objective. However, a mediator's capacity can be enlarged to develop a draft proposal to be adopted as a starting point to narrow difference along with the increase in the hope for settlement.

The functions of good offices perform a channel of communication along with the interpretation and transmission of ideas. Shuttle diplomacy provides communication means for the exchange of proposals by involving a neutral go-between role. During the Biafran civil war (1967–1970), the British Commonwealth Secretary General was engaged in shuttle diplomacy even though these attempts failed due to the Nigerian military government's intransigence. In general, shuttle diplomacy is adopted when parties are not ready to meet formally.

If their functions are limited to organizing meetings, keeping records, and providing clarity in communication, a third party is mostly concerned with a process of identifying topics to be addressed rather than shaping the actual content. Even though some mediators may limit themselves to encouragement and advice for the resumption of direct negotiation, others may advance proposals along with the interpretation of each disputant's proposals and even exert pressure for compromise. This type of mediation is effective to the extent that contestants have a high desire for settlement, but fail to make compromises due to a lack of information or an attempt at the extraction of last-minute concessions. Resolving highly intensive conflict can benefit from more active participation of an intermediary in the injection of new ideas about the nature and methods of ending hostilities.

In order to ensure the continued, constructive dialogue among disputants, active facilitation may entail determining how discussions will be conducted as well as collecting information and setting agendas. An intermediary's management of the process is not necessarily separated from their contribution to the substance of the agreement. The insistence on the exclusion or inclusion of certain agendas by the partisans can hinder substantive discussion. In January 2003 talks designed to end the civil war in southern Sudan, the opposition movement insisted on discussion about jurisdiction over Nuba Mountains, Abyei, and Southern Blue Nile not included in the previously reached agreement, despite the government's objection. In order to overcome the gridlock, the Kenyan mediators devised a supplementary negotiation just for the issue outside the official framework. It was an inevitable compromise to permit negotiations to get back on such substantive topics as the cessation of hostilities, power sharing, and distribution of resources (Khadiagala, 2007).

Mediators may make suggestions or offer advice about possible outcomes related to each party's concerns even though the ideas for solutions can be generated by the parties. Parties are assisted in formulating their expressed interests. An effective mediator shares their ideas about the situations with the parties in identifying the areas of agreement. Alternative suggestions can be based on the discovery of each party's bottom line. In ending civil wars or disputes between state entities, mediators may attempt to augment the appeal of a proposal by not only adding benefits but also subtracting loss for one party or both.

In order to bring an end to the Bosnian civil war, both American and European officials were engaged in proposal formulation, suggesting new solutions with attempts to overcome impasse in negotiation. The Carrington–Cutileiro peace plan was proposed at the European Commission Peace Conference held in February 1992. In an endeavor to stop Bosnia-Herzegovina from sliding into war, the proposal advocated the devolution of part of central government function to local ethnic communities in combination with ethnic power-sharing on all administrative levels. The plan was not adopted due to the objection of the Bosniak representative Alija Izetbegović to the split of Bosnia-Herzegovina's districts as Muslim, Serb, or Croat.

In May 1993, the UN Special Envoy Cyrus Vance and European Commission representative David Owen proposed a new peace plan based on the division of Bosnia into ten semi-autonomous regions. The self-proclaimed Bosnian Serb assembly rejected the Vance–Owen plan that emerged from negotiating with the leaders of Bosnia's warring factions with the backing of the UN. In response to continuing territorial fragmentation and ethnic cleansing caused by Serb aggression, the reshuffled UN mediating team composed of David Owen and Thorvald Stoltenberg abandoned the notion of a mixed, united Bosnia-Herzegovina in favor of further partition.

Their proposal reinforced the split of Bosnia into three ethnic mini-states; accepting gains by force, the plan formulated the territorial allotment among Serbs, Bosniaks (Muslims), and Croats according to the ratio of 52, 30, and 18 percent. As the proposals on the disproportional division of Bosnia-Herzegovina in favor of Bosnian Serbs were rejected by Serb politicians, Western powers were more directly involved in the formulation of solutions due to difficulties to expect compromise among warring factions. A new formula emerged from multilateral diplomacy conducted by the Contact Group (composed of the US, France, Germany, Great Britain, and Russia) between February and October 1994. The newest division granted 49 percent of Bosnia-Herzegovina to a Serb republic and 51 percent to a Muslim/Croat Federation. The Contact Group plan was also rejected by Bosnian Serbs despite heavy pressure on them; the Yugoslav federal republic imposed an embargo on the Drina river because the failure of Bosnian Serbs to accept the proposal meant continued international sanctions on them. Owing to the stiff resistance by Bosnian Serbs, it took another year to finally end the war by reaching a Peace Accord among federal Yugoslav, Croatian, and Bosnian presidents Milošević, Tuđman, and Izetbegović at the US air force base near Dayton, Ohio in November 1995.

When parties are not able to reach an agreement by themselves, more interventionist strategies are often necessary. The 1999 Camp David Accord between Israel and Egypt

Table 9.1 A series of mediations in Bosnia

Time of proposal	Mediators	Major content	Outcome
February 1992	Carrington–Cutileiro	Devolution of central government to local ethnic communities	Rejected by the Bosniaks
May 1993	Vance–Owen	Division of Bosnia into ten semi-autonomous regions	Rejection by the Bosnian Serb assembly
August 1993	Owen–Stoltenberg	Territorial partition among Bosnian Serbs (52%), Muslims (30%), Bosnian–Croats (18%)	Rejected by Serbs
October 1994	Contact Group	Partition between the Muslim/Croat Federation (51%) and Serb Republic (49%)	Rejected by Serbs
November 1995	Contact Group	New territorial division among Bosnian Serbs (49%), Muslims (30%), Croats (21%)	Signed in Paris, December 1995

was formulated and adopted by the active engagement of President Carter who was deeply committed to "drafting agreements and talking to each of the parties in turn, trying to persuade them to make concessions" (Kleiboer, 1998, p. 111). In fact, Prime Minister Begin and President Sadat spent more of their time individually with the mediator Carter than each other.

The main motivation for participation in the mediation for both sides was the significance of their relations with the US rather than with each other. Even though he anticipated the entire Arabic world's condemnation for agreeing to a treaty which did not guarantee the sovereign rights of Palestinians in the West Bank and Gaza, Egyptian President Sadat accepted the Camp David Accord since he did not want to alienate the US (Quandt, 1986). President Carter's main priority was producing a substantive outcome which could be agreeable to both sides rather than improvement in inter-personal or political relationships between the two parties. Thus the continuing US engagement was pivotal to ensure that the deal would not break down.

At the agreement stage, a mediator may improve the outcome for one or both parties in order to make the deal more attractive (e.g., the release of imprisoned IRA terrorists by the British government). Imbalances need to be removed to entice the dissatisfied party to the agreement. A third party may promise to provide the financial aid needed for carrying out changes when the mediator has considerable resources and engagement in the implementation process. In implementing the 1978 Camp David Agreement, the US government offered loan guarantees and extra funding needed for the Israeli withdrawal from the Sinai and the rebuilding of a new airfield on the Israeli side. Any future agreement on Palestinian refugees (created since the establishment of Israel in 1948) would be likely to demand compensation for their loss not only by Israelis but also by Western donors. Although it was not accepted by Iran, in the early 1980s, Saudi Arabia and other moderate Middle Eastern countries offered war compensation to Iran as a condition for agreeing to an armistice with Iraq.

From less to more directive mediation

In their most basic functions, mediators can be limited to passively transmitting ideas without any investment in the mediation's outcome. On the other extreme, mediators can be highly directive with the authority to control and direct the actions of the parties (although a directive mediator role still requires the cooperation of the parties). Mediators can be less or more directive, depending on various circumstances. The less directive form of intervention is limited to message deliveries via shuttle diplomacy; chairing meetings or clarifying issues in formal mediation sessions.

More directive mediators may even decide acceptable settlement terms beyond generating and sharing information while changing the way parties interact. In their more directive role, mediators may press hard reluctant parties to accept a deal to prevent the collapse of talks. When the warring factions in Burundi had difficulty in choosing an interim president at the final stage of settlement negotiation held in July 2001, Nelson Mandela (as a mediator) proposed that the incumbent Pierre Buyoya should lead the first 18 months with a main Hutu group leader, Domitien Ndayizeye, as his deputy. His proposal was unanimously backed by the Organization of African Union summit as well as the leaders of the Great Lakes region. This left very little room for various factions to continue political squabbles among themselves.

Even though its direct effects in the partisan's actual behavior are not yet been known, former Nigerian President Olusegun Obasanjo, serving as UN chief mediator, even scolded Congo's Tutsi rebel leader, Laurent Nkunda, for starting a new offensive along the border with Uganda. The mediator was angry with the rebel leader for violating a cease-fire which had been in place since the first round of peace talks in the middle of November 2008. In a muscle mediation designed to break an impasse, directive approaches involve a push for a particular option; a strong leverage by mediators and their allies helps more forceful mediation.

In putting pressure on the parties to accept a proposed settlement or make concessions, each mediator has a different leverage. In a more directive approach, a full gamut of influence includes reward, persuasion, legitimacy, and information sharing as well as the threat of sanctions. In strengthening the hands of the mediators, in the late 1990s, neighboring regional states brought sanctions to the governments of Sudan and Burundi prior to a drop in their uncompromising positions which served as an obstacle. Power-driven mediation is more outcome oriented than process management which may put priority on empowering both adversaries to come up with a joint formula.

While more directive approaches can be effective in cajoling or coaxing reluctant or intransigent parties to reach an agreement, a facilitative approach is more suitable for the development of long-term, mutually reinforcing outcomes presuming that each party is sufficiently motivated. In general, directive approaches may pay less attention to deeper causes in seeking a compromised agreement. In applying the mixture of push and persuasion strategies, more intensive engagement benefits from an established relationship. Premature adoption of directive approaches can ruin credibility and acceptability of a mediator. In the absence of friendly or trust relationships, directive activism of a mediator may damage trust and goodwill.

Intervention strategies

The application of leverage involves different skills from bringing parties together at the table. In order to induce cooperation, a mediator may utilize the strategies of persuasion, compensation, and pressure. Mediators working in a private capacity adopt persuasion tactics to influence disputants. In changing the perceptions of the parties, the effectiveness of persuasion depends on the appeal to the needs, tangible and intangible, to be satisfied. While reward can be made to compensate for concessions, it may be combined with forceful, pressing tactics. As part of pressure tactics, a mediator may criticize one of the sides (e.g., Israeli housing projects which create more hurdles in the transfer of the West Bank to Palestinians that is essential to a final peace deal).

The threat of cessation of mediation may be adopted as a tactic to push for agreement when an intermediary feels frustrated with each party entrenched in their positions. The success of the mediator's threat to quit depends on the fear of being blamed for scuttling the process. If threats or coercive tactics are frequently used in the absence of a long-term positive relationship between the mediator and disputants, it risks exacerbating mutual distrust and insecurity.

Depending on strategic relationships and the leverage held by mediators, high or low degrees of pressure can be exerted. When Egyptian President Sadat wanted to leave Camp David out of frustration in the middle of peace negotiations, President Carter warned him of irrevocable damage to their friendship which the former valued greatly. Powerful interveners are capable of pulling out a deal with high-pressure tactics, making the continuing conflict unattractive. Both the British and Irish governments put heavy pressure on the IRA to cease terrorist attacks by precluding their political ally Sinn Féin from peace talks designed to obtain a negotiated settlement.

Negotiation between rebel forces led by Robert Mugabe and the white government in 1979 was assisted by Britain to end bi-racial rule in Rhodesia. The British government's effort was supported by President Samora Machel of Mozambique who put pressure on Mugabe to accept the mediated proposal. Mugabe found it difficult to ignore the pressure given that the Mozambican government provided a support base for his military operations.

Facilitative versus evaluative mediation

Mediators have a diverse range of interest and capacity to bring successful settlement. If a mediation function is limited to supporting communication, mediators do not need to be experts on the subject. Facilitative mediation stresses the informal and consensual nature of the process that is suitable for creative solutions. In the absence of coercive power, an equitable settlement stems from persuasion and compromise. The involvement of intermediary communication helps proposals be considered on their own merit (rather than who proposes them). In concession making, proposals can be redefined and reframed to increase their acceptability.

A facilitator's role is oriented toward process management rather than the substantive deal making. Relationship management is necessary to enhance confidence and credibility along with reduction in hostility and tensions. In fact, procedural interventions may aim at keeping negotiation orderly and functioning along with testing ideas. In carrying messages, mediators are gatekeepers for the flow of information. Negative emotions and feelings tend to be controlled in the process of reframing the substance or facts of the message. Trust and confidence of the disputants can be gained by avoiding taking sides. As presented by such examples as mediation in Guatemala, El Salvador, and Angola, the UN mediators tend to depend more heavily on facilitative methods (than the US or other powerful states).

In evaluative mediation, an intermediary should be capable of making a judgment in assessing the disputants' arguments about a fair deal. In the implementation of the Beagle Channel award by international arbitration, Pope John Paul II set the terms that confirmed Chile's sovereignty over all of the islands but permitted the Argentine access to the territorial water along with navigation rights. The golden rule was that Chile retain the territorial ownership but share equal participation in resource exploitation, scientific investigation, and environmental management with Argentina by creating an ocean area known as the Sea of Peace. Whereas principles, opinions, and values need to be separated from facts, a focus on the disputants' underlying interests or goals may still need to be regarded as crucial to evaluative mediation. Given the Pope's overwhelming traditional influence and moral authority in the Catholic countries of Latin America, the Pope's role was more acceptable than others.

In a domestic setting, retired judges, senior lawyers, or politicians are more likely to be respected when in charge of evaluative meetings due to the depth of their experience in a particular field (such as business contracts or wage disputes). Partisans ought to be persuaded to accept the merit of mediators' judgment, even though the evaluative process can be characterized as muscle mediation (Stitt, 2004, p. 2). In a mediation oriented toward technical issues, an intermediary may draw on their expertise and experience for reaching conclusions about the relative merits of the arguments. Trade or environmental treaties may prearrange settlement of any disputes arising from their implementation through evaluative mediation or arbitration commissions. Evaluative mediators may bring about an end to interest-based conflicts more quickly and easily than adjudication.

Mediators are likely to have more leverage over reluctant partisans if failure of mediation is followed by arbitration. Under a prior agreement between parties, a third party may act as a mediator but can have power to move into the role of an arbitrator when mediation is not successful. Breakdown (in negotiation and mediation) means arbitration and going to court with great uncertainty. Parties are more willing to reach an agreement if they do not want to face the risk of loss in arbitration. On the other hand, the possibility of arbitration inhibits honest expression of feelings and opinions.

Transformative mediation

Transformative mediation focuses on the improved relationships that help disputants develop their own capacity to resolve a number of disputes as they arise. The clarification of underlying issues and interests is essential to reframing and prioritizing the issues as well as clearing up assumptions. Trust and cooperation derive from the minimization of the effects of stereotypes through a communication process in mediation. Reduction in cognitive distortions contributes to the creation of a setting for mutual cooperation; empathy and sympathy can facilitate caring responses.

Conflict resolution reflects political norms closely tied to social expectation and regularity about the way one ought to be treated and cared for. Most importantly, the psychological dynamics of transformative mediation offer an opportunity to negotiate for increasing self-esteem and empowerment. Parties can define issues and decide settlement terms for themselves with a better understanding of one another's perspectives (Marshal and Ozawa, 2003). A disputant's ability to participate in a problem-solving process enhances self-perceptions of power. Even though it can bring long-term positive relationships, transformative mediation is not easily adopted for crisis situations.

Transformative approaches are contrasted with the development of contact being limited to specific narrow issues without regard to relationship issues. US Secretary of State Alexander Hague developed separate communication channels with Britain and Argentina during the Falklands War (1982). His main concern was how to avert a war between the two American allies, rather than a search for a long-term solution along with the recovery of trust. Not every mediation involves face-to-face meetings even though it can later evolve into direct negotiations under the sponsorship of a third party. A series of broad prisoner swaps took place in June 2008 after indirect talks between Israel and Hezbollah sponsored by Germany.

Phases and steps in mediation

There are diverse phases from initial contact to discussion of formal agreement. In general, a mediation protocol features the style and formality of meetings. After the initial stage of contact, process functions can be set up to establish ground rules, clarify communication, define issues, and set agendas. At the opening stage, setting ground rules and structuring the agendas may move on to discussion about expectations. Setting up ground rules can minimize the negative effects of unproductive tactics. Keeping the process focused on the issues is essential to devising a framework to achieve an acceptable outcome.

In shifting from the opening to proposal development stage, trust building can emerge from perceptional changes. In reaching the Good Friday Agreement to settle communal conflict in Northern Ireland, the multi-party talks sponsored by the British and Irish governments benefited from the influence of two main moderate parties (Ulster Unionist Party;

Social Democratic and Labour Party) in toning down hard-line positions by other particip-ants. The rejection of certain members of an adversary's delegation as a legitimate negoti-ating partner can derail or protract a process of moving into more substantive discussion. In a mediation conducted by Kenyan President Moi in 1985 to end the Ugandan civil war, the opposition leader accused the absence of the military government head at the initial round of talks held in Nairobi as showing a lack of seriousness in negotiation. The initial stage was also complicated by wrangles over the representation and identity of negotiation teams (as related to issues of legitimacy). Discussion among low-level delegations is more suitable for settling differences in more technical issues.

In a more structured mediation, procedural rules may focus on the format of discussion. In the mediation of warring factions in the Burundi civil war (1995–2001), a mediating team headed by the former Tanzanian president Julius Nyerere organized a plenary and five committees which negotiated separate topics ranging from peace and security to demo-cracy to reconstruction and transitional institutions. The progress in negotiation in each committee was reported to the mediating team's chairman. The proposals produced by the committees were further discussed at the plenary session prior to approval via collective decision making. In order to manage the complex process of committee negotiations, a sec-retariat in support of the mediating team monitored progress in proposal development by regular contact with the committee chairs who were neutral outsiders.

The 1978 Camp David mediation provides a unique model which does not adopt formal rules or procedures. The high-ranking delegations of Israel and Egypt led by the head of states spent 13 days discussing various terms and conditions for the return of the Sinai and the status of the West Bank and Gaza. In order to protect the leaders from public pressure, the Camp David Summit was kept confidential with the exclusion of the mass media.

It started without prepared agendas, and utilized informal meetings that did not have regular set hours. Various complaints and pressure for change in positions were made in a series of intense private meetings between US President Carter and each of the disputing parties, namely, Israeli Prime Minister Begin and Egyptian President Sadat. The occasional meetings of senior level officials and advisors were used to provide input into discussion among the state heads (Quandt, 1986).

A mediating team led by President Carter developed a single draft based on the identifi-cation of the issues and differences in positions. The initial draft was revised after presen-tation in caucus and relay of opinions and criticisms by both Israelis and Egyptians. The revised drafts were introduced to incorporate their main concerns. The continued amend-ment was made prior to the emergence of a draft that cannot be further revised without risking the danger of failure. In general, the discussion can start from a skeleton draft agreement until different interests are represented in the final agreement (Stitt, 2004, p. 112). The evaluation of proposals and counterproposals propels the process of bargain-ing and trade-off.

In moving toward an agreement, the identification of substantive and procedural inter-ests of the parties results in assessing options for settlement. A possible settlement agree-ment can be forged by seeking a proposal that balances the views expressed on different issues. At the stage of formulating and drafting proposals, mediators may remind the parties of the consequences of non-settlement and press the parties to be flexible along with supplying and filtering information. Faced with a bleak impasse on the Camp David Sum-mit's tenth day, pressure was exerted on the Egyptian side to budge due to difficulties in breaking the intransigent Israeli positions on the status of Palestinians in the West Bank (Quandt, 1986).

The formulation of viable options can be based on the assessment of what is minimally acceptable to each party. In order to avoid the derailment in reaching an agreement, in the case of Camp David, Palestinian issues were excluded to be left with separate negotiations in the future. A tentative agreement can be reached on a particular issue if a final commitment should emerge from reaching an agreement on all other issues. Less complicated issues can be resolved first in order to develop an atmosphere of accomplishment. That allows negotiation to continue until everyone is ready to accept the final draft as an agreement. The settlement can be formalized by establishing an evaluation and monitoring procedure along with the creation of an enforcement mechanism.

In the Camp David negotiation, President Carter played a decisive role in determining the satisfactory level of progress. The summit mediation (which ended on September 17, 1998) achieved an accord which covered Israeli withdrawal from the Sinai peninsula in return for Egyptian establishment of diplomatic relations with Egypt as well as the cessation of economic boycott. The other accord simply served the purpose of face saving for President Sadat by leaving such agendas on the determination of West Bank and Gaza's status with future negotiation (Quandt, 1986). These accords provided the basis for formulation of details in the negotiation of a formal treaty signed in March 1979. In this final process, both parties pressed for US support to extract last-minute concessions from their opponent.

Failure of summit mediation: Camp David II

In order to forge final settlement terms for an Israeli–Palestine peace process, the summer 2000 Camp David II emulated the Carter model of summit mediation by inviting both Israeli Prime Minister Ehud Barak and Palestinian head Yasir Arafat, but it fell short of expectations of achieving a formal peace treaty. In contrast with the methodically prepared Camp David I, many important issues such as sovereignty over East Jerusalem and the Temple Mount were not fully discussed prior to the summit mediated by President Bill Clinton (Dowty, 2008, p. 152). Given insufficient readiness for engaging in a compromise, the summit ended up with finger pointing at each other's lack of seriousness and goodwill (Swisher, 2004). While Palestinians regarded the Israeli proposal as deficient of significant substance, Israelis felt that they had offered enough and had already made many concessions.

Even though Camp David II was not successful due to poor chemistry between the leaders as well as unconstructive maneuvering tactics (related to insistence on infeasibility of making concessions), it actually helped being engaged in more serious bilateral negotiations; by the end of January 2001, the momentum reached the point that the two sides felt they had never been so close to reaching agreement on previously deadlocked issues. This sentiment was well expressed in their closing statement that described the talks as "in-depth and practical" and "unprecedented in their positive atmosphere." Yet it was "impossible to reach an agreement on all the issues" due to time constraints imposed by upcoming elections and circumstances of violence beyond the negotiators' control (Sher, 2006, p. 228). Unfortunately, substantive progress made on all the issues was nullified by the defeat of Israeli Prime Minister Barak to the hard-line Likud party leader Sharon in the February 2001 Israeli election.

The missed opportunity at Camp David II was accompanied by violent street confrontations between Israeli forces and Palestinians, pushing the time clock of the Israel–Palestinian peace process back indefinitely even though serious post-summit efforts by all sides signaled the feasibility of mutual compromise needed for the final agreement. Often timing is an important factor in pushing for a final deal, since political circumstances are not always ripe for reaching a serious settlement.

The papal mediation of the Beagle Channel disputes

The six years of the Pope John Paul II's engagement in averting a war between the Argentine and Chile present dramatic features of conflict management and settlement. The papal mediation went through different stages, starting from crisis diplomacy, assessment of claims, Vatican proposal, and rejection by the Argentine military regime, and its reversal by a new civilian government. Being alarmed by the Argentine military's preparation for the invasion of the islands around Cape Horn (awarded to Chile by the International Court of Justice ruling in 1952), the Pope dispatched his personal envoy Cardinal Antonio Samoré to Buenos Aires on December 25, 1978. This preventive diplomacy bore fruit in the Act of Montevideo (signed by both Chile and Argentina on January 9, 1979) to request mediation by the Vatican with the commitment to the non-use of force.

This initial stage was critical in opening communication channels while saving face for the military regime of the predominantly Catholic country Argentina in calling off armed operations. The aversion of a serious military confrontation permitted probing and exchange of each side's views along with the visit of the Chilean and Argentine delegations in Rome (May 1979 to December 1980). The third stage started with the December 1980 presentation of the first papal proposal for settlement terms. The rejection of the proposal by the Argentine military junta created a long stalemate (featured by protracted negotiations), running from the beginning of 1981 until December 1983. The eventual settlement came through the arrival of a newly installed democratic government president, Raúl Alfonsín, in Buenos Aires in late 1983. The end of the long-running territorial conflict (traced back to 1952) was finally celebrated by the signing of the 1984 Treaty of Peace and Friendship by the two countries.

Types of mediators

The myriad of mediators have diverse ranges of roles and strategies. State versus non-state intermediaries can be compared in terms of their diverse motivations, skills, capacity, and leverage on disputing parties as well as differing values and principles. Individual mediators rely on their communicative exercise, while states have the advantage of bringing tangible resources to the negotiation. Various types of mediators have different degrees of leverage, ranging from the persuasion of alternative future and benefit to threat of withdrawal from their mediating efforts. Mediators can be favored by their different ability to produce an attractive outcome to disputants.

Individual states, alone or collectively, may intervene in a conflict which adversely affects their political interests or as a way of enhancing their influence or status. In controlling the crises between Ecuador and Peru in 1935, 1941, 1981, 1991, and 1995, the United States, Argentina, Brazil, and Chile served as guarantors of the 1942 Rio Protocol. Mediation is often mandated or promoted by international or regional organizations. The UN Secretary General's office successfully conducted mediation in ending civil wars in El Salvador and Guatemala with the assistance of the Organization of American States (Shamsie, 2007). The Organization of African Union carried out mediation in Somalia in an attempt to bring stability. In ending a civil war in Liberia, the Economic Community of West African States (ECOWAS) acted as both a peacekeeper and mediator, contributing to the formulation of the Cotonou Agreement of July 1993 and the Abuja Accords of 1995 and 1996. An official representative of a government or organization such as the Arab League carries out mediation as part of their organizational mandate. Arab mediators focus on the restoration of harmonious relationships, preserving Arab unity.

Individual mediators tend to be motivated by a desire to be instrumental in change. Their initiatives heavily rely on a personal capacity with communication, facilitation strategies. In the absence of government authority, individual mediators can make flexible arrangements, providing an input to formal mediation. The involvement of individuals is not common and is limited to informal mediation prior to direct negotiations compared with a state's involvement in mediation. World-known political figures such as former US President Jimmy Carter or Finnish President Martti Ahtisaari can muster more resources due to personal prestige and ability to easily obtain institutional endorsement of their initiatives. Especially in the African context, elder statesmen, in particular, respected state heads Julius Nyerere (Tanzania) and Daniel arap Moi (Kenya) were tipped as mediators in managing a negotiation process to end civil wars in Burundi and Uganda respectively. Former high-ranking officials can be backed up by powerful governments, as exemplified by the mediating role of former US Secretary of State Cyrus Vance and David Owen (on behalf of the US, British, German, and French governments) in an attempt to end civil war in Bosnia-Herzegovina.

By utilizing his political weight as former US president, Jimmy Carter has successfully intervened in diffusing several international crises. In the midst of the major confrontation with implications for another war in the Korean Peninsula, President Carter visited the North Korean capital Pyongyang in the summer of 1994 and carried a proposal (which he privately forged with the North Korean leadership) to Washington. Even though the US government did not officially sanction the deal, they followed through the steps laid by him to overcome the most serious crisis prior to reaching negotiated settlement in the fall. Carter's mission in 1994 to Haiti negotiated the conditions for the exile of the ruling junta who faced imminent US military intervention. In the latter case, his political credibility was fully backed by the US government and Congress with the accompaniment of Joint Chief of Staff Colin Powell and Senator Sam Nunn.

In contrast with former politicians, religious leaders carry moral and persuasive ability. Especially active in international mediation have been the Quakers, Brethren, and other peace churches. The World Council of Churches intervened in the Sudanese war for humanitarian purposes (1972). The Pope's successful intervention in averting a looming war between Chile and Argentina over the disputed islands (known as one of the most successful international mediations by religious organizations) is ascribed to his highly respected moral and religious authority. The Community of Sant'Egidio (a Catholic lay group based in Rome) was able to bring the warring parties in the Mozambican civil war to peace talks (1991) in that its relief activities gained the trust of all sides along with its informal, nonthreatening status.

Even among state mediators, there are differences between geostrategic powers and small states. Strong states can apply carrot and stick to press for concessions, offer proposals, and alter the pay-offs and motivations. By involving great powers as intermediaries, a power brokerage model contributes to the maintenance of stability of the international system (Kleiboer, 1998). On the contrary, small and middle-rank states are engaged in low profile strategies of dialogue and communication to improve their prestige and status. Algeria provided good office for the US and Iran to resolve a hostage crisis in 1980. It is often historic links, familiarity with the conflict or parties that invite intermediaries to take an intermediary role. In the Biafran conflict, the UK and the OAU were lead mediators due to historic or geographic links.

At a geostrategic hot spot, different mediators can get involved at different times. The Soviet mediation of the India–Pakistan war in 1965 was ascribed to concerns about stability on its southern border. Even though the US was not seen as neutral due to its critical stance against India during the earlier Kashmir conflict, the US was invited to mediate the 1999 India–Pakistan conflict because of changing regional political interests. Given its geopolitical interests, the US government mediated the negotiation between Israelis and their neighbors, ranging from Lebanon to Egypt to Palestine after the Yom Kippur War (1973). Regional interests drag a major power into the conflict to avert collusion among its allies. These mediation examples include Russian involvement in the mediation of conflict in the Caucasus (Nagorno-Karabakh), Saudi Arabia in the Yemen and Lebanese conflict, and Kenya and Zimbabwe in the Mozambican war. Neutral third states tend to be more trusted, as is illustrated by the 1963 Ethiopian mediation between Algeria and Morocco over border disputes.

Some state actors have more actively promoted their status as a peacemaker. While Norway initiated peace processes between the Israelis and Palestinians and offered mediations in Sri Lanka and other conflicts around the world, Qatar and Costa Rica's reputation comes from their role in mediating regional crises and disputes (in the Middle East and Central America, respectively). Nonthreatening actors, mostly being limited to communication, take less directive approaches than mediating authorities which can make proposals to be taken seriously by disputants. Different motivations have diverse ramifications in the mediation process and outcomes. In general, a highly motivated intermediary (especially with moral visions) can produce a better result than disinterested ones.

Coordination of multiple mediators

Multiple types of mediators may join combined initiatives or develop separate contacts with contestants. As is illustrated by various experiences in Mozambique, the Democratic Republic of Congo, Burundi, Sudan, and Somalia, some mediators are self-invited to launch competitive mediation initiatives in a parallel manner; others may proceed simultaneously with loose coordination. The coordinated mediation initiatives can be sequentially executed upon the failure of previous ones. A series of international mediations (during the time span between 1992 and 1995) were launched one after another sequentially until the relentless efforts finally brought an end to the atrocious civil war in Bosnia-Herzegovina (refer to Table 9.1).

In a peace process, multiple activities can be complementary to supporting the entire process of negotiated settlement. Non-state mediators may open the door for formal negotiations involving state or other entities which have to carry out the agreement. In ending the 18-year-old civil war in Mozambique, non-state mediator Sant'Egidio was supported by the Assistant Secretary General of the Organization of African Unity. The Community of Sant'Egidio has ties both to the government and rebel forces through their humanitarian work. The Italian government provided consultation for the negotiators along with the input from an international community (the UN, etc.). The Rome General Peace Accords (signed in October 1992) to end the Mozambican Civil War was brokered by a four-person mediation team (composed of two Sant'Egidio members, the Archbishop of Beira, and an Italian parliament member). The treaty's credibility was backed by an array of states, including the US, Italy, Portugal, Russia, etc., who assisted the negotiation process.

In contrast with the above example, the involvement of multiple intermediaries (with different motivations and roles) might complicate each other's work in ending a protracted conflict with a tumultuous history. The sequencing of multiple initiatives among intermediaries can converge and supplement each other under unified goals, generating synergy in expediting the peace process. Yet often mediators (endowed with competing expertise and networks) may interfere in the existing process with their own efforts, creating an opportunity for manipulation by some of the obstructive parties. Due to the competing motives and diverse approaches to disputing parties, intermediaries rely on intricate links with the parties to conflicts instead of forging common objectives among themselves.

In the absence of cooperation and consultation, new actors may take initiatives that contradict the existing process with a turf war in a crowded peace-making field (e.g., Burundi, Sudan, Somalia). Whereas the world attention on Darfur attracted a plethora of would-be peacemakers, mediation attempts have become unnecessarily complex due to difficulties in forging unity among various interveners about how to resolve the crisis. In the endeavor to bring an end to civil wars in Burundi, former Tanzanian President Nyerere's mediation was undercut by the secret Sant'Egidio-mediated talks in Rome (supported by Western European countries) from July 1996 to May 1997 (Maundi, 2003). The Sant'Egidio's intervention was intended to break the ice between the military government and the main Hutu rebel group Conseil National pour la Démocratie (CNDD). However, the Tutsi-dominated government took the Sant'Egidio involvement as an opportunity to sideline and circumvent the Nyerere-led mediation backed by regional states. The Sant'Egidio was favored by the Tutsi-led military leadership since contrary to the regionally sponsored mediation, it did not demand change in its uncompromising position on negotiating conditions.

As the Sant'Egidio talks hit deadlock, Nyerere's mediating authority was reaffirmed in the early September 1997 consultative meeting of regional heads of state and Western representatives in Dar es Salaam. While the Sant'Egidio's intervention was based on benign motives, the Egyptian–Libyan initiatives in Sudan (summer, 2001) were politically motivated to rival the existing mediation of Intergovernmental Authority on Development coordinated by Kenya. The Egyptian–Libyan's "nine point plan" was condemned by the regional states for assisting in the Sudanese military government's objectives to reestablishing its hegemony in southern Sudan instead of seeking genuine peace.

Assessing mediations

In the simplest assessment, a mediation outcome is regarded as successful if it contains conflict and prevents armed clashes. A mediation outcome can be assessed in terms of either reaching an agreement or improvement in relationships that can pave a road for bilateral negotiations. The terms agreed in haste under pressure can be resented or overturned in the future. As hard bargained agreement falls apart, renewed enmities occur under new conditions. In contrast with a simple compromise, accommodation can be based on deeper understanding. The feelings of equity felt by the parties as well as the mediator can motivate a durable change. Parties have diverse motivations to accept mediated outcomes. The acceptance or rejection of settlement terms can be based on the consideration of its diverse consequences. The stakes are reputation, political fortunes, prospects for sustained relationships, ally support, or world public opinion.

Various mediators have different degrees of influence over the process and outcome, depending on the partisans' relationships with the mediators. The success of the 1978 Camp David negotiation is, in part, attributed to a more directive approach of President Carter in combination with his commitment to Middle East peace and skills to handle deadlocked situations created by the tough personalities of Sadat and Begin. In 2000, on the contrary, besides insufficient pre-summit preparation to probe differing positions, President Clinton was not successful in utilizing all his capacity to put substantial proposals acceptable to both the Palestinian and Israeli sides. A more forceful mediator role can be beneficial, but it also has to involve strong incentives for the partisans to accept the dominant role of a mediator. In Israeli–Palestinian negotiations, each party had little to retrieve if they receded from their key positions on Jewish settlement in the West Bank and the control of Jerusalem in contrast with the situation which permitted Israel and Egypt to exchange land for security.

A mediator's skills and ability are likely to have a limited impact on each party's positions if negotiations between opponents entail diametrically opposed principles and interests. Prior to the Falklands War, the Argentine wanted to have control over the island, but Britain insisted on the wishes of the inhabitants as a condition for relinquishing its territorial rights; only one party could achieve its original aims. It is certainly easy to formulate win–win solutions if disputants have complementary goals. The Beagle Channel mediation proposal by Cardinal Samore satisfied Chile's sovereignty over the island in return for recognizing the Argentine's economic and navigation rights in South Atlantic waters. Mediators have to be able to recognize both tangible and intangible needs of the parties.

New dynamics of mediation might emerge along with the evolution of a conflict which changes the perceptions of stakes. Mediation strategies may need to be adjusted to unexpected conflict situations (such as tipping military balance). Even though Kenyan President Moi successfully mediated to achieve power-sharing arrangements between the Ugandan government and opposing forces, the political divisions among political factions within the government and its weakened military capabilities in the final days of arranging mediated settlement led to the opposition force's military takeover of the government in December 1985.

If one of the parties clings to its position, it will be difficult to make a breakthrough. US and other parties tried to get humanitarian aid to the Biafrans with pressure on both sides to agree to the cease-fire. While Biafrans were interested in an unconditional cease-fire first, the Nigerian government wanted to have negotiation prior to cease-fire (as well as its outright refusal to accept the Biafran position on independence). Arnold Smith, a Canadian career diplomat, secretary general of the Commonwealth secretariat, had little success in his May 1968 attempt to arrange reduced hostilities, hopelessly watching the starvation of the civil population caused by the blockade of the Nigerian government. In a lopsided power situation when one side begins to win in a war, mediation is not likely to succeed. Military imbalance often works against a mediation attempt, as seen in the Democratic Republic of Congo and Sudan.

Good mediation is fair and efficient while improving the climate of the relationships. The success or failure of mediation represents not only internal but also external variables, ranging from the intervention timing to a shift in an international political environment. When the conflict becomes internationalized, official government envoys may operate within an institutionalized structure set up by either UN or regional organizations such as the Organization of African Unity (OAU), Organization of Security and Cooperation in Europe (OSCE), limiting the salience of personality and personal ability in informal mediation. The Kenyan foreign ministry served as a secretary of the mediation for the Sudanese People's Liberation Movement and the military government on behalf of the Intergovernmental Authority on Development (IGADD), a seven-country regional development organization in East Africa. Kenyan mediators had to maneuver within the established diplomatic intercourse, involving the European donor's perspectives as well as the regional states' concerns. Beyond a mediator's skills, effectiveness in mediation is also related to disputant motivation as well as each side's internal power distribution and nature of their decision-making process. In the case of the Falklands War, the US mediation was bound to fail due to the strong-willed personality of the British Prime Minister, Margaret Thatcher and intransigent positions of the Argentine military leadership as well as the misreading of partisan intentions by US government officials.

Ethical issues and power imbalance

Manipulative strategies (based on the presentation of erroneous facts and ambiguous statements) are not likely to produce genuine settlement, eventually tarnishing one's reputation and credibility. In addition to procedural justice, substantive justice featured by a fair and equitable outcome should be one of the main criteria that guide the mediator's judgments. The support for unjust relationships can sow seeds for future atrocities and more conflict. At the same time, mediators will not avoid balancing ethical concerns and political feasibilities affected by power imbalance. In the mediation in Bosnia-Herzegovina, partition of ethnic territories became the only feasible solution due to the resistance of opposing ethnic groups to the coexistence of mixed populations. The main dilemma was the sacrifice of fairness to stop the war by recognizing the Serb territorial gains achieved by military aggression.

One of a few tools possessed by mediators in the equalization of power is to let a marginalized party be aware of their own power as well as guaranteeing equal access to information. Yet, mediation is not easily adaptable to dealing with an unequal distribution of power established in social institutions. In general, mediators do not have authority and capacity to rectify conditions of injustice created by the disproportionate distribution of power and do not have a veto power over the outcome. Mediation may have to be conducted within a given political process which may not be suitable for serving the interests of marginalized parties. The powerful party can manage conflict to their advantage by restricting the political agenda as well as co-optation. "The informality of mediation (when compared to litigation) may present inherent difficulties for weaker parties if the safeguards of more formal procedures are lacking" (Amy, 1987). The uneven distribution of power limits a weaker party's ability to have access to the resources or the political process.

Further reading

Bercovitch, J. and Houston, A. (2000) "Why do They do it like This? An Analysis of the Factors Influencing Mediation Behavior in International Conflicts," *The Journal of Conflict Resolution*, 44: 170–202.

McCorkle, S. and Reese, M. (2005) *Mediation Theory and Practice*, Boston: Pearson/Allyn and Bacon.

Picard, C. *et al.* (2004) *The Art and Science of Mediation*, Toronto: Edmond Montgomery Ltd.

Quandt, W. B. (1986) *Camp David: Peacemaking and Politics*, Brookings Institution.

Robert, M. (2007) *Developing the Craft of Mediation: Reflections on Theory and Practice*, London: Jessica Kingsley Publishers.

10 Facilitation

Reaching consensus or some kind of agreement by facilitative methods is often essential to finding acceptable options for different parties. Mutual satisfaction stems from innovative and flexible solutions made by the maximum involvement of participants along with individual capacity building. As a nonauthoritarian and nonjudgmental mode of decision making, facilitative methods have been applied to a broad set of issues in a wide range of settings from promotion of mutual understanding in a protracted conflict to reconciliation. Even though the official peace negotiation process has been stalled, civil society sectors have been engaged in organizing dialogue projects to build a bridge between Israelis and Syrians, Russians and Georgians, and Armenians and Azerbaijanis along with an attempt to reduce mutual misunderstandings and hostilities.

A facilitative process can also be utilized for communal problem solving as well as creating an opportunity for informal contact between members of antagonistic communities that might lead to official negotiations. A series of meetings among people representing communities of various warring parties in Tajikistan were engaged in the analysis of the causes of the conflict and joint exploration of solutions. The dialogue showed the possibility of negotiated settlement, prompting official negotiations to end the civil war in 1996. In post-apartheid South Africa, several series of facilitative meetings were organized to improve the policing service, and communal groups were invited to generate practical solutions.

This chapter covers procedures which contribute to unfreezing conflict relationships by developing a common understanding of deeper issues that underlie adversarial relationships. The participants' control over conflict outcomes can be promoted by their enhanced skills in constructive interaction. In general, a dialogue process is informal and unstructured in the promotion of collective understanding, but talks designed for developing action plans may adopt a more organized structure in agenda setting and debates.

Features of facilitation and dialogue

In facilitation (designed to tackle militia violence or stop civil war), group discussion is designed for a collective search for problem solving based on mutual understanding of the issues and sources of problems. In many intractable conflict settings, negotiations may not be easy or feasible due to the refusal of adversaries to talk to each other or wide gaps between opposing positions. In this kind of situation, facilitated meetings can be utilized as the first step to unfreeze the relationship of old animosities.

Inter-group contact is designed to create favorable circumstances for dialogue with the promotion of an ability to develop procedures for change. There are a variety of objectives and procedures of facilitation. These include problem-solving workshops for influential social actors, forums for the empowerment of women's voices for peace, and an informal conference for the recognition and respect for different cultural traditions. The products of facilitation can be the development of an ability to understand and empathize with the other's situations in tandem with the validation of one's own claims.

An increase in understanding is supported by various communication methods which influence group dynamics. Facilitated dialogues can support mutual understanding of each other's concerns, building solidarity, paving moments of transition, or helping to develop transformative insights. The process has been used for shared communal decision making or relationship building in many war-torn societies. The network of women's groups affected by brutal civil wars in Liberia (1992–1996), for instance, organized a series of meetings themselves, eventually deciding to put pressure on the warlords to stop fighting. These activities strengthened women's role in society with the election of a woman president in the post-conflict political transition.

Dialogue and other processes of facilitation differ from negotiation in that it does not involve bargaining processes nor does it promote compromise. In contrast with negotiation, facilitation is not based on evaluating ideas according to fixed criteria. The "art of the possible" is derived from bringing the adversaries to forge mutual understanding on specific issues instead of position taking (Lynch, 2005). Indeed, a facilitated process is more oriented toward developing mutual understanding prior to formal negotiations designed for the satisfaction of everyone's interests. Various methods of facilitation (such as problem-solving workshops and dialogue projects in Colombia, Guatemala, Somalia, Democratic Republic of Congo, and Tajikistan, Moldova, Georgia, and other former Soviet republics) rely on the analysis of deep causes of hostile relationships for the exploration of desirable solutions. Sufficient time and commitment are essential to relationship building and sustained collaboration.

In facilitated dialogues, moments of transition can be created by each party sharing the opposing party's concerns through empathetic listening. The transitional moments can unlock or dissolve polarized positions, serving as a vehicle for developing new "insights and actions by the participants" (Isenhart and Spangle, 2000, p. 108). Transformational processes are necessary to promote the major change in conflict relationships whether they take place in private or in public.

The goal of a dialogue process is to develop a framework to arrive at shared meaning and understanding along with the group ownership of the facilitative process and outcome. In a search for ending violence, elders and women's groups representing diverse kin groups in Somalia organized communal meetings. Although they do not have the power to stop militia warfare, they came up with specific suggestions and requests for the UN and other international actors. Since solutions cannot be unilaterally imposed, the lateralization of power is vital to supporting a collaboration process. By sharing authority and accountability for the result, parties co-own more than knowledge and information. The creation of future visions and joint strategies is an effective way of working toward common goals beyond the purview of an individual party.

Facilitation serves as a method of adjusting interaction in an environment conducive to flexible decision making. Owing to the group ownership of the process along with the promotion of participant involvement, outcomes (mutual understanding) cannot be unilaterally imposed. Collaboration within deeply divided communities is no longer threatening with a shift in mindset from control to learning (derived from a full examination and discussion of group issues). At the same time, giving up our preconceived ideas about solution is not a required condition for collaboration in searching for common ground.

Group facilitation

By accepting a joint accountability for the process, individual participants can develop a high stake in the outcome of dialogue. Participants should be able to commit the resources (time, energy, money, and facilities) needed for the process to address, discuss, and resolve issues. Trust is gained by a feeling of security and confidence that allows for open, candid discussion. In dialogue projects which include staunch members of adversarial communities (e.g., ethnic conflicts in Tajikistan), several meetings are needed to pass through the initial difficulties in getting involved in discussion, since the facilitated process may bring in foes who were not willing to talk about the past. Successful facilitation is based on realistic expectations about what can be achieved as well as re-examination of preconceived assumptions about an appropriate process. There are intentional or unintentional effects of individual, group, or organizational interaction processes.

The participant's control over dialogue outcomes is developed by an ability to design a process for change. The creation of new understanding helps cultivate interdependent relationships with a shared future. No decision-making authority (which controls a group process) is necessary in that the process has to be acceptable to all the participants. In accommodating different perspectives, high assertiveness and competition need to be converted to cooperation by a collaborative process.

Indeed, different types of facilitation represent varying goals, circumstances, and targeted audiences. Small, facilitated problem-solving workshops or seminars (as organized in Israeli–Palestinian relations, Cyprus, etc.) are suitable for cultivating personal relationships in a microcosm that may grow to increased interactions between adversarial communities. This method has been adopted to help representatives of adversarial communities in Somalia, Ethiopia, and elsewhere understand the conflict from their opponent's perspectives. This is the first step toward developing joint solutions to shared problems.

A positive atmosphere of discussion about communal conflict is created by group dynamics based on strong cohesion, goodwill, and morale. Relationship building through informal contact during the meetings can offer an opportunity to learn about each group's interests and motivations. Facilitated dialogue for mitigating ethnic tensions is essential to conflict resolution in a highly interdependent relationship. The willingness to ignore power differentials leads to solving a common problem through collaborative efforts instead of making an attempt to undermine another party's preferred solution.

By encouraging adversaries to move beyond the status quo, dialogue furnishes a potential for transformative action. It is contrasted with mediation which is limited in its scope of interaction to formal proposal making. Clearly defined issues can be easily handled in direct or assisted negotiation, but complex and unclear problems may be more suitable for facilitation. In fact, collective decision making based on a deeper understanding of each participant's main concerns is contrasted with mediation based on compromise.

The exclusion of any group is opposed to the principle of collaborative decision making. It is a delicate matter to deal with confrontational groups. In the multi-party talks to end communal violence in Northern Ireland in 1996–1997, it was a challenging decision to admit Sinn Féin to a Forum for Political Dialogue despite their links to the IRA that continued terrorist bombings. Leaving out extremist or confrontational groups such as Hamas in the Palestinian/Israeli peace talks may be desirable to reach a conclusion efficiently, but it can have long-term negative effects. It is essential to have a bridge builder who can moderate the extremists while translating their views for others.

A broader set of issues tends to involve a large number of multiple stakeholders with an even distribution of decision-making power. In the Northern Ireland peace talks, multiple groups, moderate and extreme within both Republican and Unionist communities, were invited to a group process which determined their common future. They shared differing views about development, policing, and power sharing, all built into a broad relationship.

Whereas narrow topics (associated with a dispute over interests and questions of how to achieve certain goals) permit a more focused discussion in a formal setting, certain issues become nonnegotiable due to their intrinsic value. Ethnic, religious, linguistic, and other identity-related issues representing particular communities are not likely to be amenable to compromise. Existential needs can be better understood through dialogue or other types of less formal process of exchange of views.

Facilitation and empowerment

The core value of facilitation is empowerment by enhancing, in direct and indirect ways, a positive personal, relational, and systemic change. In their struggle, partisans may strive for self-esteem by gaining the awareness of rights and responsibilities; social participation enhances access to psychological and material resources. Public participation in problem solving is crucial in upholding democratic ideals as an antidote to dysfunctional organizations especially when those in authority are not in touch with the majority of people affected by their decisions (Sidaway, 2005). In the transition to post-apartheid rule in South Africa, such communal groups as the Community Policing Forum played an important role in reshaping policing priorities. Government decisions have a severe adverse effect on public interest when plans are approved without proper examination by appropriate decision-making bodies.

Promoting civil discourse is seen as enhancing the quality of a democratic system by overcoming the challenge of a declining level and quality of participation. Indeed, constructive dialogue among citizens generates a transformative dynamic, inspiring a vital communal life (needed to adap to economic, social, or environmental changes). Institutions and practices of governance can be improved by increased societal input to solve problems especially in multi-ethnic or multi-racial societies such as Northern Ireland and South Africa.

Responding to conflict through empowerment and recognition of problems is important for not only settling disputes but also for transforming relationships (Marshal and Ozawa, 2003). Conflict can provide an impetus for growth in human morality if it is resolved in a way to eliminate political oppression and economic inequities (for instance, apologies and compensation for the indigenous populations in Australia and New Zealand). As best illustrated by the Chinese oppression of Tibetans and Uighur Muslims, repression of conflict is intended to conceal unjust relations, while denying the dignity of the oppressed. The process of relationship transformation is, in part, driven by accepting and honoring diverse worldviews that may originate from racial, linguistic, and ethnic differences.

If empowerment is designed to achieve a specific outcome from a conflict such as social justice (as seen, the indigenous population's demand of equity in Bolivia), the question remains as to under what circumstances this goal can be achieved. Self-efficacy comes from expanded access to psychological, social, and material resources which boost knowledge and skills. In the peasants' struggle against the land owners in Latin America, empowerment is more than an ability to define issues and decide settlement terms. The self-esteem of individuals is gained by control over a decision-making process with improvement in communication skills. In searching for a specific conflict outcome, empowerment embraces more than the awareness of self-interest by incorporating such concerns as social justice. Emotional strength and perceptions of personal power (exhibited by the Mothers of the Plaza in the Argentine who demanded information about the whereabouts of their loved ones abducted by the military dictatorship in the early 1980s) would enhance the ability of a weaker party to gain confidence in bringing about changes.

The elements, methods, and goals of empowerment have certain moral, ethical, and policy implications. In breaking the impasse, the weaker party (for instance, the Mayan Indians who were major victims of violence by security forces of the Guatemalan government in the 1980s and early 1990s) should be empowered to negotiate new relationships and structures. "Empowerment is often conceived of as an individual's sense of confidence, which has perhaps resulted from a self-realization of oppression or lack of freedom and opportunity" (White and Nair, 1999, p. 49). The complex and multiple networks of power relations are revealed by empowerment in promoting the role of conflict resolution in social change. The content and context of conflict resolution can be understood in terms of the adjustment of human institutions to the need for changes in the system of distribution of power and resources.

Designing a transformative process

By motivating reason, an appropriate expression of affection and emotional support can be complementary to rationality. The productive use of emotion stimulates the cognitive processes needed for creative thinking. Dialogue develops a shared inquiry in a search for a common meaning by means of thinking and reflecting together. In addressing deep issues, collective mindfulness can be cultivated by reflective thinking and listening. Good questions increase understanding of other viewpoints. Participants should be ready to "learn how to think together – not just in the sense of analyzing a shared problem or creating new pieces of shared knowledge." Informal procedures permit face-to-face meetings to "consider a range of possible solutions" (Isaacs, 1999, p. 359).

A common goal can be achieved by a relationship built on the appreciation of needs for attention, recognition, and shared power (e.g., South Africa). By promoting respect, dialogue is opposed to an adversarial argument culture which approaches "issues as polarized debate, criticism and attack" along with the advocation of positions (Foley, 2003, p. 250). In comparison with arguments which often lead to polarization, deep listening, discussion, and reflection are intended to discover differences and explore new information and insight.

In response to rising communal violence and hikes in crime rates, civil society sectors in the Western Cape, South Africa, were engaged in developing a proposal for crime prevention strategies. A local NGO organized Community Policing Forums to provide an input into this process. By going beyond a narrow focus (of criminal detection), the forum identified the diverse local safety and security needs of individual communities (such as more vigilance of the growing drug trade).

Thanks to training programs for the participants, the forum sessions avoided descending into a tit-for-tat battleground about community politics which interfere in constructive dialogue. Most importantly, the forum's devotion to relationship building contributed to the development of a new local partnership model which stresses the new roles and responsibilities of community members. The assistance of those who know local relationships as well as the input of community senior stakeholders helped clarify conceptual differences between social crime prevention versus law enforcement techniques.

Promotion of participatory democracy

The goals of various national dialogue initiatives have been the reduction of prejudice rather than the resolution of specific disputes by clearing up misunderstanding between groups. In a deliberate effort to improve the quality of participatory democracy, some study circles have developed small group and citywide processes which help everyone's voice, beliefs, and experiences to be heard. These grassroots study circles have been engaged in self-education, establishment of new community networks, organization of collaborative projects, and eventual changes in communal decision-making structures. Various dialogue forums have designed a process whereby people get together as equal participants to discuss a specific issue. At these forums ranging from small study circles to town meetings, a non-adversarial environment has permitted "citizens to take a fresh look at the topic and their own perspectives" by stressing empathetic listening and non-judgmental attitudes.

Transformative possibilities stem from uncovering a multiplicity of meanings and mutual understanding of each other's identity that emerges from interaction. A community is formed by a collection of people within a defined area overlaid with political and social structures. The goal of conflict resolution investigates the origin and nature of an existing order and helps explore alternative strategies to overcome institutional deficiencies. The careful organization and facilitation of a dialogue process is necessary without a loss of structural flexibility. Successful dialogue forums have attempted to cultivate social and political capacities to provide input to important communal issues.

While some processes are better suited for conflict over interests and questions of how to achieve certain goals, a consensus decision-making process may not be effective in responding to differences in strong preferences or beliefs about what is right and virtuous. Value conflict needs to be differentiated from the issues of wants and desires. Instead of reaching an agreement, a dialogue process needs to "make value differences transparent" while validating diverse perspectives (McCorkle and Reese, 2005, p. 123).

At the same time, commonalities can be searched by focusing on a larger, common goal. The relationship can be redefined by creating the joint frame of references that identify shared experience and belief systems. The existence of a common universe of discourse is necessary for the development of cooperation. Especially in deeply divided societies such as South Africa and Northern Ireland, common values shared by all the parties can emerge from a safer environment for interaction.

Diverse application of facilitation

There is no single uniform method of facilitation since it arises from the necessities of responding to a particular conflict. Administrative rule making on policy issues such as the regulation of industrial waste (which draw concerns about public health) tends to be generally public. However, the exploration of issues and solutions among long-term antagonists tends to be informal given the negative effects of publicity. The level of conflict is low to moderate (e.g., forums for the input of citizen views in communal development projects), but is likely to be moderate to high (in the case of unofficial meetings between government officials and armed opposition). A high level of polarization creates difficulties for achieving consensus on politicized issues. In contrast with seeking an agreement, informal dialogue is not too much concerned about a joint decision-making outcome such as the formulation of a common standpoint.

As is presented in Table 10.1, various types of facilitation projects can be understood in terms of the setting of their application, the nature of activities, and the overall objectives. In managing resistance by major stakeholders against decisions which have a larger social effect, negotiated rule making enhances collaboration among those who have diverse perspectives on public issues (such as the impact of building new roads and bridges, etc.). Public, consensus building is based on an attempt to aggregate diverse interests represented by stakeholders for efficient government policy even though not everyone may agree to every aspect of administrative regulations. The final decisions can meet less resistance if various stakeholders and supporters of certain policies have an opportunity to provide input.

Various international projects on community capacity building have been introduced to overcome economic difficulties and social divisions of poor countries. While grassroots development projects can empower the underprivileged to mobilize their own resources to overcome economically and socially disadvantaged groups, this process can lead to building solidarity through collaborative decision making. Development projects can be designed to overcome communal divisions by promoting equitable allocation of resources. Psychological, social capacity building has also been introduced to support healing in war-traumatized communities.

In polarized conflict, members of groups in opposing communities can be invited to join civil society dialogue which is aimed at promoting mutual understanding. Their understanding of the conflict and exploration of options to end conflicts may result in generating proposals that arise from a civil society level. Protracted conflicts with history of various levels of violence often perpetuate themselves. The problem-solving workshop has been introduced to promote an analytical process of discovering the deep roots of conflict and to explore collaborative efforts to initiate negotiated settlement. This approach has been applied to many ethnic conflicts in the Middle East, south-east Asia and former Soviet republics.

Participatory process in community building

Beyond conflict settings, a facilitative process has been widely adopted to overcome tension derived from disputes over resource management. The concept of human development popularized by the UN Development Program and other UN agencies has focused on capacity building at the grassroots. For instance, a model of building community through participatory approaches has been actively integrated by the Community Forestry Unit of the UN Food and Agricultural Organization (Simon, 1999).

Table 10.1 Types of facilitation

	Settings of application	*Facilitation process*	*Objectives*
Negotiated rule making	Public policy disputes	Representation of stakeholder interests	Efficient decision making
Community capacity building	Unmet socio-economic needs	Empowerment, collaborative decision	Communal development
Civil society dialogue	Polarized societal conflict	Promoting mutual understanding	Confidence building
Problem-solving workshop	Protracted, often ethnic, conflict	Confidential, analytical	Pre-negotiation initiatives

International donors utilized aid meetings to promote joint resource management projects in building bridges in a conflict-torn triangle of the Ferghana Valley region shared by Kyrgyzstan, Tajikistan, and Uzbekistan. These regions that were divided by the new borders of the three newly born states after the collapse of the Soviet Union have developed a rivalry along with support for their kin ethnic groups in other countries. Despite animosities among the central governments, the local residents have to work together on joint projects of water and forest management. Given the political difficulties, international development agencies have served as a main facilitator for community peace building.

New norms of respect, trust, tolerance, and reciprocity can be developed in handling community disputes. Consensus-based collaboration serves as an effective tool for community building by fully engaging grassroots people in the process of development. Instead of fighting over scarce water or fertile land, villagers can be linked together by communication in collective action to become self-reliant. Dialogue forges participatory communication as a two-way interaction of giving and taking in talking over differences. Democratic forms of communication relationships are socially committed, culturally sensitive, empathetic in inter-personal interactions, and psychologically prepared for social action.

The diagnostic process (for instance, related to dwindling water resources) can be framed within a problem-posing and -solving framework by asking relevant questions regarding the needs and alternatives for meeting communal needs. It is accompanied by the development of courses of action, their pursuit, evaluation, and reflection on the outcomes. By linking reflection and evaluation to action, the participatory research process is geared toward producing critical analysis and collective knowledge, making connections between individual and structural problems.

Multi-party decision making

The complexities of handling a communal conflict involve how to manage polarized positions developed over issues ranging from irreversible environmental effects of exploiting natural resources to permission to build a coal power plant. For instance, development projects in an ecologically sensitive natural habitat are characterized by discussion about complex public issues that usually touch upon the interests of multiple parties, including a range of constituents such as land owners, developers, elected politicians, local conservation groups and their national allies, residents, the local council, and the state government. The large number of participants makes the process more complicated, as each has a separate position.

To reach consensus among multiple parties demands a collaborative decision-making process. Managing complex issues (such as the protection of endangered species) through negotiation may start from the development of a context for discussion by laying out the background information as well as educating participants about the process. Defining the issues is related to the identification of problems and crystallization of questions. This initial process is followed by the generation of options, the exploration of possible decisions on actions, or other outcomes.

Multiple options can be compared with the development of evaluation criteria based on group interests and external constraints as well as the integration of factual information in the assessment. Group discussion can be invigorated by encouraging members to volunteer ideas without any fear of criticism; all ideas can be shared and evaluated to discover the most suitable option through discussion. Creative solutions to seemingly insoluble problems are likely to emerge from the maximization of brainstorming.

Negotiated rule making

Negotiated rule making in a domestic setting has been enacted to prevent policy disputes with the creation of collaborative relationships among multiple stakeholders in developing administrative regulations. As many municipal, provincial, and federal governments begin to consider various types of regulations aimed at reducing greenhouse gases, policy makers have been concerned about how to reduce the resistance of industries opposed to costly administrative measures. In some Western industrialized countries, a broad level of consensus in key public policy areas has been sought by eliminating misunderstanding and clarifying different interests (for instance, the control of air pollution).

The process is designed to resolve differences or provide input into policy making by discovering a common ground among participants in a more relaxed non-adversarial environment. If it is properly designed, a negotiated rule-making process should be inclusive in terms of the balanced representation or coverage of interests, accountability to constituencies, and the free flow of information. Ideally speaking, all phases are open to every interest group (e.g., residents, environmental groups, and businesses) so that the participants retain the control over the outcome. The public needs to be fully informed of a decision-making process. Stakeholders are supposed to be equal partners in a communication and planning exercise.

In understanding authority in decision making, it is important not only to determine the extent to which authority has been delegated to the group but also to make sure who ultimately holds power to commit resources for implementation. While those affected can make moral claims to public sympathy, the agreement can be blocked by those who have political clout. Some may have an interest, but not have the power to block the decision. The group stance may reflect an organizational mission such as the advocation of protection of endangered species. Even when the process may be purely local, the issue may attract the attention and participation of national or international stakeholders as secondary participants in a supporting role.

Balancing representational power is considered essential to public policy making. Since each participant has a different financial and technical ability to be committed to the meetings, various procedural measures are adopted to ensure the representation of all interests and concerns. In public forums, the overrepresentation of industry and government interests leads to underrepresentation of public interests. Financial assistance can provide access to consultants and other needed resources for poorly funded groups. National or international advocacy groups can be invited to directly participate in a group process or support smaller, local advocacy groups. Even brief training can be provided for novice groups at the first facilitated meeting to inform them of the process knowledge, skills of participation, and articulation of their group positions.

Dialogue forums and process

In general, dialogue is designed to enhance mutual understanding and induce change in adversarial behavior. Dialogue is dubbed both as a diplomatic tool between states and as a means to bring an end to communal violence. Regarding human rights issues, consultative meetings between China and the European Union respectively have been held in the hope of bringing about improvement in Beijing's notorious treatment of political prisoners. In addition, dialogue has been adopted as part of strategic meetings to exchange different views about economic and trade issues with China during the Bush administration. In addressing concerns with China's environmental pollution, Germany held bilateral meetings in order to explore technical assistance.

Forums of dialogue involving small groups or entire communities have also been organized to discuss diverse issues, ranging from specific local resource conflicts to racial and ethnic tensions. As part of grassroots peace building, the long-term objective of dialogue is to promote peace "from below" by encouraging collaboration among people who share an interdependent fate. Mutual understanding can emerge among widows and orphans of war, and children of victims and perpetrators who have similar experiences of being affected by a violent past (e.g., dialogue between German and Israeli youth). Joint actions can be taken to improve their situations or communicate similar interests. A dialogue process can go hand in hand with institution building, networking, and practical projects which generate confidence building. As was illustrated in Tajikistan, a dialogue process may be institutionalized in the form of "inter-ethnic advisory bodies," "reconciliation commissions," or can be utilized for capacity building for NGO networks (Ropers, 2004).

In managing human relations, dialogue has been, in a more general sense, referred to as a communal problem-solving process through building solidarity and mutual understanding within and between group members. The central elements here are personal encounters and eliminating barriers to communication. As seen in meetings between deeply divided community members in Tajikistan and Moldova, the initial stage of dialogue may go through the expression of anger and grievances. Once this stage moves on to probing the conflict's roots, the dialogue process is used to explore and propose alternatives to the current situation (e.g., desirable political system changes).

Dialogue represents critical practice of sense making and community building. In talking about highly contentious issues, communication is feasible only by permitting tolerance of diverse perspectives (Kellett and Dalton, 2001). Deep questioning is an essential part of communication for shared understanding and action for transformation. Initiatives for peace involve an essential task of building empathy and confidence as well as reframing and reconceptualizing the problems. As people perceive the ethnic other as a threat to their national and personal security as a result of state propaganda, overcoming mutual fears of competing ethnicities can be the central focus of civic society dialogue projects.

In response to the intractable Kurdish problems in Turkey, developing discussion among local intelligentsia has promoted the efforts to bring pressure on the government to reform its policies in conformation with the international standards of democracy. The Center for the Research of Societal Problems has challenged the status quo to transform the perceptions of the Turkey–Kurdish relationships from ethnic strife to democratic responsibility of a state. The Center (founded in 1997 by two Kurds and two Turks) has played a pioneering role in seeking conciliation between citizens from the two communities of Turkey by disseminating the culture of democracy with multiculturalism (Ergil, 2004).

The intent of a dialogue "is not to come to consensus over an issue, but to find common ground" by understanding the thought processes of others (Foley, 2003, p. 248). The main goal is a deeper understanding of the complex issues that divide communities, facilitating decision making for action. In seeking to uncover areas of common understanding, dialogue adopts the format of listening, reflection, and deliberation.

Mutual understanding through dialogue can be more easily achieved by improved knowledge about their conflict as well as participants' skills in interacting constructively with one another. In a long series of talks between the representatives of the Sudanese government and its opposition People's Liberation Movement (SPLM), a facilitating team began to introduce expert lectures and seminars as a means to complement official negotiation (Khadiagala, 2007). Inquiry and learning (based on shared information) facilitate a search for solutions, while encouraging interaction to move forward with greater clarity and depth. Mutual influence stems from a willingness to be persuaded as well as gaining important insights and observations.

The expression of differences may lead to challenge any social or organizational norms inhibiting the exploration of diverse perspectives. Space for explicit reasoning in dialogue is created by commitment to openness. Dialogue fosters trust, bonding, and connecting. It is helpful to bring forth everyone's own assumptions about each other's behavior so that misunderstanding would not arise from mistrust (Saunders, 2003). As illustrated by Jewish–Palestinian dialogue projects, relationship building through communication contributes to the humanization of transactions.

In ending the civil war in Guatemala, dialogue between left-wing guerrilla insurgents and civil society groups developed space for connecting diverse interests. As an initial step of the peace process, the Guatemalan National Revolutionary Unity (URNG) met with members of civil society and political groups under the auspices of the Lutheran World Federation in Oslo, and produced the Basic Agreement on the Search for Peace by Political Means in March 1990. In addition to this meeting, from June to October, URNG was engaged in a series of continuing meetings with leading Guatemalan political parties (in Spain), business associations (in Canada), clergy (in Ecuador), and popular organizations and academics (in Mexico) respectively. These meetings set out arrangements to open negotiation with the government in April 1991, promoting broad understanding of social, economic issues as well as confidence building.

Interaction in multi-group process

Facilitation is designed to examine issues and explore alternatives. The expectations need to be clarified with the input of participants. It can be based on brainstorming and productive problem solving. An open forum leads to increased participation. In terms of the environment of group interaction, the atmosphere needs to be managed to achieve optimum conditions needed for discussion. Procedures designed to enhance collaboration help a group reach its goals more easily.

In many deeply divided societies, group interaction navigates via a multifarious web of confrontation, cooperation, and compromise. A key to the successful facilitation is the creation of an unbiased and impartial environment for group interaction. An interaction process can be more complex with the involvement of a large number of participants. Challenges to listening, regulating, and synthesizing the exchange of diverse perspectives are common in a large group environment. This is particularly the case when a facilitation process moves from a general discussion to a more goal-oriented one involving specific ideas.

In a large group setting, the conference can be divided into a plenary and committee structures. The representatives of diverse group members, for instance, in peace conferences (e.g., Burundi), can be assigned to small committees which permit close interactions to develop proposals on designated areas (such as democracy, peace, and security). Then each committee presents their report at a plenary session that included all the participants. The committee structure provides an opportunity to forge a common bond and unity among opposing group members who worked on the same issues. In spite of their ethnic, cultural, or ideological differences, committee members have shared responsibility for not only formulating proposals on designated areas but also for ensuring their successful presentation and acceptance at the plenary session that included all the participants. The collaborative process develops new group dynamics manifested in a common identity and even loyalty attached to each committee. The close relationship built around the committee assignment can nurture even long-term friendship among delegation members of warring factions.

The regulation of member participation helps prevent a few participants from dominating discussion. Yet balanced participation is essential to building the diversity and strengths of the group. In multi-party talks such as the constitutional assembly (e.g., Ethiopia, South Africa in the early 1990s), it was essential to create a mechanism for marginalized groups to have their views heard. The exclusion and marginalization of the Inkatha Freedom Party in transition to a new majority rule in South Africa provoked pre-election violence in 1994.

Once opposing perspectives surface, facilitators need to heed bringing a rocky point of the process back on track with the adoption of ground rules that promote such a protocol as "disagree but do not be disagreeable." A discussion plan includes a strategy to promote full, equal participation. In Northern Ireland's multi-party peace talks (1996–1997), a ground rule was established to permit all the participants to freely raise any aspect of constitutional issues.

Ground rules are generally designed to establish communication geared toward cultivating mutual respect and minimizing self-righteousness by emphasizing "listen to understand." In addition, the rules can help prohibit any participant from making irrelevant comments at excessive length. The protocol also needs to be established to prevent emotional abuse with verbal attacks and threats of walk-away as well as inflexibility in modifying one's positions.

Polarizing discussion (especially in such settings as Israeli–Palestinian dialogues) can be moderated and altered by the clarification of misunderstanding as well as using partial agreement as encouragement for further discussion. A destructive exchange of arguments can be controlled by stepping back to bring in meta-communication perspectives as well as a call for a break or caucus. Tensions can be diverted or reduced by restricting the amount of time allocated to emotionally charged topics as well as reframing toxic comments. By promoting an open climate for discussion, participants are encouraged to expand the agendas, and develop alternative views with new insights.

In a large group setting, there are diverse techniques to increase the input of participants. In its simple form, a census method assists in the identification of problems by permitting the audience to individually write down ideas. The canvassing of views by participants through an open-ended, initial questionnaire can be accompanied by ranking each of the ideas on the collected list according to specific criteria. After the identification of frequently referred themes, participants will have an opportunity to modify their earlier views in relation to the majority opinions while having the option of keeping and justifying their dissenting opinion. In contrast with open discussion forums, limited interaction (resulting from the dispersion of constituents) would require dependence on the utilization of mail, fax, or email.

In exploring some kind of resolution to the crisis after the cease-fire of the 1992 civil war in Moldova, representatives of the residents of Transdnestra (the majority of whom are Russians) were engaged in facilitated dialogue with their Moldovan counterparts. The meetings often turned out to be unproductive due to the fact that the tendency of each party to keep repeating positions, sometimes even with the same words. In order to break a logjam, facilitators asked each participant to write on a piece of paper three things they would like to get help from the other side, and three things they could do for the other side. As a result of this process, some 72 propositions emerged to be condensed down into nine "principles," which served as the agenda (Webb, 2001).

The precise sequence and rate at which issues are discussed differ in each facilitation. By nurturing empathy, the participants can share and understand their experiences; diverse ideas blend into orderly concepts through synthesis. The successful outcome of facilitation is deduced from skillful and effective integration of separate concepts into a large whole. Synthesis may emerge from rewording or rephrasing participant comments. A rank-ordered list of suggestions can be a product of group facilitation. The outcomes of discussion can be categorized in terms of a list of action items for the group, recommendations to be passed to the authority and issues to be further discussed later.

Facilitator roles: procedural responsibilities

Facilitation procedures can be coordinated by someone who is able to offer inputs into a group process with sufficient background information and broad knowledge base. Facilitators help a group identify outcomes to achieve (e.g., action plans to eliminate hate crimes or proposals to curb the harmful effects of water pollution). Positive group functioning comes from the protection of a group against its own bad habits (of developing stereotypes and continuously blaming each other for communal violence), while fostering and enhancing participation. At community meetings involving multiple participants, facilitators may spell out the prohibition of personal attacks as well as attacks on motivations and intentions of participants. In keeping the group focused on objectives, a facilitator needs to periodically summarize the group's progress.

Facilitators can nurture a conducive environment for a group process by properly balancing the human and physical dynamics. The ability of scanning the surroundings based on observation skills is needed to "guide through the challenging labyrinth of conflict and resolution" (Zimmerman and Evans, 1993, p. 38). As illustrated by the role of former US Senator Mitchell in organizing hearings of decommissioning paramilitaries in Northern Ireland, seasoned technical skills and the intuitive insight of facilitators would blend into concentrating on monitoring emotion and translating the ideas into proposal making as well as the development of an agenda. As the parties' positions fell too far apart, the 1999 pre-negotiation meetings between Renamo and Frelimo in Mozambique had to address relationship issues (involving each party's political legitimacy) prior to setting agendas. The dialogue sponsored by Rome-based Catholic lay group Sant'Egidio was devoted to carefully cultivating conditions for improved relationships by appealing to positive personal emotions and generating hope for the future (Bartoli, 2005).

In maintaining the direction and purpose of the discussion, thus, skilled facilitators can do a lot more than merely responding verbally and nonverbally to participant input. The guidance by a facilitator can help groups create a positive climate for conversation and identify the main steps needed to move toward the overall goal. The impartiality and objectivity of a procedure are essential to the expression of diverse views. The process can be constructively managed by information sharing and consultation with constituents. In an attempt to explore options for a shared future and bring peace to southern Sudan, a Kenyan mediator traveled widely to canvas diverse opinions as part of his consultation with the warring factions.

Facilitator skills

The main job of facilitators is not a leader's role but is probing, observing, developing rapport with participants (Foley, 2003). The task also entails providing feedback in guiding a participatory process without being obtrusive. Facilitators need to have diverse interpretive skills, ranging from listening to rephrasing. Skilled listening is needed to comprehend the denotative and connotative parts of a message. Facilitators should be able to rephrase concepts without altering their original meanings. In distinguishing issues and providing a logical framework, facilitators need to be flexible to accept unknowns as assets in goal attainment. Openness encourages acknowledging, understanding, and managing emotions. This is important in racial and ethnic conflict settings especially when past violence did much harm to either one or both of the communities.

Relational skills permit the expression of differences in opinions. Trust and confidence can be derived from empathetic listening that enables speakers to talk through their own problem and feelings (McCorkle and Reese, 2005). A general strategy of empathetic listening is validation and acknowledgment of each other's concerns or feelings (about insecurity, for instance, felt by rival ethnic factions in Kenya). Supportive statements can be accompanied by the expression of feelings, affirmation of each other's contribution. This is opposed to devaluing behavior such as downgrading the other's competence or discounting their capability and contribution along with tangential statements and interruptions.

Process skills entail properly sensing the flow of interaction as well as developing common meanings from different perspectives. Facilitators should lay down, prepare, and work out explicit procedures and schedules. The absence of clear systems for communication (all parties are expected to adhere to) can result in "laxity, lack of seriousness, laissez-faire attitude of the parties" (Khadiagala, 2007, p. 143). In the initial sessions of Burundi's multi-party forum to search for peace (June 1998), 18 factions submitted lengthy papers, creating a slow, clumsy process. While facilitation sessions should be frank and democratic, someone should be in charge of taking decisions about time frames for the talks.

Blending into discussion as a member of the group may result in the loss of objectivity and leverage. This can be compared with avoiding seriously assisting in reaching group goals. The observer's presence in group interaction without participation can be positive through their quiet influence. Selected, temporary intervention in diffusing tension can be compared with active engagement in relationship building. In facilitating talks to end Burundi's civil war in the late 1990s and early 2000s, former Tanzanian President Nyerere's facilitating role permitted the expression of anger and hostilities before gradually forging consensus while his successor Nelson Mandela brought morality and justice concerns in his interventionist approaches (Maundi, 2003).

Intervention can be designed to moderate attacking and defensive statements which produce refusal to cooperate. Stress and emotion during difficult discussion generate a defensive reaction (McCorkle and Reese, 2005). Negative emotions are obstacles to the exchange of views since they cause the loss of proper judgment. When emotions get into a negative spiral, it is time to break off discussion to have time to let the tension subside. Stepping aside to recompose is needed to resist similar emotional display to avoid worsening the matter. It takes time to step away from emotional triggers and to revert back to substantive discussion.

Facilitators need to watch out for the derailment of the group process arising from turf battles. Balanced and cool attitudes help a facilitator remain unfazed and focused even in the midst of chaos. Diverse techniques to interrupt the cycle of provocation and reduce the impact of emotion on discussion involve acknowledging feelings as well as withdrawal from discussion. A response to an emotionally laden message is reframing the issues in less stressful terms. The depersonalization of issues helps separate feelings from substance. Facilitators can urge the participants to put themselves in the other's shoes for greater openness with more flexibility in attitudes and goals.

Conditions for successful facilitation

What is most desired at the end of facilitation is the emergence of trust and respect. Because facilitation is not likely to "produce immediate solutions to all problems," an attempt to control the group process and outcome is not desirable (Zimmerman and Evans, 1993, p. 36). The initial facilitation sessions can be used to help groups form their own concept of closure. Productive facilitation would not take place without a conducive environment that has a positive impact on the participants' perceptions. The psychologically and physically flexible atmosphere (such as informal meetings held at a castle during peace talks in Northern Ireland) helps communication be free of bias as much as possible.

In any kind of group process, there are such questions as the clarification of the purpose and forms of the meetings which all need to agree to. In Sudan's Darfur, not all the participants were clear about the aims of the conferences. The agenda needs to be balanced to cover the full range of issues which represent all key interests. This process should not be restrained by a proposition held by powerful interests. Seeking a balance in the power situation is necessary to boost the capacity of participants for full expression of their views so that any power differential would not inhibit the exchange of views.

Reaching consensus is time consuming or even fails if we are not able to overcome the challenge of how to discuss deeply held views that are not negotiable. Polarized debates prohibit partisans from gaining insight into the beliefs and concerns of the other side. Understanding the perceptions of other parties is essential in a joint diagnosis of obstacles to progress. Intellectually reverse roles are needed for looking behind statements for underlying interests.

Public peace process: the role of dialogue

In various settings of international conflict, improved relations arise from new communication patterns that facilitate the mutual clarification of perceptions. The existence of various forms of dialogue suggests their multiple objectives and functions. These range from contact and confidence building to joint conflict analysis to explorative problem solving to pre-negotiations. Some are limited to mere acknowledgment of opposing views and positions, while others are oriented toward removing stereotypes (for perceptual changes in relationship improvement and increased respect).

Grassroots peace-building initiatives shed light on interacting constructively with one another, eventually leading to institutional, network building (inter-ethnic advisory boards, NGO networks). The dialogue methods have been applied to dissolving tensions in civil conflicts of Tajikistan, South Africa, and Northern Ireland as well as US–Soviet relations. The Dartmouth Conference established in 1960 achieved its objective by stimulating policy-relevant, citizen-to-citizen dialogue on relations between the US and the USSR.

In Northern Ireland, cross-community NGOs working on dialogue and understanding between communities played a very important role in consolidating the peace process in support of an official negotiation. In particular, advocacy agencies such as the Belfast-based Community Development Centre built a bridge between a government agency and the community by establishing the Interagency Working Group for Displaced Families.

Dialogue (i.e., confidential problem-solving workshops) is utilized as a pre-negotiation to inspire official negotiations. Various initiatives were taken in preparing steps for peace in Syria–Israel, Palestine–Israel relations (Sultan, 2006). For instance, Syrians and Israelis (from nongovernmental sectors) met in Geneva to discuss conditions for the return of the

Golan Heights (Lerner, 2004). Dialogue groups may get engaged in a search for common ground and joint actions as is presented by the Geneva Accord between private Israeli and Syrian citizens. Problem solving in intractable conflict has been designed to resolve substantive differences. These meetings are considered "non-official" but involve political preliminaries especially when they are "joined by officials who have access to the leadership decision making" (Ropers, 2004, p. 177).

The clarification of different viewpoints can be accompanied by the acknowledgment of substantive issues. In fostering empathy, group encounters supported by face-to-face communication promote personal confidence building. A series of dialogue events (in protracted conflicts) are designed to reveal underlying needs and fears as well as values. Reflecting on the experience of conflict, participants seek each other's knowledge about conflict history. An understanding of the substantive issues results in the identification of shared interests (and needs). Discussion about practical measures and implementation can focus on joint efforts and collaborative action.

Dialogue initiatives eventually have to build "peace constituencies or alliances" (Ropers, 2004, p. 182). When dialogue projects are utilized as pre-negotiation, the most ambitious dialogue-based undertakings are those designed to exert influence on the regulation of the conflict at the political-leadership level. Yet one of the main challenges still remains how to sustain them and most importantly how to move beyond exploratory talks to building consensus for joint actions at an official level. In an attempt to end a protracted civil war in Colombia, civil society dialogues between NGOs and each of the guerrilla groups, namely the Revolutionary Armed Forces of Columbia (FARC) and the National Liberation Army (ELN) were held separately in Europe, Mexico, and Cuba (Chernick, 2003). These talks produced a series of proposals on economic reform, human rights, and constitutional changes (that can serve as negotiation between the government and rebel groups) by the early 2000s. Even though these proposals were actively supported by Germany, Sweden, Mexico, and Cuba and other foreign sponsors of the civil society initiated dialogue projects, they failed to provide a momentum for reaching a peace accord due to deteriorating security situations.

National forums have also been used either to supplement or support a negotiation process to end civil wars or to develop a framework for political transition (e.g., South Africa). Bridge-building functions were provided by national assemblies to resolve intercommunal issues. In post-conflict settings, a dialogue process was adopted to discuss constitutional changes in Ethiopia, Somalia, and Afghanistan. Prior to reaching the 1999 Lusaka Agreement for a cease-fire, a parallel national dialogue process (involving armed and unarmed Congolese groups) discussed the future institutions and interim government of their country as well as the disarmament of armed groups and departure of foreign troops. The six-week-long dialogue sessions reflected the frustration felt with at least 20 failed mediation attempts to end the second Congo war.

Informal, nonofficial communication: track II diplomacy

A clearer understanding of interests and constraints might emerge at an informal meeting to set the stage for subsequent official negotiation. Meetings prior to reaching a formal agreement can also be designed to explore options. Various discussions can take place either with public knowledge or through back channel communication. In general, official government actions (equated to track I) are distinguished from unofficial efforts by non-governmental professionals called track II.

In the more adversarial setting of a formal, official process, the main communication goal is to score points. A hostile opinion within the community or country often does not encourage politicians to contact the opposing sides. While the Israeli–Palestinian track did not produce tangible agreement in the 1991 Madrid Peace Conference, the 1993 Oslo Agreement was the fruit of negotiation conducted secretly in Norway between the PLO and the Labor government of Israel. An informal process brought about the breakthrough in Israeli–Palestinian negotiations from 1992 to 1993 while official Israeli–Palestinian negotiation stalled in the peace process invigorated by the end of the first Gulf War. Norwegian diplomats led by Johan Jorgen Holst facilitated the track II meetings held near Oslo. The informal setting provided the atmosphere for forging close relationships between the representatives of the two long-term antagonists. This process was eventually advanced to formal negotiations approved by high-level authorities.

As official representatives are engaged in formal interaction based on government instructions, track I official diplomacy is likely to be constrained by power politics. On the contrary, track II relies on nongovernmental, informal, unofficial interaction between private citizens for the exploration of security and esteem of each other, bypassing the formal government power structure. Its main goal is lowering fear and tension through improved communication and better understanding of each other's viewpoints. In general, informal confidence-building processes invite multiple groups to diverse settings of contact and exchange, ranging from scholarly meetings to communal development.

As a parallel process, track II is not a substitute for but is rather complementary to track I. In fact, tracks I and II are often interconnected to each other. Informal bridge building was increasingly endorsed or supported by EU and other official governmental actors as part of an attempt to end armed conflicts in Sri Lanka, Guatemala, Colombia, and post-Soviet independent states such as Armenia–Azerbaijan. In order to build up public support for a settlement, unofficial contacts were supported by OSCE and other international organizations. They have sponsored the organization of workshops for journalists and business groups, academic exchanges, and study trips (in such places as Moldova and Georgia), many of which emerged from civil society. While informal meetings serve as a means for confidence building, these meetings can evolve into mediated negotiations.

Indeed, nonofficial track II diplomacy focuses on understanding and communication through direct encounters. Its main function is the education of the public in creating a safe political environment for leaders to negotiate, but immediate success depends on effectiveness in changing the perceptions of influential policy makers. Dialogue in Tajikistan sponsored by both the Americans and Russians represents one of the examples which illustrate how official and unofficial processes can be linked to each other in ceasing the hostilities of a civil war (1992–1997). Various proposals developed in official meetings were actually adopted in formal negotiations. In fact, some of dialogue group members participated in either an official negotiation process or national reconciliation commission. Others have started their own dialogue process in different regions to develop shared understanding about the relationships between Islam and democracy (Saunders, 2003).

In a nonofficial engagement with an adversarial community, no one is an official representative even though government officials may participate in an unofficial capacity. Most participants are likely to be influential community members, not decision makers who are constrained by an official commitment. Even though government officials are not authorized to make decisions, they are free to explore options in an informal setting. It is not about negotiation, being designed to enhance understanding. Prior to the government decision to negotiate with the African National Congress (ANC) in 2001, the members of the South African intelligence service were involved in secret contact with ANC leaders via channels developed by Afrikaner academics.

The major distinction between official and unofficial diplomacy is differing legitimacy. Power-political options of states are contrasted with the different understanding of conflict by societal groups in contact with each other. As protracted conflict is ascribed to a failure to satisfy basic needs in regard to security, recognition, and participation, the need for social change is not only a matter of substance but also troubled relations. In human needs perspectives, tackling substantive conflicts is regarded as a shared problem.

People in the media, business, and other sectors across states can be engaged in promoting intercultural understanding. As is illustrated by various events in post-1945 Europe, "increased contact could help eliminate prejudices and enemy images with the creation of new loyalties" (Ropers, 2004, p. 177). Preceding the Israeli–Palestinian accord of 1993, various informal forums (which were used to air new ideas) helped develop networks of personal relationships in tandem with the socialization of future leading figures. The civil society's influence is considered generally indirect; sustained engagement supported by citizen participation needs to be built on a long time horizon in order to overcome substantial psychological and procedural reservations of government officials who hold power-politics perspectives.

Deeper communication: a problem-solving workshop

In identifying and understanding each other's needs, parties should analyze the causes of conflict and examine conditions for its resolution. The new patterns of behavior emerge from the learning process of the protagonists in a relaxed setting. New information about root causes of conflict gained in the analytical process should give participants an opportunity to alter their perceptions about the conflict and their adversaries. An acceptable compromise between the parties is more likely to be forged by sufficient knowledge of the sources of conflictual relationships. The conflict can be more easily restructured from a zero-sum to positive sum definition by eliminating the assumptions of power politics (Burton, 1997). Problem-solving workshops seek mutual understanding of security and other ontological issues which contribute to the deep polarization of positions between parties.

An academically based, unofficial third-party approach is manifested particularly in problem-solving workshops. Representatives of community members are brought together for communication in interactive problem solving. It was first initiated in the 1960s by American social psychologist Leonard Doob in an attempt to apply academic theories and skills to inter-group and international conflict. His workshop on Kenya invited the social and cultural elites of various ethnic communities who were approved to attend the gathering by their political leaders. In its continuing experiment, different variations of the workshops were later developed by J. W. Burton (for ethnic conflict in Malaysia in the early 1960s) and Herbert Kelman (on the Israeli–Palestinian conflict) based on the participation of a broad spectrum of elites, former politicians, diplomats, and academics. A facilitated process in workshop settings brought close working relationships between moderate Israelis and Palestinians over more than a decade prior to the 1994 Oslo Peace Accord (Kelman, 2008).

An action-oriented workshop approach has drawn the attention of other scholars who were devoted to playing a positive role in resolving Arab–Israeli conflict. The workshops for Lebanon started in 1984 and continued during the civil war period; the participants were nominated by the leaders representing various Christian and Muslim factions. The interactive process of conflict resolution has also been applied to newly emerging tensions in Modova, Georgia, and other newly born states of the former Soviet Union in the mid- and late 1990s. These workshops paid growing attention to dehumanization, victimization, and other psycho-dynamic processes. Interactive problem solving has been further utilized for reconciliation by developing a group process of mourning and forgiveness.

In these workshops, the analysis of human motivations and competitive social processes embedded in a particular conflict is an essential first step toward resolving a deep-rooted communal problem which entails the marginalization of certain social groups. Thus the role of facilitators is devoted to promoting analytical thinking by workshop participants themselves with the increased knowledge of each other. The sources and origins of a conflict need to be analyzed to grasp the complexities of social and political rifts. In reconceptualizing the totality of a problem and its source, a social structure is considered a function of a shared frame of mind. Thus, conflict-generating social reality is interpreted as a process rather than an entity that cannot be fixed.

The meetings are held confidentially to prevent public backlash and criticism against any contact with adversaries. Initially, a small group of expert panelists guide the participants to analyze the causes of conflict and examine conditions for its resolution. In the process of analyzing the root causes of contentious relationships, adversarial group members can develop sufficient knowledge of the sources of conflict (often associated with suppressed basic human needs). In contrast with mediation, which seeks an acceptable compromise between the parties, the main task of the workshop is not bargaining different interests but reconceptualizing conflict relationships through the analysis of the parties' needs.

The motivational aspects of social action are explained in terms of a desire to fulfill a set of deep-seated psychological and physical needs; threats to the fulfillment of basic needs or their actual nonfulfillment are often powerfully played out in protracted political or ethnic conflict. Through the workshop process, participants may eventually realize that fears in inter-group conflict situations are driven by perceived threats to identity and security associated with the denial of ontological needs.

The merit of problem-solving workshops is related to their unconventional ability to change the socio-psychological environments of participants by avoiding the assumptions of power politics. The exploration of a needs-based solution has emerged as a remedy to mediation which enhances communication between parties, but is not designed for a sufficient understanding of the main cause of problems. In order to transform conflict embedded in long-term hostilities, parties have to be willing to change the patterns of their interactions that may entail the need for structural changes. Historical animosities cannot be dissipated by limited, short-term solutions. The interactive process of conflict resolution is geared toward the understanding of each other's perceptions and motives in getting to the real source of recurrent tensions and violence.

Relationship transformation

The views of political leaders and public opinions can be reconfigured by social and cultural elites who have developed new understandings of problems through informative facilitation sessions. The search for a new solution can certainly be motivated by frustration with the traditional *realpolitik* paradigm which guides politicians and diplomats to carve out their gains and make a compromise according to the logic of power. While the settlement of relatively specific, containable inter-state disputes can be obtained by a political agreement, the involvement of the collective identities and concerns of group well-being and survival demand a collaborative effort to explore solutions. Groups in a communal conflict are less inclined to give up their demands due to their power inferiority. Since they are not likely to be content with mere short-term settlement (e.g., ethnic rivalry between Hutus and Tutsis), understanding an inter-societal phenomenon requires interactive communication designed to discuss the sources, not symptoms of adversarial relationships.

The initial stage of conflict-resolution workshops needs to be oriented toward overcoming demonized enemy images of each other because mutually hostile perceptions are an obstacle to collaboration on the projects of common interests. Indeed, antagonistic identity boundaries can be redefined, along with attitudinal changes, in the negotiation of security and autonomy. The main assumption of the workshop is that the eventual transformation of relationships between long-term adversaries is a precondition for overcoming a history of intense hostilities. The immediate goal of a workshop is to generate a learning process with the injection of new knowledge and information through informal meetings. Yet its ultimate objective is to provide a positive input to an official negotiation process.

Workshop process and dynamics

The workshop's goal can be best achieved by selecting participants in a position to politically influence their respective communities. However, they do not need to be directly responsible for policy making, while their active and credible role in the political debate is necessary to bring about a change in the political environment (Kelman, 2002). A panel, composed of half a dozen facilitators, encourages parties to get to the bottom of the problem which is not easily understood in power bargaining situations. The credibility and legitimacy of facilitators come from their academic credentials. The input provided by expert panelists consists of general theories about human behavior applicable to a particular conflict.

It is important to manage effectively an initial workshop which tends to be full of tensions. In the Moldovan workshop organized by Keith Webb, Andrew Williams, and his colleagues at the University of Kent, the participants initially refused to travel together in the same airplane or bus. They also insisted on speaking in their own languages (Russian, Moldovan) even though they were fluent in both languages, reflecting the nature of conflict. Thus management of communication between facilitators and participants and between participants became an important issue. In the seven-year-long workshop, progress came by slowly along with frequent deadlocks. These meetings were complemented by numerous visits to Moldova and Transdnestra, monitoring agreements as well as post-conflict reconstruction seminars.

In their sponsoring role, the third party assists in the clarifications and interpretations of facts and events by offering knowledge about relevant patterns of behavior drawn from other situations (with their wider knowledge base for conflict-resolution processes). At the Moldovan conflict workshop, participants were brought in to the conflict sites of Northern Ireland to develop a more in-depth analysis of their own case (Webb, 2001). In examining their own struggle, Israelis and Palestinians also referred to the Northern Ireland conflict, benefiting from the analysis of the overall, generic nature of conflict. In a confidential setting, parties feel comfortable in disclosing information, improving the quality of discussion. Informal, exploratory interactions need to be hidden from public attention at least prior to the emergence of an acceptable basis for negotiation, in that public misperception can interfere in an attempt at honest talks.

The workshop should support mutual examination of each other's perceptions and assessment of the consequences of their conflictual tactics in a search for alternatives. In interactive decision making, false assumptions are screened out along with the examination of existing knowledge, cultural, and ideological orientations and personal prejudices which constitute the participants' frame of reference. A workshop process is not designed to advocate particular solutions; its detailed outcome is not known in advance although the principles of reciprocity and equity are adopted to produce enduring solutions. Possible outcomes acceptable to all are likely to stem from information about alternative means of attaining their goals as well as avoiding the costs of pursuing present policies. The collaborative process is necessary to form new ideas, perceptions, and attitudes (Burton, 1997).

The careful examination of situations leads to the new definition of the relationship which helps create the joint frame of references with the establishment of new facts, norms, and practices. Interaction can be based on the identification of relevant experiences by the participants. Strongly held belief systems can serve as an obstacle to the internalization of new information and knowledge and learning from interaction. In building bridges among themselves, participants are encouraged to develop a common universe of discourse. Workshop proceedings can be designed to examine the impact of each community's action on the other side by utilizing role plays. Based on the analysis, participants can eventually become partners for problem solving.

New frames of reference can facilitate a process to produce a change in the structures of interactions by putting each party's action and content of communications in the light of their contexts. A separate frame, held by each protagonist, inhibits communication, and deforms perceptions of reality. Parties to a problem-solving exercise should be able to develop a common frame which helps interpret and evaluate their opponent's role in a more acceptable term. Indeed, continuing meetings can result in further development of a temporary frame into a shared belief which produces a collapse of categories, eventually redefining the opponents as partners.

The criteria for success of a workshop include its impact on the participants' attitudes. Changes in the perceptions of adversaries tend to be more easily achieved within a small group setting. Yet the biggest hurdle is to transfer psycho-dynamic changes in a small group setting to a large social relationship. Most importantly, the product (such as proposals and ideas) needs to be fed into a political process. The second-track intervention in the Moldova–Transdnestra conflict paralleled the official negotiated constitutional settlement process. Despite the experience of much frustration, the workshop played an important role in gauging new possibilities for Transdnestra and Moldova (Webb, 2001). The involvement of more opinion leaders or people connected to government leaders is designed to have long-term effects in a broad macro-political context. In the Israeli–Palestinian conflict, more than a decade of workshops were conducted prior to the 1994 Oslo Accord.

Further reading

Broome, B. J. (2004) "Reaching across the Dividing Line: Building a Collective Vision for Peace in Cyprus," *Journal of Peace Research*, 41: 191–209.

Burton, J. W. (1997) *Violence Explained: The Sources of Conflict, Violence and Crime and Their Prevention*, Manchester: Manchester University Press.

Chataway, C. J. (2002) "The Problem of Transfer from Confidential Interactive Problem-solving: What is the Role of the Facilitator?" *Political Psychology*, 23: 165–189.

Fisher, R. (2007) "Assessing the Contingency Model of Third Party Intervention: Successful Cases of Prenegotiation," *Journal of Peace Research*, 44 (3): 311–329.

Foley, D. (2003) "The Methods of Dialogue: Promoting Understanding between Hawaiians and Non-Hawaiians," in W. Pammer, and K. Jerri (eds) *Handbook of Conflict Management*, New York: Marcel Dekker, Inc. 243–256.

Lieberfeld, D. (2007) "Overcoming Intractability in South Africa and Israel/Palestine: The Role of Semi-official Meetings," *American Behavioral Scientist*, 50: 1542–1562.

Mitchell, C. (2001) "From Controlled Communication to Problem Solving: The Origins of Facilitated Conflict Resolution," *The International Journal of Peace Studies*, 6 (1): 59–68.

Nan, S. (2004) "Track One and a Half Diplomacy: Searching for Political Agreement in the Caucasus," in M. Fitzduff and C. Church (eds) *NGOs at the Table: Strategies for Influencing Policies in Areas of Conflict*, New York: Rowman and Littlefield.

Perich-Anderson, J. (2003) "The Only Game in Town: Managing Multistakeholder Conflicts," in W. J. Pammer and J. Killian (eds) *Handbook of Conflict Management*, New York: Marcel Dekker, Inc.

Pruitt, D. G. (2008) "Back-channel Communication in the Settlement of Conflict," *International Negotiation*, 13: 37–54.

Saunders, H. (2003) "Sustained Dialogue in Managing Intractable Conflict," *Negotiation Journal*, 19: 85–95.

Senehi, J. (2002) "Constructive Storytelling: A Peace Process," *Peace and Conflict Studies*, 9 (2): 41–63.

Webb, K. (2001) "Mediation in Moldova: A Case of Second-track Diplomacy in Negotiations," in D. Goodwin (ed.) *International Conflict: Understanding Persuasion*, London, Frank Cass. 137–150.

11 Reconciliation

Once conflict is resolved, relationship changes are necessary to remove negative emotional residues that can ignite future hostilities. In overcoming violence and building peaceful relations, fractured social bonds need to be reconstructed, resetting people's expectations of themselves and others. However, the remnant of deep divisions among communities based on fear and anger creates serious challenges to putting a broken social fabric back together. A post-conflict process in such places as Cambodia, Sierra Leone, and Bosnia-Herzegovina is fraught with emotional injury and pain brought about by the death of family members, the shock of exposure to atrocious acts, as well as the loss of property. Difficulties in the suppression of grief and fear often result in a strong desire for justice and revenge.

This chapter reviews the emotional, psychological aspects of post-conflict relationships in the context of the elimination of fear and hatred. It sheds light on various activities of curing wounds and healing traumas in cultivating healthy and sustained relationships. Social healing in civil war situations is laden with such priorities as repatriation and reintegration; resentment toward former militia group fighters hinders intra-community reconciliation after their return. Reconciliation entails steps toward psychic, attitudinal, and behavioral changes beyond the settlement of issues which have immediate consequences such as cessation of war. The emotional and psychological "residues" of conflict – trauma, fear, and hurt – poison future relations, since they continue to fuel revenge motives. The act of aggression is often justified by the creation of myths/heroes in the conflict history of perpetrators.

Properties of reconciliation

Reconciliation activities need to be set in the context of overcoming marginalization, alienation, and other psychological and social effects of violent conflict. Overall, the initial peace-building process is set in the past trajectory of horrific conflict. In order to realize coexistence, the most essential element is a change in the attitudes and behavior of adversaries. The appreciation of common humanity and respect for each other's identity are necessary to affirm a new future.

In overcoming anger and frustration accompanied by loss, social space is needed to express grief in tandem with naming and confronting fears. Social bonds are recreated by the process of remembrance and mourning (Daly and Sarkin, 2007). Rehumanizing the enemy may start from a commitment to take the risk of a journey for reconciliation and to accept the choice to forgive. The process of restoring justice starts with the admission of guilt by perpetrators and public apology. Joint planning is necessary for reviewing history and navigating solutions.

Agreements about constructive engagement can be based on learning about the other community's experiences of the effects of a conflict. More complex narratives emerge from listening to each other's stories honestly. Most importantly, acknowledging harm and empathizing with suffering should lead to exploring truth and redressing injustices. The entire gamut of psychological interaction involves perpetrators' repenting and apologizing before victims relinquish bitterness in favor of forgiveness.

It is a daunting task to embark on reaching into a society full of inexpressible shame, fear, and self-loathing. The experience of violence deprives people of the abilities to listen and to express themselves that are very basic to relationship building. The absence of the capacity to trust does not generate a creative imagination of the future. A learning process entails expanding the meaning of one's own concepts as well as dislodging what was formerly believed to be true.

The capacities of people and communities are limited given their disorientation after the experience of widespread violence and long-standing oppression. The webs of relationships disappear along with the destruction of a community which sheltered everyday life (bombed-out villages and desecrated shrines). The textures of people's lives are lost in the aftermath of the death or injuries of loved ones.

Helping adversaries appreciate their common humanity is the basic condition for coexistence along with accepting a former enemy as a member of a newly shared community. In fact, people can certainly be convinced to channel their grievances without descending into cycles of violence. The questions of injustice, inequities, and historical grievances (embedded in power asymmetry) cannot be ignored to sustain reconciliation.

The context of reconciliation

Deceit, manipulation, control, and violence are often manifested in the abusive inter-communal relationships of war, genocide, extreme oppression of rights, and dignity for the marginalized. Democratic, consensual, or healthy inter-communal relationships are managed by agreed-upon procedures and structures. Functional families, friendships, and fellowships are warranted by the well-being of all members in tandem with a shared understanding of interdependence of each other's welfare.

The main challenge in many post-conflict settings is nourishing the attitudes, values, and capacities for respect and cooperation, if not immediately, then over time. A healing process and justice are necessary to overcome the circumstances responsible for victimization. Building a new relationship has to go hand in hand with continuing efforts to settle unresolved issues in tandem with looking into the circumstances responsible for victimization (Jeong, 2005). The psychological aspects of reconciliation are particularly relevant to the elimination of residues of victimization feelings. Reconciliation and healing remain an important part of a conflict-resolution process given that the legacy of past violence serves as a latent source of future confrontations. The establishment of a harmonious relationship requires the confrontation of past grievances and historical traumas.

The readjustment of various aspects of communal relations has to be made beyond resolving differences at a negotiation table. It is a far more complicated process to rebuild a community after conflict was institutionalized through a cycle of mutual victimization. Indeed, direct inter-personal violence can be linked to destruction of the deeper structures of social bonds such as social identity. Justice cannot be fulfilled by continuously condoning and extolling violence. Social exclusion is engendered by bullying, gendered oppression, and homophobic violence.

Reconciliation is thus a process to tackle the central needs and fears of the societies which grapple with the wounds of conflict. Group healing and other activities can focus on individual and social well-being in overcoming the pathological, psychological and social conditions that are likely to harbor the conflict. Reconciliation and healing should be supported by social and institutional changes (such as democratization and equitable development as well as security reform). It is not merely psychological but also institutional–structural.

Overcoming the psychology of victimization

The experience of systematic, ruthless, and indiscriminate mass violence adds an additional dimension to the process of conflict resolution. Violence directed against defenseless women, children, and old men deprives human beings of a sense of community and self-identity. The psychology of victimhood sustains political antagonism and deep divisions between groups through the mobilization of communal symbols. The victims both consciously and unconsciously fear that the offenders may commit more aggression and violence by denying the injustice of their past acts. Building trust has to follow overcoming the past wounds of victimization by such means as the acknowledgment of crimes and the expression of contrition.

Recovering people's common sense of reality is crucial since violence has been incorporated into everyday life. Desire for expressing grievances with revenge would remain high without overcoming hatred and fear. Reconstructing people's destabilized social world has to concentrate on the transformation of abnormal violent relations. In a situation where violence has become a social norm, reconciliation constitutes part of a social process for conflict resolution. Regaining lost honor and recovering from emotional wounds are associated with changes in the psycho-dynamics of power relations. Overcoming a major traumatic loss of physical and mental capacity has become an important issue in undoing the cycle of violent conflict.

Since intense struggle creates the psychological conditions for dehumanization, reconciliation is part of a process toward establishing a constructive relationship. Whereas political and social relations have to be renegotiated in the process of guaranteeing mutual security, healing focuses on nonnegotiable psychological tasks in an inter-communal conflict characterized by political strife and violence by carrying out contrition/forgiveness transactions. By changing the psychological bases of violent conflict, reconciliation is supposed to remove the sources of current and future animosities and tension.

The rebuilding of divided societies has to address such questions as the basis on which a new relationship ought to be forged. The involvement of communal groups is critical in peace building associated with the elimination of existing feelings of threat. The arrangement of a new inter-communal relationship is needed for creating a social space for cooperation, and it has to be based on the recognition that interdependence helps meet the critical needs of both sides.

Steps toward overcoming past enmity

Preventing the cycle of historical enmity requires overcoming the past history of conflict relationships. Reconciliation as a social process is generated by shared understandings of problems, empathy, changes in public discourse, and concerns with social justice. Reconciliation focuses not only on substantive issues (of how to remedy past harms) but also on the restoration of relationship. Abusive and manipulative relationships need to be tackled in transforming conflict. Restoration of a broken relationship is made possible by acknowledging past misdeeds, exploring common purposes, and respecting different interests. Exposure and full accounting of the past ought to lead to an apology on the part of aggressors. The expression of remorse and apology are essential to ending long-term resentment.

The process of restitution involves forgiveness and compensation being accompanied by the show of remorse. Material compensations as well as apologies can be offered at both an individual and institutional level to make good for past damages. In addition, punishment of offenders can be made in the form of social censure, public embarrassment, social vengeance, and retributive justice. Reconciliation is not likely to occur without forgiveness given that past wounds would not be undone in themselves; any hurt cannot be genuinely compensated in the aftermath of killings, torture, and imprisonment.

This process is designed to transform relationships of hatred and suspicion into relationships of trustworthiness. Former enemies should be able to acknowledge each other's humanity, empathizing with the suffering of victims. In redressing past injustice, remorse can be expressed with an offer of reparations by a perpetrator prior to granting forgiveness. Thus a reconciliatory process based on inclusiveness and mutual acceptance relies on relationship transformation even though it may involve a punitive process (such as concrete repayment). On the part of perpetrators, reconciliation reflects a role shift from being blamed to taking responsibility for the attitudes and actions of one's self and one's own community.

Acknowledgment and forgiveness

Truth telling and acknowledgment of the past harm should assist societies in restoring the dignity of those whose rights have been violated. Acknowledging political, economic, educational, and personal injustice enhances healing in tandem with honoring feelings of victims. Apology is an initial step toward "healing of memories (though not forgetting) and moving on from us and them to become just us; moving from human wrongs to human rights and responsibilities" (Hogan, 2007, p. 265). The review and release of pain has to lead to the development of a new reciprocal respect by reconciling the past with future hope. In order to gain forgiveness, perpetrators have to admit guilt, and give a solemn promise to correct the misdeed. Restitution for the wrong can reverse the harmful effects.

Confession is the authentic acknowledgment of bearing responsibility for one's acts and their consequences by avoiding justification, rationalization, and attribution of blame to others. A cultural setting can determine the style and degree of content disclosure from radical openness to intense guardedness. Disclosure of past acts should be followed by remorse and contrition for healing. Repentance is not punitive self-condemnation but appropriate expression of sorrow for one's behavior and acceptance of consequent compensation for the injury.

Hindrance to forgiveness and healing by victims of horrific violence can be attributed to feelings of personal diminishment vis-à-vis an offender in conjunction with a continued real or imagined threat. Future relationships are undermined by a refusal to take responsibility or at least the rectification of injuries. It is difficult to let bitterness go in the absence of a proper response to alienation. Many horrific war crimes by the Japanese during World War II still revive anger among their victims, since the government has refused to take responsibility for such incidents as the abduction of young Asian women as sex slaves for their soldiers.

Forgiveness "is not an arbitrary, free act of pardon" and is distinguished from resuming interaction without repairing a broken relationship (Augsburger, 1992, p. 283). The relationship can be reestablished by the release of past guilt and the pain of suffering, the removal of fear and suspicion, and the renegotiation of present differences. Apology based on a heartfelt expression of sorrow opens the door for the offender to return to the moral community. Forgiveness can bring about benevolent acceptance with restored mutuality by redressing past power differentials felt in the wrongdoing.

There are situations such as the experience of genocide that defy the comprehension required for any meaningful apology and forgiveness. Many survivors of the genocide in Cambodia feel the impossibility of forgiveness. "The very idea of it [forgiveness] can be offensive after horrible events like the Holocaust, the genocide in Rwanda, or the genocidal violence in Tibet. Even to people outside the victim group, the idea that survivors should forgive following genocide is an affront, an anathema" (Staub *et al.*, 2001, p. 197). In some religious traditions (e.g., Islam and Judaism), the repentance of the wrongdoer is prioritized over forgiveness of the injured.

Post-conflict justice

A wide range of judicial and non-judicial mechanisms from criminal prosecutions to a truth commission have been developed in coming to terms with large-scale past abuses. Many of these activities (individual prosecutions, reparations, truth-seeking, institutional reform, vetting, and dismissals, or a combination thereof) have been applied to a range of cases over the past several decades with differing levels of international involvement (or none at all). One instrument after another, or perhaps in tandem with another (e.g., the establishment of a restorative mechanism like the truth commission in advance of any kind of legal accountability or vice versa), needs to be considered in a unique local setting. Retributive justice searches for prosecutions and punishment through legal procedures. On the other extreme, a passive approach is derived from national amnesia (e.g., the closure of past memories in Spain after the death of the long-term dictator General Franco in 1975) or blanket amnesty (Guatemala and El Salvador after the end of civil wars in the early 1990s).

Each conflict resolution puts different priorities on rectifying injustice. Norms for obtaining justice depend on the social and political context of a conflict. Justice is rarely a univocal concept to refer to different outcomes. A sense of fairness emerges in diverse dimensions of the relationship. Whereas distributive justice may focus on land reform to achieve economic equity, access to power is critical to the attainment of political and social justice (e.g., various policies pursued by President Evo Morales in Bolivia since 2006). Based on the notion of retribution or punishment for crimes committed, the trial can be conducted by a panel of judges who determine guilt and subsequent penalty. Whereas legal processes focus on procedural justice, reparations policies aim for compensatory justice. The reestablishment of historical justice is critical to truth commissions.

Reflecting on the evolution of transitional justice, Sierra Leone simultaneously created a truth commission in tandem with a Special Court in prosecuting the leaders of the Revolutionary United Front and other rebel group leaders who bore the greatest responsibility for atrocious human rights crimes. In its investigation of atrocities following the brutal civil war, the credibility of the truth commission was hurt by the court due to a direct clash of their activities. It is essential to endow truth commissions with proper authorities to fulfill their functions of promotion of justice through truth seeking.

Retribution is widely associated with the principles of both criminal and civil laws carried out by traditional justice based on trials and tribunals. Community courts (such as the Gacaca courts in Rwanda) derived from the traditional legal system of centuries have been revived and reshaped to accommodate the government's dire need to bring perpetrators to trial.

Restorative justice overcomes the inconsistency between justice and reconciliation. Genuine relationships between victims and offenders cannot be restored by punitive measures. As part of a conciliatory process, punishment for perpetrators can be combined with or replaced by rehabilitation. Restorative justice permits offenders to have an opportunity to accept and be accountable for their acts. The recreation of a moral framework agreed upon between victim and offender instigates moving into the future. Whereas the fulfillment of justice is aimed at the empowerment of victims, it creates constructive relationships between victims and perpetrators. In general, past wrongs are rectified by reinstatement of justice in a legal system but without the creation of communication between victims and offenders.

Restitution and reparation

Repayment or reparation as well as compensation for loss are ways to acknowledge wrongful acts and restore justice. Reparation seeks societal restoration by apology and restitution. Government apologies take the form of activities like "Sorry Day" in Australia for the Aborigines, or the Canadian Government's apology to descendants of Métis rebel leader Louis Riel. Most commonly reparation entails the obligations of perpetrators to make restitution by giving up their gains (e.g. seized land, properties, etc.). As part of reestablishing mutual justice (resolving guilt and responsibility), restitution means the return of confiscated belongings or possessions. In addition, restitution takes the form of financial compensation, as in the award of $21,000 to Canadians of Japanese origin who were interned during World War II under the Japanese Canadian Redress Agreement.

At the end of a war, a victorious party often unilaterally imposes its own terms of restitution on the defeated. For several years after Germany's surrender, the Allies transported large numbers of huge dismantled manufacturing plants and machinery to France, Russia, and the UK. The United States government vigorously pursued scientific and technological know-how as well as all patents in Germany (Bottigliero, 2004). Germans were also forced to make compensation, in part, in the form of forced labor by approximately four million German prisoners of war and civilians under such titles as "reparations labor."

Punitive measures against the populace of the losing side (such as the imposition of war reparations) are, in general, regarded as unjust especially in such a situation that they had little or no power over, such as decisions to go to war. The impoverished populations (overburdened by destruction in a lost war) are not likely to make actual payment demanded by the victorious party. Heavy war reparation payments were forced upon Germany after the 1919 Treaty of Versailles, resulting in hyperinflation and economic exacerbation that contributed to the fall of the democratic Weimar Republic. After World War II, the victorious powers took reparations in the form of confiscating machines and transferring movable goods of the defeated nations to their own countries instead of money.

Tension between justice and forgiveness

In terms of sequence questions, most people feel uneasy about offering forgiveness prior to satisfying the demands of justice. Justice can contribute to healing wounded people in several ways. The public acknowledgment of crimes against victims puts pressure on the offenders to see the truth. Criminal justice can have a deterrent effect in preventing future human rights violations (e.g., Bosnia-Herzegovina). Exposing the guilt of individual perpetrators reduces the human tendency to assign collective guilt to a particular ethnic or national group. The process of reconciliation can be helped by understanding the psychodynamics of political conflicts.

The challenge to peace building often remains with respect to the appropriate balancing point between the establishment of harmonious relations and the pursuit of justice. In the realm of transitional justice, punishment of humanitarian crimes does not need to be sacrificed for the sake of the cessation of hostilities or political solutions. Justice can be promoted by democracy and reconciliation with sensible sequencing of activities to restore harmony in society. The success of retribution depends on functioning democracy which can bring dignity and respect for victims.

Restorative practice

Restorative practice is to manage conflict and tensions by repairing harm through education, counseling, social work, or organizational management. It is concerned with not only repairing the harm done by an offense but also proactively building new relationships. Thus its main focus is not only on responsibility for past acts but also on prospects for the co-creation of future steps. Primary stakeholders in restorative practice are victims, offenders, and their networks of care; their aims are connections among individuals and redeveloping communities. The assumption of restorative practices is to induce positive changes in human behavior by forming bonds on the basis of trust, mutual understanding, shared values and behaviors.

The mutual exchange of expressed affect is geared toward establishing community, creating the emotional bonds that connect people (Weine, 2006). Trust and shared values bind people together, making cooperative action possible. People are allowed to openly air their emotion in the development of connections among individuals. Restorative conferences and circles provide a safe space for the expression and exchange of emotion such as anger, rage, fear, terror, distress, and anguish.

Restorative practice consists of victim–offender mediation, circles and conferences. Victim–offender mediation offers an opportunity for victims to speak about their feelings and pain incurred by the offender's actions. An offender listens and eventually responds to a victim's statements, feelings, and needs. Then the victim may be ready to listen to the offender's perspectives and reflect their feelings and talk back to the offender. The session is also composed of a request from the victim to the offender, and feedback from the offender back to the victim as part of a reconciliation process. Restorative sessions for victims of the violence were introduced to individual healings in Israel, Palestine, Rwanda, Colombia, and Sierra Leone.

Whereas a victim–offender mediation attempts to bring healing to an inter-personal level, responsibility and reparation can be established through engaging stakeholders in a collaborative process at an inter-group level. In particular, the family plays an important role in a juvenile offender's life by offering a sense of community, identity, and stability. The engagement of families is essential in making plans for their members' well-being.

The widened circles of support and accountability are extended to communities of care beyond a family network of victims and offenders. A community restorative board, composed of a small group of citizens, can conduct public, face-to-face meetings with offenders and victims in discussion about the nature and consequences of offensive behavior. These sessions can forge a voluntary agreement on reparation for the crime.

Restorative circle

Participation in collaborative processes called "conferences" and "circles" involves primary victims, offenders, and people connected to them (Umbreit and Coates, 2006). Restorative circles make collective decisions on how to repair harm by involving not only victims but also offenders. Their respective family members and friends are also invited to share their feelings and experiences in meeting their own emotional and psychological needs. Restorative circles encourage participants to own the process in understanding human needs and other motivations by empowering the participants and minimizing the role of a facilitator.

After a multi-step procedure, the offender's participation in a healing circle results in a restitution agreement and follow-up in conjunction with monitoring the progress of the offender. Restorative conferences, groups, and circles are formed to facilitate communication of people's feelings while reflecting on behavioral implications. Emotional bonds are created by the expression of affect by such means as affective questions and statements. Free expression helps a release of feelings about shame–humiliation. The circle reflects the legacy of traditional aboriginal and Native American social processes of speaking from the heart. In a restorative circle, participants speak around the circle as many times as necessary, before all the participants said everything they wanted. The ritual of a traditional circle creates an atmosphere which enhances collective understanding and development of the steps for healing and prevention of future incidents.

Conferencing

In contrast with a counseling or a mediation process, conferencing adopts forthright problem-solving strategies as well as promotion of healing. Restorative conferencing with a wider circle of participants is designed to explore ways to tackle wrongdoing in various settings. The reintegration of offenders into their community or workplace becomes possible after their taking accountability. The conferences of community accountability focus on a response to crimes.

The conference facilitator keeps statements focused on the offender's deeds, thoughts, and feelings as well as the perspectives and experiences of victims and their family members. Offenders, victims and their families and friends discuss consequences of the crime and decide an appropriate method to repair the damage. At the same time, victims and their family members express their suffering and feelings, and have an opportunity to ask questions. The first-hand encounter with victims helps the offenders grasp the harm caused by their behavior. Personal or community service work as well as financial restitution can be accompanied by apologies.

Empowerment and humanization

A well-managed reconciliation process invigorates changes for the betterment and empowerment of community or organizational members. It provides an opportunity to hear the voice of the oppressed side with the involvement of wider social sectors beyond elite negotiation. What is important to the victims is clearly expressing their perspectives and feelings so that the perpetrators know what is important for those who suffered from unjust treatment.

The struggle of the oppressed against an oppressor can be characterized by a protest against dehumanization and a demand for human dignity. In healing to overcome traumas and hurts, especially the weaker party needs to gain a greater sense of self-reliance, confidence, and respect. Thus empowerment is defined in terms of controlling one's own destiny; power imbalance can be redressed by the creation of space for dialogue and arts which lead to self-expression of the marginalized. Empowerment of the vulnerable for a better chance of obtaining equitable conflict outcomes is developed by a sense of fairness and justice.

Path to healing

Healing starts from the confessions of guilt and acceptance of responsibility for past wrongs by perpetrators so that the victims of trauma can regain a sense of normal life. The sense of self can be recovered only in a climate of expectation for creating a safer world. Communion (designed for positive inter-communal relations) would not be formed without the expression of feelings of guilt on the part of offenders as well as the acceptance of apologies by victims. A long-term process of healing would be supported by a psychologically informed conflict resolution strategy. Healing is designed to reaffirm the value of the self-concept and restore the loss of self-esteem of the victimized. A group process might be designed to nurture new relationships that have to be based on a commitment to justice, equity, and mutual respect.

In overcoming pain, the first step of healing is listening to intuition "without interruption or discussion, to bear witness to the story" (Hogan, 2007, p. 264). The recovery from the assault to one's dignity demands substituting subjugation by a respectful relationship of human dignity. Unfreezing identities requires holding space for co-construction of events. Group healing is often supported by solidarity among victims (as exemplified by the Child Bereaved Families Forum, Neva Shalom/Wahat al-Salam and Oasis of Peace for Jews and Palestinians). In their campaign to break the cycles of violence and revenge, these organizations are dedicated to honoring the memories of the victims and utilizing their collective experience and skills to promotion of nonviolence and conflict resolution. In particular, the Child Bereaved Families Forum has developed a global network of people across diverse communities affected by various types of violence, ranging from war to political torture to genocide.

Group dynamics provided by a psychologically sensitive problem-solving workshop can generate insights about how to genuinely resolve conflict and stop violence. The agenda for healing in a conflict resolution workshop can only be revealed by honest expression of basic emotional preoccupations. A psycho-dynamic workshop allows victimized groups to present grievances, fears, and political demands. Examining the history of a conflict relationship leads to understanding symbolic meanings for a profound sense of victimhood nourishing feelings of unacknowledged injustice.

The scope, scale, and extent to which actors participate in a healing process may differ. In dealing with the behavior of groups, healing involves a large number of people who have been wounded psychologically or physically in all their complex social settings. Psychological defenses against unexpected emotional loss and mental pain stem from adhering to such social institutions as family and community support networks.

Mourning losses

Grieving loss is essential to victims who want to move beyond past losses and look to the future. Mourning losses is also a vital step toward riding over the suffering of one's own group. The failure of mourning leaves the victim's self-esteem bound up with images of what has been lost in the past, looking for future circumstances of revenge. Intensive anger and rage often interfere with the ability to complete the cycle of mourning. Losses, not having been mourned, are likely to be transmitted to future generations as trauma (Volkan, 1998). Each loss has its own unique response, circumscribed by the surrounding cultures, the scope and outcome of the violence, the proximity in time to the traumatic events, and the degree of persisting inequities.

Remembrance

The general feeling of justice can be obtained in a historical and restorative sense by museums, monuments, and other installations. Any scheme of reparations or punishment would never bring back loved family members and friends (whose bodies were dismembered) or the abducted children. However, respect for victims' dignity can be protected by acknowledging injuries and atrocities hidden under a carpet of silence. Argentina's Memoria Abierta commemorates those who were tortured and killed under the military dictatorship during the 1970s and 1980s.

The preservation of the memory of the past is designed to insure the history of atrocities will not repeat itself. 'International Legacy Project' initiatives covered the Armenian Genocide, mass killings in Cambodia, and the Vietnamese–American War. Through a Phnom Penh cultural organization known as "Reyum" Cambodian artists were encouraged to reflect on the inheritance of genocide victims during the Khmer Rouge period. Eight human rights organizations worldwide have developed a project on the contemplation of the period of state terrorism under military dictatorships.

The International Coalition of Historic Sites of Conscience is a consortium of museums dedicated to honoring the victims of extreme human rights abuses. The incorporation of diverse artistic genres (photographs, sculpture, children's art) helped keep memory alive by documenting history. A sense of dignity has been restored by inviting viewers to reflect on the contemporary implications of the history displayed in the exhibits. One of the Coalition's member institutions, The District Six Museum in Cape Town, South Africa, has demonstrated a vivid role in redressing the grievances of victims sacrificed by apartheid forced removal.

In reflecting on the activities of the International Coalition of Historic Sites, the Museums of Conscience 2003 Conference Report underscored the importance of preserving local history and culture in enhancing the capacity for reparations. The member museums of the International Coalition of Historic Sites of Conscience utilized monuments and memorials that rekindle historical memories, thus contributing moral awakening of their own societies. Linking together dialogue projects across war-torn regions can engage people by connecting the past to contemporary questions of justice and human rights.

Empathy with the suffering of the other

Empathy with the suffering of one's enemy is a scarce commodity during violent conflicts and in their aftermath. Perpetrators and those who bear their legacies may tightly cling to defensive postures in order to avoid feelings of guilt and shame, usually interfering with compassionate response and flexible thinking. Recurring victimization deprives a capability of empathizing with the suffering of another group. The little capacity and inclinations of offenders to grieve for the hurts of other peoples result in a refusal to take responsibility for their victims created by their warlike actions. Empathy comes from the ability of former adversaries to attach importance to each other's suffering; former enemies' capacities to develop heartfelt empathy with each other can truly convert the violent relationships.

The strength in grassroots peace building comes from sharing the same fate as well as interdependence. Personal encounters and elimination of barriers to communication between groups include "bringing children of victims and perpetrators for sharing and exploring ways of integrating the violent past"; the challenge is how to "move beyond one-off encounters, build up longer-term personal relations, and create shared structures" (Ropers, 2004, p. 178).

Healing through storytelling and listening

Grievances need to be fully aired and communicated with the appropriate expression of strong feelings and emotions. In healing, avoiding harmful statements or acts especially by the perpetrator side is helpful for a more amicable solution. Speaking our mind, listening seriously and remaining reasonable to possible accommodations are basic conditions for empathy. Understanding the feelings of the victims permits the situation to be seen from their perspectives.

The situations of communication are often altered by exploitation based on class, race, ethnicity, gender, sexual orientation, religious, or linguistic differences. The suppressed groups are forced to adopt the language and perceptive world views of an oppressive group. Survival in the context of long-standing oppression demands the subordinate group's control of one's own mental world by defining their own experiences (Freire, 1970).

The sharing of stories requires the capacity to listen as well as to speak, but these capacities are severely limited in the aftermath of violence and fear. Various situations of oppression inflict rigid boundaries on verbal expression. Traumatized victims may desire silence to protect themselves from the fear of being engaged in listening and speaking. In oppression, victims may use silence as a sanctuary and as psychological space of bonding. Silence may serve as exile, preserving a victim's identity (Cohen, 2005). The experience of oppression and violence can removes people's ability for expression and listening with the maintenance of a deeper wound.

Shared stories can assist former enemies in coming to terms with each other's experiences. In collective narratives, life-shattering traumas related to sexual assault, loss of loved ones, and other community-uprooting events (cast outside of the normal realm of life) need to be comprehended and recounted. Social, emotional, and intellectual space for more nuanced understandings of a victim's identity can be linked to putting our stories in a new context. In the process of grasping moral sensibilities each community attaches to historical events, former enemies may revisit stories and their meanings.

Through attentive listening, participants in dialogue can demonstrate their respect for each other. Emotional sensitivity is crucial in listening. By showing various types of attitude, ranging from trust to skepticism, listeners can show reluctance or enthusiasm. Hostility or reverence indicates the listener's attitudes toward the speaker. The quality of communication is also revealed by superficiality or genuine curiosity. Listening merely for information is different from more keenly seeking to understand feelings surrounding words.

The inner healing of the wounded is supported by receptiveness and non-intrusive support. Surrounding emotional circumstances (for instance, related to fear and anxiety) as well as a social atmosphere affect capacities to listen and speak. After periods of violence, fear and guilt of survival (after the death of beloved family members or friends) is likely to shut down receptive capacities.

Listening to perpetrators in the aftermath of violence carries a high level of emotive sensitivity. Listening in the context of oppression is not inductive to enthusiastic feelings. Receptivity to what has not been spoken is as important as attention paid to what is expressed overtly. Restoring the capacity to attend to each other is essential to a genuine, compassionate dialogue.

The endeavor to end the cycle of oppression begins with opening the myth of the past to new information and new themes. The original myths are resistant to change in developing a narrative which can serve as a basis to form new identity. Personal identities of narrators and listeners flourish with changes in movements between narrative roles. The process to embrace complexity of our experience depends on how to tell stories, listen, and revise narratives. In projects on targeting the Australian Aboriginal and other indigenous groups, storytelling has focused on the historical context for a journey of well-being as well as role reversal.

In many cultural awareness workshops, telling a stranger an intimate story is not only a risk but also a gift. This can be a very emotional experience for the storyteller as well as the participants. Some storytellers use the story as a form of healing for both themselves and others. The story can re-traumatize the teller and/or listeners. The ideal outcome of facilitated dialogue is a positive experience for the storyteller and acknowledgment without shame. In every story, there are "hooks" to connect many previous experiences, "so one story which is well debriefed is often enough to get your points across" (Hogan, 2007, p. 256). Owing to different emotional space possessed by the speaker and participants, role reversal is essential to developing empathy with shifts in the attitudes.

Empowerment through cultural work

The uneven quality of communicative ability is manifested across communities. The arts and cultural work can be crafted to remind people of the humanity of their adversaries. Diverse artistic forms or media can be crafted in diminishing the defenses that adversaries have against listening to each other's stories. Poems, films, exhibitions, and novels can mediate stories as part of efforts to supplement or restore impaired communication capacities (Zeigler, 2003). Stories from enemy communities can be presented in a play, mural, or quilt to inspire rethinking about their own stories in more nuanced ways. Receptivity to an adversary's experience can be increased by oral history projects based on interviews.

Communication capacities are nourished by the incorporation of the ritual, aesthetic, and social dimensions of art. In theater performance, the narrative expands from gaining another kind of understanding with a deepened use of language, sound, and movement. A story is re-enacted by switching roles back and forth between tellers and listeners. The members of the audience can sometimes, themselves, become actors by sitting in the teller's chair to comprehend the real aspects of the story as not being experienced before. Tellers feel heard and respected on the spot by the audience through enactment of their stories. A keen sense of ritual supports the ability to tell and receive stories, even for those who could otherwise have been locked up silently in shame, confusion, or fear.

The role of arts

Community rituals and art influence a non-conscious domain of the human mind, contributing to the transformation of a desire for revenge into a desire for affiliation. Emotional wisdom can be tapped by ritual and art. The occasions of reflexivity and innovation stem from the special qualities of attention and response created by artistic work. Indeed, the beauty and power of art works induce cognitive alertness and blissful serenity. Non-linguistic forms of communication are more readily received than dialogue alone. Rituals help the traumatized victims act out their terrors, reclaiming their voices. This process of empowerment needs to be engaged in political dialogue about their future.

The availability of public space for the creative communication of private experience supports a cooperative community. Unheard voices can be invited to share a story and feeling of hope. Folk expression (accessible across cultures) embodies the spirit of victimized groups. Shared humanity can be discovered through folklore projects centered around intergenerational and cross-cultural sharing of children's games.

In African contexts, drum performance (favored in African folklore) facilitates the discovery of common roots among former enemies. Dancing and drumming are the modalities that support the expression of complex African philosophy and experience. The rhythm of the universe and the dance convey the connecting thread binding all being in completing the universe whole.

Further reading

Baum, S. K. (2008) *The Psychology of Genocide: Perpetrators, Bystanders and Rescuers*, New York: Cambridge University Press.

Chaitin, J. (2008) "Bridging the Impossible? Confronting Barriers to Dialogue between Israelis and Germans and between Israelis and Palestinians," *International Journal of Peace Studies*, 13 (2): 33–58.

Cohen, C. (2005) "Creative Approaches to Reconciliation," in M. Fitzduff and C. Stout (eds) *The Psychology of Resolving Global Conflicts: From War to Peace*, Portsmouth, NH: Greenwood Publishing Group.

Gyatso, T. (2001) *The Compassionate Life*, Boston: Wisdom Publications.

Hawes, D. (2007) "Crucial Narratives: Performance Art and Peace Building," *International Journal of Peace Studies*, 12 (2): 17–29.

Huyse, L. and Salter, M. (2008) *Traditional Justice and Reconciliation after Violent Conflict*, Stockholm, Sweden: International IDEA.

Kriesberg, L. (2007) "Reconciliation: Aspects, Growth, and Sequences," *International Journal of Peace Studies*, 12 (1): 1–21.

Lederach, J. (1997) *Building Peace – Sustainable Reconciliation in Divided Societies*, Tokyo: United Nations University Press.

Lerche, C. (2000) "Peace Building through Reconciliation," *International Journal of Peace Studies*, 5 (2): 61–76.

Long, W. J. and Brecke, P. (2003) *War and Reconciliation: Reason and Emotion in Conflict Resolution*, Cambridge, MA: MIT Press.

Umbreit, M. S. and Coates, R. (2006) "Restorative Justice Mediated Dialog," in M. S. Herman, *The Blackwell Handbook of Mediation*. Malden, MA: Blackwell Publishing.

Zeigler, C. (2003) "The Role of Artistic Processes in Peacebuilding in Bosnia-Herzegovina," *Peace and Conflict Studies*, 10 (2): 62–76.

Bibliography

Abrams, D. and Hogg, M. A. (2001) "Collective Identity: Group Membership and Self-Conceptions," in M. Hogg and R. Tindale (eds) *Blackwell Handbook of Social Psychology: Group Processes*, Malden, MA and Oxford: Blackwell, pp. 425–460.

Abrams, D., Hogg, M., and Marquez, J. (2005) "A Social Psychological Framework for Understanding Social Inclusion and Exclusion," in D. Abrams, M. Hogg, and J. Marquez (eds) *Social Psychology of Inclusion and Exclusion*, NY: Psychology Press.

Allport, G. W. and Pettigrew, T. F. (1998) "Intergroup Contact Theory," *Annual Review of Psychology*, 49: 65–85.

Amy, D. (1987) *The Politics of Environmental Mediation*, New York: Columbia University Press.

Anderson, M. (2004) *Cultural Shaping of Violence: Victimization, Escalation, Response*, West Lafayette, IN: Purdue University Press.

Augoustinos, M. and Reynolds, K. (2001) *Understanding Prejudice, Racism, and Social Conflict*, London: Thousand Oaks, CA: Sage.

Augsburger, D. W. (1992) *Conflict Mediation Across Cultures: Pathways and Patterns*, Louisville, KY: Westminster/John Knox.

Autesserre, S. (2007) "D. R. Congo: Explaining Peace Building Failures, 2003–2006," *Review of African Political Economy*, 34: 423.

Avruch, A. (2004) "Culture as Context, Culture as Communication," *Harvard Negotiation Law Review*, 9: 391–407.

Avruch, K. (2002) "Cross-Cultural Conflict," in K. Hipel (ed.), *The Encyclopedia of Life Support Systems*: *Conflict Resolution*, Oxford, UK: UNESCO, Eolss Publishers. Available at: www.eolss.net.

Bartoli, A. (2005) "Learning from the Mozambique Peace Process," in R. Fisher (ed.) *Paving the Way*, Lanham, MD: Lexington Books.

Baum, S. K. (2008) *The Psychology of Genocide: Perpetrators, Bystanders and Rescuers*, New York: Cambridge University Press.

Bazerman, M. (2005) *Negotiation, Decision Making and Conflict Management*, MA: Edward Elgar.

Beal, J. and Khechog, N. (2003) *Tibet, Cry of the Snow Lion*, New York: Karuna.

Bercovitch, J. and Houston, A. (2000) "Why Do they Do it like this? An Analysis of the Factors Influencing Mediation Behavior in International Conflicts," *The Journal of Conflict Resolution*, 44: 170–202.

Bingham, L. and Nabatchi, T. (2003) "Dispute System Design in Organization," in W. Pammer and J. Killian (eds) *Handbook of Conflict Management*, New York: Marcel Dekker, Inc.

Black, P. and Avruch, K. (1999) "Cultural Relativism, Conflict Resolution, Social Justice," *Peace and Conflict Studies*, 6 (2): 24–41.

Blalock, H. M. (1989) *Power and Conflict: Toward a General Theory*, Newbury Park, CA: Sage Publications.

Blau, P. (1964) *Exchange and Power in Social Life,* Edison, NJ: Transaction Publishers.

Botes, J. (2003) "Conflict Transformation," *International Journal of Peace Studies*, 8 (2): 1–28.

Bottigliero, I. (2004) *Redress for Victims of Crimes under International Law*, Leiden: Martinus Nijhoff Publishers.

Bourdieu, P. (1991) *Language and Symbolic Power*, Cambridge, MA: Harvard University Press.

Boutros-Ghali, B. (1995) *Agenda for Peace*, New York: United Nations.

Broome, B. J. (2004) "Reaching across the Dividing Line: Building a Collective Vision for Peace in Cyprus," *Journal of Peace Research*, 41: 191–209.

Burton, J. W. (1997) *Violence Explained: The Sources of Conflict, Violence and Crime and Their Prevention*, Manchester: Manchester University Press.

Burton, J. W. (2001) "Conflict Prevention as a Political System," *International Journal of Peace Studies*, 6 (1): 23–32.

Byrne, S. (2001) "Consociational and Civic Society Approaches to Peacebuilding in Northern Ireland," *Journal of Peace Research*, 38 (3): 327–352.

Byrne, S. and Irvin, C. (2002) "A Shared Common Sense: Perceptions of the Material Effects and Impacts of Economic Growth in Northern Ireland," *Civil Wars*, 5 (1): 55–86.

Carayannis, T. (2005) "The Complex Wars of the Congo: Towards a New Analytic Approach," in R. M. Kadende-Kaiser and P. J. Kaiser (eds) *Phases of Conflict in Africa*, Toronto: de Sitter Publications.

Cashman, C. (2000) *What Causes War?: Introduction to Theories of International Conflict*, Lanham, MD, and Cumnor Hill: Lexington Books.

Chacham, R. (2003) *Breaking Ranks: Refusing to Serve in the West Bank and Gaza Strip*, New York: Other Press.

Chaitin, J. (2008) "Bridging the Impossible? Confronting Barriers to Dialogue between Israelis and Germans and between Israelis and Palestinians," *International Journal of Peace Studies*, 13 (2): 33–58.

Chataway, C. J. (2002) "The Problem of Transfer from Confidential Interactive Problem-solving: What is the Role of the Facilitator?" *Political Psychology*, 23: 165–189.

Chernick, M. (2003) "Colombia: International Involvement in Protracted Peacemaking," in S. C. Lekha and K. Wermester (eds) *From Promise to Practice: Strengthening UN Capacities for the Prevention of Violent Conflict*, Boulder, CO: Lynne Rienner.

Cohen, C. (2005) "Creative Approaches to Reconciliation," in M. Fitzduff and C. Stout (eds) *The Psychology of Resolving Global Conflicts: From War to Peace*, Portsmouth, NH: Greenwood Publishing Group.

Coleman, P. (2000) "Intractable Conflict," in M. Deutsch and P. Coleman (eds) *The Handbook of Conflict Resolution*, San Francisco: Jossey-Bass, pp. 428–450.

Conteh-Morgan, E. (2004) *Collective Political Violence*. New York: Routledge.

Cordesman, A. H. (2005) *The Israeli–Palestinian War: Escalating to Nowhere*, Westport, CT: Praeger.

Coser, L. A. (1956) *The Functions of Social Conflict*, Glencoe, IL: The Free Press.

Curtin, P. A. and Gaither, K. (2007) *International Public Relations: Negotiating Culture, Identity, and Power*, Thousand Oaks, CA: Sage.

Dahrendorf, R. (1959) *Class and Class Conflict in Industrial Society*, Stanford, CA: Stanford University Press.

Daly, E. and Sarkin, J. (2007) *Reconciliation in Divided Societies: Finding Common Ground*, Philadelphia, PA: University of Pennsylvania Press.

Das, S. K. (2005) *Peace Processes and Peace Accords*, Sage Publications.

Davidio, J. F. (2005) "Social Inclusion and Exclusion: Recategorization and the Perception of Intergroup Boundaries," in D. Abrams, M. Hogg, and J. Marques *The Social Psychology of Inclusion and Exclusion*, New York: Psychology Press.

Dedring, J. (1999) "On Peace in Times of War: Resolving Violent Conflicts by Peaceful Means," *International Journal of Peace Studies*, 4 (2): 1–21.

Deutsch, M. (2006) "Justice and Conflict," in M. Deutsch, *The Handbook of Conflict Resolution*, San Francisco: Jossey-Bass.

Domenici, K. and Littlejohn, S. W. (2001) *Mediation: Empowerment in Conflict Management*, Prospect Heights, IL: Waveland Press.

Donohue, W. A. (2001) "Defining Relationships in the Negotiation Context: Features of the Negotiation Context," in W. Eadie and P. Nelson (eds) *The Language of Conflict and Resolution*, Thousand Oaks, CA: Sage Publications.

Dowty, A. (2008) *Israel/Palestine*, Oxford: Polity.

Druckman, D. (2001) "Turning Points in International Negotiation," in *Journal of Conflict Resolution*, 45 (4): 519–544.

Ellis, D. G. (2006) *Transforming Conflict: Communication and Ethnopolitical Conflict*, Lanham, MD: Rowman & Littlefield.

Ergil, D. (2004) "Reframing the Problem," in M. Fitzduff and C. Church (eds) *NGOs at the Table: Strategies for Influencing Policies in Areas of Conflict*, New York: Rowman and Littlefield.

Erikson, E. H. (1994) *Identity: Youth and Crisis*, New York: W. W. Norton & Company.

Esman, M. J. (2004) "Ethnic Pluralism: Strategies for Conflict Management," in A. Wimmer, R. J. Goldstone, D. L. Horowitz, U. Joras, and C. Schetter (eds) *Facing Ethnic Conflict Toward a New Realism*, Lanham, MD: Rowman and Littlefield.

Faure, G. O. (2003) *How People Negotiate: Resolving Disputes in Different Cultures*, Dordrecht, Boston: Kluwer Academic Publishers.

Fisher, R. (2007) "Assessing the Contingency Model of Third Party Intervention: Successful Cases of Prenegotiation," *Journal of Peace Research*, 44 (3): 311–329.

Fisher, R. and Ury, W. (1983) *Getting to Yes: Negotiating Agreement Without Giving In*, New York: Penguin Books.

Foley, D. (2003) "The Methods of Dialogue: Promoting Understanding between Hawaiians and Non-Hawaiians," in W. Pammer and K. Jerri (eds) *Handbook of Conflict Management*, New York: Marcel Dekker, Inc. 243–256.

Forbes, H. D. (1997) *Ethnic Conflict: Commerce, Culture, and the Contact Hypothesis*, New Haven, CT: Yale University Press.

Forester, J. (2000) *The Deliberative Practitioner*, Cambridge, MA: MIT Press.

Foucault, M. (1977) *Politics, Philosophy, Culture, Interviews and Other Writings, 1977–1984*, London: Routledge.

Franke, Volker (2006) "The Peacebuilding Dilemma: Civil–Military Cooperation in Stability Operations," *International Journal of Peace Studies*, 11 (2): 5–24.

Frazer, T. G. (2008) *The Arab–Israeli Conflict*, Basingstoke: Palgrave Macmillan.

Freire, P. (1970) *Pedagogy of the Oppressed*, New York: Continuum Publishing Co.

Gaertner, S. L. and Davidio, J. F. (2000) *Reducing Intergroup Bias: The Common Ingroup Identity Model*, Philadelphia, PA: The Psychology Press.

Galtung, J. (2007) "Conflict Formation and Transformations: Deep Culture and Structure," in C. P. Webel and J. Galtung (eds) *Handbook of Peace and Conflict Studies*, New York: Routledge.

Gamson, W. A. (1992) "The Social Psychology of Collective Action," in A D. Morris and A. D. Mueller (eds) *Frontiers in Social Movement Theory*, New Haven, CT: Yale University Press.

Giddens, A. (1986) *The Constitution of Society*, Berkeley, CA: University of California Press.

Giannakos, S. A. (2002) "Introduction," in S. A. Giannakos, *Ethnic Conflict: Religion, Identity and Politics*, Athens, OH: Ohio University Press.

Goffman, E. (1963) *Stigma: Notes on the Management of Spoiled Identity*, New York: Penguin.

Goodwin, D. (2002) *Negotiation in International Conflict: Understanding Persuasion*, London: Frank Cass.

Gudykunst, W. B. and Mody, B. (1989) "Language and Intergroup Communication," in M. Asante, W. Gudykunst, and E. Newmark (eds) *Handbook of International and Intercultural Communication*, Newbury Park, CA: Sage Publications.

Gyatso, T. (2001) *The Compassionate Life*, Boston, MA: Wisdom Publications.

Habermas, J. (1987) *The Theory of Communicative Action*, Boston, MA: Beacon Press.

Haugaard, M. (1997) *The Constitution of Power*, Manchester: Manchester University Press.

Hawes, D. (2007) "Crucial Narratives: Performance Art and Peace Building," *International Journal of Peace Studies*, 12 (2): 17–29.

Heitler, S. M. (1990) "From Conflict to Resolution," in M. Isenhart and M. Spangle, *Collaborative Approaches to Resolving Conflict*, Thousand Oaks, CA: Sage Publications.

Helsing, J. W. (2004) "The Regionalization, Internationalization, and Perpetuation of Conflict in the Middle East," in S. E. Lobell and P. Mauceri (eds) *Ethnic Conflict & International Politics: Explaining Diffusion and Escalation*, New York: Palgrave.

Hogan, C. (2007) *Facilitating Multicultural Groups: A Practical Guide*, Philadelphia, PA: Kogan Page.

Hogg, M. A. (2001) "Social Categorization, Depersonalization, and Group Behavior," in A. M. Hogg and R. S. Tindale (eds) *Blackwell Handbook of Social Psychology: Group Processes*, Malden, MA: Blackwell Publishers.

Huyse, L. and Salter, M. (2008) *Traditional Justice and Reconciliation after Violent Conflict*, Stockholm, Sweden: International IDEA.

Isaacs, W. (1999) *Dialogue and the Art of Thinking Together*, New York: Currency.

Isenhart, M. W. and Spangle, M. (2000) *Collaborative Approaches to Resolving Conflict*, Thousand Oaks, CA: Sage Publications.

Jeong, H. W. (1999) "Research on Conflict Resolution," in H. Jeong (ed.) *Conflict Resolution: Dynamics, Process and Structure*, Aldershot: Ashgate.

Jeong, H. W. (2005) *Peacebuilding in Postconflict Societies*, Boulder, CO: Lynne Rienner.

Jeong, H. W. (2008) *Understanding Conflict and Conflict Analysis*, Thousand Oaks, CA: Sage Publications.

Kalpakian, J. (2004) *Identity, Conflict and Cooperation in International River Systems*, Aldershot: Ashgate.

Kaplan, M. (1957) *System and Process in International Politics*, New York: Wiley.

Kellet, P. M. and Dalton, D. G. (2001) *Managing Conflict in a Negotiated World: a Narrative Approach to Achieving Dialogue and Change*, Thousand Oaks, CA: Sage Publications.

Kelman, H. C. (2002) Interactive Problem-Solving: Informal Mediation by the Scholar-Practitioner," in J. Bercovitch and J. Rubin (eds) *Studies in International Mediation*, New York: Palgrave Macmillan.

Kelman, H. C. (2004) "The Nature of International Conflict," in H. J. Langholtz and C. E. Stout (eds) *The Psychology of Diplomacy*, Praeger, pp. 59-78.

Kelman, H. C. (2008) "Evaluating the Contributions of Interactive Problem Solving to the Resolution of Ethnonational Conflicts," *Journal of Peace Psychology*, 14: 29–60.

Khadiagala, G. (2007) *Meddlers Or Mediators?: African Interveners in Civil Conflicts in Eastern Africa*, Leiden and Boston: Martinus Nijhoff.

Kheel, T. W. (2001) *Keys to Conflict Resolution: Proven Methods of Settling Disputes Voluntarily*, New York: Four Walls Eight Windows.

Kimmel, P. R. (2000) "Culture and Conflict," in M. Deutsch and P. Coleman (eds) *The Handbook of Conflict Resolution*, San Francisco: Jossey-Bass Publications.

Kleiboer, M. (1998) *The Multiple Realities of International Mediation*, Boulder, CO: Lynne Rienner Publishers.

Kolb, D. M. and Williams, J. (2003) *Everyday Negotiation: Navigating the Hidden Agendas in Bargaining*, San Francisco, CA: Jossey-Bass.

Kriesberg, L. (1998) *Constructive Conflicts*, Lanham, MD: Rowman & Littlefield Publishers.

Kriesberg, L. (2007) "Reconciliation: Aspects, Growth, and Sequences," *International Journal of Peace Studies*, 12 (1): 1–21.

Lebow, R. N. (1996) *The Art of Bargaining*, Baltimore: Johns Hopkins University Press.

Lederach, J. (1997) *Building Peace – Sustainable Reconciliation in Divided Societies*, Tokyo: United Nations University Press.

Lederach, J. (2003) *The Little Book of Conflict Transformation*, Intercourse, PA: Good Books.

Lee, H. (2001) "Cultural Confrontation and Compromise: The Response of Non-Western Societies to Western Political Ideas," *International Journal of Peace Studies*, 6 (2): 53–74.

Legro, J. W. (2005) *Rethinking the World: Great Power Strategies and International Order*, Ithaca, NY: Cornell University Press.

Lerche, C. (2000) "Peace Building through Reconciliation," *International Journal of Peace Studies*, 5 (2): 61–76.

Lerner, M. (2004) *The Geneva Accord: and Other Strategies for Healing the Israeli–Palestinian Conflict*, Berkeley, CA: North Atlantic Books.

Lesch, D. (2008) *The Arab–Israeli Conflict*, Oxford: Oxford University Press.

Lewicki, R. J. *et al.* (2001) *Essentials of Negotiation*, Boston, MA: Irwin/McGraw-Hill.

Lewin, K. (1997) *Resolving Social Conflict, and Field Theory in Social Science*, Washington, DC: American Psychological Association.

Lieberfeld, D. (2007) "Overcoming Intractability in South Africa and Israel/Palestine: The Role of Semi-official Meetings," *American Behavioral Scientist*, 50: 1542–1562.

Littlejohn, S. W. and Domenici, K. (2001) *Engaging Communication in Conflict: Systemic Practice*, Thousand Oaks, CA: Sage Publications.

Long, W. J. and Brecke, P. (2003) *War and Reconciliation: Reason and Emotion in Conflict Resolution*, Cambridge, MA: MIT Press.

Lynch, E. F. (2005) *Negotiation and Settlement*, St Paul, MN: Thomson/West.

McCorkle, S. and Reese, M. (2005) *Mediation Theory and Practice*, Boston: Pearson/Allyn and Bacon.

Marcus, E. C. (2000) "Change Processes and Conflict," in D. Morton and C. Peter (eds) *The Handbook of Conflict Resolution*, San Francisco: Jossey-Bass Publications.

Marshal, G. and Ozawa, G. (2003) "Mediated Negotiation and Democratic Theory," in W. J. Pammer and J. Killian (eds) *Handbook of Conflict Management*, New York: Marcel Dekker, Inc.

Mason, D. T. and Meernik, J. (2006) *Conflict Prevention and Peacebuilding in Post-war Societies: Sustaining the Peace*, London, New York: Routledge.

Mauceri, P. (2004) "Internationalization as an Explanation? The Development of Ethnic Conflict in Latin America," in S. Lobell and P. Mauceri, *Ethnic Conflict & International Politics*, New York: Palgrave, pp. 95-132

Maundi, M. O. (2003) "Preventing Conflict Escalation in Burundi," in S. C. Lekha and K. Wermester (eds) *From Promise to Practice: Strengthening UN Capacities for the Prevention of Violent Conflict*, Boulder: Lynne Rienner.

Menkel-Meadow, C. (2003) *Dispute Processing and Conflict Resolution: Theory, Practice, and Policy*, Burlington, VT: Ashgate/Dartmouth.

Merrills, J. G. (2005) *International Dispute Settlement*, 4th edition, New York: Cambridge University Press.

Miall, H. (2004) "Transforming Ethnic Conflict: Theories and Practices," in A. Wimmer, R. J. Goldstone, D. L. Horowitz, U. Joras, and C. Schetter (eds) *Facing Ethnic Conflict Toward a New Realism*, Lanham, MD: Rowman and Littlefield Publishers Inc.

Miall, H., *et al.* (1999) *Contemporary Conflict Resolution: The Prevention, Management and Transformation of Deadly Conflicts*, Malden, MA: Blackwell Publishers.

Midgley, J. R. (2002) "Guests Overstaying Their Welcome: The Demise of the Peace Accord Structures in South Africa," *The International Journal of Peace Studies*, 7 (1): 77–90.

Mitchell, C. (2001) "From Controlled Communication to Problem Solving: The Origins of Facilitated Conflict Resolution," *The International Journal of Peace Studies*, 6 (1): 59–68.

Mitchell, C. (2002) "Beyond Resolution: What does Conflict Transformation actually Transform?" *Peace and Conflict Studies*, 9 (1): 1–24.

Moshin, A. (2005) "Gendered Nation, Gendered Peace: A Study of Bangladesh," in S. K. Das, *Peace Processes and Peace Accords*, New Delhi: Sage Publications.

Nan, S. (2004) "Track One and a Half Diplomacy: Searching for Political Agreement in the Caucasus," in M. Fitzduff and C. Church (eds) *NGOs at the Table: Strategies for Influencing Policies in Areas of Conflict*, New York: Rowman and Littlefield.

Northrup, T. A. (1989) "The Dynamic of Identity in Personal and Social Conflict," in L. Kriesberg (ed.) *Intractable Conflicts and Their Transformation*, New York: Syracuse University Press.

Operario, D. and Fiske, S. T. (1999) "Integrating Social Identity and Social Cognition: A Framework for Bridging Diverse Perspectives,", in A. Dominic and M. A. Hogg (eds) *Social Identity and Social Cognition*, Malden, MA: Blackwell Publishers.

Opotow, S. (2000) "Aggression and Violence," in M. Deutsch and P. Coleman (eds) *The Handbook of Conflict Resolution*, San Francisco: Jossey-Bass Publications.

Osgood, C. E. (1962) *An Alternative to War or Surrender*, Urbana, IL: University of Illinois Press.

Perich-Anderson, J. (2003) "The Only Game in Town: Managing Multistakeholder Conflicts," in W. J. Pammer and J. Killian (eds) *Handbook of Conflict Management*, New York: Marcel Dekker, Inc.

Picard, C. *et al.* (2004) *The Art and Science of Mediation*, Toronto: Edmond Montgomery Ltd.

Poneman, D. B. *et al.* (2004) *Going Critical: The First North Korean Nuclear Crisis*, Washington, DC: Brookings Institution Press.

Premdas, R. R. (2003) "Fiji: Peacemaking in a Multiethnic State," in C. L. Sriram and K. Wermester (eds) *From Promise to Practice: Strengthening UN Capacities for the Prevention of Violent Conflict*, Boulder, CO: Lynne Rienner.

Pritchard, R. (2007*)* *Failed Diplomacy*, Washington, DC: Brookings Institute.

Pruitt, D. G. (2007) "Social Conflict: Some Basic Principles," *Journal of Dispute Resolution*, 1: 151–156.

Pruitt, D. G. (2008) "Back-channel Communication in the Settlement of Conflict," *International Negotiation*, 13: 37–54.

Quandt, W. B. (1986) *Camp David: Peacemaking and Politics*, Washington, DC: Brookings Institution.

Quandt, W. B. (2005) *Peace Process: American Diplomacy and the Arab–Israel Conflict since 1967*, Washington, DC: Brookings Institution Press and University of California Press.

Raiffa, H. *et al.* (2002) *Negotiation Analysis: The Science and Art of Collaborative Decision Making*, Cambridge, MA: Belknap Press of Harvard University Press.

Reilly, C. A. (2008) *Peace-Building and Development in Guatemala and Northern Ireland*, New York: Palgrave.

Robert, M. (2007) *Developing the Craft of Mediation: Reflections on Theory and Practice*, London: Jessica Kingsley Publishers.

Rodney L. (2002) *Forgiveness and Reconciliation*, Philadelphia, PA: Templeton Foundation Press.

Ropers, N. (2004) "From Resolution to Transformation: Assessing the Role and Impact of Dialogue Projects," in W. Andreas, R. J. Goldstone, D. L. Horowitz, U. Joras, and C. Schetter (eds) *Facing Ethnic Conflict Toward a New Realism*, Lanham, MD: Rowman and Littlefield Publishers Inc.

Ross, M. H. (2006) *Cultural Contestation in Ethnic Conflict*, Cambridge, UK: Cambridge University Press.

Ross, W. H. and Conlon, D. E. (2000) "Hybrid Forms of Third-Party Dispute Resolution: Theoretical Implications of Combining Mediation and Arbitration," *The Academy of Management Review*, 25: 416–427.

Rouhana, N. and Bar-Tal, D. (1998) "Psychological Dynamics of Intractable Conflicts: The Israeli–Palestinian Case," *American Psychologist*, 53: 761–770.

Rubin, J. *et al.* (1994) *Social Conflict: Escalation, Stalemate, and Settlement*, Boston, MA: McGraw-Hill.

Rummel, R. J. (1976) *Understanding Conflict and War*, Beverly Hills, CA: Sage Publications.

Sandole, D. (1998) "A Comprehensive Mapping of Conflict and Conflict Resolution: A Three Pillar Approach," *Peace and Conflict Studies*, 5 (2): 1–30.

Saunders, H. (2003) "Sustained Dialogue in Managing Intractable Conflict," *Negotiation Journal*, 19: 85–95.

Schlee, G. (2008) *How Enemies are Made*, New York: Berghahn Books.

Scimecca, J. A. (1993) "Theory and Alternative Dispute Resolution: A Contradiction in Terms?," in D. Sandole and H. van der Merwe (eds) *Conflict Resolution Theory and Practice: Integration and Application*, Manchester: Manchester University Press.

Scott, J. C. (1985) *Weapons of the Weak: Everyday Forms of Peasant Resistance*, New Haven, CT: Yale University Press.

Senehi, J. (2002) "Constructive Storytelling: A Peace Process," *Peace and Conflict Studies*, 9 (2): 41–63.

Shamsie, Y. (2007) "Moving beyond Mediation: The OAS Transforming Conflict in Guatemala," *Global Governance*, 13: 409.

Sher, G. (2006) *The Israeli–Palestinian Peace Negotiations, 1999–2001: Within Reach*, London: Routledge.

Sidaway, R. (2005) *Resolving Environmental Disputes: From Conflict to Consensus*, London: Earthscan Publications Ltd.

Simon, A. (1999) "Synergizing Participation," in S. White (ed.) *The Art of Facilitating Participation: Releasing the Power of Grassroots Communication*, Thousand Oaks, CA: Sage Publications, pp. 68–79.

Simon, B. and Klandermans, B. (2001) "Politicized Collective Identity," *American Psychologist*, 56: 319–331.

Simon, H. A. (1996) *The Sciences of the Artificial*, 3rd edn, Cambridge, MA: MIT Press.

Singer, J. D. (1971) *A General Systems Taxonomy for Political Science*, New York: General Learning.

Singer, J. D. (1990) *Models, Methods, and Progress in World Politics*, Boulder, CO: Westview Press.

Singer, J. D. and Small, M. (1972) *The Wages of War, 1816–1965: A Statistical Handbook*, NJ: John Wiley & Sons.

Spangle, M. and Isenhart, M.W. (2003) *Negotiation: Communication for Diverse Settings*, Thousand Oaks, CA: Sage.

Spencer, D. and Brogan, M. (2006) *Mediation Law and Practice*, Cambridge: Cambridge University Press.

Sprout, H. and Sprout, M. (1971) *Toward a Politics of the Planet Earth*, New York: Van Nostrand Reinhold Co.

Starkey, B. *et al.* (2005) *Negotiating a Complex World: an Introduction to International Negotiation*, Lanham, MD: Rowman & Littlefield Publishers, Inc.

Staub, E. *et al.* (2001) "Healing, Reconciliation, and Forgiving after Genocide and Other Collective Violence," in R. Helmick and R. Petersen (eds) *Forgiveness and Reconciliation*, Philadelphia, PA: Templeton Foundation Press, pp. 195–218.

Stein, J. G. (1989) "Getting to the Table: The Triggers, Stages, Functions and Consequences of Pre-Negotiation," in J. G. Stein (ed.) *Getting to the Table*, Baltimore, MD: Johns Hopkins Press.

Stein, K. W. (2000) "Comparing the Camp David Summits," *The Middle East Insight*, 5: 7–14.

Stetter, S. (2007) *Territorial Conflicts in World Society*, London: Routledge.

Stitt, A. J. (2004) *Mediation: a Practical Guide*, London: Cavendish.

Swisher, C. E. (2004) *The Truth about Camp David*, New York: Avalon Publishing Group.

Tajfel, H. (1981) *Human Groups and Social Categories: Studies in Social Psychology*, Cambridge: Cambridge University Press.

Tillet, G. and French, B. (2006) *Resolving Conflict: a Practical Approach*, Victoria, Australia: Oxford University Press.

Touval, S. and Zartman, W. I. (2001) "International Mediation in the Post-Cold War Era," in C. Crocker *et al.*, *Turbulent Peace*, Washington, DC: US Institute of Peace Press.

Tritter, R. P. (2000) *Control Self-assessment: a Guide to Facilitation-based Consulting*, New York: John Wiley.

Umbreit, M. S. and Coates, R. (2006) "Restorative Justice Mediated Dialog," in M. S. Herman, *The Blackwell Handbook of Mediation*, Malden, MA: Blackwell Publishing.

van Atta, R. H. (1973) "Field Theory and National International Linkages," in J. Wilkenfeld (ed.) *Conflict Behavior and Linkage Politics*, New York: David McKay Company Inc.

Volkan, V. (1998) *Bloodlines*, Boulder, CO: Westview Press.

Walker, R. A. (2004) *Multilateral Conferences: Purposeful International Negotiation*. New York: Palgrave Macmillan.

Wallerstein, I. (1980) *The Modern World-System: Mercantilism and the Consolidation of the European World-Economy, 1600–1750*, New York: Academic Press.

Waltz, K. N. (2001) *Man, the State, and War: a Theoretical Analysis*, New York: Columbia University Press.

Webb, K. (2001) "Mediation in Moldova: A Case of Second-track Diplomacy" in D. Goodwin (ed.) *Negotiations in International Conflict: Understanding Persuasion*, London, Frank Cass. pp. 139–150.

Weine, S. (2006) *Testimony after Catastrophe: Narrating the Traumas of Political Violence*, Evanston, IL: Northwestern University Press.

White, S. A. and Nair, K. S. (1999) "The Catalyst Communicator: Facilitation without Fear," in S. A. White (ed) *The Art of Facilitating Participation: Releasing the Power of Grassroots Communication*, Thousand Oaks, CA: Sage Publications.

Wilmot, W. and Hocker, J. (2001) *Interpersonal Conflict*, Boston, MA: McGraw-Hill.

Wilson, M. S. (2003) "Social Dominance and Ethical Ideology: The End Justifies the Means?" *Journal of Social Psychology*, 143: 549–558.

Wittkopf, E. R. and McCormick, J. M. (2008) *The Domestic Sources of American Foreign Policy: Insights and Evidence*, Lanham, MD: Rowman & Littlefield Publishers.

Womack, B. (2006) *China and Vietnam: the Politics of Asymmetry*, New York: Cambridge University Press.

Zartman, I. W. (2005) "Structures of Escalation and Negotiation," in I. W. Zartman and G. Faure (eds) *Escalation and Negotiation in International Conflicts*, New York: Cambridge University Press.

Zeigler, C. (2003) "The Role of Artistic Processes in Peacebuilding in Bosnia-Herzegovina," *Peace and Conflict Studies*, 10 (2): 62–76.

Zimmerman, A. L. and Evans, C. J. (1993) *Facilitation – from Discussion to Decision*, East Brunswick, NJ: Nichols Publishers.

Index

An environmentally friendly book printed and bound in England by www.printondemand-worldwide.com

PEFC Certified

This product is
from sustainably
managed forests
and controlled
sources

www.pefc.org

MIX
Paper from
responsible sources
FSC® C004959

This book is made entirely of sustainable materials; FSC paper for the cover and PEFC paper for the text pages.

Reprint of # - C0 - 246/174/14 - PB - Lamination Gloss - Printed on 13-Jan-17 17:21